THE PULITZER PRIZE STORY

RAISING THE FLAG ON MOUNT SURIBACHI, *by Joe Rosenthal*

PULITZER PRIZE, 1945 ASSOCIATED PRESS

THE PULITZER PRIZE STORY

NEWS STORIES, EDITORIALS,
CARTOONS, AND PICTURES
FROM THE PULITZER PRIZE COLLECTION
AT COLUMBIA UNIVERSITY

Edited, with commentaries, by JOHN HOHENBERG

COLUMBIA UNIVERSITY PRESS
New York and London

For Dorothy

FOREWORD

"What does it take to win a Pulitzer Prize?"

"Where can I find some examples of the work of winners of the Pulitzer Prizes in Journalism?"

These are the questions that have been asked of me most frequently since I became secretary of the Advisory Board on the Pulitzer Prizes five years ago.

As to the first, I can't answer it. I wish I could.

As to the second, Columbia University decided something should be done about it. This book is the result.

BASIS FOR THE TEXT

A total of 251 Pulitzer Prizes for Journalism has been awarded from 1917 through 1958—41 gold medals for public service for newspapers and 210 cash prizes for individuals in varying amounts up to $1,000. (Most individual prizes have been $1,000, but for a time they were reduced to $500; moreover, some prizes have been shared.)

Ninety-eight newspapers and 187 individuals, seven entire newspaper staffs, three wire services, three syndicates, and one group award for war correspondents have figured in the prizes. Twenty-nine news organizations or their staff members have been multiple winners. There have also been 13 special citations for journalism.

With so large a selection to choose from, it became obvious from the first that not everyone could be represented; nor was it possible even to choose the best. Trying to pick the best of the Pulitzer

Prizes would be like trying to select the best gold from the vaults at Fort Knox, Kentucky. It can't be done.

The idea of presenting some of the winners from each of the eight categories in the Pulitzer Prizes for Journalism, although it was the most logical, therefore turned out to be the least possible for a collection of this kind.

Dr. William Bridgwater, editor-in-chief of the Columbia University Press, suggested organizing the volume on the basis of subjects that had figured most frequently in the award of prizes. Under this plan, subject categories had to be picked, stories classified under each, some material had to be chosen, and much that was just as good or better had to be left out. My apologies for that, and my regrets.

Whatever sins may have been committed in doing this job, they are all mine. And since there are just as many opinions about newspaper work as there are newspapermen and women, I have no doubt there will be voices of dissent. If there weren't a lot of stiff arguments, the newspaper business would dry up and blow away.

SOME PULITZER PRIZE SUBJECTS

Knowing in advance that not everybody was likely to agree with me, I made the following breakdown of subject matter for the Pulitzer Prizes in Journalism from 1917 through 1958:

Exposing graft and corruption in government on local, state, and national levels	33 prizes
War reporting	22 prizes
U. S. racial conflict	16 prizes (7 for editorials)
Crime reporting	12 prizes
Civil liberties	12 prizes (4 for editorials)
Reporting from Russia (except war)	9 prizes
General international coverage	8 prizes
Science (including the atom)	8 prizes
Human interest	6 prizes
Storms, accidents	6 prizes
General Washington coverage	6 prizes
Cold War (domestic results)	4 prizes

There was a scattering for labor, economics, international conferences, sports, education, medicine, and other subjects. Ten of the eleven parts of this volume were drawn from this list. A section on general assignment was added to provide some idea of the breadth of a reporter's work. The pictures and cartoons were included after the text had been decided upon.

SELECTION AND ARRANGEMENT

Most Pulitzer Prize exhibits are quite bulky. As will be seen by even the most casual inspection of the Special Collections files at Butler Library, Columbia University, few awards are given for just one story, one editorial, one picture, or one cartoon. Most careful scholars readily understand this, but there's no accounting for the ones who glance, run, and write.

Public service, for instance, requires a large documentation of news, editorial support, cartoons, and pictures. Reporting calls for a "distinguished example," which may be a story, a series, or even a year's work in some cases. Editorial writing is often based on the writer's work for a year, as is the case with cartoons; but in these categories requests are made to hold down the size of actual exhibits to a dozen examples where possible. Photographs, until 1957, were supposedly held to one picture but the rule was never seriously observed and was changed to accord with reality. The New York *Daily News's* winning exhibit is a whole bookful of pictures.

Obviously, a single exhibit could have been larger than the space allotted for this book, if an attempt had been made to reproduce it. Because of this unhappy reality, it became necessary for me to check over the exhibits and try to select those stories, editorials, pictures, and cartoons that could give the reader some appreciation of a whole category of work on the same subject.

Sometimes there was a guide in the example that was made public of the whole range of the winning work. Occasionally, there was a story, picture, or cartoon that could stand by itself. This was not so true of editorials, but some were found—notably those of William Allen White and Hodding Carter. But in all cases except that of Anne O'Hare McCormick, the work presented here was from the winning file of the newspaper or writer. Mrs. McCormick is the only writer in the history of the journalism prizes for whom there is no exhibit, and I tried to do the best I could to give a selection typical of her work at the approximate period covered by her prize.

For the most part, the various sections of the volume fell into a natural arrangement in point of interest and time. But now and then, as was the case with general assignment, it didn't matter too much whether chronological order was followed. The story was the thing. Nor was there any artificial separation between news and editorial comment. If the material belonged together, that's the way it went.

ACKNOWLEDGEMENTS

I am most grateful to President Grayson Kirk of Columbia University for his encouragement in the preparation of this volume. At a time when I had serious doubts as to whether it could be done at all, he resolved them for me very simply. Such a book, he said, was necessary; and with that, I am sure, there will be no disagreement.

I am thankful, also, to Joseph Pulitzer Jr. and my other associates of the Advisory Board on the Pulitzer Prizes for their support and their friendship.

It should be made clear, however, that neither the university, its trustees, nor the Advisory Board is in any way responsible for the selection or arrangement of the work presented here, or of the comments that have been made in the presentation. This is by no means an "official" text. It is, to repeat, the sole responsibility of the editor and commentator who has learned one thing about the newspaper business in a quarter-century of active work—it's impossible to please everybody.

I am indebted to Dean Edward W. Barrett of the Graduate School of Journalism, Columbia University, for his keen interest in this project. And to many other friends and associates I also owe a great deal, among them Charles G. Proffitt, Dr. William Bridgwater, Joan McQuary, and Melvin Loos of Columbia University Press; Dr. Richard H. Logsdon, director of Columbia University Libraries, Charles W. Mixer, the assistant director, and their Special Collections staff. All helped in many ways.

FOR THE FUTURE

Finally, in thanking the organizations and individuals who have generously permitted use of their material, I want to draw attention to the needs of the Pulitzer Prize collection itself. Some of it already has disintegrated and efforts are being made to replace such material. But for the future, there is only one solution if this priceless collection is to be preserved and that is microfilming. The share of the Pulitzer Prize proceeds from this book will be set aside for that purpose. I can only hope, somehow, that sufficient funds will be found for this necessary work.

JOHN HOHENBERG

Aquebogue, New York
January, 1959

CONTENTS

CONTENTS

CONTENTS xix

CONTENTS

ILLUSTRATIONS

CARTOONS

INTRODUCTION:
THE VALUES OF JOURNALISM

The American newspaper is a friendly neighbor.

It is the best source of news and opinion in the communities it serves. It brings the world to Main Street. It is a bulwark against injustice, a strong force for better government and a better life.

It has deep convictions. It has a conscience and a heart. It is not afraid to fight for its principles and frequently does, win or lose.

Such is the image of the American newspaper that emerges from the files of the Pulitzer Prizes in Journalism after more than four decades of awards.

SOME OTHER IMAGES

Yet, this is not precisely the image that the American newspaper itself has tried to project before the public for much of this century. The newspaper's concept of itself is stern and forbidding—impersonal, objective, authoritative.

Nor do the Pulitzer Prizes sustain the rather sinister image drawn of this country's press by its critics. That image is based on the "devil" theory of the press. It presupposes that the press is a profit-laden monster, swollen and arrogant, whose cruel purpose is monopoly, one-party political journalism, and monolithic supervision of opinion-molding.

After having blinked at such a horrendous vision, one is tempted to rush to the map and make sure that Sauk Center somehow has not changed places with Moscow.

The joke, if any, does not dispel the seriousness of the questions that inevitably must be raised by these conflicting views:

Which is the real image of the American newspaper?

Which ones are artificial?

What is the public truly to believe about its press?

What can the press and its people do to sustain an honest image of their work?

Let's take another look at the model, even if it is very familiar, somewhat plain, and maybe a little homely.

THE LESSON OF HISTORY

There wasn't much argument about what the American press was like in colonial days. Benjamin Franklin, James Franklin, John Peter Zenger, and their associates among colonial editors nourished the spirit of independence with their attacks on the colonial government. They were not afraid to lead.

Theirs was a small, struggling, brawling, courageous, personal kind of newspaper. It led the people in a venture that brought war, independence, and the creation of a free nation. More than that, it helped lay the foundations for a democratic government that has grown to world leadership.

Yet, even this press, so clear in its purpose and so willing to stake its existence on principle, had its detractors. James Rivington, the Tory publisher, would have sketched in quite easily a fine "devil theory" of the press of those times, complete with horns and a tail.

When it comes to newspapering, all prospect of firm agreement on what it is and what it should be goes out the window.

Let me illustrate. Suppose some day that there should be a perfect newspaper. Its news columns would be unsullied by distortion. Its editorials would be undefiled by low self-interest. Its pictures would consist exclusively of dignified people, rather than some "love-goddess" suing her fourth husband.

Would all the good people cheer and subscribe by the tens of thousands? You can be sure somebody would rise up and exclaim, "No, take the blamed thing away! It's damn dull!" And he'd be right.

WHAT IS OBJECTIVITY?

Now this doesn't mean a less-than-perfect newspaper is worth settling for. It is merely a mild and, I hope, good-humored caution against expecting perfection from journalism, of all things, in a less than perfect world.

Consider, if you will, the American newspaper's image of itself. The vision, at best, is not clear; at worst, it is artificial.

American editors argued for years that there was a distinction between the news and editorial columns. They contended that the news was entirely factual while the editorial was entirely opinion, or at least that was the theory when I last looked.

This might possibly have been true, in a sense, for relatively simple news items—vital statistics, arrivals and departures, accidents, social notes, weather, and the like. But even here, the least sophisticated reader often failed to make a distinction between what was news and what was comment. If asked about the weather forecast, he was as likely as not to reply, "Well, I dunno. The paper says . . ."

And where was the editor with all his fine talk about the distinction between the news and editorial columns? The public just didn't believe it.

Because, in truth, the concept of pure objectivity in newspaper work or in life itself is a myth. It doesn't exist and it never did. The sooner it is recognized, the better it will be for both the American newspaper and its readers.

What editors mean by objectivity, if I may dare to read the editorial mind, is nothing more nor less than plain honesty in the news. That is attainable, as any issue of a good newspaper will demonstrate. But the degree of detachment and lack of comment implied by the use of the word objectivity in its traditional sense is beyond humankind.

When Gabriel blows his horn on Judgment Day, you may be sure he really will try to hit that high note hard. There won't be any nonsense about objectivity here. He'll put his heart into it. Should an humble newspaperman do less?

WHAT NEWSPAPERMEN BELIEVE

Now, no one in or out of newspaper work advocates a news story so overgrown with weedy interpretation, personal bias, and plain and fancy writing that it moves the reader to little moans of anguish. Any sensible newspaperman of experience will insist that a substantial account of events must tell not only what happened but also, if possible, why it happened.

There isn't really too much uproar about this any more. Even the Associated Press has got religion. Today, except for the arch-conservatives of journalism who aspire to be the only voice of the press, the cause of interpreting the news is won.

How well it is being done is quite another story, and how much it has contributed to public understanding is open to serious debate. It is also questionable whether all the interpreters of the news are as qualified as they think they are to do the job.

But as to the right to give meaning to the news, that is established. The American newspaper today has many voices, not one. The problem is to get them into harmony.

AN EDITORIAL VIEW

Walter Lippmann explained it clearly, as he nearly always does. In a piece for the Bulletin of the American Society of Newspaper Editors, he said: "We have all become more sophisticated about what are facts and what are opinions."

If I may embellish this from my own experience, without being accused of using the space for a commercial, I well remember my own instruction from a city editor long, long ago:

"Just write what the man said, and not what he meant or what you think he meant. That's why we pay editorial writers. They do the thinking. You get me the quotes."

It was like life in vertical unions, where the carpenter and painter can't do each other's work. The reporter got the facts and, figuratively wagging his tail, laid them at the feet of the editorial writer like a bone. The editorial writer thereupon brooded and eventually pointed with pride or viewed with alarm. To continue with Lippmann:

"In the course of time, most of us have come to see that the old distinction between fact and opinion does not fit the reality of things. This is in part because the 'facts' have become enormously more complicated than they used to be when the federal government was so much smaller and when the United States was still an isolationist country. . . .

"These developments have made obsolete the old distinction

between reporting and editorial writing. . . . The editorial writer's first function is to interpret and to explain the news, and no clear line can be drawn as to where the work of the reporter and the correspondent ends and where the work of the editorial writer begins."

TOWARD A NEW IDEAL

It follows, therefore, that the American newspaper is not exactly what it thinks it is. The concept that it is impersonal, objective, and authoritative requires some changes.

The growth of interpretation has reintroduced the personal note to journalism in the United States. In place of the rigid writing that went under the heading of "objective," and conjured up the image of the oracle at Delphi uttering even a paragraph about the decline of the horse trough, the American newspaper is more relaxed today. It is friendly, considerate, willing to concede it doesn't know all the answers, anxious for advice from its readers.

This split between the self-image and reality is symptomatic of at least one thing. The average newspaper isn't quite sure what its own role should be in today's world. For the very function of the newspaper is changing.

News is not enough for a newspaper now. Radio can put out news much faster and in greater volume. Television, if it could ever overcome the repugnance of advertisers to the featuring of news rather than soap opera, plain hokum, and bedraggled comedy, would be a far more dramatic news medium.

Except for newspapers that use the finest newsprint and the best photographic and reproduction material, the slick paper picture-magazines and the newsreels do a better job of photographic journalism. The news weeklies can hold their own with even the largest and best qualified newspaper staffs in reviewing and explaining the news. The technical press is more learned.

But there is one field in which the newspaper of general circulation has always excelled: public service. It is in this area, I am sure, that the newspaper of today and tomorrow will find the projection of an image of itself that has greater fidelity to truth than the old "objective" and "impersonal" know-it-all image.

And this the public will accept.

THE "DEVIL THEORY" OF THE PRESS

The reader must excuse me if I do not take too much stock in the "devil theory" of the press.

There is nothing new in it. Well-intentioned social critics have always belabored the press. And there are others whose purposes are not so clear, who let fly at a juicy target in the hope of hearing a yelp of anguish.

The press, having handed it out on this continent for about two and one-half centuries, is well able to take it. But its critics really ought to adapt themselves to the conditions of 1959, when bloated press plutocrats are in somewhat scarce supply in the economy.

With the growth of industrial America, and the combination of both industry and labor into gigantic units, the press also has felt the great economic pressures of the times. For the past four decades or more, the tendency has been toward fewer papers and larger circulations. Weaker units have died out or sold out.

The census of 1910 reported 2,200 daily English language newspapers of general circulation were published in the United States, and 2,600 daily publications of all types. In the same year, there were 14,000 weeklies.

Today there are some 1,750 dailies and less than 10,000 weeklies. But the daily newspaper circulation has increased from 24,000,000 copies in 1910 to about 58,000,000 today which, although impressive on the surface, still has not kept pace with population growth.

It is the sheerest nonsense to credit this primarily to manipulation. For if the "devil theory" is correct, then publishers are rascals and editors fools, reporters and writers are craven wretches and readers are idiots. The theory has to be stretched to cover some 250,000 persons employed in the industry, which would seem to be an additional difficulty. The legions of the devil aren't quite so numerous—in journalism, at least.

THE STORY OF MERGERS

Publishers like Frank Munsey gave the critics of journalism— and the friends of journalism as well—a lot of the substance for their complaints. Yet, as Munsey's own failures showed, there is no security in mergers. Munsey became one of the most hated men in newspaper work and did harm to journalism as a profession.

Cyrus H. K. Curtis is another who couldn't make a go of his newspaper ventures.

And if anyone thinks chain newspapering automatically insures a big profit today, a study of the revenue produced by larger chain newspapers and their parent corporations will dispel still another illusion. The Hearst interests didn't sell International News Service because they were rolling in profits. Nor, for that matter, did United Press buy to get rid of excess profits.

The myth of the bloated profit certainly was not upheld when so great and worthy a newspaper as the New York *Times* was able to show a profit in 1957 on its newspaper operation after taxes that represented only 1.7 percent of total operating revenues. True, some newspapers do better. But the lords of the press don't seem to be living up to their reputation. The little fellows in the medium-sized American cities, who are lords only of their mortgages, seem on the whole to be in a more favorable position than the big fellows. But that doesn't call for stinging social criticism, so to hell with it.

THE ONE-PARTY PRESS

As for the one-party press, an offshoot of the "devil theory," this one gives the public a lot of concern—and it should.

There can be no argument about the tendency of a majority of publishers to support Republican administrations. But in a country that has elected Democratic Presidents for twenty of the past twenty-eight years, and Democratic Congresses with even greater regularity, the matter of advocacy hasn't seemed very compelling to large numbers of newspaper readers.

The fact is that the principal complaints to the publishers come from their own editors, in many cases. The very editors, mind you, who are supposedly bound hand and foot to the "one-party press." Moreover, the historic conflict in journalism today is not between cruel publishers and readers whom they lead by the nose (a likely story!) but between those courageous editors who are forever battling for the betterment of their communities and lethargic public servants. It is no wonder that there seems to be a growth in the number of newspapers devoted to public service and to satisfying those readers who look for impartial news presentation.

It would also seem to be considerate of all those Republican publishers to hire so many Democrats to write their news for them, and permit interpretive by-lined comment on Page 1. To say nothing of Democratic copyreaders, of whom a few may still be found.

The sarcasm may be lost on the uninitiated. To state the case bluntly, therefore, it would seem that a publisher is well within his rights to be a Republican. It's a free country. He has a right, as one of them said recently, to try to create the kind of economic climate that will help him meet his payroll. Of course he may get a stiff argument from that bull-headed editor of his, but there's no accounting for editors. Or readers. They don't know they're supposed to be docile. he falsely claims that an overabundance of healthy interpretation draw readers of press

But whether the publisher votes for the Republican or Democratic Party, he owes it to his public to run a decent newspaper with a fair and honest representation of news on both sides. There is more than enough evidence to show that good newspapers try to do this with reasonable success—on the north as well as the south side of the Mason-Dixon Line.

There is no other way for them to retain the respect of a community. And to prosper at all, a newspaper must have the trust of the people for whom it is published or it dies—and if that trust is abused the paper deserves to die. left pure

THE RESPONSIBILITY OF THE PRESS

To cite just a few examples of such press responsibility from the Pulitzer Prize files, the Kansas City *Star* exposed a Republican National Chairman and forced him out of office. Most of the supposed one-party press did the same, with enthusiasm, for a Republican Secretary of the Air Force. Nor was ex-Presidential Assistant Sherman Adams treated very gently, even though President Eisenhower "needed" him, after his relationship with a Boston financier was developed in that same one-party press.

The Chicago *Daily News* showed that a Republican state auditor was a thief and helped put him behind the bars. The same paper, combined with the St. Louis *Post-Dispatch*, disclosed that newspaper editors were on the Illinois state payroll to praise a Republican governor. Of these newspapers, only the *Post-Dispatch* has normally supported Democrats and even that newspaper has occasionally strayed.

On the Democratic side, the Pulitzer Prize files fairly bulge with instances of press opposition to Southern segregationists—the Ku Klux Klan, White Citizens Councils, and the like—which is not calculated to earn big profits in today's angry South. The *Arkansas Gazette* risked its very existence to stand for moderation in the Little Rock riots, but its 85-year-old publisher softly and courteously insisted that he must keep faith with the country and its laws.

There are many more. For every prize-winner, there are scores who stood unflinchingly for principle without thought of an award. The evidence is conclusive that the serious, responsible press of America takes its role of public servant with deep concern and tries faithfully to discharge its duties to its readers. Conscience is more than a word.

THE COMMERCIAL PRESS

There is, to be sure, a sizeable commercial press in this country. I would not say these lighthearted, fun-loving papers are in the majority although their circulations are usually impressive in terms of numbers. But even for a commercial newspaper interested primarily in journalism as a business rather than a profession, there comes a time sooner or later when the support or abandonment of the principles of journalism becomes a serious matter.

That time is now. Television, within a few years, has developed into a much finer entertainment medium than any newspaper could be. Once, it might have been possible to halt a dip in circulation by turning on the old tap labeled "blood, money, and broads." Or maybe buying up two more pages of comic strips and hoping one of them was another "Blondie" or "Dick Tracy." Comic strips still sell.

But newspapers—and magazines—that solely rely on old methods for pleasing the customers are finding that circulation is slipping. With newsprint at $135 a ton (it was $40 a ton during the great depression), that means an initial saving. But the commercial newspaper won't keep its share of a $2.5 billion press income from advertising revenue for very long, if circulation keeps sagging. So, what price amusement by the press in a television era?

It takes something more than good clean (or not-so-clean) fun to intrigue the customers nowadays. Because they're not so anxious to read for amusement any more. They reach for the TV set.

Not that a newspaper has forfeited the right to be entertaining. God forbid! But entertainment for its own sake no longer can insure the kind of mass circulation it once did. The limit has been reached. Even the commercial press has come to see that the old images are not enough. Something new must be added.

THE PULITZER PRIZES

We return to the image of the American newspaper that is cast by the Pulitzer Prizes in Journalism. It is, no doubt, a more idealistic concept than is presented by the average newspaper. That is because the Pulitzer Prizes, for more than four decades, have endeavored to represent the best in American journalism year by year.

Here is the superior image of the American newspaper.

It is created by a press that has never feared to pioneer in public service, whether it meant gain or loss, and it is unfortunately true that some crusading newspapers have not been able to survive. The responsible press has gone on despite that.

Such newspapers have fought civic graft and corruption, the excesses of mismanagement in state and nation, in corporations, and in labor unions, and even in the ranks of the press itself.

Such newspapers have stood for freedom of speech and the press, not only for themselves but for the persecuted. They have raised their hands against injustice. They have fought hatred and intolerance. They have stricken down malefactors, whether wealthy or not. They have raised up those who were unfairly stigmatized and freed some who were unjustly imprisoned.

Just as these newspapers have striven for principle, there are thousands of newspapermen and women who have worked and sacrificed—some giving up their lives—to bring the news and the meaning of the news to the American people.

This is the heritage of the Pulitzer Prizes, of those who have striven for them and those who have won them. If these awards have now achieved some measure of fame, it is because the journalists of yesterday and today have made them famous, and because the journalists of tomorrow will without doubt follow their example.

THE TRUE IMAGE

To anyone who is familiar with the Pulitzer Prizes, the American newspaper's stiff and lifeless image of itself and the "devil" image shaped by its critics are equally unacceptable. The truth is closer to the image cast by the Pulitzer Prizes—the friendly neighbor, the warm, personal, fighting partisan for the best interests of the community.

Here, then, is the substance of that image. In the pages that follow are recorded some of the great moments of American journalism. These typical examples, and the great body of work from which they were taken, are a permanent contribution not only to American journalism but to the history and the literature of the nation as well.

Joseph Pulitzer, the founder of the prizes that bear his name, truly wrote of newspaper people long ago:

"What is a journalist? Not any business manager or publisher, or even proprietor. A journalist is the lookout on the bridge of the ship of state. He notes the passing sail, the little things of interest that dot the horizon in fine weather. He reports the drifting castaway whom the ship can save. He peers through fog and storm to give warning of dangers ahead. He is not thinking of his wages or of the profits of his owners. He is there to watch over the safety and the welfare of the people who trust him."

The proudest moment of a newspaperman's life comes when he knows he has lived up to that trust.

I. GENERAL ASSIGNMENT:
THE FACE OF THE AGE

"Do we ever overlook any questions, Mr. President?"

There was a roar of laughter from the more than 200 White House correspondents. The reporter who had asked the question tried to adopt a blandly innocent air, as reporters will on occasion.

President Eisenhower grinned, then replied,

"I will say this: Once in a while, when some member of my staff comes in and says—just almost shakes his finger in my face, 'That is what you are going to be questioned on this morning,' I will go back and say, 'Who was that that was so smart?' So I don't think you overlook them, they probably just don't interest you."

There is, the President of the United States notwithstanding, very little that doesn't interest a reporter. In the city halls, legislatures, and courts of the nation, they are always listening, always turning the pages. Just as they throng to the weekly White House news conferences, they confront lesser officials at regular intervals with requests for an accounting. With the clang of the fire alarm or the sound of a shot, they are on their way to the story. At home or abroad they serve the right of the people to know.

As Rebecca West wrote,

"It is the presentation of the facts that matters, the facts that put together are the face of the age; the rise in the price of coal, the new ballet, the woman found dead in a kimono on the golf links, the latest sermon of the Archbishop of York, the marriage of a Prime Minister's daughter. For if people do not have the face of the age set clearly before them, they begin to imagine it."

It is the reporter, rather than the historian or novelist or play-wright or even the editor, who truly depicts the face of today's age. He is first on the ground, first to see, to hear. He is no mere stenog-rapher, parroting the lines that others speak. His fact-gathering, his impressions, his interpretation—like it or not—place bands of steel about the shape of events. Sometimes he even makes these events happen.

When the Pulitzer Prizes were first awarded in 1917, there was but one prize for reporting. Today there are four—a testimonial to the impressive growth of news-gathering. Out of this spangled array, the following pieces show the reporter at work on general assignments all over the nation in many of his most useful—and sometimes glamorous—roles.

James Reston has said that if the nineteenth century was the era of the novelist, the twentieth is the era of the reporter. No reporter will dispute him, least of all those who have won a Pulitzer Prize.

1. HOW TWO CUB REPORTERS
SOLVED THE LOEB-LEOPOLD CASE

The "story of a story" that won a prize
for Alvin H. Goldstein and James W. Mulroy

Pulitzer Prize for Reporting, 1925

It is nearly four decades since the Chicago *Daily News* carried a Page 1 story beginning as follows on May 22, 1924:

"Robert Franks, the fourteen-year-old son of a wealthy South Side watch manufacturer, was found today, murdered by kidnapers who demanded $10,000 ransom.

"The boy's naked body was found early in the morning, stuffed into a culvert under the Pennsylvania Railroad tracks at 118th Street, but it was late afternoon before the Franks family suspected the truth."

Such was the first news of what later became known as the Loeb-Leopold case—the "thrill murder" committed by two wealthy students, Richard Loeb and Nathan Leopold. Nearly everything about the story has been told and retold—how Clarence Darrow's supreme courtroom effort saved the two defendants from the death penalty, how Loeb was killed in a fight with a fellow-prisoner while serving a life term, how Leopold finally won parole after over thirty years behind bars.

Yet, the story of an inhuman crime continues to exert a morbid fascination for Americans of all ages, even those unborn when the killing occurred. It has been the subject of novels and plays, replete with the disgusting detail culled from testimony, and even fairly recent newspaper serialization. But, buried in the yellowed and cracked clippings in the Pulitzer Prize files, there is one story that isn't quite as familiar as the rest—the Chicago *Daily News's* own account of how its two brilliant young reporters, Alvin H. Goldstein and James W. Mulroy, broke the story and within a week trapped both Leopold and Loeb.

In a preface to its account, known to the trade as a "box precede," the *Daily News* reported with somewhat grim humor how Loeb had been put to work "hunting for himself" by acting as a chauffeur for the two reporters who had known him in college. The box went on:

"He helped the reporters locate the drug store to which he and Leopold had tried to lure Jacob Franks [the victim's father, and target of the ransom demand], and in the course of the day's work he made significant statements that were turned against him to bad effect after the two newspapermen had produced the evidence that brought about his confession and Leopold's."

Here is the *Daily News's* "story of a story."

CUB REPORTERS WIN GLORY

From the Chicago Daily News, May 31, 1924

Two "cub" reporters of the *Daily News* staff, James W. Mulroy and Alvin H. Goldstein, contributed more than most of the police force and the legions of rival newsmen combined to the solution of the Franks kidnaping mystery.

"O'Connor and Goldberg," their scornful rivals called them—a wheeze inspired by the almost fanatic zeal with which Mulroy and Goldstein wore out shoe leather in their search for clews. "O'Connor and Goldberg" they may be until they're gray and reading the copy of cubs yet unborn, but the names will be service medals, not taunts. Nobody's kidding the pair today.

It's the story of a story—a perfect realization of the dreams of all the thousands of cubs who come stumbling into the dusty local rooms of all the newspapers of the land, green and unskilled and ambitious. To jump from picture-chasing to triumph over the whole town in the biggest story of a generation sounds like the poppycock of newspaper fiction, but "O'Connor and Goldberg" did it.

They dug up the truth about the kidnaping before any one but friends of the Franks family knew about it. They accomplished a scoop which would have given most reporters glory enough for a lifetime when they brought about the identification of the kidnaped boy's body a full jump ahead of every other newspaper in Chicago. They ran and taxied and poked about day and night through the week of frenzy that followed, turning up valuable information under the noses of the police and their rivals.

All unaided they got the evidence that broke the kidnapers' resistance today. "O'Connor and Goldberg" solved the mystery if anybody did. Without them it might have remained a mystery forever.

Ten days ago they were legging it all over town, hunting pictures, getting statements from press bureaus, checking up on minor details that real reporters didn't have time for. A good-natured, breezy pair, doing the dreary routine that lies back of the news. Nobody paid much attention to them; they were just a pair of cubs.

Mulroy was sitting in a back corner of the local room of the *Daily News* office, killing time, on the morning of Wednesday, May 21, when a tip came in about a kidnaping "that Sam Ettelson knows all about." He was sent to see Ettelson.

Now Ettelson wasn't anxious to have the newspapers get hold of the fact that the fourteen-year-old son of his old friend Jacob Franks had been kidnaped. But Mulroy has the priceless kind of personality that can't be resisted—the kind that's worth a Rolls Royce income in the bond business. He talked the story out of Ettelson.

The story wasn't printed. Publication might imperil the life of the kidnaped boy. But Mulroy didn't let that bother him. He got his pal Goldstein and they set to work.

Goldstein was sent hustling out to Hegewisch, where the body of an unidentified boy had been found crammed into a railroad culvert. Mulroy went out to the Franks home.

The description Goldstein phoned to Mulroy at the Franks house apparently didn't fit the kidnaped boy. Eyeglasses had been found near the Hegewisch body and young Franks had never worn eyeglasses.

The Franks couldn't be interested at first, but at last Goldstein and Mulroy got an uncle of the missing boy into a taxicab, headed for the Hegewisch morgue.

The activities of "O'Connor and Goldberg" had caused Ettelson to phone to the city editor of another afternoon paper by this time lest the story leak into print there, and a reporter for that paper horned in on the ride to the morgue. But he wasn't a match for the relentless cubs. They ran circles around him and had the news of the identification into their office an edition ahead of their winded rival.

Well, a kidnaping-murder was too good a story for a pair of cubs, of course. Veterans were assigned to the case. Every newspaper in town, including the *Daily News,* put its best talent to work on the mystery—big leaguers.

Goldstein and Mulroy? Oh, they just stuck. "Leggers" were needed and anyhow they would have refused to leave the job. They are reported to have slept and eaten in relays, so that one of them would be on the case if anything happened.

Day and night they were at it, never sitting still. Hunting them by telephone was a mystery in itself. One minute they'd be at the Franks home, almost the next minute one of them would bob up at a police station and the other on some mysterious errand they had no time to explain, off in some other sector of the field of action.

Thus they canvassed all of East 63d Street until they located the drug store which was to have been the kidnapers' rendezvous with Franks—an important find.

Also in the course of their investigations they bumped into young Loeb and incidentally got from him a chance statement that was proved of great value later.

"If I was going to kill any kid," said Loeb to Goldstein, "I'd pick just such a fresh little ———— as that Franks kid."

Yesterday saw their supreme triumph. While rival reporters and detectives were pounding their skulls for a hunch on Leopold and Loeb, Goldstein and Mulroy went out to the University of Chicago campus and scouted about until they had found samples of typewriting done by Leopold on the very typewriter that produced the kidnapers' ransom letter.

They turned the stuff over to the police (after reporting their scoop, of course) and then, still forgetting sleep, they rounded up four college witnesses who popped into the case along about midnight to break down the alibis and the nerve of the two kidnapers.

They were there at the Criminal Court Building all night and they were still on the job at daybreak with volumes of exclusive material for their paper's first edition.

They're at it somewhere (maybe chasing pictures again) as this is written. They'll get their sleep when the excitement dies down and the paper doesn't need their help.

So it was that in the Chicago newspaper world of Ben Hecht and Charles MacArthur, of Bob Casey and Carl Sandburg and so many other great ones, the then unknown Goldstein and Mulroy beat the town and jointly won the Pulitzer Prize for Reporting for 1925.

As might be expected after such a beginning, the glamor of journalism never wore off for the Chicago *Daily News's* triumphant pair. Goldstein, the New York correspondent for the St. Louis *Post-Dispatch*, is still after the big story—the biggest of all stories now. For at the United Nations, which he has covered intensively from the beginning, he is regarded as one of the few journalistic experts on the intricate negotiations on atomic diplomacy between the United States and the Soviet Union. Mulroy, after a lifetime in journalism, rose to managing editor of the old Chicago *Sun*. He died on April 29, 1952.

2. THE MERCURIAL RISE AND FALL
OF THE STATE OF JEFFERSON

Stanton Delaplane of the San Francisco Chronicle
records the saga of the mining camps

Pulitzer Prize for Reporting, 1942

Once there was a forty-ninth state called Jefferson. It lived gloriously, but all too briefly, in the headlines of the nation's press. Its 75,000 inhabitants, who used to secede each Thursday from Oregon and California, are now sober and more orthodox citizens of the United States.

The story began, as such stories often do, with a brief piece from a San Francisco *Chronicle* "stringer" late in 1941. He reported that the northern California counties of Del Norte, Siskiyou, Modoc, and Lassen and the southern Oregon county of Curry were threatening secession to form the forty-ninth state of Jefferson.

The *Chronicle* sent Reporter Stanton Delaplane 1,000 miles north to record the birth of the new state, which on the map assumed the un-Jeffersonian shape of a dachshund. Delaplane faithfully reported the setting up of roadblocks by booted miners, the huge signs warning motorists, "Stop! State of Jefferson!" and he had pictures taken showing pretty girls being told the story of the rebellion.

There was, of course, a serious side. The people had agreed (without consultation) to become Jeffersonians temporarily in order to draw attention to their need of roads and their reluctance to pay sales taxes until they got roads. Roads, it seems, were the key to the mineral wealth of the back country and everybody in Yreka and Happy Camp and Hard Scrabble Creek and Pistol River wouldn't take no for an answer.

Of course there had to be a leader of the rebellion and Delaplane found him, too. He was Mayor Gilbert Gable of Port Orford, Oregon, who styled himself the "hick mayor of the westernmost city of the United States." As it turned out (and it does more often than not in such cases), Mr. Gable also happened to be an agile and imaginative publicity man who had worked for the Bell Telephone Company and the Liberty Loan drive in World War. I.

Between gulps of hot buttered rum to fortify himself against the more impressionable adventures of Mr. Gable and the State of Jefferson, the visitor from San Francisco told the story in daily dispatches from the scene that had no rivals. He was far ahead of the competition.

Here is one of the stories that was typical of the recorded history of the State of Jefferson. It provided a brief but welcome comic relief to a nation that was heading into the worst war in its history.

REBELLION EVERY THURSDAY

By Stanton Delaplane

From the San Francisco Chronicle, Dec. 1, 1941

PISTOL RIVER (Secession State of Jefferson), Nov. 30.—Until Curry County, Oregon, began talking secession, it got as little attention as a hitch-hiker trying to thumb a ride on a Vanderbilt yacht.

The Cinderella county was unique in the United States. It had no incorporated city, no telegraph line, no railroad.

It had 10 percent of the standing timber of the nation within a 100-mile radius, chromite and copper deposits, and fish in the river here so thick that residents swear you can walk from bank to bank without wetting your feet.

Curry County, with Mayor Gilbert Gable of Port Orford leaping from copper deposit to cinnabar mine, is calling for a meeting of a provisional state legislature today.

Miners from the back country are ready to put up hard cash and get the legal talent to petition Congress for the 49th state of Jefferson.

Jefferson already is in existence. Each Thursday, citizens of Modoc, Siskiyou, Del Norte, and Lassen Counties are in patriotic rebellion and operate as a separate state. It raises some fine legal problems.

For example, does California dock State Senator Randolph Collier's pay on Rebellion Thursday when he acts as provisional Governor of Jefferson?

Who does State of Jefferson Comptroller Homer Burton, the Yreka mortician, pay on Thursday and what does provisional Treasurer Heine Russ use for money?

The lumber counties have offered to mint wooden nickels for the rebellion and have warned Governor Olson of California that the penny sales tax will be impounded by the new state.

"If he wants copper," say the Jeffersonians, "let him come up and dig it out of the Siskiyous."

What they really want to do is to give the Governor a ride over the back country roads to the copper deposits and show him why trucks have to blow off the sides of mountains to get through.

All across the California-Oregon border the Jefferson state seal of a double cross on a mining pan is spreading from town to town.

Mayor Gable spoke at a meeting at Cave City in Josephine County just the other night and Fifth Columnists of the Jefferson movement are active in other border counties. Everyone in these counties has a piece of a mine, a copper or chrome deposit, and thinks he would be rich with present prices and development.

The gas station man and the restaurant owner will tell you about their cinnabar claim up creeks with names out of Bret Harte.

This is the amazing and unknown land of America. This is the last frontier and the hardy stand of rugged individualism that is not a political slogan.

This is where miners swarm around building excavations and wash gold dust from the new earth.

Housewives slit open a duck's gizzard and their husbands are off for the backwoods farm where those ducks picked up the gold nuggets that popped out of their giblets.

Youngsters are making Christmas money by washing small amounts of gold dust from old tailings of the Sixties when prodigal miners with crude equipment sent as much dust downstream as they took out of the ground.

Now the rush is on. Chrome for hardening steel is double the usual price. Copper is up to 14 cents a pound. The rocks that old-timers threw away are big money now and they want money for roads to bring them to ships on the coast.

I have seen enough fallen timber rotting on the ground to stoke the fireplaces of San Francisco for the next ten years. Lumber mills, they tell me, are burning all but the choice center boards of the logs. Transportation would solve a lot of problems up here. And until Oregon and California give it to the mountain men, I wouldn't sell short on this movement for a new 49th State of Jefferson.

The Jeffersonian movement collapsed two days after this story was written. Mayor Gable, its chief publicist, died of acute indigestion on December 2, 1941 at the age of fifty-five—"And perhaps," wrote Delaplane in an unorthodox obituary, "he was too tense."

"Gable probably knew," Delaplane went on, "that his forty-ninth state and secession movement would not be accomplished. But he knew the weaknesses of state legislatures and the pin pricks of adverse publicity, and he used them neatly. But death beat him to the knockout punch."

The tragic news of Pearl Harbor washed over the feeble remnants of humorous comment on the forty-ninth state of Jefferson five days later. And in the broiling midsummer heat of Washington, D. C., in 1958, William H. Seward's $7,200,000 iceberg, the fabulously vast and rich expanse of Alaska, was voted the forty-ninth state. In 1959 it joined the union.

Jefferson lives on, a pleasant and harmless myth, in the Pulitzer Prize Collection. Not without the wry ghost of a smile in the bleak America that faced the Axis after Pearl Harbor, the Trustees of Columbia University voted Stanton Delaplane a Pulitzer Prize in reporting for 1942.

3. ARTHUR KROCK INTERVIEWS TRUMAN
AND IS UPHELD EIGHT YEARS LATER

The story that didn't win a Pulitzer Prize
because its author was on the Board

Former President Harry S. Truman was testifying before the House
Banking Committee. Republicans were pressing him to admit that he
once had conceded a certain amount of unemployment was supportable,
that "it is a good thing that job-seeking should go on at all times . . ."
Truman denied it.

He was told he had said exactly that in an interview he had granted
to Arthur Krock of the New York *Times,* published on February 15,
1950. This was now eight years later—April 14, 1958.

Truman thrust out his chin defiantly. "May I say that exclusive interview never happened! That came out of the air!"

Krock charged to the offensive in the *Times* next day. He disclosed
that Truman himself had proposed the exclusive interview at a dinner
on February 7, 1950.

In excellent humor, the President had joined Chief Justice Vinson and
Krock after leaving the table. Nodding at Krock, he had said, "I want
to talk to the Brains Trust."

"He has a few questions, Mr. President, that he would like to ask
you," Justice Vinson had said.

"Just come and see me and ask 'em!"

After that, Krock had gone to the White House February 13, 1950,
had his interview, and later he had shown the text to the President and
obtained his approval.

All this Krock recalled in the *Times* and commented tartly: "The most
tolerant conclusion is that memory . . . fails Mr. Truman when the event
is a part of his own and recent experience."

Truman backed down. A week later, after reviewing the facts, he
apologized to Krock and to the House committee. He wrote that he had
been taken by surprise by the Republicans and "thought that an effort
was made to embarrass me at your [Krock's] expense."

"My memory fails to work quickly . . ." he added.

To which Krock magnanimously added his comment that the Republicans "were indeed using me to make a whipping boy out of you."

All of which prompted one observer to write: "I'd rather be Krock than President."

The Krock interview is a curiosity for still another reason. It never was awarded a Pulitzer Prize but achieved the rare distinction of blocking all other candidates for the National Reporting award for 1951. Because Krock that year was a member of the Advisory Board on the Pulitzer Prizes, the Board ruled as follows:

"The Advisory Board on the Pulitzer Prizes as a policy does not make any award to an individual member of the Board, and whereas the outstanding instance of National Reporting in 1950 was the achievement of Mr. Arthur Krock in obtaining an exclusive interview with the President of the United States, Be it resolved that the Board make no award in the National Reporting category."

Krock had won two Pulitzer Prizes before becoming a member of the Advisory Board, in 1935 and 1938. His second was for exclusively interviewing President Franklin D. Roosevelt. In the history of the prizes, only one other reporter ever received an award for exclusively interviewing a President—Louis Seibold of the New York *World* for publishing an authorized talk with President Wilson.

Here is the essential text of the Krock interview with President Truman, which led the *Times* for February 15, 1950 under a three-column head.

THE PRESIDENT RECEIVES A REPORTER

By Arthur Krock

From the New York Times, Feb. 15, 1950

WASHINGTON, Feb. 14—In the age of atomic energy, transmuted into a weapon which can destroy great cities and the best works of civilization, and in the shadow of a hydrogen detonant which could multiply many times that agent of destruction, a serene President of the United States sits in the White House with undiminished confidence in the triumph of humanity's better nature and the progress of his own efforts to achieve abiding peace.

This President, Harry S. Truman, is a controversial figure in the world and in domestic politics. But to those who talk with him intimately about the problem of global life and death, his faith that these good things will happen, and probably in his time, shines out with a luminous and simple quality which no event or misadventure of policy can diminish.

The following is an account of the President's current views on the international and domestic issues of his time which I can vouch for as to accuracy. It may serve further to reveal to doubters and critics what manner of man he really is, and crystalize in the minds of those who instinctively supported him in the campaign of 1948 what were the personal qualities they sensed but did not always comprehend.

He sits in the center of the troubled and frightened world, not a world he ever made; but the penumbra of doubt and fear in which the American nation pursues its greatest and most perilous adventure—the mission to gain world peace and security while preserving the strength of the native experiment in democracy—stops short of him. Visitors find him undaunted and sure that, whether in his time or thereafter, a way will be discovered to preserve the world from the destruction which to many seems unavoidable, as moral force is steadily weakened by the conflict of two great rival systems and by new skills in forging weapons of destruction that make the discovery of gunpowder seem like the first ignition of the parlor match.

His reasons for this serenity and this sureness emerge from current conversations with the President on the issues of the time. For Mr. Truman is the kind of American who must be observed at firsthand, free to speak with the candor and natural piety of his makeup, to be wholly understood.

In such meetings he answers questions that bear directly on the problems before him. And these questions and his answers that follow (the latter put mostly in the indirect discourse which is due a President for his own protection and that of the country) reveal the man and what he conceives to be his mission and his methods of accomplishing it better than the formal record can do.

Q. You recall the hopeful prospect of peace that surrounded you, and you expressed, at San Francisco in 1945 when the United Nations was organized. What has happened since to bring about deterioration to the point where a member of your Cabinet can say of it: "The cold fact is that we are still in a hot war"? When did you conclude that normal negotiation with the Kremlin was hopeless?

A. The President said he remembered that time well, and with what good will toward the Russian people and their rulers he went to Potsdam shortly thereafter. There he planned to offer help for

THE LAWS OF MOSES AND THE LAWS OF TODAY
by D. R. Fitzpatrick

PULITZER PRIZE, 1926   ST. LOUIS POST-DISPATCH

reconstruction, of Russia as well as the rest of the world, on a very large scale. He remembered with pride and sympathy how Russians had smashed the German armies in the East, and he believed their assistance was necessary to win the war against Japan. But he found that all Stalin wanted to talk about was the abrupt cessation of lend-lease; hence the atmosphere was unfavorable to what President Truman had in mind.

"To abolish lend-lease at the time was a mistake." But he was "new" then; the papers had been prepared for Roosevelt and represented a Government decision. He felt there was nothing else he could do but sign. He had no staff and no Cabinet of his own. Now he has both.

The agreement the Russians made at Yalta to enter the war against Japan was the only one they ever kept out of nearly forty. He has no hope they will keep any which now it would be good policy to seek. But he remains hopeful of the outcome. . . .

Q. In view of your background, training, and dislike of debt, how do you reconcile these with your toleration of deficit spending and your advocacy of new spending programs? Critics of the Fair Deal program say it proposes permanently to burden the more able, diligent, and successful with the cost of "insuring all others against the results of their own improvidence, ill-luck, or defective behavior"; that this is very nearly the Marxian doctrine, "to each according to his need, from each according to his ability."

A. In no sense does the President tolerate deficit spending. There wouldn't be any now if the Republicans had not cut the income taxes in the Eightieth Congress. Tax changes should not have been made piecemeal at any time, but conformed to a general and revised plan. This was equally true when he approved the repeal of the excess profits tax. He wishes he had not done this, because it was piecemeal also. But then again he was new at the job.

His object is steadily to expand the economy so as to provide jobs and careers for the million and a half young people who come annually into the stream of commerce. This cannot be done without the measures outlined in the Fair Deal. From a peak of 59.6 millions of persons employed in civilian activities last September, the number has gone down to 56 millions, with 4.8 millions unemployed. A certain amount of unemployment, say from three to five millions, is supportable. It is a good thing that job-seeking should go on at all times; this is healthy for the economic body. But the main thing is to keep the economy rising to absorb the new entrants into the stream of commerce. There are now 62 millions employed in the labor force in the United States, including the military. Ten years ago whoever suggested that this could happen would have been written down a fool or a dreamer. . . .

He has no policy which contemplates permanently burdening the more able, diligent, and successful with the cost of insuring all others against the results of their own improvidence, ill-luck, or defective behavior. This charge—also that the Fair Deal approximates the Marxian doctrine—is absolutely untrue. The President's aim is to preserve life and property and expand opportunity and the standards of living. "There isn't a drop of Marxist or Socialist blood" in him.

The globe shows vast areas inhabited by hundreds of millions of people who want to improve their lot, and this can be done with our American surpluses and with a moderate amount of our assistance, financial and technical. When that is done, the chief threat of international communism will pass, and this is the primary objective of his policy. . . .

Q. Will you explain your use of "red herring" and "hysteria" in the context of the spy trials and hunts since you are charged (1) with not comprehending the gravity of this situation or (2) playing for votes of groups under suspicion?

A. When Mr. Truman on several occasions spoke of "hysteria" and "red herrings" in connection with revelations about espionage, etc., he was criticizing the *methods* employed by the Un-American Activities Committee and by individuals in Congress and out of it. The objective of having only loyal citizens in Government service and in positions of importance and responsibility has been his fundamentally, too.

His loyalty board (Chairman Seth W. Richardson) has done much more effective screening of this kind without headlines and personal publicity than the Congressional spy hunts, which have been animated chiefly by quests for headlines and personal publicity. These produced the "hysteria" he was talking about, reminding him of the public excitement in the days of the Alien and Sedition Acts, the Know-Nothing Movement, the Ku Klux Klan, and the Red scares of 1920. And he has never changed his opinion that the way the Un-American Activities Committee handled the Hiss and other cases was a "red herring" to distract public attention from the blunders and crimes of the Eightieth Congress.

When the President was chairman of the special Senate committee during the war, he followed a method which he sought to endorse by contrast when he made the above comments about "hysteria" and "red herrings." Whenever he found something wrong or some indication of potential wrong in the war program, he privately communicated the facts to the departments concerned, and usually it was corrected or averted without the kind of publicity that unfairly shakes public confidence and spreads through the more than two millions in Government employ a feeling of insecurity in their jobs which hampers and damages their work.

The result was that no major scandal occurred in the war. This is the responsible method which, because it was not followed in these other matters, impelled him to say what he did. The Government service is 99 percent plus loyal and secure.

If the facts about a Government employee show the contrary, out the man will go at no expense to public stability—though, it is true, without a headline for a politician who has that chiefly in his mind.

Such are the President's statements of his views.

Those who have the privilege, necessarily a limited one, of searching in this way the mind and purpose of Harry S. Truman usually come away with faith in his honesty and courage. They usually come away also with the conviction that, whether or not he has the greatness which the times require—a question that must be left to the verdict of history—he means to preserve the basic system by which this nation attained its greatness and to achieve and maintain that peace which has been its highest aspiration since 1783.

4. WHY THEY INSIST
ON BEING CANADIANS

Austin Wehrwein of the Milwaukee Journal
interprets our northern neighbors

Pulitzer Prize for International Reporting, 1953

"Why don't they like us?"

Many Americans solemnly fold their hands, look worried, and wonder aloud over the anti-American outbursts abroad.

"We want to be friends . . . we give them money . . . we protect them . . ."

Yes, it's very true. It was true when Vice-President Richard M. Nixon sallied south of the border in 1958. It was true when he came back after the roughest reception ever given any Norte Americano by our Latin American friends.

It raises the question: "How can we achieve a decent appreciation of friendly peoples by our own people?"

After all, as any reporter who has ever worked abroad knows, it is an unhappy truth that our friends are much more aware of us than we are of them. Also, that they tend to become annoyed, even embittered, because we sometimes don't know what they are, what they have done, what they wish to be.

Sometimes they suspect, quite wrongfully, that we don't really care about them as people.

Of course, there have been many articles in the press to promote international understanding. It's like promoting going to church, living right, subscribing to the Red Cross. Everybody's for it. But it isn't often that reporters can do a job that is original, interesting, and worth re-reading. Now and then it does happen. One such series was on "Canada's New Century" in the Milwaukee *Journal* in 1952. It was awarded the Pulitzer Prize for International Reporting in 1953.

Austin C. Wehrwein, a Texan with a rich and varied background, wrote the twenty-five articles after a considerable study of Canada and wide travel among Canadians. He had a B.A. in economics from Wisconsin, a law degree from Columbia, and wide experience as a reporter and also as a staff member of the Economic Cooperation Administration abroad. Here is the substance of his concluding article.

CANADA TO AMERICA

By Austin C. Wehrwein

From the Milwaukee Journal, Dec. 28, 1952

VANCOUVER, B. C.—On the surface Americans and Canadians have much in common, but below the surface a visitor finds variations in the daily social and business life. The Canadian tempo is slower and the manner more modest. The general atmosphere is, for lack of a better word, more sober.

That's the impression an American gets after spending several months traveling Canada, a nation bigger than the United States by a third. He finds himself agreeing with Hugh MacLennan, one of Canada's top novelists, that Canadians live under "the tyranny of the Sunday suit."

This is reflected in many ways. In small habits of speech and accent, in their strict Sunday blue laws and restrictions on drinking, in the pomp and circumstance (by our standards) that surround their government. The atmosphere in the "bush" and on construction jobs is, of course, more "breezy" although still not quite "American."

Nothing pleases a Canadian more than to have an American notice these things. He is happy and secure in the knowledge that the stupendous country "across the border" is a friendly power. He has often crossed that border and usually has a host of relatives in "the States" but he is determined to achieve a nationalism that he can call his own.

He feels that along with this he has a mission, individually and nationally, to be a mediator and interpreter. It is a rare Canadian who doesn't tell how he "stands up" for the Yanks when talking to an Englishman, and for the English when talking to a Yank.

Yet this is somewhat of a paradox because Canadian nationalism, in the broad sense of the word, has grown stronger as Canada's ties with the United States have grown closer. It has been the development of intimate political and military ties with the United States, and the development of what amounts to a single economy, that has in large part enabled Canada to cut all but sentimental links with mother country England. However, there does remain in spots an undue deference to things "British."

In groping toward "Canadianism"—a word still used but rarely—Canadians are finding that they must do more than become different from the British and the Americans. They must find themselves.

"We do not understand ourselves," Bruce Hutchison, editor of the Victoria (B.C.) *Times* and a leading Canadian author, said recently. On another occasion Hutchison declared that Canada has reached nationhood by a method that was "obscure, amorphous, and drab."

Hutchison's "understanding" is made all the more difficult to achieve by the existence of "French Canada," whose people make up one-third of the population of 14 million. Only in cities like Montreal, it seems to a visitor, have the two cultures blended to produce something new. . . .

It is only natural for Canadians to take a world view because Canada is primarily an exporting nation. World trade to Canada is not just a way to reduce foreign aid programs. It is her economic meat and drink, bread and butter.

Nevertheless, it seems to an observer that Canada's current boom has blinded some businessmen to the degree to which the country depends on the prosperity of other countries, notably the United States. For example, there is the glee with which they remind an American that their dollar is "worth" more than ours. Actually it is "selling" at a premium in international exchange transactions partly because of United States participation in their internal business, and partly because of a heavy world demand for Canadian exports.

They also tend, as Americans have for too long, to confuse individual merit with the lucky chance that they live in a land rich in resources.

There is a firm optimism in business circles. There is none of the tendency found in the United States to be forever predicting recessions and "soft spots" to come. . . .

Canada's biggest frontier is to the north, the only frontier opened by airplane. While Finland and the Scandinavian countries have proved that a rich culture can be created in the sub-Arctic, the shape of Canada's northward development is not going to follow the pattern of the westward growth of the United States.

Nor, despite her riches, is there the same kind of business opportunity awaiting the ambitious individual. No Henry Fords are likely to emerge. The twentieth century in Canada, as in the United States, is a much more regimented century than was the last. Canada's new wealth is being turned into dollars by big corporations (many American) who move with bulldozers and airplanes, not with covered wagons and moldboard plows. . . .

The average Canadian has far more confidence than an American in the integrity of his governmental representatives and civil servants even when they do step into the field of what might be considered private enterprise.

Part of this may be the result of the orderly tradition of government inherited from Britain. Part is undoubtedly due to the smallness of the population. The atmosphere in Ottawa is more like that of Madison, Wis., than Washington, and a citizen has a far better chance to confer with a top public official than his American counterpart would have in the District of Columbia.

In 1949 the Canadians set up a royal commission on national development in the arts, letters, and sciences when their blossoming nationalism turned into a desire to establish a "native culture."

A single passage of this commission's report illustrates the "we want to be different" emotion in Canadian hearts. It said:

"American influences on Canadian life to say the least are impressive. There should be no thought of interfering with the liberty of all Canadians to enjoy them. . . . It cannot be denied, however, that a vast and disproportionate amount of material coming from a single alien source may stifle rather than stimulate our own creative effort. . . . We must not be blind to the very present danger of permanent dependence."

Thus, Canada, a nation with a far more cozy feeling than we have for tradition, even if it is secondhand, is still really a nation of futures—a nation where what is, or what has been, is less important than what will be. And what will be in Canada will have a tremendous influence on what the United States will be.

5. A LADY FROM ALICE, TEXAS, AND THE DUKE OF DUVAL COUNTY

Mrs. Caro Brown of the Alice Echo
covers the downfall of a one-man empire

Pulitzer Prize for Local Reporting, 1955

Caro Brown knows what it is to look into the end of a gun. She has worked in south Texas.

She made history there in 1954 as a reporter for the Alice *Daily Echo,* and people there have never forgotten it. More than any of her colleagues, she went after the news behind the one-man political empire of George B. Parr, a tough south Texan who was known as the Duke of Duval County. When it toppled, Caro Brown was there to tell the story.

For forty years the Parr family had dominated the county. Its political machine and its private army had been unchallenged until the Texas Rangers moved in. The Rangers came to restore the privileges of U. S. citizens to the people of Duval County. And with them went Caro Brown, the quiet and unassuming mother of a small daughter.

"More than one reporter failed to get information about Duval County," wrote Tom E. Fite, managing editor of the *Echo,* "and one died trying.

"When state and federal agencies finally went into Duval County to open the records, reporters still were not free of the threat of harm if they wrote and printed the story. But Mrs. Brown wrote her stories, and they were published, under perhaps as difficult conditions as such a story ever was."

The following incident, written by Mrs. Brown in Alice on January 18, 1954 and published in the *Echo,* shows what it was like to be a reporter in south Texas when the Duke of Duval County rode high.

"SOMETHING'S FIXING TO HAPPEN"

By Caro Brown

From the Alice (Texas) Echo, Jan. 19, 1954

I've learned never to leave the scene just because things are dull. That's when the lid usually pops off in south Texas.

That's why I stuck around today as Sheriff Archer Parr of Duval County; his uncle, George Parr, the south Texas politico; Ranger Captain Alfred Allee and Ranger Joe Bridge started what was an apparently amiable conversation in the courthouse hall.

The elder Parr was here for his hearing on a charge of unlawfully carrying a pistol. [He and an associate were accused of brandishing guns to try to break up a meeting of the opposition Freedom Party.]

I was about six feet away when Ranger Bridge slapped Archer Parr, setting off a chain of action that left spectators shaken long after it was over. As I watched I could tell that the talk between the sheriff and Bridge was becoming heated and I shushed the man who was talking to me. "Something's fixing to happen," I warned.

And it did. Faster than we could keep up with it, Bridge struck the younger Parr, knocking the latter's glasses to the floor. George Parr jumped forward at that, and immediately Allee grabbed him, and at the same time disarmed the sheriff, who had reached for his gun.

Parr's left ear received an open tear when it was twisted by the Ranger captain, who also hit Parr with his fist before sticking his gun in his ribs.

At that point I stepped into the middle, begging, "Cap, please don't, please don't."

Repeatedly the Ranger captain told George Parr, "I've had all I'm going to take off you and the way you've been handling things."

He then shoved Parr roughly into the county courtroom, motioning Sheriff Parr to come inside along with Bridge.

"We're going to get this thing settled right here," Allee told them.

Archer Parr nervously polished his glasses, which had come through the fracas unbroken, while George Parr nodded agreement to what Allee said. At one time the captain said, "I'm not going to put up with any whipping with pistols or Winchesters in Duval County. Those people have a right to have political meetings without being molested."

Parr nodded, promising that he would not interfere with such meetings.

Later Archer came to me and said, "Caro, thanks for doing what you could to stop the trouble."

A WISE ECONOMIST ASKS A QUESTION, *by John T. McCutcheon*

PULITZER PRIZE, 1932   CHICAGO TRIBUNE

I said, "Archer, please try to keep things straight—let's not have any more things happen that we'll be sorry for."

"Well, I'll try," Archer Parr replied, "but you know how our tempers get some times."

As every reporter knows, there aren't many such incidents in the coverage of even the most heated investigations. The work mostly consists of painstaking coverage of meetings and court hearings, checking of records, getting out on news breaks at all hours of the day and night and trying to discover what happened. That was what Caro Brown did mostly, and that was why she won the Pulitzer Prize for local reporting under edition deadline pressure for 1955. It was a happy coincidence that another Texan, Roland Kenneth Towery, managing editor of the Cuero (Texas) *Record*, won the Pulitzer Prize for reporting not under edition deadline pressure that same year. He exposed a scandal in the administration of the veterans' land program.

It was proof that small city journalism was small in name only. As John Ben Shepperd, Attorney General of Texas, wrote to Mrs. Brown: "You . . . have the gratitude of the people of Duval County and the State of Texas and the admiration of your profession. But your greatest compensation, I am sure, is the satisfaction of having helped bring forty years of corruption and terrorism to an end. Duval County is no longer the 'Land of Murder and Mayhem.'"

6. METRO, CITY OF TOMORROW:
WHAT IT WILL BE LIKE

George Beveridge of the Washington Evening Star
asks its readers to worry about their city

Pulitzer Prize, Local Reporting, not under deadline pressure, 1958

Few newspapers would have paid more than passing attention thirty years ago to the growing problems of urban life. It was good for the editorial page, or maybe the Sunday real-estate section.

Many an editor in those days would have argued that the subject was too general, and seemingly dull. They would have objected because it wasn't headline material, that it took too much space, that it required reporters with special qualifications. And besides, wasn't there a lot of circulation still in sex and crime?

Nowhere is there evidence of greater change in the values of American journalism than in the willingness of thoughtful editors today to try to interest their readers in population pressures, roads, housing, better schools, and all the other factors in urban life. George Beveridge's Pulitzer Prize-winning series of 1958 on "Metro, City of Tomorrow," in the *Evening Star* of Washington, D. C., was the product of just such an editorial attitude.

The *Star* had no sensations to sell, no blast of Page 1 headlines, no crooks to put in jail. It ran the Beveridge series, without by-line, as full-page stories with unexciting illustrations on succeeding Sundays. Its only purpose was to make its readers think about the problems of growth that were confronting the nation's capital.

Beveridge was no slam-bang reporter of the old school, always good for a fast quote or a colorful new fact on an edition deadline whenever the needs of a fast-breaking story demanded it. He was thorough, pains-taking, a gatherer of facts by the volume, an interpreter of municipal affairs. In one article he wrote:

"Some time before the end of this year the birth of a baby will push metropolitan Washington's population over the two million mark.

"In 1940 the population figure was only 967,985. Eight years from now it may be 2.4 million; by 1980, 3.5 million . . ."

And he warned bluntly of these two consequences:

"First, the local populations are increasing to the point where they can no longer be handled by simple extensions and improvements of old systems. As growth continues, local governments must build areawide expressway systems, look outside their own boundaries for distant water-sheds which may supply their needs—and develop new sources of revenue.

"Second, and this is the great Metro challenge here as elsewhere—the provision of these services will become so difficult and expensive that it no longer will be either practical or desirable for the present separate jurisdictions to act independently of their neighbors."

Some old-time editors, reading such passages as these in Beveridge's copy, would have sent him out to get some far less expert civic official to say the same thing in quotes—the deskman's original genuflection to the ancient journalistic god of objectivity. The *Star* scorned such devices and let Beveridge have his say, with results that neither expected. For out of nearly a hundred entries in the category known as local reporting not under edition deadline pressure, three editors composing the jury for that category were impressed with the "Metro" story. And so were the Advisory Board on the Pulitzer Prizes and the Trustees of Columbia University.

Here is Beveridge's general introduction to his series.

NEW URBAN PROBLEM NEEDS NEW ANSWERS

By George Beveridge

From the Washington (D. C.) Evening Star, Oct. 6, 1957

Expanding cities these days are up against a new problem. It is Topic A for discussion wherever sociologists or municipal planners gather. The average citizen is little concerned as yet. But this problem is not just for the experts—it matters to every one who lives near a population center. It matters a great deal to people in Washington's metropolitan area.

The problem arises as a growing city spills over its political boundaries into the land around it. The traditional pattern of gaps between the component parts are filled in and the area becomes a solid metropolis with old boundaries obliterated.

Borrowing a name coined recently in Toronto, let us call this metropolitan phenomenon "Metro." Numerous other names have been used. "Urbanization" is one. A national magazine calls it "The Exploding Metropolis." Our name, at least, has the merit of brevity. Metro, then, it is.

Now this Metro, our city of tomorrow, amounts physically to a single urban community. It has many community-wide interests. Politically, however, it has no unity, no identity even. It is a formless conglomeration of independent jurisdictions, each going its own way, often conflicting with neighboring jurisdictions in the process. How can such a fragmented community pull itself together and make some kind of coordinated sense? That is the Metro problem.

To say it is a new problem is not to say that it has burst on us out of nowhere. It has been a long time coming. Cities have been growing, of course, ever since the industrial revolution. By 1940, about half the nation's people were living in cities or their sparse suburbs. World War II saw new waves of urban migration and expansion, producing strains on the existing political machinery. Still the city areas could muddle along. While the problems raised were vexing, it was possible to cope with them on a business-as-usual piecemeal basis. Moreover, things might settle back to normal before too long.

But they never did settle. Metropolitan growth has continued and in recent years it has accelerated alarmingly. Today, nearly 100 million of 169 million Americans live in urban areas. In case after case, the point has been reached where growth problems no longer can be solved by the individual political entities which make up an urban community.

The urban trend of population movement, moreover, is established. There is nothing in sight to change its direction. Bit by bit, if the experts are right, each urban community will find itself progressively unable to cope, through the existing political setup, with this or that phase of its activities. More and more, it must recognize the necessity for Metro solutions.

And these will have to be new solutions. The Metro problem is a particularly tough one because there is now no recognized political apparatus which takes it into account. Certainly the traditional forms of local government do not. Cities, towns, and counties can deal only with affairs within their physical boundaries. State governments have direct relations only with their own counties and municipalities. Even the machinery used by the federal government to dispense aid for schools, roads, and slum clearance is geared to deal only with states, cities or counties—though the affected communities are unlikely to conform to these geographical boundaries.

In sum, although Metro is now the dominant pattern of American living, it is a pattern without legal recognition.

7. THE BOYS WHO CAME TO DINNER: FOOTNOTE TO A SENATE INQUIRY

Clark Mollenhoff of the Des Moines Register & Tribune breaks a secret meeting between Jimmy Hoffa and Bob Kennedy

Pulitzer Prize for National Reporting, 1958

Clark Mollenhoff is a digger. For five years he worked to force disclosures of racketeering in the powerful Teamsters Union. Eventually, he succeeded.

During those five years Mollenhoff poured a succession of exposés, exclusive interviews, and explanatory series into the Des Moines *Register & Tribune*. He was among the first to get into the strange and tangled affairs of Dave Beck, president of the Teamsters. He also attacked loose handling of Teamster health and welfare funds, lack of democracy in some of its elections, and "conflicts of interest" in its dealings with employers.

Both Senator John L. McClellan, the Arkansas Democrat who headed the Senate inquiry into labor racketeering, and Robert F. Kennedy, the chief counsel, praised Mollenhoff's work. Kennedy, in fact, wrote that "it was probably you more than anyone else who is responsible for this investigation."

The results of the inquiry are history. Beck was overthrown and convicted of stealing union funds. James R. Hoffa, his successor, was subjected to a thorough inquiry. A number of other Teamster officials were removed, either as a result of conflicts with the law or the disgust of their associates.

Probably one of the most intriguing stories Mollenhoff unearthed was his account of a secret dinner party at which Kennedy and Hoffa met for the first time. It was published in the Des Moines *Register* and was one of the many in the file that won Mollenhoff a Pulitzer Prize for National Reporting in 1958.

"I'M STILL ALIVE, DEAR"

By Clark Mollenhoff

From the Des Moines Register, June 7, 1957

WASHINGTON, D. C.—At 7:45 p.m., February 19, 1957, Robert F. Kennedy shook hands with James R. Hoffa.

Kennedy, chief counsel for the Senate labor racket committee, quipped: "From what I've heard about you, I probably should have worn my bullet-proof vest."

Kennedy's remark was made in good humor. Hoffa accepted it with equal confidence. It was the first face-to-face meeting of the investigator with the aggressive, 44-year-old Teamsters Union vice president who was one of his major targets.

The scene was a small dinner party at the home of Washington

FORD STRIKERS RIOT, *by Milton Brooks*

PULITZER PRIZE, 1942   DETROIT NEWS

FORD STRIKERS RIOT, by Amos Brooks

BRITISH PRESS, 1941. DETROIT NEWS

attorney Edward Cheyfitz. Cheyfitz, a friend of Kennedy and also a former public relations counsel for the Teamsters, had thought it would be nice for Hoffa and Kennedy to get acquainted without public fanfare.

The arrangements had been made weeks earlier—before either Kennedy or Hoffa had heard of John Cye Cheasty, New York lawyer-investigator. Each of these men was confident he held the top cards in the battle between Congressional investigators and the mighty Teamsters Union.

Hoffa felt he had ample reason for confidence. Only an hour earlier he had met Cheasty on the corner of Seventeenth and I Streets, N. W. Cheasty had given him a report on what witnesses Kennedy planned to subpoena for the labor racket hearings.

As they huddled outside the Service Pharmacy in a heavy snowstorm, Cheasty had told Hoffa he expected to be sworn in next day as a member of the McClellan committee staff.

Hoffa had reason to believe he had a direct pipeline into the heart of Kennedy's confidential files. What Hoffa didn't know was that Cheasty four days earlier had turned double agent and was under constant FBI surveillance in his contacts with Hoffa.

Kennedy approached the dinner in possession of more of the facts. But he had more than a slight uneasiness. He had been tempted to call off the dinner on one pretext or another.

Kennedy was afraid the meeting with Hoffa might result in an incident that would jeopardize the whole Cheasty operation. At the same time, he was afraid Hoffa would be suspicious if the dinner was canceled. He decided to go through with the dinner, and didn't even mention it to the FBI.

Cheasty had been accompanied by FBI Agents Charles Schaffer and Carl Martin at 5:30 p.m. February 19 as Cheasty phoned Hoffa from a pay telephone in the Senate Office Building. Cheasty identified himself to Hoffa as "Eddie Smith"—a code name they had arranged—said he had some information for Hoffa and asked where they might meet.

Hoffa yelled to Cheyfitz, asking him the time of the dinner with Kennedy. When Cheyfitz said it was set for 7:30, Hoffa and Cheasty agreed to a meeting at 6 or 6:15 p.m.

Cheasty, followed by two FBI agents, hurried to Kennedy's office

THE THINKER, *by Bruce M. Shanks*

PULITZER PRIZE, 1958   BUFFALO EVENING NEWS

to report he was to meet Hoffa, and received some innocuous information from Kennedy that he might pass along to Hoffa. The FBI agents took Cheasty to the corner of Seventeenth Street and Pennsylvania Avenue—two blocks from the Hoffa rendezvous. Kennedy read some newspaper articles on Hoffa's background as a last-minute preparation for the meeting.

Shortly after 7 p.m., Kennedy called home to tell his wife, Ethel, he was leaving for the dinner with Hoffa. She was nervous about it, but Kennedy quipped: "Maybe I should wear a bullet-proof vest."

He asked his wife to call around 10 p.m., so the evening wouldn't be drawn out too long.

Kennedy was fifteen minutes late when he drove up to the Cheyfitz home in suburban Bethesda, Md. It was snowing and he felt uneasy as he rang the doorbell.

Hoffa didn't drink. Cheyfitz offered Kennedy a drink but Kennedy cautiously declined.

After a few quips the conversation turned to the Teamster power abuses and business power abuses. Both Kennedy and Hoffa were guarded and careful. The talk was dull at points.

The discussions continued on generalities through the roast beef dinner. Kennedy had two glasses of milk. Hoffa had tea. Kennedy had two desserts—cheese and cake. Hoffa had none.

"If you don't ask a few embarrassing questions, then I will," Cheyfitz said. He asked about Hoffa's association with the underworld, and the "paper locals" in New York. Kennedy got into the conversation in a cautious way.

Hoffa admitted he had a lot of underworld associates, including Labor Racketeer John (Johnny Dio) Dioguardi, but said he was entitled to his own choice of friends. He assured Kennedy he was tough, plenty rough, but that he was "legal."

Just before 10 p.m., the phone rang and Julia Cheyfitz answered it. "Your wife wants to talk to you," she told Kennedy.

Hoffa took his turn at a quip: "Better hurry up, Bobby. She probably called to see if you are still alive."

At the telephone, within hearing distance of Hoffa and Cheyfitz, Kennedy answered: "I'm still alive, dear. If you hear a big explosion, I probably won't be."

Ethel Kennedy said a woman had driven a car into the bushes at their home, and she wanted Bob to come home. It was a true story. Kennedy left.

At home Kennedy told his wife and his secretary, Angela Novello, that he doubted if a guy who was really tough would talk as much about it as Hoffa did.

The next time Kennedy saw Hoffa was at the Federal Court House in Washington the night of March 13, shortly after Hoffa was arrested at the Dupont Plaza Hotel in the possession of some committee files he had received from Cheasty.

A Federal Court jury in Washington was shown pictures of Hoffa passing $2,000 to Cheasty and taking the files. Two FBI agents corroborated the story. Hoffa, taking the stand in his own defense, conceded the story was true. But he pleaded that he had hired Cheasty as a lawyer and that he hadn't known Cheasty was a member of the McClellan committee staff. Hoffa was acquitted on July 24, 1957 as a sequel to the dinner party and shortly afterward was elected president of the Teamsters Union. But the investigation went on despite that.

II. A NEVER-ENDING BATTLE:
THE FIGHT AGAINST GRAFT

A new district attorney took office in 1955 in Watsonville, Calif. The Watsonville *Register-Pajaronian,* the only newspaper in the town, soon became increasingly suspicious of him and his friends. It began investigating.

With a circulation of only 7,000, the paper couldn't afford to antagonize the community. It also couldn't afford to be wrong about the new prosecutor.

But the inquiry paid off. One cold fall midnight, a reporter and photographer for the paper found the district attorney visiting a known gambler. After they had taken pictures to confirm the visit, both newspapermen were held at gun point by the gambler's henchmen. The camera was destroyed.

In the scandal that resulted, the people of the community rallied to the paper's side. The attorney general of California began an investigation. The district attorney's principal adviser was convicted of bribery and conspiracy. The district attorney resigned.

For its work, the *Register-Pajaronian* won the Pulitzer Prize for Public Service for 1956.

It took just as much courage for this small paper to oppose a prosecutor as was required of any large paper in fighting a governor, a senator, or a powerful judge. And it has often happened in the annals of the Pulitzer Prizes that such small papers are just as effective and zealous guardians of the public welfare as any large daily.

For every Chicago *Daily News* that exposes a grafting state auditor, there is a Cedar Rapids *Gazette* to fight corruption in its Iowa home.

For every St. Louis *Post-Dispatch* that attacks wholesale registration frauds, there is a Medford *Mail-Tribune* to battle political graft in Oregon.

For every Detroit *Free Press* that leads a civic cleanup, there is a Waterbury *Republican & American* to achieve needed reforms in Connecticut.

For every Indianapolis *Times* and Miami *Daily News* that are active in the cause of good government, there is a Columbus (Ga.) *Ledger* to clean up a danger spot like Phenix City.

For every newspaper that has won the Pulitzer gold medal for public service, in fact, there are scores of others that have made valued contributions to honesty and integrity in government.

In such a cause, reporters and photographers have risked their lives. In such a cause, editors have been shot down. In such a cause, day by day, journalism proves itself.

8. ASSASSINS MOW DOWN
A FIGHTING OHIO EDITOR

How the Canton Daily News avenged the murder of Don R. Mellett, a crusader for decency and justice

Pulitzer Prize for Public Service, 1927

On New Year's Day, 1926, Don R. Mellett wrote a front page editorial for the Canton (Ohio) *Daily News,* which was published the following day. In it, he told his fellow-citizens:

"It is the opinion of the *News* that Canton needs cleaning up. Bootlegging, gambling, and houses of prostitution are running wide open in flagrant violation of the law. . . .

"The ramifications of the underworld reach rather far in Canton and touch some men of considerable standing. This condition will continue as long as the Police Department remains incompetent and lax in its program of law enforcement as it has been during the last several years."

Mellett's decision to clean up Canton had not been lightly taken. Many months before, he had gone to the owner of the *News,* former

Governor James M. Cox of Ohio, to discuss the encroachment of the underworld and the pitiful laxity of the police.

As Governor Cox later wrote:

"I subjected him to an extensive and intensive investigation. On one occasion he replied in his characteristic affable way that my inquiries seemed to imply lack of confidence in him. My response was that I only sought to save him from the mistake I made when I was his age. This seemed not only satisfying to him, but very reassuring. It seemed to form the beginning of a relationship which approached the fondness of a father for his son."

Governor Cox, who had been the Presidential nominee of the Democratic Party in 1920, quietly reminded the youthful publisher of the Canton *Daily News* that "the affairs of a community cannot be made any better than the people themselves want them to be." But Mellett stubbornly championed the people of Canton, and kept up the pressure on his employer.

"When he made his case as to existing conditions," Governor Cox wrote long afterward, "and reminded me of our professional responsibility, then there was no answer to his expressed determination to expose wrong wherever found, regardless of any conditions, political or otherwise, that might be encountered."

And so Don Mellett began firing his editorial broadsides, directing his staff in an exposé that jolted the chief of police out of office, naming names, smashing through the flimsy opposition of those who murmured that he was "giving Canton a bad name" and ought to desist.

"The big cleanup is on the way," he wrote jubilantly under his own by-line on Page 1 of the *Daily News* on March 1, 1926, naming still more names and making still more demands for action.

"Liquor law violation is only part of the vice. Dope and gambling are contributing a big share to making Canton's underworld a place to be reckoned with. During the last six years there have been committed nearly fifty murders in Stark County. Of these only two convictions were obtained. It is a common thing, rather than the exceptional, for a murder to go unexplained rather than to obtain a confession or apprehend the murderer . . ."

On July 12, 1926, he apparently felt that he should give the opposition a hearing and ordered published, on Page 1, a letter signed by Price Janson, the respectable head of the Canton Civil Service Commission at the time, which contained these two sentences:

"Mr. Mellett not so long ago blessed the state of Indiana by leaving it and brought to Canton a mouthing, slobbering, overworked jawbone and by his blackguarding, muckraking tactics has caused Canton un-measurable harm by his publicity of scandalous matter and given to Canton an unfavorable name which the facts and truth of the situation do not warrant—a man whose civic pride all rests in his overworked jawbone. In a less refined, civilized society than exists here in Canton, the community would have purged itself of this nuisance by riding him out on a rail, amidst the praise and applause of the enraptured multi-tude . . ."

A Mellett editorial on the following day gave the Janson letter a rela-tively gentle answer, saying, "Certainly there should be no division of the good citizens while the forces of the underworld stand united, ready and willing to confuse the fight for their abolishment."

Three days later, in the early hours of July 16, 1926, Don R. Mellett drove home to his wife and four small children but was shot and killed while he was putting his automobile in the garage. The Canton *Daily News* hit the street two hours later with an extra, telling the news and promising to avenge its fallen publisher in this editorial.

WE CARRY ON

From the Canton (Ohio) Daily News, July 16, 1926

Like a captain in battle leading his forces, Don R. Mellett, pub-lisher of the *Daily News*, has fallen—a sacrifice to the cause he waged against vice and what he believed were efforts to corrupt the city government. Wanton murder stalked at midnight into his home. Assassin bullets took his life, and left the widow and four small children, his only pride and joy outside of his newspaper work. Shot down in the dark without any warning or any chance to defend himself, he is the victim of cowards who were afraid to come out and fight fair. He has been laid upon the altar, a martyr to a system that is getting a stranglehold upon government. A brilliant career is cut off just at the time when this man, hardly out of his youth, began to visualize his aspirations—that of having performed a service to his fellow beings and his adopted city.

A born fighter, Mr. Mellett waged the vice war unrelentingly, and almost single-handed, his support being a few individuals who were as keenly interested as he was in the situation here. Mr. Mellett has fallen, but his ideals are emblazoned brighter than ever on his escutcheon. Canton more forcibly realizes now what he was fighting and why he was fighting. The thoughtful must now know that what Mr. Mellett charged was true. His passing does not mean the end of the battle.

The *Daily News* will carry on.

The battle was waged relentlessly.

Governor Cox, in a long tribute to Mellett, wrote the following day: "Don Mellett was not a crusader bent merely on adventure. He sought neither to exploit himself nor his newspaper. He discussed with me once how disagreeable an affair it was. He was moved purely by a sense of duty.

"How foolish were the assassins and those who goaded them on! The taking of a single life in the present circumstances is of no avail. When a general falls at the head of his army, the spectacle of sacrifice moves his followers onward to increased devotion in the cause."

Charles E. Morris, who had been Cox's secretary as governor, took over from the fallen Mellett. Within twelve hours he had left his office as editor-in-chief of the Cox Ohio News League and was demanding action from a supine police department. When he didn't get it, he brought in his own investigator, Joseph Roach of Chicago. But for all that, a grand jury failed to return any indictments.

Public officeholders were lax, and some were worse. The public conscience had been dulled. The fight to avenge Mellett was carried on with vigor wherever there were honest newspapers—but Canton remained supine.

Finally Roach filed suit in Federal Court on behalf of Mrs. Mellett, ostensibly to seek damages, and named several suspects. He also threatened to make city and county officials co-defendants unless they took a more active role in the case. The threat worked.

Five men were arrested, tried, and convicted. Three had been ex-convicts—Pat McDermott, Ben Rudner, and Louis Mazer. The fourth was Floyd Streitenberger, captain of detectives on the Canton police force, and the fifth was the police chief of Canton, S. A. Lengel.

Rudner, accused of arranging the killing, was convicted of second-degree murder and is in Ohio State Penitentiary. Mazer, who drove the getaway car, turned state's evidence and was given a five-year term which he served. McDermott, convicted of first-degree murder, was sentenced to life and is in Ohio State Penitentiary. Streitenberger also was convicted of first-degree murder, given a life sentence, and sent to the same prison. Chief Lengel, convicted of first-degree murder, was granted a new trial and acquitted when Streitenberger, who had testified against him at the first trial, refused to do so a second time. There were reports that Streitenberger had been threatened by fellow-convicts. Lengel died some years after being freed.

The Canton *Daily News* received the Pulitzer Prize for Public Service in 1927. But three years later, Governor Cox, unable to overcome his distress over what had happened, sold the *News*. It was combined with the Brush-Moore paper, the Canton *Repository*. Mrs. Mellett moved away to Indianapolis. New York University established a fund to honor Mellett's memory with an annual lecture on crusading journalism.

The gold medal, emblematic of the Pulitzer public service prize, is sealed in the cornerstone of the building now occupied by the *Repository*. And whenever a newspaper embarks on a campaign for better government in America, the name of Mellett is remembered with reverence and respect.

9. A SMALL OREGON DAILY BATTLES
BALLOT BOX THEFTS AND MURDER

Robert W. Ruhl and the Medford Mail Tribune
defeat a gang of corrupt officeholders

Pulitzer Prize for Public Service, 1934

Suppose your favorite newspaper demanded one morning: "Must we have martial law?"

You'd think, of course, that it couldn't happen. Yet, it did happen in the pleasant rural community of Medford, Oregon.

It was a time of crisis in America. The year: 1933. The situation: a world-wide depression. The threat: an overthrow of a town's free, democratic government by a corrupt, totalitarian regime.

Melodramatic? Yes, and worse. It was sheer tragedy that went far beyond the borders of Medford and surrounding Jackson County, and affected many more than the 32,000 persons in that area. The story carries ominous overtones for any time of crisis in America.

It all began quietly enough in the 1920s when Llewellyn A. Banks, an owner of orchards, came to Medford from California. He had with him a second wife, a million dollars, two new Cadillacs, and a tremendous lust for power.

As the depression gripped him, and threatened his standing, he sought a way out. He tried politics. Swiftly he founded a political organization, ironically called the Good Government Congress; ran unsuccessfully for United States Senator against Charles McNary; elected a county judge, a sheriff, and others; bought a newspaper and began playing for high stakes.

That was when the Medford *Mail Tribune*, which alone opposed him, raised the issue of martial law as follows:

"During the past few days, the writer has been visited by well-known and responsible citizens, urging that we advocate the declaring of martial law so that bloodshed can be avoided, respect for our courts and our laws enforced, and those threatening bombs and the noose can be put behind the bars where they belong . . ."

The writer was the energetic young editor and publisher of the *Mail Tribune*, Robert Waldo Ruhl, out of Phillips Andover and Harvard and New York journalism. Although his paper had only 4,441 subscribers and was in debt because of purchase of a new press and equipment, he turned down the idea of martial law and went after the Banks organization himself.

Crisis succeeded crisis until, in an attempt to halt a recount of an election that might have endangered their power, the gang raided the county court house, stole ballot boxes, and destroyed them. Next, Banks shot and killed a constable, George Prescott, who sought to serve a summons on him for a court action. Banks, by this time, had lost his newspaper, the Medford *News*, to its previous owners and was desperately rallying his followers for a final stand. The *Mail Tribune* charged he was about to embark on an armed insurrection.

Here is the climactic editorial.

THE CHALLENGE IS ACCEPTED!

By Robert Waldo Ruhl

From the Medford (Ore.) Mail Tribune, March 17, 1933

Do the people of Jackson County want more innocent officers shot down in cold blood behind the skirts of some woman?

Do they want continued lawlessness, continued pillaging of court houses, and burning of ballots?

Do they want this reign of terror followed by another, until this community is reduced to a shambles and advertised far and wide as a place where crime is encouraged, sedition lauded, and murder condoned?

If they do, then that is precisely what they are going to have. All they need to do now is to lie down and take it!

There is no regret for this crime on the part of those responsible for it. No remorse. No sympathy for the dead; no human feeling for the bereaved and aged living; not a thought for the mourning children.

The man who fired the fatal shot, who snuffed out the life of a man who had done him no wrong, who he knew was merely performing his sworn duty, glories in the terrible deed. He proudly tells the world that under the same circumstances he would kill again. With a set smile on his face, he walks over the body of his stricken foe, steps off the stage he had prepared with his own hands to himself escape the fatal sentence he had so pitilessly and wantonly inflicted, and is apparently surprised that he did not receive the plaudits of his "Good Government" followers.

The woman who had shielded and aided him, who at a given signal stepped aside that the bullet might find a fatal spot, proudly poses for her picture with a smile on her face. She had supposed she shouldn't smile for such a picture but her amusement couldn't be controlled. She smiled and smiled, adding, "This fight will go on."

Another woman, the president of the Good Government Congress, the woman who boasted of taking the law into her own hands, who declared that the ballot boxes that were burned should have been burned before, has the unspeakable effrontery to claim in one breath that she "regrets the tragedy" and in the next: "I would not be a real American if I did not continue to fight."

"An American!" Continue to fight for what? For ballot burning, for horsewhipping, for deliberate and premeditated murder!

There is the challenge, citizens of Jackson County! Are you going to meet it? Or are you going to laugh it off as just another one of those "funny things"?

Yesterday when the fatal shot was fired, and one of the finest and most fearless officers we have ever had lay crumpled and cold in death, we believed that the shot had at last solved our problem. We felt it would certainly remove the scales from the eyes of Banks' deluded and misguided followers, show them clearly their ghastly and tragic mistake, and put the leader of this criminal conspiracy

"TAMMANY!" by Rollin Kirby

PULITZER PRIZE, 1929   NEW YORK WORLD

to destroy this community behind the bars. We thought it would
result in the return of peace and security—too late, it is true—and at
too great a price—but we found consolation in the old adage,
"Better late than never."

We were mistaken. We frankly admit our mistake. We underestimated the extent to which this poison had spread. We failed
to appreciate the depths of human depravity to which certain
sections of Jackson County had fallen.

Only a few hours after that editorial was written, this office
received an anonymous phone call from some woman who warned
this paper to "lay off," who obviously was not only in sympathy
with the crime, but rejoiced in it. She agreed with the wife of one
of the Good Government leaders that "George Prescott merely got
what was coming to him—that there would be others!"

And today this community is informed that the fight that has
ended in this tragedy, that is solely responsible for it, "must go on."

We don't know how the people of this community feel about it.
But we know how this paper feels. With that brazenly lawless statement, we heartily agree. That challenge to everything that is right
and decent and law-abiding in Medford and Jackson County is
promptly accepted.

The fight must go on!

Yes, the fight must go on—

Until every individual directly or indirectly involved in this murder is brought to justice.

Until every person involved directly or indirectly in the pillaging
of the court house and the burning of the ballots is put in the penitentiary where he—or she—belongs.

Until every person involved, directly or indirectly, in this out-
rageous and diabolical conspiracy to destroy this community and
overturn the government under which we live, who has contributed
in any way to the campaign of falsehood, character assassination
and calumny which forms now and has always formed the fertile
field in which seeds of hatred and spite have flowered into outright
murder, is either placed behind the bars or forced to leave this
section of Oregon and never return.

Ruhl and the *Mail Tribune* kept their word. Banks was tried and convicted of murder, sentenced to life imprisonment, and died in a jail cell. The county judge who was his principal henchman also went to jail for the ballot theft conspiracy. His "Good Government" organization was wrecked. And the Medford *Mail Tribune* won the Pulitzer Prize for Public Service for 1934.

"The show is over," Ruhl wrote. "The play is played out. But it was a close call."

10. JOSEPH PULITZER II DEMANDS
MINE REFORM IN ILLINOIS

The St. Louis Post-Dispatch makes an issue
out of the tragedy of Centralia No. 5

Pulitzer Prize for Public Service, 1948

This is a story that shocked the nation. It is the tragedy of a coal mine in Illinois known as Centralia No. 5, where a blast in 1947 killed 111 miners.

The sacrifice of life was needless. It could have been averted. Numerous advance warnings had been given by a forthright mine inspector to comply with safety regulations. But all the warnings were ignored.

And so, the explosion occurred. The nation's press was clogged with black headlines over the story of Centralia No. 5 and with pictures of the widows and orphans the miners left behind them.

The St. Louis *Post-Dispatch* printed the news in grim detail, putting every man it could spare on the story. Then, even before the bodies of the last miners had been taken from their dark tombs, the newspaper began a historic fight that swept an Illinois governor from office and led to the adoption of state and federal reforms in coal mining.

Joseph Pulitzer, the editor of the *Post-Dispatch* and a son of the founder, began it all with one of his familiar yellow memos. This one, to Ben Reese, the *Post-Dispatch's* managing editor, fairly burned with a demand for action.

"Has not the time come," J. P. wrote, "for a concise, terse review of the Centralia tragedy, covering these angles . . . the responsibility of the Governor . . . what is likely to be done, and how, to improve and to enhance safety through federal and state government . . . what may be done for the miners' families . . . are the guilty likely to be punished?"

When J. P. demanded action of his staff, he got it. Ben Reese swung the *Post-Dispatch* into high gear. Under the constant prodding of Joseph Pulitzer, one of the finest of the *Post-Dispatch's* many campaigns got under way.

The following summary of the disaster at Centralia No. 5 was published in its issue of April 30, 1947—a special section that was devoted entirely to the crusade for mine reform.

SUDDEN DEATH AT CENTRALIA NO. 5

By Harry Wilensky

From the St. Louis Post-Dispatch, April 30, 1947

The clock in the office of the Centralia Coal Company's Mine No, 5 ticked toward quitting time on the afternoon of March 25. As the hands registered 3:27 and the 142 men working 540 feet under ground prepared to leave the pit at the end of their shift, an explosion occurred.

The blast originated in one of the work rooms in the northwestern section of the workings. Fed by coal dust, it whooshed through the labyrinth of tunnels underlying the town of Wamac, Ill., on the southern outskirts of Centralia. Thirty-one men, most of whom happened to be near the shaft at the time, made their way to the cage and were brought out alive, but the remaining 111 were trapped. Fellow-workmen who tried to reach them shortly after the explosion were driven back by poisonous fumes.

As rescue crews with special equipment hurried from Belleville, West Frankfort, Herrin, DuQuoin, Eldorado, and other Illinois mine towns, relatives of the trapped miners gathered in tense, silent groups around the tipple. It was a raw day, and an icy wind whipped the coal dust through the air, begriming faces and clothing; but the wives, sons, and daughters stayed on, hour after hour.

Here and there a woman wiped tears from her eyes, but few broke down. After darkness fell, many of the relatives retired to a washhouse where they sat on the benches the miners had used in changing their clothes. Overhead, suspended on chains and pulleys, hung the street clothing of the men who had failed to come up. In some cases wives recognized their husbands' garments and selected their places for the long vigil.

It rained. Then it snowed. Still most of the wan, tight-lipped

relatives stayed on, refusing to go home "until we can find out."
The Red Cross and the Salvation Army set up canteens which
served coffee and sandwiches.

It was twenty-seven hours before the rescue crews brought the
first trapped miners to the surface. An eerie hush fell over the
crowd, held back by police, as the first stretcher was carried from
the cage to the line of waiting ambulances. When it was observed
that the blanket in which the huddled form was wrapped covered
the face, some women turned their heads and wept. Sixteen other
victims followed out of the shaft, but all were dead.

The next day, after eighteen additional bodies were brought out,
those in charge began to refer to their work as "recovery operations"
instead of rescue activities, and hopes for the men still unaccounted
for faded.

Penetration of the underground passageways was a laborious as
well as extremely hazardous operation involving removal of debris,
sealing off of side tunnels, and partial restoration of the mine's
ventilating system.

On March 28, the rescue volunteers threatened to quit when
Robert M. Medill, director of the Illinois Department of Mines
and Minerals, sought to turn the electric power on in the blast-torn
mine to "speed the work." Driscoll Scanlan, state mine inspector
who had been overruled in repeated efforts to close the mine as
unsafe months before the explosion occurred, upheld the workers'
contention that this might result in a new explosion.

A chemical test of the air in the mine disclosed the presence of a
mixture of gases that could be ignited by an electric spark, and
Medill conceded he was wrong.

The day-and-night operations proceeded with mules instead of
power-driven equipment, and on March 29 the farthest corner of
the mine was penetrated, disclosing that all of the remaining miners
were dead.

The victims left 99 widows and 76 children under the age of
eighteen.

The toll of the disaster of 111 dead made the Centralia explosion
the nation's worst mine disaster in twenty-three years. Only once
before had Illinois experienced a mining tragedy of such proportions; this was at Cherry in 1909, when 250 men were killed.

After an intensive study, a team of five experts from the United States Bureau of Mines reported the Centralia explosion "was caused by coal dust raised into the air and ignited by explosives fired in a dangerous and non-permissible manner."

The inspectors found explosives had been tamped with combustible coal dust, in violation of regulations. They pointed out that the mine was not using electric detonators, as had been recommended. State and federal experts agreed the explosion was spread from the point of ignition to distant reaches of the mine by excessive quantities of coal dust blown into the air and ignited.

Both Scanlan and federal mine inspectors had notified the management prior to the disaster that accumulations of coal dust in the mine were excessive, and had recommended use of rock dust. When blown into the air by an explosion, rock dust lessens the combustibility of coal dust, thereby localizing and smothering the blast.

In his inspection reports on Mine No. 5, Scanlan time and again had cited the danger of a dust explosion and had urged rock-dusting, thereby resisting pressure from higher-ups in the State Department of Mines who considered his concern for the miners' safety excessive. On one occasion the inspector had risked the loss of his job by forcing the Centralia mine partially to suspend production until it corrected the dust hazard.

Conditions in the mine remained safe for only a short time, however, Scanlan reported, and soon his official complaints and his recommendations for corrective steps were resumed.

At the conclusion of the recovery operations, which Scanlan had directed personally, going down into the mine with the volunteers, the weary inspector made this bitter comment:

"Every one of my recommendations could have been complied with, could have saved the company money, and could have saved these men's lives."

Seven *Post-Dispatch* reporters headed by Theodore C. Link were detailed to dig into Governor Dwight H. Green's part in the disaster at Centralia No. 5. But Green, despite an exposé, ran for reelection anyway. Through the Illinois machine's efforts, Reporter Link was indicted with several other persons on trumped-up charges, but Joseph Pulitzer fought back with all the energy at his command.

He directed the *Post-Dispatch* to run an editorial captioned, "The

Green Machine Strikes Back." Then he bought space in Illinois papers representing 3,000,000 circulation and ran an ad based on the editorial, which denounced Green and all his works. Green was overwhelmingly defeated for reelection.

That was one of the results of the Centralia No. 5 campaign. Illinois approved laws giving mine inspectors indefinite tenure in order to take them out of politics and also made it a crime for any state mine official to solicit campaign funds from an operator, miner, or union. The state also stepped up its mine inspection program. And the Centralia Coal Co., indicted for willful neglect, pleaded no defense and paid a fine.

After forty-three years of active direction of the *Post-Dispatch*, Joseph Pulitzer died on March 30, 1955 at the age of seventy. His son, Joseph Pulitzer, Jr., succeeded him in carrying on a tradition of conscience at the *Post-Dispatch*.

The newspaper's platform is the platform of the three Joseph Pulitzers who have been its editors and publishers. It was written by the first of the line, the donor of the Pulitzer Prizes, upon his retirement April 10, 1907:

THE POST-DISPATCH PLATFORM:

"I know that my retirement will make no difference in its cardinal principles; that it will always fight for progress and reform, never tolerate injustice or corruption, always fight demagogues of all parties, never belong to any party, always oppose privileged classes and public plunderers, never lack sympathy with the poor, always remain devoted to the public welfare; never be satisfied with merely printing the news, always be drastically independent, never be afraid to attack wrong, whether by predatory plutocracy or predatory poverty."

For its crusade to avert another Centralia No. 5 and punish the guilty, the *Post-Dispatch* was awarded the Pulitzer Prize for Public Service in 1948. After thirty-eight years as city editor and managing editor of the paper, Ben Reese retired in 1951 to become co-chairman of the American Press Institute advisory board at Columbia University.

11. TWO NEWSPAPERS EXPOSE
A SCANDAL ABOUT THE PRESS

The St. Louis Post-Dispatch and Chicago Daily News
find fifty-one newspapermen on the Illinois state payroll

Pulitzer Prize for Public Service, 1950

The press has exposed many a scandal in government, with beneficial results. When the St. Louis *Post-Dispatch* and the Chicago *Daily News* discovered a scandal involving the press, they were just as prompt to publish the nauseous details. Their indignation, editorially expressed, took the form of scathing rebukes to those in their own profession who were involved and demands for an end to abuses of a privileged position.

The story broke on April 14, 1949 simultaneously under the by-lines of Roy J. Harris in the *Post-Dispatch* and George Thiem in the *Daily News*. They had discovered that the editors and publishers of at least thirty-two Illinois newspapers were carried on the Illinois state payroll during the administration of Governor Dwight H. Green, collecting more than $300,000 in salaries.

Harris commented as follows on the activities of the men who also controlled small daily and weekly newspapers:

"A few of the payrollers . . . actually worked regularly at the State house. Chief function of many of the others, however, was to print canned editorials and news stories lauding accomplishments of the Republican state administration."

Continuing their investigation, Harris and Thiem were able to report by May 6, 1949 that the total number of newspapermen on the Illinois payroll was fifty-one, and that they had collected more than $480,000. The combined circulation of the dailies and weeklies affected was 350,000.

In news stories, editorials, and cartoons, and in bitter captions under pictures of the men involved, the two newspapers went after the backsliding editors and publishers. Some resigned their posts immediately, despite a defense made of them by Governor Green. The rest were removed from the state payroll when the incoming administration of Governor Adlai E. Stevenson abolished their jobs.

It made no difference whether newspapers commenting on the disclosures were Republican or Democratic. After the Associated Press distributed the story to the nation, the press unanimously praised the exposé and demanded measures to prevent a recurrence of the scandal.

Typical was the comment of the Milwaukee *Journal:*

"Perhaps there is no machinery by which these men can be disciplined. But there are ways in which they can be repudiated. Newspapers should go on record, organizations of newspapermen should express themselves. And if these men are members of press associations in Illinois or in the nation, their ouster should be seriously considered. They are not deserving of membership.

"If the American press wants to maintain the respect of the American people, it had better be firm on this Illinois mess."

The St. Louis *Post-Dispatch* and the Chicago *Daily News* set an example for disclosures by other newspapers that have been made since, which have had the net effect of discouraging the practice throughout the country in whatever guise it takes. Here is the first editorial of protest published in the *Post-Dispatch,* a part of the vast amount of material that brought the Pulitzer Prize for Public Service for 1950 jointly to that newspaper and the Chicago *Daily News.*

BETRAYAL BY THE PRESS

From the St. Louis Post-Dispatch, April 14, 1949

A particularly nauseous footnote to the history of the Green administration in Illinois is the revelation that editors and publishers of at least thirty-two downstate newspapers were on the state payroll. Since January, 1943, they hijacked more than $300,000 from the pocket of the people of Illinois.

Some of these newspaper men did work at their state jobs. The chief function of many of the others, however, says *Post-Dispatch* correspondent Roy J. Harris, "was to print canned editorials and news stories lauding accomplishments of the Republican state administration."

No doubt many of these double-dealers could often be heard in pious praise and fervent defense of the great American principle of freedom of the press. Yet they prostituted their own press freedom by taking money from the state treasury.

Did any of these editors tell their readers the truth about the Green administration? Does a dog bite the hand that feeds him?

The scandals of the Green administration were an open book to any independent investigator and to any honest newspaper man.

ALL SET FOR A SUPER-SECRET SESSION IN WASHINGTON
by James T. Berryman

PULITZER PRIZE, 1950   WASHINGTON EVENING STAR

The people were entitled to be told about them. Yet the editors' mouths were closed and their consciences, if any, stilled by pieces of silver.

Fortunately the people of Illinois learned about the Green scandals from sources other than their local newspapers. They buried Green and his gang under an avalanche of votes. But what do they think of a press which had sold out to the same Green gang?

Even the editors who actually worked on their state jobs were in a questionable ethical position. How can an editor serve two masters? How can he take a job as state employee and still bring to the high calling of editorship that disinterestedness necessary to a decent newspaper? . . .

There has been a good deal of discussion recently about the gulf between the American press and the people. The Illinois revelation will widen the gulf. Readers of those Illinois papers whose editors were on the payroll must rightly feel that they have been betrayed.

It is humiliating to be compelled to report and comment on this shameful chapter in American journalism.

12. ALICIA PATTERSON CHALLENGES
A LABOR RACKETEER

And "Big Bill" DeKoning goes to jail
in Newsday's trotting track scandal exposé

Pulitzer Prize for Public Service, 1954

In 1940, prelude to one of the darkest years in American history, Alicia Patterson started a new newspaper in a Long Island garage. Its name was *Newsday*. Its prospects, by all ordinary standards, were slim.

But its energetic and bold young editor refused to be dismayed by circulation or advertising problems, by wartime shortages, by the dismal predictions of her friends—and her enemies. Being the daughter of Captain Joseph Medill Patterson, the founder of the New York *Daily News*, she would have been hard to discourage, anyway.

Within six years, *Newsday* was in the black. Miss Patterson and her husband, Harry F. Guggenheim, worked hard over their paper and Long

Islanders read it faithfully. It had much more than the local news that was passed up by the loftier New York dailies. It also had a lot of fight.

Under the direction of Alan Hathway, its managing editor, and a former reporter and deskman on the New York *Daily News* staff, *Newsday* went out looking for trouble—and found it. The biggest target on Long Island was Big Bill DeKoning, then at the height of his power as a labor czar. With the control he exercised over a number of unions, he could threaten picketing, boycotts and strikes and bring employers to terms—his terms. He was even able to get into Roosevelt Raceway, the kingdom of the trotting horse, and dictate who was to be hired and who was to be turned away.

Newsday went after him and openly charged he was not a legitimate labor union leader but a racketeer. For three years, from 1950 on, the paper hammered away at the DeKoning empire. Seemingly the New York papers were uninterested in this first-rate campaign on their own back doorsteps. Seemingly the authorities were bored by *Newsday's* disclosures.

But, there was a break. A murder at Yonkers Raceway, disclosing sensational racketeering angles there, caused attention to be directed at Roosevelt Raceway, too. On October 7, 1953, in answer to the charges made by DeKoning and his friends of persecution and libel, *Newsday* ran a blistering editorial that topped anything it or any other paper had previously published.

IF THIS BE LIBEL, SUE!

From Newsday, Oct. 7, 1953

David Holman, attorney for union czar William C. DeKoning, has given *Newsday* the credit for causing all of his client's woes. Holman, who was a Nassau County assistant district attorney when *Newsday* first reported the racketeering activities of DeKoning three and one-half years ago, approved a statement that, if it had not been for this newspaper, the New York City newspapers would never have become interested in the DeKoning story, and would not have printed their own reports.

We did not ask for any credit for publishing the facts; we must admit we are honored to accept it. We are even more pleased that, because of our stories run since May, 1950, District Attorney Frank Gulotta is conducting an investigation. We are honored to have performed a public service.

It is too bad, though, that it took a killing at Yonkers Raceway to make the New York newspapers and the people interested in racketeering at Roosevelt Raceway. It took a murder before Gulotta saw fit to put witnesses under oath. Three years ago his investigation fell flat because he did not put the fear of perjury into his witnesses.

Holman, who owned while assistant DA and still owns 1,200 shares of stock in the Old Country Trotting Association and 200 shares in the Nassau Trotting Association, also challenged *Newsday's* integrity. He espoused the term "scurrilous," and stated that our reports were "untrue" and "derogatory." But he declined to say whether or not DeKoning would institute suit against us for libel.

If DeKoning thinks that we have dealt unfairly with him, that we have injured his reputation by inadvertently printing something untrue and damaging, then he owes it to himself and to this newspaper to sue us for libel.

DeKoning never sued. That same edition of *Newsday* reported, under banner headlines, that he had been indicted for extortion in connection with irregularities at Roosevelt Raceway. The harness racing scandal broke wide open.

Newsday's contemporaries were generous.

Life magazine said DeKoning's activities "might have remained relatively unknown even today were it not for an enterprising Long Island newspaper called *Newsday*." *Time* magazine ran a cover story on Alicia Patterson. The Associated Press told its subscribers in its weekly report: "*Newsday*, directly and indirectly, has been responsible to a very large extent for the exposé of the harness racing scandal."

For its work, which was climaxed by DeKoning's guilty plea and imprisonment, *Newsday* was awarded the Pulitzer Prize for Public Service for 1954. And Alicia Patterson, asked in jest when she intended to extend *Newsday's* circulation into New York City, smiled demurely. "Why should I?" she asked. "New York City is coming out to me."

13. CHICAGO DAILY NEWS UNMASKS
A THIEVING STATE AUDITOR

A reader's tip starts the Hodge case,
revealing a $2,500,000 larceny

Pulitzer Prize for Public Service, 1957

A newspaper can become angry and indignant, without obligation, over wrongdoing in the next city or state. It can also work up an admirable head of steam over monkey business in a foreign country to seem committed to virtue. But when it comes to rooting out official thievery at home, that takes guts. It also calls for a lot of work—and money to finance the job.

The Chicago *Daily News*, a fighting paper, went after official wrongdoing in Illinois in 1956 on nothing more than a reader's tip. Before the job was over, two city editors had heart attacks, 21 members of the city and state staffs had gone into action, and a fantastic scandal had been exposed. More than anyone else, Reporter George Thiem, a Pulitzer Prize winner in 1949, received credit for breaking the story.

State Auditor Orville E. Hodge, at fifty-two a respected businessman and former legislator, was the newspaper's target. He was so high in the Republican administration at the time that he was spoken of as a potential candidate for Governor. His wealth had been estimated at as high as $5,000,000. He had several homes. There was nothing to show that he was a crook.

And yet, the *Daily News* proved its case. It was so confident that it told the story even before Hodge was arrested. Here is the account, in condensed form.

"I'D RATHER BE A REPORTER"

From the Chicago Daily News, July 14, 1956

Two months ago, on a Saturday morning, a reader of the *Daily News* walked into the office of one of the newspaper's executives. He urged an investigation of the office of State Auditor Orville E. Hodge. The reader said he had learned there were many irregularities there. . . .

The investigation was a routine assignment for "Investigate Everything" George Thiem. From the start, Thiem was opposed by Hodge. Certain records could not be found. Others were located and produced only after persistent demands.

Hodge complained that Thiem was "trying to get" him. Office employees were instructed not to talk to Thiem.

This was unusual. As Springfield correspondent, Thiem covers the state legislature and state offices. He is on a first-name basis with state officials and hundreds of state employees.

Thiem learned that fifteen employees were laid off by Hodge after the investigation started. The list included many Democratic politicians and their relatives hired by Hodge, a Republican.

Thiem also learned that Hodge, an affable host and lavish spender, used some state funds for personal expenses, and for large hotel and entertainment bills. Also, he discovered there were some peculiar circumstances surrounding two mortgages held by the Southmoor Bank & Trust Co., 6760 Stony Island.

The aid of the Miami *Herald*, a Knight newspaper, was enlisted to run down one of the mortgages covering the Esquire Apartment hotel, a Fort Lauderdale, Fla., resort owned by Hodge. Florida records showed that Hodge took a mortgage for an undisclosed amount with the Southmoor Bank. But this was denied by the bank.

Another mortgage was held on Hodge's luxurious summer home at Lake Springfield, outside the state capital. Sangamon County records showed that Southmoor gave Hodge favorable interest terms on this mortgage.

As state auditor, Hodge hires the bank examiners for the state. This provided another story.

One article listed fifteen persons or businesses in whose names state checks totaling $180,000 had been issued and cashed. Because Hodge had barred reporters from his office, the state's attorney was asked to search for the fifteen checks, with supporting invoices, in Hodge's files.

All were missing.

State Treasurer Wright, who has been most cooperative all during the investigation, had photostats prepared from his records.

A story was prepared July 3 under the direction of City Editor Clem Lane for publication July 6. It revealed that state auditor checks had been issued and cashed to persons who never received the checks or the money. Names and amounts of checks were listed.

When the first edition of the *Daily News* of July 6 hit the street, the full scope of the Hodge scandal became immediately obvious to those who had been following Thiem's stories with rather mild interest up to that time.

When the *Daily News* reached Springfield, Governor Stratton asked State Treasurer Wright to bring along his office records and photostats of the mysterious checks issued by the auditor's office.

More questionable checks were found. Six, totaling $80,000, were traced to the Southmoor Bank where they had been cashed.

Edward A. Hintz, who resigned Friday night as Southmoor president, said through his attorney that Edward A. Epping, Hodge's top assistant, had cashed the checks and had taken the money.

The Federal Deposit Insurance Corp., Federal Reserve Bank, and Federal bank examiners started their own investigations after the *Daily News* published this statement.

Hintz, and the teller who cashed the checks for Epping, were ordered subpoenaed before the Sangamon County Grand Jury.

Hodge refused to answer questions of the state attorney. He, too, was served with a subpoena. Dozens more have been prepared for others.

State Treasurer Wright made a personal trip to the bank and demanded the immediate repayment of the money paid to Epping. He was refused and has ordered suit to recover it.

Still more checks have been found which, Hintz says, Epping cashed. Hundreds of documents are missing from Hodge's files. The total funds now under suspicion top $500,000 and may reach double that figure.

All of this because a reader thought he had a story the *Daily News* should investigate.

Hodge's thefts exceeded $2,500,000, of which part has been recovered. He, Epping, and Hintz went to jail, among others. For its work, which won the praise of some of its competitors, the Chicago *Daily News* was awarded the Pulitzer Prize for Public Service in 1957. When someone told Governor Stratton that George Thiem should be nominated for public office for his part in the exposé, Thiem cracked:

"Tell 'em I'd rather be a reporter."

III. TURMOIL OVER DIXIE:
THE RACIAL PROBLEM

The unending battle of courageous Southern editors and their newspapers against the evils of race hatred has been one of the great landmarks of American journalism.

Some have triumphed, others have failed. But no mobs and no threats have been able to silence newspapers of principle and editors and publishers of conviction.

Such an editor was Julian LaRose Harris of the Columbus (Ga.) *Enquirer-Sun*. It was his policy to wage ceaseless war against the Ku Klux Klan in Georgia even though a Klansman was governor of the state and Klan hirelings were in a position to harm the paper. In those days the symbols of conflict were the noose and the whip and the hooded night rider, not the schoolroom pointer.

Yet Harris, picking up the slogan, "It's great to be a Georgian," flung it headlong at the Klan on December 31, 1925.

"Is it great to be a Georgian?" he demanded on his editorial page. "Is it great to be a citizen of a state which is the proud parent of a cowardly hooded order founded and fostered by men who have been proved liars, drunkards, blackmailers, and murderers? Is it great to be a citizen of a state whose governor is a member of and subservient to that vicious masked gang, and whose officials are either members or in sympathy with it? . . . Is it great to be a citizen of such a state? Is it great to be a Georgian? Let each one answer as he will, but the reply of the *Enquirer-Sun* is no."

Harris won a Pulitzer Prize for Public Service for his paper in

1926—one of many such awards to Southern newspapermen who
took a position and held it in the face of threats and violence. Someone had to lead. Someone had to stand out ahead of his time and
take the abuse for advocating realistic, but unpopular measures.
Often, it was the Southern newspaperman.

It is surely not stretching a point to credit them with a measure
of such progress as has been made in the patient efforts of white
and colored people to live together peacefully in the South.

To those extremists who curl their lips in scorn at the very notion
that there has been progress, let it be said at once that force can
never solve this problem. The Klan failed. The school riots at Little
Rock in 1957 caused lessons to be taught under the guard of Federal troops brought in to keep order. The closed schools of 1958
were an even less satisfactory answer.

Where violence fosters the will to resist, there may be little more
than token integration in the South. But a few Negro students today
are in some white schools in Southern towns and cities even where
there have been fights and dynamite blasts.

The struggle goes on. But had it not been for the newspapermen
whose work is represented in the following pages, and the many
others who persisted with or without the recognition of a prize, the
path ahead might be still darker than it is at this moment of turning
in American history.

14. HATRED AND BIGOTRY FOR SALE:

THE NEW YORK WORLD ARRAIGNS THE KLAN

Herbert Bayard Swope leads the opening attack
on the Invisible Empire and its bedsheets

Pulitzer Prize for Public Service, 1922

In every age and in every region, the fires of intolerance may be kindled
by different hands but the result is always the same. If the flames cannot
be effectively fought, then they may run wild and burn all that stand
in their path.

Today, among some of those who thrive on hate as a business, the
Ku Klux Klan is no longer respected. Perhaps because it has given

intolerance a bad name. But it was a great power in the land in the 1920s when a few Southern editors and the New York *World*, and a number of other public-spirited newspapers, actively began to oppose it.

The *World's* campaign, in particular, retains meaning for the nation today. It shows what digging and documenting can do to a seemingly powerful organization that opposes the public welfare and rips the public conscience to tatters.

This was the background of the *World's* crusade. The Klan, organized in the South after the Civil War to fight the rule of carpetbaggers from the North, had gone out of business in 1869. But in 1915, William Joseph Simmons revived it primarily as a money-making vehicle. In the early 1920s, aided by Edward Young Clarke and Mrs. Elizabeth Tyler, he rode to power on a wave of race and religious hatred promoted by the Klan.

It was at this juncture that Herbert Bayard Swope crossed his path. Swope, the "snorting Caesar" among newspapermen, had just taken over as executive editor of Pulitzer's *World* in New York. In typical Swope fashion, he tore into the Klan. It was a time of rare excitement in New York journalism. People waited for his first edition beside the golden dome in Park Row—and the *World's* press time in those days was 12:30 a.m.

The *World* missed nothing. The exposé published the Klan's money-making rackets, spread the names of all its salesmen on the record, got "inside" stories from former Klan members, gave its secret aims and purposes as never before and even unearthed a police record indicating that two of the Klan's leadership had been seized and fined in a police raid on what is known euphemistically as a house of ill-fame.

While the Klan at first gained membership on the publicity, the resulting chorus of nation-wide denunciation grew so great that inevitably it became an organization of bad repute and various state-wide prosecutions did the rest. Today, except for semiliterates, the Klan is unpopular in the South even among the White Citizens' Councils.

The *World's* series carried no by-line but it is a matter of common knowledge that it was written by a competent newspaperman and magazine writer, now dead. His by-line appears below over the first article of the series which won the Pulitzer Prize for Public Service in 1922.

A SECRET EMPIRE IN THE SOUTH

By Rowland Thomas

From the New York World, Sept. 6, 1921

What is the Ku Klux Klan?

How has it grown from a nucleus of thirty-four chapter members to a membership of more than 500,000 within five years?

How have its "domains" and "realms" and "Klans" been extended until they embrace every state in the Union but Montana, Utah, and New Hampshire?

What are the possibilities of an order that preaches racial and religious hatred of the Jew and the Roman Catholic, of the Negro and the foreign-born citizen?

What are the possibilities of a secret organization that practices censorship of private conduct behind the midnight anonymity of mask and robe and with the weapons of whips and tar and feathers?

What ought to be done about an order whose members are not initiated, but "naturalized," whose oaths bind them to obedience to an "Emperor" chosen for life?

What ought to be done about an organization with such objects when the salesmen of memberships in it work first among the officers of the courts and police departments, following then with the officers on the reserve lists of the military and naval forces?

At the end of months of inquiry throughout the United States and in the performance of what it sincerely believes to be a public service, the *World* this morning begins the publication of a series of articles in which answers to these questions will be offered, set out against the vivid background of as extraordinary a movement as is to be found in recent history.

ARTICLE I

The Knights of the Ku Klux Klan, Inc., was organized October 29, 1915 in Atlanta, Ga., by William Joseph Simmons, who at one period of his life had been an itinerant Methodist exhorter; at another, professor of Southern history at Lanier University, a small and newly organized institution in Atlanta, and at still another a solicitor of members for the Woodmen of the World. On that date Simmons and 33 of his friends signed a petition for a charter as a standard

WAITING FOR ORDERS, *by Rollin Kirby*

FROM THE PRIZEWINNING FILE OF 1929 NEW YORK WORLD

fraternal secret order, which charter was issued by the Superior Court of Fulton County, Ga., on July 1, 1916.

Now the organization is active in every state of the Union but three. It has a membership of more than 500,000—of 650,000, according to the boasts of its leaders.

When it was organized, its founders claimed it was a revival of legitimate rebirth of the old Ku Klux Klan of the reconstruction period in the South and, like the original Klan, its slogan was "White Supremacy." It was directed against the Negro.

Now the Negro has become a side issue with it. Today it is primarily anti-Jew, anti-Catholic, anti-alien, and it is spreading more than twice as fast through the North and West as it is growing in the South.

How has it managed to spread out so widely and so rapidly?

First, by appeals to local or sectional prejudices and hatreds. On the Pacific Coast it has beckoned to Japophobes and whispered in their ears that the yellow man is plotting to incite the black man in America to rise against the white man. In the cities of the Central West it has pretended to devote itself to stamping out radicalism. On the Atlantic Coast it has preached that an alien-born man or woman, even though naturalized, has no place in America. Everywhere it has banned Jews from membership and made anti-Semitism one of its many missions. Everywhere, also, no less positively but not as frankly, it has barred and attacked Roman Catholics. Wherever a prospective member lives, he has been promised that his pet aversion will be made an object of Klan action.

Second, it owes its growth to the employment of a large number of professional salesmen, who net the country in an up-to-date sales organization and peddle memberships on a basis of $4 for every member taken into the Klan. These paid organizers, or Kleagles, are at work this summer on a membership drive directed from Atlanta and from the various cities where the state sales managers, or King Kleagles, have set up their headquarters.

The drive is being actively pushed in scores of communities throughout the United States. The Kleagles collect no initiation fees, but each new member makes a "donation" of $10, of which the Kleagle keeps $4 and sends the rest to his King Kleagle, who pockets another $1. The remaining $5 vanishes into the "imperial" treasury of the order.

Furthermore, the Klan itself owns the company manufacturing the regalia of cotton robe and hooded cap, which is sold to members for $6.50 and costs $1.25 to make. The whole "propagation" department is in the hands of professional drive leaders, whose sole interest in Ku Kluxism is in the "split" just outlined.

In the last five years membership "donations" and sales of regalia have yielded at least $5,000,000—probably a considerably greater sum. Ku Kluxing from the inside has been a paying enterprise and its lucrative possibilities have recently been increased by the decision to admit women as well as men to membership. The sisters can now come on in with the brothers—at only $10 per come-on.

The original Knights of the Ku Klux Klan, Inc., modestly begun five years ago, has become a vast enterprise, doing a thriving business in the systematic sale of race hatred, religious bigotry, and "100 percent" anti-Americanism.

It has become and calls itself an "Invisible Empire" ruled by an "Emperor" and "Imperial Wizard," Colonel William Joseph Simmons, who is no more legitimately a Colonel than he is an Emperor or a Wizard. Closely associated with him, and making up the triumvirate or "Big Three" which controls its affairs, are Edward Young Clarke, "Imperial Kleagle," a professional publicity man and drive promoter, and Clarke's business partner in the management of the Southern Publicity Association of Atlanta, Mrs. Elizabeth Tyler, who is the principal stockholder in the *Searchlight*, a newspaper published in Atlanta as the organ of the movement.

Efforts are being made to spread the poison of Ku Kluxism in the army and navy. For months its membership peddlers have been sending their anonymous circulars to officers on the reserve list of the military and naval forces.

Also to reach the hundreds who flew during the war and the thousands then awakened to active interest in aviation, the promoters of the Klan last spring formed in Atlanta an adjunct order headed by "Emperor" Simmons and known as "The Invisible Planet, Knights of the Air." Membership in this was open to men, women, and children, and Jews and Catholics were not barred. The price of admission was $10. Only Klansmen could be officers in the Knights of the Air, and every white, gentile, Protestant, native-born member was a hand-picked prospect for Klansmanship and another $10 donation.

The Klan organizers go out instructed by headquarters to make their first drive to secure city, town, and village authorities as members, and to center their efforts also on judges of local and circuit courts and the police forces. In the weekly news letters sent out from Atlanta by Imperial Kleagle Clarke for circulation among Klansmen, the success achieved along these lines is boasted as the reason why in so many places the Klan has ventured to work openly without fear of interference and as an incentive for pushing forward the work of setting up an invisible, Klan-controlled super-government throughout the country.

What are the possibilities of such as organization as the Ku Klux Klan?

A partial answer to this question lies in an analyzed list prepared by the *World* of outrages committed by groups of masked men wearing white robes and hoods and announcing themselves to their victims as Ku Klux Klansmen. A large majority of these attacks on individuals have involved matters of behavior along the lines of personal morality, have flagrantly violated the Bill of Rights of every state in the Union, and have involved an assumption of the Klan's authority to impose moral censorship on communities and citizens, summarily punish any "offenses," and set up and enforce its own standards covering every incident of private life. To sum up this aspect of the case, the words of a man who knows the Klan intimately from the inside might be used. He says:

"It would be impossible to imagine an attitude more essentially lawless. Ku Kluxism as conceived, incorporated, propagated, and practiced has become a menace to the peace and security of every section of the United States. Its evil and vicious possibilities are boundless. It is nothing more or less than a throwback to the centuries when terror, instead of law and justice, ruled and regulated the lives of men."

15. LOUIS ISAAC JAFFE FATHERS
VIRGINIA'S ANTI-LYNCH LAW

The editor of the Norfolk Virginian-Pilot
persuades Governor Byrd to act

Pulitzer Prize for Editorial Writing, 1929

To Louis Isaac Jaffe, a lynching meant humiliation for every Virginian. He said so. In the Norfolk *Virginian-Pilot*, of which he was editor, he campaigned for more than two years to make any lynching on Virginia's soil a state—rather than a merely local—responsibility.

But Louis Isaac Jaffe was ahead of his time. Where such a belief is elementary today, he was one of the few who held it and spoke in favor of it and fought for it in the mid-twenties—the high tide of the Ku Klux Klan. Governor Harry Flood Byrd of Virginia liked Jaffe. He was sympathetic to the editor's idea. But, he feared an anti-lynch law might in some way violate Virginia's constitution.

Jaffe never wavered. When a Negro was lynched on November 30, 1927 by a mob on the exact boundary between Virginia and Kentucky, thereby causing solemn peace officers to debate over which had jurisdiction, Jaffe appealed to Byrd personally:

"I hope you will find a means of forcing a showdown on this outrage—in the name of Virginia and in the name of decency."

Byrd asked Jaffe to outline his ideas for an anti-lynch law and the editor complied. Then began a series of editorials without precedent in Virginia's journalistic history. Alone among the newspapers of the state, the *Virginian-Pilot* pressed for an anti-lynch law that would give the state power to punish violators. And when Governor Byrd called on the General Assembly to enact it, Jaffe's campaign was won. The bill became law on March 14, 1928 and Governor Byrd wrote to President E. A. Alderman of the University of Virginia:

"Mr. Jaffe's editorials over a long period in advocacy of making the punishment of lynchers a state responsibility, supplemented by his personal representations to me, had more to do than any other single outside urging in convincing me that I should make one of my major recommendations the passage of a drastic anti-lynching law providing that lynching be a specific state offense."

Far from content with his victory in Virginia, Jaffe aroused national interest in an anti-lynching campaign with an editorial on June 22, 1928, following a lynching on the eve of the Democratic National Convention at Houston, Texas. The editorial, which helped win him the Pulitzer Prize for Editorial Writing in 1929, follows.

AN UNSPEAKABLE ACT OF SAVAGERY

By Louis Isaac Jaffe

From the Norfolk Virginian-Pilot, June 22, 1928

As the Democratic hosts prepare to rededicate themselves anew to fairness and justice, the bustling Southern city in which they are to meet is disgraced by an unspeakable act of savagery. There is no other way to describe the performance of the eight armed white men who yanked Robert Powell, 24-year-old Negro, from a hospital cot on which he lay with a bullet in his stomach, and hanged him from a bridge just outside the city. Powell was under the charge of killing a detective in a shooting match from which he himself emerged with an apparently mortal wound. In the event of his recovery, he was headed for the courts. But to this Texas mob neither Death nor Justice was an acceptable arbiter. Nothing would satisfy them but a loathsome act of murder carried out against a human being while he lay in agony with a bullet in his entrails.

Houston, which is said not to have had a lynching in fifty years, is understandably stirred by this foul thing laid on its doorstep just when it was most anxious to show itself to the world at its cleanest. The City Council made an immediate appropriation of $10,000 for an investigation to be carried out by a committee representative of both races. A grand jury has been ordered to drop all other business to conduct an immediate inquiry. The Governor has offered a reward for the capture of each participant in the lynching and sent a special detail of Texas Rangers to assist the Houston police in the hunt. Apparently the spotlight that beats on Houston at this particular time has had something to do with the energy with which the authorities have acted. Ordinarily, Texas justice proceeds in these matters with considerably less dispatch and excitement. But this is no time to inquire too closely into motives. One of the proudest cities of Texas has been polluted by one of the foulest forms of mob murder, and it is a matter for general satisfaction that the authorities are moving so energetically to repair the damage to Texas' good name. If the perseverance of the authorities is in keeping with their initial burst of energy, one or more of the group that bravely did to death a crippled man lying on a hospital cot may see the inside of the Texas penitentiary.

The year that saw four months pass without a single lynching has now accumulated five of them. Five lynchings in six months represent a proportional reduction in savagery from last year's record of sixteen lynchings in twelve months, but the year is only half gone and no one may be too confident. We have come a long way from the dark days of 1892 when America celebrated the 400th anniversary of its discovery with 255 lynchings, but we have not yet arrived at that social abhorrence of this crime that must precede its practical extinction. When eight presumably decent and rational beings can gain the consent of their conscience to rob a hospital bed for the purpose of executing summary vengeance, and when, as was the case a few days ago in Louisiana, two Negroes are torn from their guards and lynched because they were brothers of another Negro who was accused of murder, it must be recognized that the rise and fall of the lynching curve is governed by racial passions that remain still to be brought under civilized control.

16. FOLLIARD AND THE COLUMBIANS: "HATE COMES WITH THE WIND"

They wanted to be forty times as bad as the Klan,
but Atlanta would have none of them

Pulitzer Prize for National Reporting, 1947

Intolerance takes many forms. One of the strangest after World War II was the Columbians, Inc., which patterned itself after the Nazis. Its declared object, at its ramshackle office in Atlanta, Georgia, was to be "worse" than the Ku Klux Klan.

Many worthy citizens believe that such menaces to public peace are best ignored, but newspapers long ago found out that "hate" movements thrive when unopposed. Accordingly, newspapers from Atlanta to Washington and New York took a lively interest in the Columbians.

Among the reporters who came to Atlanta to look over the neo-Nazis was Edward T. Folliard, lately returned from Europe as a war correspondent. The Washington *Post* (now the *Post and Times-Herald*) wanted a series from him on the Columbians. Out of his long experience as a political writer, Folliard did a job that won him the Pulitzer Prize for National Reporting in 1947.

The Columbians died of over-exposure and their principal leader, Emory Burke, was sentenced to a three-year prison term upon conviction for rioting. Folliard went on to many other honors after a life-time of distinguished newspaper work. Among them were the presidencies of both the White House Correspondents Association and the Gridiron Club. His series in condensed form follows.

"HOW DO MEN GET THAT WAY?"

By Edward T. Folliard

From the Washington Post, Nov. 30-Dec. 1, 2, 3, 1946

ATLANTA, GA., Nov. 30—A Confederate flag hangs outside the headquarters of the Columbians, Inc., located at 82 Bartow Street, but it doesn't look right. Something alien-like has been woven in between the stars and bars. It is a jagged red streak and somehow it looks familiar.

That crazy red streak is the Columbians' insigne, a symbolic thunderbolt that proclaims the arrival of a new and spectacular hate organization in the Southland.

The motto of the Columbians is "Race, Nation, Faith," but its wild-eyed orators put it more crudely,

"This is a white man's country," they shout, and then go on to tell what they are going to do about it.

The Washington *Post* reporter has spent a week in Atlanta looking over the Columbians. He has talked to their leaders (one of whom has a gorgeous shiner) and has listened to their tirades against Negroes, Jews, the Communists, the rich, and newspaper editors who don't share their views on "Anglo-Saxon culture." He has attended their mass meetings and has checked up on their vigilante tactics that have caused Atlanta police to arrest four of them on charges ranging from assault and battery to incitement to riot.

These impressions stand out:

1. The Columbians are not, as has been said, "juvenile delin-

quents of the Ku Klux Klan." The Klan doesn't like the Columbians, perhaps it's because the kleagles are jealous and don't want these upstarts moving in on their side of Hate Street. Also it might be that the hood-and-sheet men are frightened. The word has gone out (although it's probably just talk) that the Columbians are determined to be "40 times as bad as the Ku Klux Klan."

2. The whole aura of the Columbians is Nazi. This is not surprising because two of the leaders are known to have been admirers of Hitler and his racial phobias. The Columbians, all fanatic racists, dress and swagger in the manner of storm troopers. They wear khaki shirts without coats, and on their arms are the red thunderbolt patches suggestive of the runic insignia of the late Heinrich Himmler's SS bullies. It is a startling experience, the first time, to see them swinging down Bartow Street or Peachtree Street; something like seeing an old newsreel of Munich in the days of the beer-hall putsch. After seeing them a third or fourth time, of course, they cease to be exciting.

3. The oddest thing of all about the Columbians is that the movement has brought a new kind of Yankee carpetbagger to the South. From above the Mason-Dixon line has come Homer L. Loomis Jr., not to allay racial prejudice but to whip it up. A strange fellow of thirty-two, given to nervous laughter and nonstop harangues, Loomis is a New Yorker with a Park Avenue background. He attended fashionable St. Paul's Prep School and studied at Princeton until, according to his own story, he flunked out in an alcoholic haze, after two years.

"I suppose it sounds funny to hear one crackpot talking against other crackpots," Loomis told me once, and gave his nervous laugh.

4. Atlanta is terribly embarrassed by the Munich atmosphere brought to it by the Columbians. Both of the city's newspapers—the *Constitution* and the *Journal*—are crusading against them, after first maintaining a hush-hush policy for fear of giving them free advertising. Virtually all civic and patriotic organizations are fighting them. Protestant clergymen have denounced them as prototypes of Hitler and his Nazis. The official organ of the Catholic Laymen's Association of Georgia, the *Bulletin*, has joined in the fight with a bitter editorial headed, "Heil Columbians!"

In view of this, and in view of the fact that Atlanta's police have gone all out to harass them, one would think that the Columbians were doomed. Certainly it seemed so to the *Post* reporter after watching a Columbians' rally, attended by only 200. What bothers newspaper editors and others here is a fear that they might underestimate the organization, just as a lot of people underestimated the Ku Klux Klan or, going farther afield, an Austrian with a funny little moustache.

The No. 1 man of the Columbians—nominally, at least—is Emory Burke, a scrawny, undersized Alabaman, who holds the title of president. Burke has figured in the news more than Homer Loomis, one reason being that Dan Duke, assistant attorney general of Georgia and a much bigger man physically, took a sock at him in court last week and opened a gash over his eye.

However, the Atlanta police regard Loomis as the "kingpin" of the outfit, although as secretary he rates No. 2. They believe that he is smarter than Burke, more intense in his fanaticism, and less inhibited.   · · · ·

What leads men to form a hate organization like the Columbians? How do men get that way?

The story of Burke and Loomis gives one answer; and it may be that the answer comes close to being the definitive one.

Although they have come from different social strata, one having been a "have" and the other a "have-not," Burke and Loomis both have behind them records of frustration and failure.

Burke, an Alabaman, was embittered because he wanted to go to college and couldn't.

Loomis, a New Yorker, revolted because his well-to-do family sent him to Princeton where he didn't want to go.

Back in the 1930s, both of them fancied themselves as thinkers. Burke, wandering from one New Deal transient camp to another, got so he hated "commercialism"—the placing of a "money value on men, as if they were cattle or slaves." ("It tore my soul to pieces, commercialism, commercialism!") Loomis, whose family wanted him to be a lawyer or a banker, became outraged by "man's nastiness to man, by the fact that we hadn't learned to get along with one another." He didn't see why, in school, a professor had to give you a sharp answer instead of a soft one.

Both of them, so they told the *Post* reporter, were trying to work out some philosophy, some scheme whereby discord in American society could be done away with and life made more to their liking.

Loomis racked his brain in his two years at Princeton trying to figure the thing out. But he remained baffled.

"I didn't know what I could do about it," he said. "That made me angry, so I just drank and forgot about it."

Burke probably didn't have the price of a drink in the early 1930s. Like Loomis, however, he was doing a lot of thinking and talking.

Ultimately both Burke and Loomis came up with an idea that seemed to answer the question that had been tormenting them. . . . The solution, of course, was to rid America of its 13 million Negroes and its 4½ million Jews. . . .

A mass meeting of the Columbians starts off with martial music. Then comes the Lord's Prayer, and after that a verbal flogging of Negroes, Jews, Communists, and the rich.

At the end, of course, there is the appeal for money; for "quarters, half-dollars, dollars—anything you can spare to help in our fight for the white race."

The rally Thanksgiving night was the last the Columbians will hold in the hall of the AFL Plumbers and Steamfitters, the union having notified the Nazi-like outfit that their rental contract has been cancelled. . . .

Approximately 200 persons made up the audience. They were of all ages, from a squalling baby in its mother's arms to stooped old men leaning on canes. One woman, built like a barn, wore a sky-blue uniform and an overseas cap to match. On her arm was the thunderbolt insigne of the Columbians.

The men, except for the younger ones in storm-trooper attire, nearly all wore odd coats and trousers. Once during the proceedings a dirty-looking fellow got noisy and quarrelsome and was dragged out by two Atlanta policemen. He was blind drunk. Another drunk, seeing this, wobbled out under his own steam.

Who were these people who were being asked to pay $3 to join the Columbians and $2 for "The Thunderbolt"?

Loomis, in a hair-down talk with me earlier, had explained that the Columbians were out to enroll the "little people."

"Any mass movement has to use mass tactics," he said, his eyes afire. "Hitler appealed to the little people. The Communists appealed—no, no, strike that out. . . . Our movement appeals to the little people.

"Most of them lead dull lives—work, sleep, maybe an occasional beer. We're giving them something new, something exciting. We're satisfying their lust for power. We're building up their egos, making them feel they will have a part in the victory if only they are willing to sacrifice."

At one point in the interview, Loomis grew cynical. He said that the little people were at heart "animals and capitalists"—that they had no desire to share anything with anybody.

"Of course," he said, "we don't say the same thing at our meetings that I'm saying to you here."

Atlanta's newspaper editors are not nearly as harsh as that in their judgment of Columbian audiences.

Ralph McGill, editor of the Atlanta *Constitution,* wrote a column the other day in which he asked: "Why do these things always come to roost in Georgia?" The inevitable answer was, he said, that the ringleaders thought they could succeed.

"Therein," wrote McGill, "have we all failed and therein are we all to blame."

. . . .

What can be done about a hate organization like the Columbians?

The answer, as it appears here, is in two parts: First, a short-range campaign of harassment by police and prosecutors; second, and most important, a long-range program that involves education, economics, and religion.

Governor Ellis Arnall, who soon will be making way for Gene Talmadge, gave orders recently for revoking the charter of the Columbians. He confessed, however, that this was an empty gesture except that it "takes away the sanction of the state."

What was needed, Arnall said, was a program to hit at the breeding ground of bitterness, tension and hate organization. He outlined one as follows:

1. A good dose of education.
2. Better health conditions.

3. Perfection of an economic system to enable all men by their own efforts to have a higher standard of living.

4. Start in the hearts of men a new indoctrination of religion and love to replace hatred.

The demagogues who are running the Columbians have thick skins, naturally, but it is very doubtful if they are impervious to the blast that is now coming their way.

The publicity at the same time has brought about such a revulsion of feeling against the Columbians that newspaper editors and others are gratified that the business is finally out in the open. The abhorrence shown by so many citizens goes a long way toward tempering Atlanta's first feeling of humiliation.

The Columbians fell apart. But other small and vicious hate groups sprang up to replace them. In 1958, a Jewish synagogue was dynamited in Atlanta. Hatred, once aroused, spreads its poison without pity and without shame.

17. TWO NORTH CAROLINA WEEKLIES
TAKE ON THE KU KLUX KLAN

The Whiteville News Reporter and the Tabor City Tribune
end an era of fear and floggings

Pulitzer Prize for Public Service, 1953

"In this democratic country, there's no place for an organization of the caliber of the Ku Klux Klan which made a scheduled parade through our streets last Saturday night."

In this manner, using big double-column bold face type on Page 1, the weekly Tabor City *Tribune* opened a three-year battle against the Ku Klux Klan in North Carolina on July 26, 1950. The Klan had revived there after World War II. The semi-weekly *News Reporter* of nearby Whiteville quickly joined the fight. The Klan began flogging its enemies, including Negroes.

The editors—W. Horace Carter of the *Tribune* and Willard Cole of the *News Reporter*—had a combined circulation of less than 10,000 and were quickly attacked through pressure on their advertisers. But they persisted in their campaign with fearlessness and admirable professional journalistic skill that eventually aroused the entire state, brought about the strictest law enforcement, and crushed the Klan in North Carolina.

An era of fear, threat, and floggings by hooded night riders came to an end in 1952 with the sentencing of eighteen members of the Ku Klux Klan to prison terms and the fining of many more. A four-year term for the Grand Dragon himself, Thomas L. Hamilton, following his admission of conspiracy in having led the Klan's flogging of an innocent Negro woman, caused the collapse of the movement.

As the Washington *Star* observed editorially,

"Columbus County and the state at large probably will not be bothered again—not in a long, long time—by the night-riding terrorists of the Klan."

How did Carter and Cole do it?

The way any honest and courageous newspaper does anything that is worth while. Both weeklies reported the news quickly and accurately and featured every new Klan outrage. Their headlines were bold. No punches were pulled. And in their editorials both on Page 1 and the editorial page, an incessant hammering at the issue of law enforcement in the South brought results.

Here was a typical headline from the *Tribune* on January 24, 1951:

NIGHT-RIDING TERRORISTS BEAT

DISABLED VET, CRIPPLED FARMER

AND ELDERLY NEGRO WOMAN

Here was a typical news lead from the *News Reporter* August 27, 1951:

"A 'watch your step' letter from 'a friend' sympathetic to the Ku Klux Klan was received today by the *News Reporter*. The letter contained the admonition to 'stop your yapping about the KKK,' a warning to 'watch your step hereafter,' and a request for no 'publisitie.' "

Here was a typical editorial from the *News Reporter* after the beating of a Negro woman:

"It is to be fondly hoped that the beating of a defenseless Negro woman near Chadbourn was only an isolated incident and that there will be no repeat visit from either this or a similar band of hoodlums.

"There is no sanity in such a mob and not a semblance of decency in the entire group. They represent a type that is too cowardly to come out into the open and face men when the odds are even. Since they move in gangs, in reality they are nothing less than gangsters."

The *News Reporter's* hopes were vain. The Klan, representing some 5,000 hooded men, mercilessly flogged thirteen individuals, including three Negroes, for such alleged crimes as too much drinking, non-pay-ment of debts, and loose living. It frequently threatened both weeklies with reprisals, but neither would back down. There was no comfortable escape here by such doubtful proofs of editorial courage as attacks on State Department policy in, let us say, Afghanistan. The Klan was right in the editor's front yard.

At the height of their campaign, Carter and Cole used to ask each other with rather wan humor which one would be the first to be hauled out and flogged by the irate Klansmen. It was no joking matter, as Grand Dragon Hamilton himself made clear in a bitter attack on the Tabor City *Tribune*.

With characteristic courage, Editor Carter defiantly printed the full text of Hamilton's scurrilous letter on Page 1 and just as defiantly answered it. Here is the Carter letter, the high point in the war of the two weeklies against the Klan.

OUR DEFENSE

From the Tabor City Tribune, Jan. 23, 1952

Dear Mr. Hamilton,

Thank you for your letter of January 21, even though most of your remarks are highly slanderous and untrue. However, in at least one respect we see eye to eye—we both believe in the freedom of the press and for that reason your letter is printed in this "trash sheet" word for word. I know then that you would have no objection to my offering a few remarks in my defense. Even criminals tried in legal courts have that privilege.

In your first paragraph you repeat a charge made by you months ago that my "mind is warped." Mr. Hamilton, just to deny this statement is not evidence enough, when you consider the source from which the charge came. But perhaps you will accept my challenge to appear with me before any qualified psychiatrist and let him thoroughly examine us both. It might be interesting to see just whose mind is warped. Matter of fact, I believe it would be a revelation.

You insinuate in your first paragraph that my advertisers in the *Tribune*, as well as subscribers, are affiliated with your organization. Of course, we can neither say you are right or that you are wrong. But we will make this statement. If there are any KKK members advertising with us who would like to cease doing so, we will be happy to cancel it forthwith. If there are any subscribers who would like to have their subscription money refunded, we will refund in cash the remainder of their paid-up subscription time. We ask for no assistance from the Ku Klux Klan. There are enough other people for us to make a living.

In your second paragraph you "are led to challenge" me to prove that your KKKs have had anything to do with the recent Columbus County floggings. Mr. Hamilton, please take note that the column to which you have taken such violent objection stated, "This fear is an outgrowth of the KKK and an evil thereof whether they are the guilty parties in the numerous Columbus County floggings or not."

The coming of your Klan marked the beginning of these floggings and even if your group isn't doing the job themselves, others are using the organization for a haven. But believe me, if I could prove that the KKKs are responsible for just one of them, I would be most happy to tell a jury of twelve men all about it. The group carrying out these floggings give the defendant no chance to testify for himself. They are being beaten on the theory that they are guilty without any right to plead innocent.

Your boys will seek legal counsel and a chance to plead their cases when the time necessitates such action. And that's as it should be—innocent until proven guilty.

Then, Mr. Hamilton, there is no difficulty in proving your statement wrong when you said, "I challenge any one to prove where the organization has in any way tried to administer justice to any one." By your own admission, you and your robed friends dragged Charlie Fitzgerald from his place of business in Myrtle Beach and made some violent attempts at your form of administering justice. Did you or didn't you?

And then the constitutional principles to which you refer. Have you ever read that document? A man who so roundly criticizes the law, the Negro, the Jew, the Catholics in public speeches everywhere and who still professes to believe in the principles of our democratic government is stretching an interpretation much further than I can imagine.

You have asked what was wrong with the law officers of Columbus County. As to their ability to track down these criminals, who have made one assault after another, I do not know. As to their efforts in this direction, I am confident they have done their best. Pitted against such an undercover society perhaps makes it too big a job for them.

But at any rate they are lending their assistance to a big brother, the FBI, along with the SBI (State Bureau of Investigation), from whom they have every right to request help, and it is our belief that they are making progress, and that there is no reason to believe there is anything wrong with our law enforcement.

Should they fail miserably to hang one of these crimes on the proper persons, then I will have to agree with you that there's some ability or something lacking. I do not minimize their task. It's difficult to procure the evidence. With that, they have my sympathies and best wishes.

As to the caliber of men in your Klan, I can only say "no comment." But I would like to have the membership roster held up before God to get His stamp of approval. A group of hand-picked righteous people who can hide their identity and their faces and do no wrong.

In your last two paragraphs you get back to God and Country, both dear to my heart, and to which I can only say "amen." But as to the missions given by God, I can't help but wonder if God gave you your mission, or if He gave me mine. Or if He had rather you cease your operation or me mine.

Very sincerely yours,

W. Horace Carter

The weeklies won. It was Hamilton who had to cease operations. Upon his conviction, the *News Reporter* wrote as follows on October 2, 1952.

Some of the men who rode under the banner of the Klan were honestly misguided. They got into the organization for various reasons. A few carried the Bible in one hand and a pistol in the other. Some sought political power. Others hoped for business gain.

Some wanted to control the courts. Others felt they were "lifting up" erring humanity. Some entered for adventure, getting a couple of "shots" under their belts and sallying forth to a dangerous experience. Others sought to unite for the purpose of preventing the consolidation of Negro children with white children.

Back of it all, however, was a grasping hand, linked to a man whose mind was filled with beastly thoughts of brutality. "Do a good job or you'll have to do it all over again," was one view he took of the flogging of Mrs. Evergreen Flowers. "If it isn't done right you'll only make them mad and they'll talk," was another way of expressing his thoughts.

Yesterday, the Klan rode again. This time the brains of the Ku Klux Klan, minus his satin robe, went on a ride to a prison road gang where he will have four years to form new Klaverns and perhaps elevate himself anew to Imperial Wizard.

Most of the people in Columbus County prefer that he ride there instead of in their midst. They serve notice also that they oppose any reduction of the time that Judge Clawson L. Williams set aside for his organization effort in the state institution.

The Pulitzer Prize for Public Service was awarded to the two weeklies in 1953 "for their successful campaign against the Ku Klux Klan, waged on their own doorstep at the risk of economic loss and personal danger, culminating in the conviction of over 100 Klansmen and an end to terrorism in their communities." A whole nation applauded their devotion to duty.

Publisher Carter saw the Tabor City *Tribune* prosper and bought another weekly, this one in South Carolina. Cole left the weekly field for publicity and free-lance writing. As for the Klan, it became dormant in North Carolina.

Jonathan Daniels of the Raleigh (N.C.) *News and Observer* concluded in mid-1958:

"Even though there has been some sporadic activity on the part of the Klan in the past year, there has been nothing resembling a revival of the organization (in North Carolina) . . . The truth seems to be that now even the strongest segregationists (except for the poor dopes) dislike the Klan because they think it is a discredit to their cause."

18. AN EDITOR REBUKES A MOB
IN THE AUTHERINE LUCY CASE

"If they could have gotten their hands on her,
they would have killed her," writes Buford Boone

Pulitzer Prize for Editorial Writing, 1957

Autherine Lucy was the first Negro student to be admitted to the University of Alabama. Her presence on the otherwise all-white campus at Tuscaloosa touched off four days of rioting by students and others who opposed even this mild beginning of integration in 1956. On February 6 of that year, she was barred from classes by the University administration and accordingly withdrew.

On that same day, in the Tuscaloosa *News*, Buford Boone courageously rebuked his fellow-citizens for their resort to mob rule. His newspaper of 17,000 circulation was obviously vulnerable to attack by ill-wishers. As publisher, he himself might have faced some outrage at the hands of the segregationists. But he was not deterred from speaking his mind and trying to give leadership to a distressed community sorely in need of it.

Boone, a native of Georgia, persevered in his editorial position throughout the Lucy case and afterward. His moderation, courage, and independence were accounted to have calmed the hysterical opposition in the community so that, long afterward, he was able to say that some of his subscribers had told him:

"I felt that the *News* went too far in those editorials on this situation at first, but I have come around to believe that they are right, after all."

Here is the editorial of February 7, 1956, one of the series that won Boone the Pulitzer Prize for Editorial Writing in 1957, published at the climax of the Lucy case on the day after she was barred from college.

WHAT A PRICE FOR PEACE

By Buford Boone

From the Tuscaloosa (Ala.) News, Feb. 7, 1956

When mobs start imposing their frenzied will on universities, we have a bad situation.

But that is what has happened at the University of Alabama. And it is a development over which the University of Alabama, the people of this state, and the community of Tuscaloosa should be deeply ashamed—and more than a little afraid.

Our government's authority springs from the will of the people. But their wishes, if we are to be guided by democratic processes, must be expressed by ballot at the polls, by action in the legislative halls, and finally by interpretation from the bench. No intelligent expression ever has come from a crazed mob, and it never will.

And make no mistake. There was a mob, in the worst sense, at the University of Alabama yesterday.

Every person who witnessed the events there with comparative detachment speaks of the tragic nearness with which our great university came to being associated with murder—yes, we said murder.

"If they could have gotten their hands on her, they would have killed her."

That was the considered judgment, often expressed, of the many who watched the action without participating in it.

The target was Autherine Lucy. Her "crimes"? She was born black, and she was moving against Southern custom and tradition— but with the law, right on up to the United States Supreme Court, on her side.

What does it mean today at the University of Alabama, and here in Tuscaloosa, to have the law on your side?

The answer has to be: Nothing—that is, if a mob disagrees with you and the courts.

As matters now stand, the university administration and trustees have knuckled under to the pressures and desires of the mob. What is to keep the same mob, if uncontrolled again, from taking over in any other field where it decides to impose its wishes? Apparently, nothing.

What is the answer to a mob? We think that is clear. It lies in firm, decisive action. It lies in the use of whatever force is necessary to restrain and subdue any one who is violating the law.

Not a single university student has been arrested on the campus and that is no indictment against the men in uniform, but against

higher levels which failed to give them clean-cut authority to go
along with responsibility.

What has happened here is far more important than whether a
Negro girl is admitted to the university. We have a breakdown of
law and order, an abject surrender to what is expedient rather than
a courageous stand for what is right.

Yes, there's peace on the university campus this morning. But
what a price has been paid for it!

Boone campaigned effectively to restore quiet in the community and
succeeded. This reply to a northern editor's request for comment will
explain how he did it.

A MESSAGE FROM THE SOUTH

The following request came by telegram to Buford Boone, publisher of the *News*, from Everett Walker, of the New York *Herald
Tribune*: "Would appreciate your comment and views on segregation; its status your area. Can problem be solved? How much of
Alabama situation a true reflection of situation? Will situation become more acute? Planning symposium page view of Southern
editors this Sunday."

The following telegram was sent by the *News'* publisher in reply
to that request, and is presented as further editorial opinion and
editorial evaluation of the greatest problem facing Alabama and the
South today.

Mr. Walker:

A great majority of students at the University of Alabama would
prefer that Negroes stay away. But mob violence and mob dictation
are not condoned by most of those on the campus.

Sentiment ranges from an attitude of calm acceptance of the
inevitable to a bitter determination to fight to the last against any
change. Student opinion probably reflects the feeling of the people
of the state accurately.

Some of those who were active in the mob believe that murder is
better than submission. They are far from a majority, for actually
the mob action was by a definite minority of students. And many of

those who participated were so frenzied that they wouldn't have realized what they had done until after they had killed the Negro student last Monday—if they had succeeded in getting their hands on her.

Courageous action by university authorities and law enforcement, plus an abundance of luck, kept Alabama's conscience from bearing the load of a murder. For the mob was "gone" Monday noon. Its members, white-faced and out of touch with reality, tried to do what a white-haired woman, perhaps the mother of a student, kept shouting for them to do: "Kill her, kill her, kill her!"

(Reference to "courageous action" applies only to protection given the Negro student—not to the namby-pamby policy which permitted the mob to become so strong and so vicious.)

The thinking people of the South will pay the price of maintaining respect for law, and for bringing themselves to face the realities of the present. For white Southerners, that price is an agonizing slipping away of some customs and habits as comfortable as old garments. For Negro Southerners the price is calmness, continued patience, and a measure of satisfaction in the ever-so-slow implementation of rights that are theirs as American citizens.

But white Southerners will not submit to force and intimidation, nor to all-the-way-at-once changes in a way of life. It is silly, in some people's minds, to revere a cow. But the Hindus do. It may not be sensible, intelligent, nor American in the opinions of many for Southerners to think as we do about segregation.

However, in understanding the problem, it is necessary to recognize a condition that exists, whether right or wrong. For sentiment has coalesced and congealed, over the generations and decades, into a condition.

Changes from such a status, which is a concrete fact and not something nebulous and unperceivable, are not going to come suddenly, whether the effort is to stamp out, legislate out, or order out by a decision from the bench. For our problem is one of dealing with men's minds. And those men are fiercely free, proud and independent.

The area of danger lies in friction between extremists. The area of hope lies with Southerners, white and black, who believe in law and order. It lies with people who are willing to think—to think about the truth that when one American is denied unjustly something that is justly his, we are all poorer.

Gradual change has been taking place. But sometimes change cannot be continued in slow steps. There has to be a jump. When Autherine Lucy made the jump, all hell broke loose.

Most of the "jumps" will come, for a period of years, only as a result of court order. Agitation for more will breed strong groups of Citizens Councils and Ku Klux Klaverns. The South, it appears, is going to lose this one, too. But it's going to take longer than it took before.

Personally, I know that change is here. I am neither ashamed of the past, afraid of the present, nor despondent about the future. I believe law and order will emerge triumphant. And if it doesn't, all is lost.

My newspaper, whose policy is made solely and exclusively by myself and a few but fine editors who work with me here where the problem is, will continue to stand for what is right in all issues, to champion justice for all men, to encourage spreading, instead of limiting, the blessings and privileges of true democracy.

In so far as the rest of the world is concerned, I'd ask that you let us continue to have your intelligent interest in this problem. Give us your patient understanding and your prayers. Otherwise, leave us alone.

BUFORD BOONE

19. RELMAN MORIN REPORTS
THE SHAME OF LITTLE ROCK

A mob forces the withdrawal of eight Negro students
as the Associated Press man dictates the story

Pulitzer Prize for National Reporting, 1958

Wherever there's trouble, you'll find Relman (Pat) Morin of the Associated Press. He was in a glass-enclosed telephone booth opposite Central High School in Little Rock, Ark., on the morning of September 23, 1957. The scene was quiet and calm as he dictated routine material to his office, awaiting the arrival of the first Negro students to enter the school.

Suddenly he broke off. "Hey, wait a minute! There's a helluva fight starting!"

Then began one of the most remarkable instances of on-the-spot reporting in current American journalism. From the moment the waiting crowd turned ugly and attacked four Negro newspapermen until long after the Negro students were inside the building, he dictated his story almost blow-by-blow. He kept it up until the now-threatening mob forced the students out of school, then hustled to the Little Rock bureau for the wrap-up story that drew praise from editors all over the nation and a 1958 Pulitzer Prize for National Reporting.

It will be noted that Morin's report shows that only eight Negro students were in school on that critical day for integration in the South, three boys and five girls, whereas nine were registered. Like the Arkansas *Gazette,* the AP's gifted reporter carefully noted that one of the nine was absent.

This was Pat Morin's second Pulitzer Prize. The first in his long and distinguished career with the Associated Press was for his Korean War reporting, for which he won an international reporting award in 1951. Here is his Little Rock story.

"LOOK! THEY'RE GOING INTO THE SCHOOL!"

By Relman Morin

From the AP report, Sept. 23, 1957

LITTLE ROCK, ARK., Sept. 23.—(AP)—A howling, shrieking crowd of men and women outside Central High School, and disorderly students inside, forced authorities to withdraw eight Negro students from the school Monday, three and one-half hours after they entered it.

At noon, Mayor Woodrow Wilson Mann radioed police officers on the scene, telling them to tell the crowd: "The Negro students have been withdrawn."

Almost immediately, the three Negro boys and the five girls left the school under heavy police escort. The officers took them away in police cars.

Crowds clustered at both ends of the school set up a storm of fierce howling and surged toward the lines of police and state troopers. They were beaten back.

The explosive climax came after the school had been under siege since 8:45 a.m. when the Negroes walked quietly through the doors. Police, armed with riot guns and tear gas, had kept the crowd under control.

Inside, meanwhile, students reported seeing Negroes with blood on their clothes. And some whites who came out—in protest against integration—pictured wild disorder, with policemen chasing white students through the halls, and attacks on Negroes in the building.

The break came shortly before noon.

Virgil Blossom, school superintendent, said he asked Gene Smith, assistant chief of police at the scene, if he thought it would be best to pull out the Negroes. Smith said he did.

Mann's announcement, ordering the police to notify the crowd, came minutes afterward.

Three newspapermen were beaten by the crowd before the sudden turn in the situation. They were Paul Welch, a reporter, and Gray Villette and Francis Miller, photographers. All three are employed by *Life* magazine. A man smashed Miller in the face while he was carrying an armful of camera equipment. Miller fell, bleeding profusely.

Even after the Negroes left the school, the crowds remained. Teenagers in two automobiles cruised on the outskirts yelling, "Which way did the niggers go?"

During the hours while the Negroes were in the school an estimated thirty to fifty white students left. The crowd yelled, cheered, and clapped each time a white student left the school. "Don't stay in there with the niggers," people yelled.

Four Negroes were beaten and some arrests were made before the eight students went into the school.

The initial violence outside the school was a frightening sight. Women burst into tears and a man, hoisted up on a wooden barricade, roared, "Who's going through?"

"We all are," the crowd shouted. But they didn't.

The drama-packed climax of three weeks of integration struggle in Little Rock came just after the buzzer sounded inside the 2,000-pupil high school at 8:45, signaling the start of classes.

Suddenly on a street leading toward the school, the crowd spotted four Negro adults, marching in twos, down the center of the street. A man yelled, "Look, here come the niggers."

They were not the students. One appeared to be a newspaperman. He had a card in his hat and was bearing a camera.

I jumped into a glass-windowed telephone booth on the corner to dictate the story. As the crowd surged toward the four Negroes they broke and ran.

They were caught on the lawn of a home nearby. Whites jumped the man with the camera from behind and rode him to the ground, kicking and beating him. They smashed the camera.

This, obviously, was a planned diversionary movement to draw the crowd's attention away from the school. While I was dictating, someone yelled, "Look! They're going into the school!"

At that instant, the eight Negroes—the three boys and five girls— were crossing the schoolyard toward a side door at the south end of the school. The girls were in bobby sox and the boys were dressed in shirts open at the neck. All were carrying books.

They were not running, not even walking fast. They simply strolled toward the steps, went up and were inside before all but a few of the 200 people at that end of the street knew it.

"They're gone in," a man roared. "Oh, God, the niggers are in the school."

A woman screamed, "Did they get in? Did you see them go in?"

"They're in now," some other men yelled.

"Oh, my God," the woman screamed. She burst into tears and tore at her hair. Hysteria swept the crowd. Other women began weeping and screaming.

At that moment a tall, gray-haired man in a brown hunting shirt jumped on the barricade. He yelled, waving his arms: "Who's going through?"

"We all are," the people shouted.

They broke over and around the wooden barricades, rushing the policemen. Almost a dozen police were at that corner of the street. They raised their billy clubs.

Some grabbed men and women and hurled them back. Two chased a dark-haired man who slipped through their line, like a football player. They caught him on the schoolyard, whipped his coat down his arms, pinning them, and hustled him out of the yard.

Another man, wearing a construction worker's hard hat, suddenly raised his hands high in front of a policeman. It was only a dozen yards or so in front of the phone booth.

I couldn't see whether the officer had a gun in the man's stomach, but he stopped running abruptly and went back. Two men were arrested.

Meanwhile a cavalcade of cars carrying state troopers, in their broad-brimmed campaign hats and Sam Browne belts, wheeled into the street from both ends. They came inside the barricades and order was restored for a moment.

The weeping and screaming went on among the women. A man said, "I'm going in there and get my kid out."

An officer said, "You're not going anywhere."

Suddenly another roar—and cheering and clapping—came from the crowd. A white student, carrying his books, came down the front steps. He was followed by two girls wearing bobby sox. In the next few minutes, other students came out. Between fifteen and twenty left the school within the next half hour.

Each time they appeared, the people clapped and cheered. "Come on out," they yelled. "Don't stay in there with the niggers. Go back and tell all of them to come out."

Inside, it was reported, the eight Negro students were in the office of the principal. A moment later, two policemen suddenly raced into the building through the north door. When they came out, they were holding a girl by both arms, rushing her forcibly toward a police prisoner's wagon.

For an instant it looked as though the crowd would try to break the police lines again to rescue her. But the police put her in the car and drove swiftly down the street. Screams, cat-calls, and more yelling broke out as the car raced down the street.

A man, distraught, came sprinting after it. "That's my kid in there," he yelled. "Help me get my kid out."

But the car was gone. Soon afterward four white students ran down the steps of the school and across the street. Policemen were chasing them.

One of the boys said they had caught a Negro boy outside the principal's office in the school. "We walked him half the length of the building and we were going to get him out of there," they said. They refused to give their names.

Meanwhile, on the streets, at both ends of the school, clusters of troopers took up their stations, reinforcing the police. The crowd heckled them, hurling insults and some obscenity.

"How you going to feel tonight when you face your neighbors?" a man shouted.

The people called the police "nigger lovers" and insulted them. The officers stood, poker-faced, making no response.

Then the crowd, lacking any other object, turned on the news-papermen and photographers. A boy jumped up, caught the tele-phone wire leading from one of the three booths to the main wire and swung on it, trying to break it. The booth swayed and nearly toppled to the street.

Someone said, "We ought to wipe up the street with these Yankee reporters."

"Let's do it right now," another replied.

But it was only words. Nothing happened. The same woman who had burst into tears first buttonholed a reporter and said, "Why don't you tell the truth about us? Why don't you tell them we are peaceful people who won't stand to have our kids sitting next to niggers?"

People in the crowd reported gleefully—and shouted it at the other officers—that one policeman had torn off his badge and thrown it on the ground.

"There's one white man on the police force," a burly slick-haired youth in a tee-shirt yelled at the policeman in front of him.

Sporadic tussles broke out, from time to time, when men tried to pass the police and trooper lines. The police wrestled one man to the street and then, taking him by the hands and arms, hauled him into the squad car and drove off.

A number of plainclothesmen—some reported to be FBI agents—kept circulating up and down in front of the school.

Inside there was no sign that this was different from any other school day. Students who came out at the 10:30 recess said that, in one class of thirty students, only one stayed in the classroom when a Negro entered.

20. "WE ARE GOING TO HAVE TO DECIDE WHAT KIND OF PEOPLE WE ARE"

*Harry S. Ashmore and the Arkansas Gazette
lead the fight for decency in Little Rock*

Pulitzer Prizes for Public Service and Editorial Writing, 1958

"Somehow, some time, every Arkansan is going to have to be counted. We are going to have to decide what kind of people we are—whether we obey the law only when we approve of it, or whether we obey it no matter how distasteful we may find it. And this, finally, is the only issue before the people of Arkansas . . ."

So wrote Harry S. Ashmore. The title of that calm, reasoned editorial in the *Arkansas Gazette* was "Reflections In A Hurricane's Eye." The date: September 9, 1957. The place: Little Rock.

The school integration crisis there already had blazed its way to the front pages of the nation and world attention as well. There was no doubt where Ashmore stood. The executive editor of the *Arkansas Gazette,* with the full support and blessing of its publisher, 85-year-old John N. Heiskell, was defying the governor of the state of Arkansas and a powerful segregationist element in his own community.

When the day came that saw a violent mob force the first Negro students out of Central High School in Little Rock, the day so vividly described by Relman Morin of the Associated Press, the *Gazette* stood up to be counted. And when President Eisenhower rushed 1,200 Army paratroopers into the capital of Arkansas on September 24 to see that the Negro children went to school in safety, the *Gazette* gave stunning and complete coverage, undeterred and unafraid.

And spread across six columns was a dramatic picture taken by a staff photographer of Army trucks rumbling into Little Rock, headlights stabbing the night, past a brightly-lit sign: "Who will build Arkansas if her own people do not?"

For courage, leadership, and devotion to duty, Ashmore and the *Gazette* both were awarded Pulitzer Prizes in 1958—the first for editorial writing and the second for public service—an honor never before duplicated in the history of the prizes. Here, in selected editorials, is the temper of a man and a newspaper.

THE CRISIS MR. FAUBUS MADE

By Harry S. Ashmore

From the Arkansas Gazette, Sept. 4, 1957

Little Rock arose yesterday to gaze upon the incredible spectacle of an empty high school surrounded by National Guard troops called out by Governor Faubus to protect life and property against a mob that never materialized.

Mr. Faubus says he based this extraordinary action on reports of impending violence. Dozens of local reporters and national correspondents worked through the day yesterday without verifying the few facts the governor offered to explain why his appraisal was so different from that of local officials—who have asked for no such action.

Mr. Faubus contends that he has done nothing that can be construed as defiance of the federal government.

Federal Judge Ronald N. Davies last night accepted the governor's statement at its face value and ordered the school board to proceed on the assumption that the National Guard would protect the right of the nine enrolled Negro children to enter the high school without interference.

Now it remains for Mr. Faubus to decide whether he intends to pose what could be the most serious constitutional question to face the national government since the Civil War. The effect of his action so far is to interpose his state office between the local school district and the United States Court. The government, as Judge Davies implied last night, now has no choice but to proceed against such interference or abandon its right to enforce its rulings and decisions.

Thus, the issue is no longer segregation vs. integration. The question has now become the supremacy of the government of the United States in all matters of law. And clearly the federal government cannot let this issue remain unresolved, no matter what the cost to this community.

Until last Thursday the matter of gradual, limited integration in the Little Rock schools was a local problem which had been well and wisely handled by responsible local officials who have had—and we believe still have—the support of a majority of the people of this city. On that day Mr. Faubus appeared in Chancery Court on behalf of a small but militant minority and chose to make it a state problem. On Monday night he called out the National Guard and made it a national problem.

It is one he must now live with, and the rest of us must suffer under. If Mr. Faubus in fact has no intention of defying federal authority now is the time for him to call a halt to the resistance which is preventing the carrying out of a duly entered court order. And certainly he should do so before his own actions become the cause of the violence he so professes to fear.

NOW WE FACE FEDERAL TROOPS

From the Arkansas Gazette, Sept. 24, 1957

The march of events in Little Rock over the last three weeks has now led to an inevitable climax.

Yesterday President Eisenhower made the hard and bitter decision he has sought to avoid. He will use federal troops to restore law and order to the city of Little Rock.

The President's language made his meaning unmistakable. To the White House reporters at Newport he read a statement in the numbered paragraphs of the old military man:

"I want to make several things very clear in connection with the disgraceful occurrences of today at Central High School in Little Rock.

"1. The federal law and orders of a United States District Court implementing that law cannot be flouted with impunity by an individual or any mob of extremists.

"2. I will use the full power of the United States—including whatever force may be necessary to prevent any obstruction of the law and to carry out the orders of the Federal Court."

We can hope that we may yet escape the tragic spectacle of federal soldiers deployed on the streets of Little Rock for the first time since the post-Civil War period of Reconstruction.

The decision is up to the members of the riotous mob which assembled yesterday at Central High School and finally passed beyond the control of the local police—who did their duty and did it well.

If these reckless men force the issue again this morning, the federal troops will march—as they must march to restore order and end the intolerable situation in which the city now finds itself.

THE HIGH PRICE OF RECKLESSNESS

From the Arkansas Gazette, Sept. 25, 1957

This is a tragic day in the history of the republic—and Little Rock, Arkansas, is the scene of the tragedy.

In one sense we rolled back our history to the Reconstruction era when federal troops moved into position at Central High School to uphold the law and preserve the peace.

Yet there was no denying the case President Eisenhower made in solemn words on television last night.

Law and order had broken down here.

The local police could not restore the peace with their own resources.

Governor Faubus had refused to use his state forces to enforce the law, and instead had used them to defy the order of a federal court—and in so doing had made this last, painful step inevitable.

And so the reckless course the governor embarked upon three weeks ago has raised old ghosts and tested the very fiber of the Constitution. And, the greatest irony of all, he has by his acts and words dealt a major and perhaps a lethal blow to the cause of segregation which he purported to uphold.

We in Little Rock had perfected a plan to meet the Supreme Court's new racial requirements in education gradually and largely on our own terms. The federal courts had sustained us. But now Mr. Faubus and the angry, violent, and thoughtless band of agitators who rallied to his call may well have undone the patient work of responsible local officials.

We can still hope that this will not be the case. Unhappy though it may be, the action of the President in using federal force will serve to restore the calm that is essential to an orderly approach to any problem. In the days ahead we, as a people, will, we believe, regain our perspective and accept the clear course of duty.

That is the job for all of us now—to restore the peace and sustain the law.

ATTACK ON A FOOTBALL PLAYER
by John Robinson and Don Ultang

PICTURES OF THE DRAKE-OKLAHOMA A & M FOOTBALL GAME OF OCT. 20,
SHOWING (UPPER RIGHT) HOW PLAYER JOHNNY BRIGHT'S JAW WAS BROKEN
BY HIS OPPONENTS.

PULITZER PRIZE, 1952   DES MOINES REGISTER & TRIBUNE

THE MODERATES VS. THE EXTREMISTS

From the Arkansas Gazette, Oct. 20, 1957

In the emotional atmosphere of these last few weeks, some important words have lost their real meaning.

There are those, for example, who attempt to reduce the Little Rock school impasse to a conflict between "Segregationists" and "Integrationists."

We only wish the matter were that simple.

If "segregationist" means one who would prefer to keep the white and colored races separate in all things social the term would embrace practically all the white population of Arkansas and a substantial proportion of the black.

If "integrationist" means one who believes all the legal and extra-legal barriers between the races should be dropped overnight it would apply to only a small minority of the colored population.

The truth, deliberately obscured by those who have been loudest in arguing the case, is that neither of these concepts is or was really at issue at Central High School.

For example, the members of the Little Rock school board would without exception qualify as segregationists. Indeed, they felt (as do we) that they were working to preserve the existing pattern of social segregation when they evolved a plan which would, in compliance with the new federal law, result in the admission of only a few carefully screened Negro students to a single white high school.

Yet these conscientious men are now under attack as "integrationists"—as is this newspaper for its consistent support of their position.

Perhaps the only terms that now have any real validity are "extremist" and "moderate." An extremist is one who would defy the law and use force if necessary to prevent the entry of Negroes to any school heretofore reserved for whites. A "moderate" is one who will obey the law, no matter how distasteful it may be to him personally —and who under no circumstances will condone violence against any person for any reason.

If we divide the population of the state on this basis—as ultimately we will have to do—we believe the extremists would account for only a small minority. . . .

The problem of the moment is that they have at least the tacit support of a fairly substantial number of citizens who are still bemused by the false fear and the false hope that have beset the South for the last century—and there are demagogues abroad in the land who are deliberately playing one against the other.

The false fear is that the striking down of the legal barriers of segregation and the rising aspirations of our Negro people will bring about a vast and sudden social change in the South. Our own experience should prove to anyone who will consider the facts that this is not even a remote possibility—that the barriers of the mind have never needed to be sustained by the strictures of the law. Does anyone who has considered the matter dispassionately believe that the casual proximity of a few Negroes and a few whites in our classrooms is going to change the social pattern we have always lived by? If so, we invite an examination of the record of our state university and colleges which began desegregation some eight years ago.

The false hope is that the rest of the United States, by persuasion or force, can be brought to abandon the declared public policy of the nation and let the South alone. The presence on our streets of a detachment of the 101st Airborne Infantry, ordered here by the most conciliatory President in modern times, should disabuse us of that notion.

The point is that sooner or later we have got to make some adjustment of our legal institutions to comply with the public policy of the United States—or once again secede from the Union, which no one seriously contemplates. We were given a chance to make those adjustments largely on our own terms; we lost it the day the extremists took over and persuaded Governor Faubus to embark upon a course of defiance of federal authority. But there is still a chance to regain it—if, in time, we also regain our perspective and begin behaving like the moderates most of us really are.

The federal troops were withdrawn at the end of the school year. But in September, 1958, a new crisis began—the era of the closed school. As an election device, it brought victory to Governor Faubus and to his followers. But the Supreme Court stood firm. The law of the land and the will of the American people were summed up in one word: "Integrate."

IV. IN DEFENSE OF JUSTICE: THE REPORTING OF CRIME

On the blustery afternoon of March 1, 1954, Puerto Rican fanatics began shooting up the House of Representatives in Washington, D. C.

Reporters in and around the august chamber heard gunfire at 2:32 p.m. Suddenly, incredibly, they saw one representative collapse. Another staggered outside and slumped to the floor. Still others ducked.

Within three minutes, flashes and bulletins broke into the orderly news routine of the nation's city rooms. And for hours afterward, reporters who had been in or near the line of fire developed the fantastic story that created an uproar in the nation's capital.

It is given to few reporters to cover such an outbreak. Many can go through a lifetime of newspapering without hearing a shot fired in anger. But always, there is that chance. Always, a good reporter remembers the lessons of his first police story . . . get the facts straight . . . go to the nearest phone . . . let the desk know what's going on.

True, after the hazards of two world wars and the still greater dangers of the new era of atomic bombs, rockets, and outer space missiles, the fancied glamor of crime reporting has paled for many a newspaperman. And for editors, even on the liveliest papers, there is no longer much point to stretching out a crime story for days and weeks. Today, except for the very biggest spot news breaks, such a story often lasts only an afternoon, or an evening, and then is dropped in favor of something more important. In fact, the more serious journals are not inclined to feature crime news except when it is safe to consider it as sociology.

And yet, sometimes, the unexpected happens. In the most sensible and least sensational city rooms, that indefinable tension grows. There is a certain strain to the usually even, mild voices of the editors. The rewrite men, even the most bored, reach for the telephone with a bit of eagerness to take a reporter's call. Even the copyreaders begin asking what's going on. All that is the trademark of the big story.

In the files of the Pulitzer Prizes, there are crime stories that have brought honor to individuals, to editors, to entire staffs. With few exceptions, the awards were bestowed for cool work under great pressure, for the exceptional job that nobody else could do. Such a prize went to the Providence *Journal and Evening Bulletin* staff in 1953 for covering a bank robbery and police chase that led to the capture of a bandit.

Others have won awards for extended investigations. One such was Westbrook Pegler who, while on the New York *World-Telegram,* helped expose and convict a labor racketeer. Still others were Wallace Turner and William Lambert of the Portland *Oregonian,* who dug into vice and corruption in their city and involved some municipal officials as well as some officers of the Teamsters Union.

The following stories are representative of the work of reporters who followed the trail of a crime, no matter where it led, and by their own efforts achieved extraordinary results.

21. A 70-YEAR-OLD REPORTER SMASHES
THE "ALMOST PERFECT" CRIME

A. B. Macdonald of the Kansas City Star cracks
the Payne murder case in Amarillo, Texas

Pulitzer Prize for Reporting, 1931

When Alexander Black Macdonald was seventy years old, the Kansas City *Star* sent him to Amarillo, Texas, to solve a murder.

The trail was cold. The crime was five weeks old. Nobody had been arrested. So far as Macdonald could tell, nobody was even under suspicion. To most reporters, and probably to all except the kind of paperback novel detective who slugs a blonde in the opening paragraph, it would have seemed hopeless.

But old Macdonald was a crime reporter who had spent his life at the business, except for a brief period when he had quite unaccountably hit the sawdust trail with Billy Sunday. On the way to Amarillo, he considered the details of the crime.

The date: June 27, 1930. The place: a decent residential section of Amarillo. The family: that of A. D. Payne, a respected lawyer who had the reputation of loving his wife and three children to the exclusion of all other interests.

That morning, A. D. Sr. had decided to walk downtown to his office, leaving the family coupe to his wife who wanted to do some shopping chores. One of his two small daughters, Bobbie Jean, begged off from riding with her mother and he good-naturedly let her stroll along with him. The other daughter remained at home.

Mrs. Payne and A. D. Jr. rode off. After they had gone about six blocks, smoke poured from under the hood. Junior sniffed. "Mother," he said in shrill alarm, "that smells exactly like the smoke of that powder fuse I found in the back yard and burned."

Mrs. Payne smiled serenely. "Daddy told me to drive faster if the car smoked."

In a few moments there was a blast that tore the car apart, hurled Mrs. Payne forty feet through the roof of the car and her son even farther. Mrs. Payne was dead when help arrived. The eleven-year-old boy, although badly hurt, lived to tell the story.

But no one would believe that A. D. Payne could have done such a thing, even though there had been some peculiar incidents in recent months such as the accidental discharge of a shotgun when Mrs. Payne opened a closet door, the birdshot riddling her hand. In any case, the husband was above suspicion. To all intents and purposes he, like Macdonald, was following a cold trail to try to find the slayer.

Yet, Macdonald got him, played a key role in forcing a confession from him, and saw him placed behind the bars for trial. Here is the story, in its essentials, of how he did the detective job that won him the Pulitzer Prize for Reporting in 1931.

"THE MEANEST MAN THAT EVER LIVED"

By A. B. Macdonald

From the Kansas City Star, Aug. 24, 1930

When A. D. Payne murdered his wife in Amarillo, Texas, he believed he had planned and executed the "perfect crime."

Payne is a lawyer. He has been a college man, a school teacher and principal of a city high school. He has taken a college course in criminology. In his law practice, he has defended criminals and studied their crimes.

For ten months Payne was continuously and patiently planning the murder of his wife and children. His trained mind worked out five different schemes of murder, but in each there was a flaw that might direct suspicion toward him and he abandoned it.

At last he hit upon the idea of blowing up the wife and two of their children with dynamite. This plan he carried out and it was so perfectly done that five weeks afterward the death of Mrs. Payne was as much a mystery as it was the day it occurred.

Gene Howe is editor and half owner of the only two newspapers in Amarillo, the *News* and the *Globe*. Howe writes a column or two a day in his Evening *Globe* under the name of "Old Tack." One day there appeared a paragraph stating that "Old Tack" would have himself appointed a deputy sheriff and work to solve the Payne case.

This was meant as a joke but it had an unexpected result. It brought Payne himself into Howe's newspaper office. He came to thank Howe for the interest he was taking in trying to find out who slew his "dear wife." He urged Howe to go ahead on the mystery.

This set Howe to thinking along a new line. He wrote the *Star* and asked that someone be sent to work on the mystery.

The *Star* wired Howe that I would come, and that same day Howe called Payne by telephone and told him that the *Star* was sending a reporter.

"That's fine," said Payne. "When he gets here bring him to see me and the children. I will give him all the help I can."

I reached Amarillo late the afternoon of August 2. Howe met me at the train.

My first question was: "What do you think of it?"

"I don't know," he replied. "Sometimes I think Payne killed her and again I think he did not. I am completely baffled. So are all the authorities. Ninety percent of the people here suspect Payne killed her, but there isn't a shred of proof. It is all suspicion and gossip. Not a tangible clue."

By agreement he came for me next morning, Sunday, at 9.

"Let's drive out to see Payne," I suggested, and on the way we talked about the case. . . .

She (Mrs. Payne) was heavily insured and so was each of the three children, with Payne as the beneficiary, and Payne's life was heavily insured for the benefit of his wife and children, and nearly all the policies carried "double indemnity," that is, twice the face of the policy would be paid if death was by accident. For some reason I did not think that this insurance, alone, was motive enough for Payne to kill his wife and children.

"There may be a woman in the case," I suggested.

"That's just about impossible," Mr. Howe said. "Payne was a devoted husband."

Payne welcomed us cordially. We sat and talked. There was something about him that made me suspect him. He was nervous. His long fingers kept fidgeting and pulling at his cheeks and chin. Behind his thin-lipped mouth and leathery face I felt there was a cruel, heartless nature. I never once thought he was innocent after I first saw him and heard his even-toned voice. It seemed unnatural.

No matter what question was asked him, he always dwelt on how he loved his wife, how much she loved him, and how they just lived for each other. He overdid that.

His eldest daughter, who will be fourteen next February, was getting dinner. Every once in a while she would come to the door and gaze in at us where we sat talking, and I imagined there was a frightened look in her eyes.

Near noon Payne's little girl, Bobbie Jean, came in with a Bible under her arm. "This is our little girl coming from Sunday School," said Payne.

The morning on which Mrs. Payne was killed, it had been planned that Payne would walk downtown and Mrs. Payne and her son, A. D. Jr., and this little girl would ride in the car. Had the child accompanied her mother she might have been killed or maimed terribly as her brother was. Payne had planned the death of the three of them, but when Payne had walked two doors from his home that morning his telephone rang. It was a man downtown wanting to talk with him and Mrs. Payne called him back. That little incident saved the life of Bobbie Jean. As Payne finished talking over the telephone, she came running in from next door and begged to be allowed to walk downtown with her daddy and he took her with him.

I asked Bobbie Jean about that. She sat in a chair answering my questions. Once her father corrected her: "No, honey, it wasn't that way, don't you remember, it was this way," and he began to set her right.

Into the face of the child came a look of fright and fear as she looked at her father and heard him correct her. She burst into tears and sobs choked her. Her sister hurried in from the kitchen, nervously wringing her hands, and tears were in her eyes.

I could see that the whole household was on high tension and that the two girls had been coached by Payne to tell their stories in a certain way. Little Bobbie Jean had forgotten and told the truth. I left then, and I know now, that both knew their father had killed their mother and were in mortal fear lest they might say something that would disclose it.

From the moment I saw that child burst into tears and beheld the look in her face, I knew for a certainty that Payne was guilty, but I pretended to be agreeing with him as he talked.

Something convinced me that there was a strange woman somewhere in the background. With that in mind I decided to see every stenographer that had worked for him since he began to practice law in Amarillo six years ago. I asked him if he had ever been enamored of another woman.

"No," he said emphatically, "I was never untrue to my dear wife even in thought, let alone in deed."

He gave me a list of his different stenographers and I wrote down what he said of each. . . .

"I've had several different stenographers in the last year. The first one was Vera Holcomb. She stayed with me only a short while. I don't know what became of her. The next was Verona Thompson. She came to work for me last August, a year ago, and I let her out in December. She is twenty-four or twenty-five years old, just an ordinary-looking woman; no man would ever get sweet on her. The next was Mabel Bush. She lives on Pierce Street; she worked for me till the Monday before my wife's death. She wants to go back to work for me now. She's doing housework for her brother. She's young and very attractive, red-headed and full of pep and wide-awake. She is only about nineteen or twenty. You might see her. My stenographer now is Miss Ocie Lee Humphries."

Nothing suspicious in that as it reads, but in the way he spoke it there appeared a design to steer us away from suspicion that Miss Thompson might have any attraction that would lure him, while Miss Bush was dangerously alluring.

As we were leaving his home Mr. Howe asked me: "What do you say about it?"

"He's guilty," I said. "He killed her and those little girls know it. There's a woman in it and I believe the Thompson girl knows all about it."

We waited for her a minute or two in the reception room at the Maples apartments, and I noticed when she came in the door that there was a look of wonder in her face. I noticed instantly that there was something about her that might be thought very attractive by many men. My first question was:

"Verona, how many times has Payne had you out to lunch?"

"Many times," she answered without a moment's hesitation. "But there was always another girl with us."

"And you have been out in the Panhandle with him?"

She thought I meant the town of Panhandle, and she replied, "Yes, I've been to Panhandle with him."

"And to Borger?"

"Yes, to Borger."

"Why did you go with him?"

"It was on business. He had business in those places and he took me along for company."

"Give me the names of all the hotels where you and Payne stayed as man and wife."

"We never did that," she said.

"That is all now, Verona. The police will send for you and when they do you go and tell all that has happened between you and Payne. Don't try to conceal anything."

"Do you think he killed her?" she asked.

"Yes, I think so."

She shook her head and said: "My! It was an awful thing, wasn't it?"

After we reached the street Mr. Howe said: "That's the woman he killed her for."

"Yes, that's the woman."

Sitting in Mr. Howe's office, I said to him:

"Gene, for heaven's sake, isn't there any one in authority in this town with nerve enough to make this girl sign a statement and then bring Payne in and confront him with it? I believe, if that were done, he might break down and confess."

Howe smote his desk with his fist as an inspiration came to him and said:

"There's one man, Ernest Thompson, the mayor. He will do it."

"Call him right now, get him here," I suggested, and within fifteen minutes Mayor Thompson came bustling in. As soon as he heard the story he exclaimed:

"My God! That's evidence enough to convict him. What do you want me to do?"

"Bring her to the police station. Have her make a written statement and sign it in the presence of witnesses. When it is about finished, bring in Payne and confront him with her and the statement."

Well, I guess everybody knows the rest of it; how Payne was brought in . . . Peering at the girl, hardly believing his sight that she was there; and she watching him with a curious sort of sneer. He almost broke down there and would have confessed then, but word of his arrest had spread and mobs were forming, and the police spirited him away to a safe jail in the little town of Stinnett. He began that very night to confess; it took him twenty hours to tell it all . . . and now he is begging for death in the electric chair as soon as the law will permit.

Payne confessed not once but many times, and he invariably had a different reason for his crime. But always he came back in one way or another to the first thing he told Chief of Police McDowell of Amarillo:

"Mac, I am the meanest man that ever lived. . . . I love that girl,

Verona Thompson. Her statement made last night was the truth—every word of it. She is as pure as the driven snow."

While awaiting trial, he managed somehow to get a vial of nitroglycerin which he wore around his neck. On August 30, 1930 he blew himself up in his cell at the Potter County Jail in Amarillo. At their last visit, he had told Macdonald that he hated him, which suited the crime reporter. Macdonald returned to the Kansas City *Star,* retired in 1937 and died in 1941 at the age of eighty-one, having spent forty-five years in reporting—and making—the news.

22. "CRIME ON THE WATERFRONT" STINGS EASY-GOING NEW YORK

A New York Sun reporter lifts the curtain
on a reign of violence in the city

Pulitzer Prize for Reporting, 1949

"New York's great waterfront, representing an investment of approximately $900,000,000 in port facilities, has been aptly described as an 'outlaw frontier' where organized crime flourishes unchecked at a cost of untold millions of dollars annually to the port's shipping."

That was the beginning of Malcolm (Mike) Johnson's "Crime on the Waterfront" series in the New York *Sun* on November 8, 1948. In 1950, the *Sun* was merged with the New York *World-Telegram* and Johnson moved on to other pursuits.

But for years afterward, his stories in the *Sun* served as primary source material for new investigations, for novels, radio and TV shows and movies. It is difficult to trace the results that have flowed specifically from the series, but there is no doubt of the overall effect. In the city, state, and nation, the rule of murder and mayhem on the New York waterfront became common knowledge—and a common shame.

Some of the gang leaders who controlled the docks and union locals in 1948 are no more. Some are behind the bars. Some were thrown out of office when their sham unions were exposed. Still others, such as Albert Anastasia, the cold-blooded executioner of Murder, Inc., were mowed down by rival gang guns.

There have been many investigations since Johnson's exposé. Without doubt, there will be more. But nothing has approached the fearlessness and candor of that first series, a part of which is republished here. It won for its author the Pulitzer Prize for Reporting in 1949. The extract is from an article about the "hot piers" on Manhattan's West Side.

MEET THE BOYS

By Malcolm Johnson

From the New York Sun, Nov. 9, 1948

How does a gang obtain control of a rich waterfront section?

It's easy if you are strong enough—and God help you if you are not. All you do is move in and declare yourself in control. That's how the Bowers mob did it.

Listen to an informant whom we'll call Joe, because that's not his name and Joe feels that he's marked for death for having crossed the Bowers mob. He says that one attempt has been made on his life and that all he craves now is to get out of town. That's Joe, who looks meek and mild, but isn't.

"While I was in Sing Sing back in 1933, doing time for robbery, I met Johnny Applegate," said Joe. "Apple was in for burglary. We got to be friendly. Apple told me to look him up when I got out.

"Some months later I looked up Apple on the waterfront. He introduced me to a union delegate they called The Bandit, who got me a union membership book without me having to pay for it. I got steady work as a longshoreman, though I had never done a day's work on the waterfront in my life. I got to know all the ins and outs. How the rackets worked. You know."

At that time a mobster named Beadle was in control of the piers above 42d Street. Beadle, himself suspected of several killings, was murdered in December, 1939. Then Richard Gregory, the union delegate known as The Bandit, was killed just a year later.

"After The Bandit was knocked off," said Joe, "there was a fight for power on the upper West Side. Suddenly a new mob walked in and took over. That was the Bowers mob and I started paying dues to these boys. We got a membership book for $26, a cut rate. The official rate was $150. The mob never put no stamps in our books. I guess 2,000 men paid off in this way. The collector was Harold Bowers, Mickey's cousin."

The Bowers gang has been in control ever since. Mickey Bowers, a growing power on the waterfront, has been arrested fourteen times, his record dating back to 1920, when he got an indeterminate prison sentence in New Jersey for violating the highway law. In 1924 he got another sentence up to three years for grand larceny and in 1930 he was sent away for ten years in New Jersey for a payroll robbery. He was released on parole in 1937 and two years later arrested for bank robbery and discharged.

Bowers's lieutenants, John Keefe and John Applegate, also have lengthy records. Keefe has been arrested eight times and convicted twice. In 1925 he was sent to Elmira Reformatory for assault. In 1928 he was sentenced to twelve years in the New Jersey State Prison for assault and battery and robbery.

Applegate, arrested five times, was sentenced in 1933 to two and one-half to ten years in Sing Sing for burglary and paroled in 1936.

John T. Ward, the husky six-foot president of Bowers's company, Allied Stevedoring, has no record and because of this was recently described by Assistant District Attorney William J. Keating as "the luckiest man in New York."

When questioned as to how Ward happened to become president of Allied Stevedoring, in view of his complete lack of experience, on the waterfront, Mickey Bowers glared at his questioner and retorted: "Hell, if you'd been up there and put up $2,000, we'd have made you president!"

Curious about Ward, District Attorney Frank S. Hogan's office early last summer picked him up on a vagrancy charge though he owns a $15,000 home in Queens and had $350 in his pocket when arrested. He explained that he got the money booking horses. . . .

On being discharged for lack of evidence, Ward, who weighs 245 pounds and has a plump, babyish face, attempted to bribe a New York *Sun* reporter to keep his name out of the paper.

"Go buy yourself a smoke," Ward said, handing the reporter a $10 bill. The reporter returned the money. Ward then tried to stuff the bill in the reporter's coat. The reporter again returned it, and Ward shrugged and walked away with his attorney.

23. MIKE BERGER RECONSTRUCTS
A MASS MURDER IN JERSEY

A celebrated report of a shocking crime
by a veteran of the New York Times

Pulitzer Prize for Reporting, 1950

There was only one Mike Berger.

He was a tall, lean New York newspaperman, slightly stooped, with a mild look of constant inquiry in his eyes and the shadow of a smile about his lips. He was a reporter of the old school, which means that he could be found taking notes crossing Times Square on a bright day if he happened to be doing a weather story.

Mike Berger was a reporter's reporter. When he covered a story, somehow it seemed to have gained a little in importance. In a difficult and demanding business whose purpose it often is to raise the dappled banner of doubt, no one ever doubted him. Yet, he was never particularly pleased with either himself or his fellow-reporters. There was always one more fact he might have had, one more colorful phrase he might have turned.

In his by-line, his name was Meyer Berger. He was born in New York City in 1898, one of eleven children, and began running copy in 1909 in the hallowed, if dusty, city room of the New York *World*. His formal schooling therefore was limited, but his talent was not. In his fifty-year career as a newspaperman he covered and wrote some of the classic stories of his day.

From the *World*, to a local news agency called Standard News and finally in 1927 to the New York *Times*, his career was always to follow the news. There was a brief and unhappy period at *The New Yorker* in 1938, which Berger always described with good humor— "They were sophisticates and I am not." But otherwise, his work as a reporter kept him thoroughly occupied, whether he was covering a Texas school disaster or the strange death of Abe (Kid Twist) Reles, squealer on Murder, Inc.; the solemn and moving return of the first World War II dead from Europe or the ghastly crimes of Howard B. Unruh, the mass slayer of East Camden, N. J. It was the Unruh story that won him the Pulitzer Prize for reporting in 1950.

"HE'S KILLING EVERYBODY"

By Meyer Berger

From the New York Times, Sept. 7, 1949

CAMDEN, N. J., Sept. 6—Howard B. Unruh, twenty-eight years old, a mild, soft-spoken veteran of many armored artillery battles in Italy, France, Austria, Belgium, and Germany, killed twelve persons with a war souvenir Luger pistol in his home block in East Camden this morning. He wounded four others.

Unruh, a slender, hollow-cheeked six-footer paradoxically devoted to scripture reading and to constant practice with firearms, had no previous history of mental illness but specialists indicated tonight that there was no doubt that he was a psychiatric case, and that he had secretly nursed a persecution complex for two years or more.

The veteran was shot in the left thigh by a local tavern keeper but he kept that fact secret, too, while policemen and Mitchell Cohen, Camden County prosecutor, questioned him at police headquarters for more than two hours immediately after tear gas bombs had forced him out of his bedroom to surrender.

The blood stain he left on the seat he occupied during the questioning betrayed his wound. When it was discovered he was taken to Cooper Hospital in Camden, a prisoner charged with murder.

He was as calm under questioning as he was during the twenty minutes that he was shooting men, women, and children. Only occasionally excessive brightness of his dark eyes indicated anything other than normal.

He told the prosecutor that he had been building up resentment against neighbors and neighborhood shopkeepers for a long time. "They have been making derogatory remarks about my character," he said. His resentment seemed most strongly concentrated against Mr. and Mrs. Maurice Cohen, who lived next door to him. They are among the dead.

Mr. Cohen was a druggist with a shop at 3202 River Road in East Camden. He and his wife had had frequent sharp exchanges over the Unruhs' use of a gate that separated their back yard from the Cohens'. Mrs. Cohen had also complained of young Unruh's keeping his bedroom radio tuned high into the late night hours. None of the other victims had ever had trouble with him.

Unruh, a graduate of Woodrow Wilson High School here, had started a GI course in pharmacy at Temple University in Philadelphia some time after he was honorably discharged from the service in 1945, but had stayed with it only three months. In recent months he had been unemployed, and apparently was not even looking for work.

His mother, Mrs. Rita Unruh, fifty, is separated from her husband. She works as a packer in the Evanson Soap Company in Camden and hers was virtually the only family income. James Unruh, twenty-five years old, her younger son, is married and lives in Haddon Heights, N. J. He works for the Curtis Publishing Company.

On Monday night, Howard Unruh left the house alone. He spent the night at the Family Theatre on Market Street in Philadelphia to sit through several showings of the double-feature motion picture there—*I Cheated The Law* and *The Lady Gambles*. It was past 3 o'clock this morning when he got home.

Prosecutor Cohen said that Unruh told him later that before he fell asleep this morning he had made up his mind to shoot the persons who had "talked about me," that he had even figured out that 9:30 A.M. would be the time to begin because most of the stores in his block would be open at that hour.

His mother, leaving her ironing when he got up, prepared his breakfast in their drab little three-room apartment in the shabby gray two-story stucco house at the corner of River Road and Thirty-second Street. After breakfast he loaded one clip of bullets into his Luger, slipped another clip into his pocket, and carried sixteen loose cartridges in addition. He also carried a tear-gas pen with his six shells and a sharp six-inch knife.

He took one last look around his bedroom before he left the house. On the peeling walls he had crossed pistols, crossed German bayonets, pictures of armored artillery in action. Scattered about the chamber were machetes, a Roy Rogers pistol, ash trays made of German shells, clips of 30-30 cartridges for rifle use and a host of varied war souvenirs.

Mrs. Unruh had left the house some minutes before, to call on Mrs. Caroline Pinner, a friend in the next block. Mrs. Unruh had

BOY GUNMAN AND HOSTAGE, *by Frank Cushing*

PULITZER PRIZE, 1948   BOSTON TRAVELER

sensed, apparently, that her son's smoldering resentments were coming to a head. She had pleaded with Elias Pinner, her friend's husband, to cut a little gate in the Unruh's back yard so that Howard need not use the Cohen gate again. Mr. Pinner finished the gate early Monday evening after Howard had gone to Philadelphia.

At the Pinners' house at 9 o'clock this morning, Mrs. Unruh had murmured something about Howard's eyes; how strange they looked and how worried she was about him.

A few minutes later River Road echoed and re-echoed to pistol fire. Howard Unruh was on the rampage. His mother, who had left the Pinners' little white house only a few seconds before, turned back. She hurried through the door.

She cried, "Oh, Howard, oh, Howard, they're to blame for this." She rushed past Mrs. Pinner, a kindly gray-haired woman of 70. She said, "I've got to use the phone; may I use the phone?"

But before she had crossed the living room to reach for it she fell on the faded carpet in a dead faint. The Pinners lifted her onto a couch in the next room. Mrs. Pinner applied aromatic spirits of ammonia to revive her.

While his mother writhed on the sofa in her house dress and worn old sweater, coming back to consciousness, Howard Unruh was walking from shop to shop in the "3200 block" with deadly calm, spurting Luger in hand. Children screamed as they tumbled over one another to get out of his way.

Men and women dodged into open shops, the women shrill with panic, men hoarse with fear. No one could quite understand for a time what had been loosed in the block.

Unruh first walked into John Pilarchik's shoe repair shop near the north end of his own side of the street. The cobbler, a 27-year-old man who lives in Pennsauken Township, looked up open-mouthed as Unruh came to within a yard of him. The cobbler started up from his bench but went down with a bullet in his stomach. A little boy who was in the shop ran behind the counter and crouched there in terror. Unruh walked out into the sunlit street.

"I shot them in the chest first," he told the prosecutor later, in meticulous detail, "and then I aimed for the head." His aim was devastating—and with reason. He had won marksmanship and sharpshooters' ratings in the service, and he practiced with his

Luger all the time on a target set up in the cellar of his home.

Unruh told the prosecutor afterward that he had Cohen the druggist, the neighborhood barber, the neighborhood cobbler, and the neighborhood tailor on his mental list of persons who had "talked about him." He went methodically about wiping them out. Oddly enough, he did not start with the druggist, against whom he seemed to have the sharpest feelings, but left him almost for the last.

From the cobblers' shop he went into the little tailor shop at 3214 River Road. The tailor was out. Helga Zegrino, twenty-eight years old, the tailor's wife, was there alone. The couple, incidentally, had been married only one month. She screamed when Unruh walked in with his Luger in hand.

Some people across the street heard her. Then the gun blasted again and Mrs. Zegrino pitched over, dead. Unruh walked into the sunlight again.

All this was only a matter of seconds and still only a few persons had begun to understand what was afoot. Down the street at 3210 River Road is Clark Hoover's little country barber shop. In the center was a white-painted carousel-type horse for children customers. Orris Smith, a blonde boy only six years old, was in it, with a bib around his neck, submitting to a shearing. His mother, Mrs. Catherine Smith, forty-two, sat on a chair against the wall and watched.

She looked up. Clark Hoover turned from his work, to see the six-footer, gaunt and tense, but silent, standing in the doorway with the Luger. Unruh's brown tropical worsted suit was barred with morning shadow. The sun lay bright on his crew-cut brown hair. He wore no hat. Mrs. Smith could not understand what was about to happen.

Unruh walked to "Brux"—that is Mrs. Smith's nickname for her little boy—and put the Luger to the child's chest. The shot echoed and reverberated in the little 12 by 12 shop. The little boy's head pitched toward the wound, his hair, half-cut, stained with red. Unruh never said a word. He put the Luger close to the shaking barber's hand. Before the horrified mother, Unruh leaned over and fired another shot into Hoover.

The veteran made no attempt to kill Mrs. Smith. He did not seem to hear her screams. He turned his back and stalked out, unhurried. A few doors north, Dominick Latela, who runs a little restaurant, had come to his shop window to learn what the shooting was about.

He saw Unruh cross the street toward Frank Engel's tavern. Then he saw Mrs. Smith stagger out with her pitiful burden. Her son's head lolled over the crook of her right arm.

Mrs. Smith screamed, "My boy is dead. I know he's dead." She stared about her, looking in vain for aid. No one but Howard Unruh was in sight, and he was concentrating on the tavern. Latela dashed out, but first he shouted to his wife, Dora, who was in the restaurant with their daughter, Eleanor, six years old. He hollered, "I'm going out. Lock the door behind me." He ran for his car and drove it down toward Mrs. Smith as she stood on the pavement with her son.

Latela took the child from her arms and placed him on the car's front seat. He pushed the mother into the rear seat, slammed the doors and headed for Cooper Hospital. Howard Unruh had not turned. Engel, the tavern keeper, had locked his own door. His customers made a concerted rush for the rear of the saloon. The bullets tore through the tavern door panelling. Engel rushed upstairs and got out his .38 caliber pistol, then rushed to the street window of his apartment.

Unruh was back in the center of the street. He fired a shot at an apartment window at 3208 River Road. Tommy Hamilton, two years old, fell back with a bullet in his head. Unruh went north again to Latela's place. He fired a shot at the door, and kicked in the lower glass panel. Mrs. Latela crouched behind the counter with her daughter. She heard the bullets, but neither she nor her child was touched. Unruh walked back toward Thirty-second Street, reloading the Luger.

Now the little street—a small block with only five buildings on one side, three one-story stores on the other—was shrill with women's and children's panicky outcries. A group of six or seven little boys or girls fled past Unruh. They screamed, "Crazy man!" and unintelligible sentences. Unruh did not seem to hear, or see, them.

Alvin Day, a television repair man who lives in nearby Mantua, had heard the shooting, but driving into the street he was not aware of what had happened. Unruh walked up to the car window as Day rolled by, and fired once through the window, with deadly aim. The repair man fell against the steering wheel. The car seemed to wobble. The front wheels hit the opposite curb and stalled. Day was dead.

Frank Engel had thrown open his second-floor apartment window. He saw Unruh pause for a moment in a narrow alley between the cobbler's shop and a little two-story house. He aimed and fired. Unruh stopped for just a second. The bullet had hit, but he did not seem to mind, after the initial brief shock. He headed toward the corner drug store, and Engel did not fire again.

"I wish I had," he said later. "I could have killed him then. I could have put a half-dozen shots into him. I don't know why I didn't do it."

Cohen, the druggist, a heavy-set man of forty, had run into the street shouting, "What's going on here?" but at the sight of Unruh hurried back into his shop. James J. Hutton, forty-five, an insurance agent from Westmont, N. J., started out of the drug shop to see what the shooting was about. Like so many others he had figured at first that it was some car backfiring. He came face to face with Unruh.

Unruh said quietly, "Excuse me, sir," and started to push past him. Later Unruh told the police: "That man didn't act fast enough. He didn't get out of my way." He fired into Hutton's head and body. The insurance man pitched onto the sidewalk and lay still.

Cohen had run to his upstairs apartment and had tried to warn Minnie Cohen, sixty-three, his mother, and Rose, his wife, thirty-eight, to hide. His son, Charles, fourteen, was in the apartment, too. Mrs. Cohen shoved the boy into a clothes closet, and leaped into another closet herself. She pulled the door to. The druggist, meanwhile, had leaped from the window onto a porch roof. Unruh, a gaunt figure at the window behind him, fired into the druggist's back. The druggist, still running, bounded off the roof and lay dead in Thirty-second Street.

Unruh fired into the closet where Mrs. Cohen was hidden. She fell dead behind the closed door, and he did not bother to open it. Mrs. Minnie Cohen tried to get to the telephone in an adjoining bedroom to call the police. Unruh fired shots into her head and body and she sprawled dead on the bed. Unruh walked down the stairs with his Luger reloaded and came out on the street again.

A coupe had stopped at River Road, obeying a red light. The passengers obviously had no idea of what was loose in East Camden and no one had a chance to tell them. Unruh walked up to the car, and though it was filled with total strangers, fired deliberately at them, one by one, through the windshield. He killed the two women passengers, Mrs. Helen Matlack Wilson, forty-three, of Pennsauken, who was driving, and her mother, Mrs. Emma Matlack, sixty-six.

Mrs. Wilson's son, John, twelve, was badly wounded. A bullet pierced his neck just below the jawbone.

Earl Horner, clerk in the American Stores Company, a grocery opposite the drug store, had locked his front door after several passing men, women, and children had tumbled breathlessly into the shop panting "crazy man . . . killing people . . ." Unruh came up to the door and fired two shots through the wood panelling. Horner, his customers, the refugees from the veteran's merciless gunfire, crouched, trembling, behind the counter. No one there was hurt.

"He tried the door before he shot in here," Horner related afterward. "He just stood there, stony-faced and grim, and rattled the knob before he started to fire. Then he turned away."

Charlie Petersen, eighteen, son of a Camden fireman, came driving down the street with two friends when Unruh turned from the grocery. The three boys got out to stare at Hutton's body lying unattended on the sidewalk. They did not know who had shot the insurance man, or why, and, like the women in the car, had no warning that Howard Unruh was on the loose. The veteran brought his Luger to sight and fired several times. Young Petersen fell with bullets in his legs. His friends tore pell-mell down the street to safety.

Mrs. Helen Harris of 1250 North Twenty-eighth Street, with her daughter, Helen, a six-year-old blonde child, and a Mrs. Horowitz with her daughter, Linda, five, turned into Thirty-second Street. They had heard the shooting from a distance but thought it was auto backfire.

Unruh passed them in Thirty-second Street and walked up the sagging four steps of a little yellow dwelling back of his own house. Mrs. Madeline Harrie, a woman in her late thirties, and two sons, Armand, sixteen, and Leroy, fifteen, were in the house.

A third son, Wilson, fourteen, was barricaded in the grocery with other customers.

Unruh threw open the front door and, gun in hand, walked into the dark little parlor. He fired two shots at Mrs. Harrie. They went wild and entered the wall. A third shot caught her in the left arm. She screamed. Armand leaped at Unruh to tackle him. The veteran used the Luger butt to drop the boy, then fired two shots into his arms. Upstairs Leroy heard the shooting and the screams. He hid under a bed.

By this time, answering a flood of hysterical telephone calls from various parts of East Camden, police radio cars swarmed into River Road with sirens wide open. Emergency crews brought machine guns, shotguns, and tear gas bombs.

Sergeant Earl Wright, one of the first to leap to the sidewalk, saw Charles Cohen, the druggist's son. The boy was half out the second-floor apartment window, just above where his father lay dead. He was screaming, "He's going to kill me. He's killing everybody." The boy was hysterical.

Wright bounded up the stairs to the druggist's apartment. He saw the dead woman on the bed, and tried to soothe the druggist's son. He brought him downstairs and turned him over to other police-men, then joined the men who had surrounded the two-story stucco house where Unruh lived. Unruh, meanwhile, had fired about thirty shots. He was out of ammunition. Leaving the Harrie house, he had also heard the police sirens. He had run through the back gate to his own rear bedroom.

Edward Joslin, a motorcycle policeman, scrambled to the porch roof under Unruh's window. He tossed a tear-gas grenade through a pane of glass.

Other policemen, hoarsely calling on Unruh to surrender, took positions with their machine guns and shotguns. They trained them on Unruh's window.

Meanwhile, a curious interlude had taken place. Philip W. Buxton, an assistant city editor on the Camden *Evening Courier,* had looked Unruh's name up in the telephone book. He called the number, Camden 4-2490 W. It was just after 10 A.M. and Unruh had just returned to his room. To Mr. Buxton's astonishment, Unruh answered. He said hello in a calm, clear voice.

"This Howard?" Mr. Buxton asked.

"Yes, this is Howard. What's the last name of the party you want?"

"Unruh."

The veteran asked what Mr. Buxton wanted.

"I'm a friend," the newspaperman said. "I want to know what they're doing to you down there."

Unruh thought a moment. He said, "They haven't done anything to me—yet. I'm doing plenty to them." His voice was still steady without a trace of hysteria.

Mr. Buxton asked how many persons Unruh had killed.

The veteran answered, "I don't know. I haven't counted. Looks like a pretty good score."

"Why are you killing people?"

"I don't know," came the frank answer. "I can't answer that yet. I'll have to talk to you later. I'm too busy now."

The telephone banged down.

Unruh was busy. The tear gas was taking effect and police bullets were thudding at the walls around him. During a lull in the firing the police saw the white curtains move and the gaunt killer came into plain view.

"Okay," he shouted, "I give up. I'm coming down."

"Where's that gun?" a sergeant yelled.

"It's on my desk up here in the room," Unruh called down quietly. "I'm coming down."

Thirty guns were trained on the shabby little back door. A few seconds later the door opened and Unruh stepped into the light, his hands up. Sergeant Wright came across the morning glory and aster beds in the yard and snapped handcuffs on Unruh's wrists.

"What's the matter with you?" a policeman demanded hotly. "You a psycho?"

Unruh stared into the policeman's eyes—a level, steady stare. He said, "I'm no psycho. I have a good mind."

Word of the capture brought the whole East Camden populace pouring into the streets. Men and women screamed at Unruh and cursed him in shrill accents and in hoarse anger. Someone cried, "Lynch him," but there was no movement. Sergeant Wright's men walked Unruh to a police car and started for headquarters.

Shouting and pushing men and women started after the car, but dropped back after a few paces. They stood in excited little groups discussing the shootings, and the character of Howard Unruh. Little by little the original anger, born of fear, that had moved the crowd, began to die.

Men conceded that he probably was not in his right mind.

Those who knew Unruh kept repeating how close-mouthed he was, and how soft-spoken. How he took his mother to church, and how he marked scripture passages, especially the prophecies.

"He was a quiet one, that guy," a man told a crowd in front of the tavern. "He was all the time figuring to do this thing. You gotta watch them quiet ones."

Unruh was committed to a State hospital for the criminally insane. Berger never was very curious about the case after exhausting all the facts in a single day. He said he never re-read his own story—which put him in a class by himself. After his death on February 8, 1959, it was revealed that he gave his $1,000 Pulitzer Prize money to Howard Unruh's mother.

24. HOW A LIFER WAS CLEARED
AND RESTORED TO FREEDOM

A New York World-Telegram and Sun reporter
proves Louis Hoffner innocent of murder

Pulitzer Prize for Local Reporting, 1953

Ed Mowery knows how to listen, the priceless gift of a good reporter. He has compassion, too, and a blazing sense of moral indignation.

In 1945, while a reporter for the New York *World-Telegram* (now the *World-Telegram and Sun*), Mowery listened to Bertram Campbell. It was a fantastic story. Campbell, a respected Wall Street customer's man, claimed he had been wrongfully convicted as a forger and sent to Sing Sing for 48 months.

Mowery proved Campbell was right and the state wrong. A victim of mistaken identity, the ex-prisoner collected $115,000 when he sued the state for false imprisonment. The real forger had turned up in Chicago, a heroin addict.

Due to his success with the Campbell case, Mowery was besieged with appeals for help. Out of scores, he listened to the story of Louis Hoffner, a penniless Brooklyn clerk who was serving a life sentence at Dannemora Prison for a barroom payroll holdup he swore he had never committed.

Mowery cleared Hoffner, too, but it took him five years and seventy stories, many of them gathered on his own time, to do it. Here are the salient portions of the *World-Telegram and Sun* stories of November 21, 1952, with background that was published on November 10, 1952, which climaxed the fight to save an innocent man.

"YOU'VE TAKEN ME OUT OF THE GRAVE"

By Edward J. Mowery

From the New York World-Telegram & Sun, Nov. 10 and 21, 1952

In a drama-packed courtroom in Long Island City today, Louis Hoffner watched the legal shackles of twelve long years melt away as Queens District Attorney T. Vincent Quinn eloquently pleaded for the lifer's freedom.

A few minutes later, the diminutive convict, no longer branded a murderer, heard Judge Peter T. Farrell grant Mr. Quinn's motion.

Mr. Hoffner stared a moment at the bench. He gulped and smiled. And a murmur of gratification came from the spectators' benches, jammed with Mr. Hoffner's relatives, friends, and members of the famed Hoffner Committee of distinguished New Yorkers.

Today's court procedure, a technical rearraignment of Mr. Hoffner for the 1940 killing of a Queens bartender, was actually anti-climactic.

Judge Farrell on November 10 had set aside the Brooklyn man's conviction and in a precedent-making decision paved the way for Mr. Quinn's forthcoming motion to dismiss the indictment.

Judge Farrell ruled then that certain evidence which might have helped Hoffner at his trial in 1941 was not introduced in the courtroom.

This evidence consisted of the stenographic minutes of the police lineup in which a waiter named Steve Halkias picked Hoffner as the man who killed a bartender in the holdup of a Jamaica tavern. At the trial it was brought out that Mr. Halkias could not pick out Mr. Hoffner the first time he was taken into the lineup room, but that he did pick him out the second time.

Mr. Halkias testified at the trial that he failed the first time because he did not see Mr. Hoffner's profile. He testified that on his second trip to the lineup room he did see the profile.

But the stenographic minutes—which never were introduced at the trial, showed conclusively that Mr. Halkias on his first visit did see Mr. Hoffner's profile. Judge Farrell indicated that had the trial judge known that, he would have directed a verdict of acquittal.

Hoffner's joy at learning his fate was unbounded. Alternately crying and smiling he talked in a voice choked with emotion and thanked the people who worked for many years to help him gain his freedom.

The *World-Telegram and Sun* entered the case in 1947 when Hoffner's friends pointed out certain irregularities in his conviction and sentence, and this newspaper has worked steadily ever since to get the conviction set aside.

Blinking in the light of television cameras and flash bulbs, Hoffner stood in an anteroom in the Long Island City court house and shook hands with his attorneys, Harry G. Anderson and former Magistrate Leo Healy, and with Detective Bernard Arluck, who has worked unceasingly to get Hoffner out of Dannemora.

"Are you bitter, Lou?" asked a reporter.

"No, I can't feel bitter," said Hoffner with a gulp. "How can a man feel bitter when men like Detective Arluck, Mr. Anderson, Judge Healy, and Mr. Ed Mowery went to bat for him through the years? I don't think this could happen in any other country—that so many people would try so hard to help a man they didn't know."

How did Mowery do it? Essentially the story is undramatic, because it took painstaking, tireless plugging—the ingredient of so many big stories. B. O. McAnney, then the managing editor and now vice-president of the *World-Telegram and Sun*, wrote:

"Mowery located seven jurors who sat on the trial panel and obtained their agreement to a new trial. He analyzed the trial judge's confusing jury charge, obtained affidavits from missing alibi witnesses, and sought the legal knowledge of many jurists and lawyers in attacking the legality of the conviction.

"He located a witness to the killing and obtained from him the admission that he (the witness) could not honestly identify Hoffner as the killer. He discovered perjury at the original trial, six years previously;

coercion by police, and suppression of vital evidence by prosecuting authorities.

"In 1947, after another court refused to intervene, he continued his crusade and through the years used his own time in the evening and on week-ends to bolster the case for the lifer. When vindication came, he formed a committee of noted New Yorkers to raise a fund for Hoffner, get him employment, and medical attention."

Mowery, in a lecture for the Don R. Mellett Memorial Fund, said:

"Hoffner, a penniless nobody, became a free man because a virile press refused to compromise in perpetuating traditional American justice."

And Hoffner said to those who had helped him:

"You've taken me out of the grave."

Mowery was awarded the Pulitzer Prize for Local Reporting, not under edition deadline pressure, in 1953.

V. WITH GALLANTRY AND DEVOTION: REPORTING TWO WORLD WARS

Barney Darnton was one of the 2,500 American correspondents who covered the fighting fronts in World War II. He needn't have gone. He was forty-five years old, with a wife and two children at Westport, Connecticut, and a perfectly good desk job at the New York *Times*.

But Barney was a newspaperman—one of the best in the business—and you simply can't expect a good newspaperman to play it safe forever. So, although he was nearsighted and frail and handicapped by years, he talked the *Times* into letting him go to the Pacific. It was the biggest story of his life, after all.

At dawn off New Guinea, Barney Darnton went under fire. He was on an old ferryboat bearing invasion-bent American soldiers on October 18, 1942 when a bomber suddenly roared at them. The pilot keeled over, struck by a bomb fragment. The GIs had hit the deck, as they had been trained to do under attack. But Barney leaped to the wheel and tried to zig-zag the boat out of danger until a bomb got him, too. Probably he never knew that the attacker was an American bomber pilot who had made a tragic error.

General Douglas MacArthur wrote this message to Barney's paper: "It is my painful duty to inform you of the accidental death in New Guinea of Barney Darnton. He served with gallantry and devotion at the front and fulfilled the important duties of war correspondent with distinction to himself and to the New York *Times* and with value to his country."

In World War II and in the Korean War, eighty-two reporters

gave their lives while on active duty. Some, like Webb Miller of the United Press, survived the greatest hazards of battle but died in accidents. Miller fell from a suburban London train during a blackout. Others, like Ernie Pyle, were killed in battle by enemy fire. But all served "with gallantry and devotion" at the front when duty brought them under fire.

In this selection of the work of Pulitzer Prize-winning war correspondents, there is much that was typical of all war correspondents in the field—their risks, their constant search for the news, their eye for detail that would interest people at home. The task of selecting the prize-winners, therefore, must have been tremendous.

Anyone can understand, then, the motives that impelled the Trustees of Columbia University and the Advisory Board on the Pulitzer Prizes to recognize all American war correspondents in 1941 as follows:

"In place of an individual Pulitzer Prize for foreign correspondence, the Trustees approved the recommendation of the Advisory Board that a bronze plaque or scroll be designed and executed to recognize and symbolize the public services and the individual achievements of news reporters in the war zones of Europe, Asia, and Africa from the beginning of the present war."

It would have pleased such great ones as Webb Miller and Barney Darnton, as it did all those who served and sacrificed to cover the war news. Who can say what motivated them to do the things they did? Was it duty or daring or searching for fame or the love of adventure? Or was it perhaps something deeper than any of these—something that Barney Darnton tried to put into the lead of his last dispatch from New Guinea?

"SOMEWHERE IN NEW GUINEA, Oct. 7 (Delayed)—From the hill near the airdrome a man can see his countrymen building with blood, sweat and toil the firm resolution that their sons shall not die under bombs, but shall have peace, because they will know how to preserve peace."

The end is not yet. The war correspondent, for all his hopes of peace, must carry on.

25. HERBERT BAYARD SWOPE SEES
"THE ORDEAL ON THE SOMME"

The New York World sends its top reporter
to the battlefields of World War I

Pulitzer Prize for Reporting, 1917

If ever a newspaperman dominated the news, it was Herbert Bayard Swope. For sheer strength, alertness, foresight and audacity, there wasn't another to compare with him in his day. As a reporter, he never merely covered the story. He took it over. As an editor, he wasn't content with just publishing the news. He made it.

When he left his native St. Louis and joined the staff of Pulitzer's New York *World* in 1909, he was just another young reporter—a 6-foot, 200 pound dynamo. Within a year he was cutting a wide swath both in journalism and on Broadway. And on the early morning of July 14, 1912, when Gambler Herman Rosenthal was shot and killed outside the old Hotel Metropole, Swope swept into action. While others covered the crime, he raged into the bedroom of District Attorney Charles Seymour Whitman and stormed, threatened, and cursed until he had prodded the prosecutor into going to the scene of the slaying.

The rest is journalistic history. Whitman was able to forestall a corrupt police investigation and, with Swope's help, rolled up damning evidence that convicted Police Lieutenant Charles Becker of directing the four assassins—Lefty Louie, Gyp the Blood, Dago Frank and Whitey Lewis. All went to the electric chair, Whitman became Governor and Swope hurried on to the battlefields of World War I.

With that supreme combination of skill and a gambler's sureness of instinct, he turned up at General von Hindenburg's headquarters after the great victory over the Russians at Tannenberg. He beat the competition again on interviews with the commander of the German submarine U-9, Captain von Weddingen. He toured the Western front, and in particular the bloody Somme, and wrote the series of articles that won him the first Pulitzer Prize for reporting in 1917. Long before the day of Guntherized history, Swope entitled his series, "Inside the German Empire"—the first of the "inside" books.

At the Versailles peace conference, Swope got the first draft of the League of Nations Covenant with the help of President Wilson and published it in the *World*. Barred from the august halls of Versailles, he dressed in top hat and diplomatic formal attire, hired the longest and shiniest black car he could find and was driven into the thick of the peace conference as if he had been the fifth of the Big Four. When the disgruntled correspondents petitioned to have him removed therefore as the head of the press delegation, he signed his name to the petition with a flourish—and killed it.

Nothing really ever stopped his drive and his determination. When he became the executive editor of the *World* in 1920, he went right after the Ku Klux Klan and helped to totter it, winning a Pulitzer Prize for public service in 1922. In 1923 he led the *World* in another crusade, this time against the use of Florida convicts in peon labor, and won for his paper a second Pulitzer Prize for public service in 1924. He developed the celebrated "op-ed" page of the *World,* now only a cherished memory, with such great names as Woollcott, Broun, Bolitho, Deems Taylor, and many another.

He left the *World* in 1929 for still another career, that of publicist and adviser extraordinary to industry and government. No one will ever know whether he could have persuaded the heirs of Joseph Pulitzer to continue the *World* newspapers had he remained on the job, but he liked to recall that he did try to avert their sale to the Scripps-Howard newspapers. He failed. In 1931, the successor newspaper, the New York *World-Telegram* (now the *World-Telegram and Sun*) extinguished the light under the golden dome on Park Row and the building itself was razed years later to make way for a new approach to the Brooklyn Bridge. A small plaque replaced it.

Swope went on in his many-faceted career, appearing as the spokesman for the first United States Atomic Delegation to the United Nations, under the chairmanship of his friend of nearly fifty years, Bernard M. Baruch. He became chairman of the New York State Racing Commission for eleven years, an unpaid post, and he served as a special adviser to the Secretary of War during World War II. He died at the age of seventy-six on June 20, 1958—and made Page 1 for the last time in the New York *Times* and the New York *Herald Tribune*.

The following extracts are from his prize-winning work as a World War I war correspondent.

"WAR TO THE NTH POWER"
By Herbert Bayard Swope

From *Inside the German Empire*, copyright 1916
by the Press Publishing Company

The Somme represents war raised to the nth power.

At different times one can see and hear every phase of activity—drumfire, light field pieces, machine guns, hand grenades, mine-throwers, infantry attacks, mine explosions, liquid fire gas, observation balloons, anti-aircraft cannon.

Aeroplane observation and flights are so common that they fail to stir up any excitement even among visitors. I counted as many as sixty machines aloft in half an hour a few weeks ago. The large majority of them were French and English, for the German machines are heavily outnumbered, so much so that their value as observers is sharply curtailed.

Where a division covered about three miles of front, the fighting is so intensive on the Somme that it now holds less than one mile. This is true on both sides.

In one day the Third (German) Division, standing opposite the Courcelette-Martinpuich line, shot away 160 heavy truck loads of ammunition. This is a fair example of the tremendous drain on supplies. The reserve men and supplies are brought up at night. That is why the roads on both sides are generously sprayed with cannon-fire after sunset.

The Germans have pushed the railroad construction right up to the firing lines to facilitate replenishment of supplies. It is rather incongruous to see locomotives puffing away, with harvesters at work on one side (the Germans till the ground right up to the volcano's edge) and heavy guns shooting on the other.

As you pass through the villages in the line of fire you notice that every house has a sign on it indicating how many soldiers can find place in the cellar when bombardment begins.

Bapaume, one of the greatest objectives of the British just now, is under almost constant fire, yet many French villagers still stay there. They no longer live in the houses; they live entirely in the

LEAGUE OF NATIONS

WAR

TOPPLING THE IDOL, *by Nelson Harding*

PULITZER PRIZE, 1927   BROOKLYN EAGLE

cellars and the improvised chimneys stick up along the street in a weird manner.

In this era of supersonic flight and air-to-air missiles that are attracted by the heat of enemy aircraft, Swope's reporting of World War I air combat is a stunning reminder of the growth of air power in less than fifty years.

Describing the exploits of Captain Boelcke of the German Flying Corps, who shot down 38 opponents, he wrote:

"Boelcke had had five machines smashed under him but always volplaned to earth successfully until the fatal trip late in October, 1916. His favorite machine had the lines of a bird.

"He used a specially cooled machine gun, firing ordinary rifle ammunition. The gun had a pistol grip and trigger, and he fired it with one hand, steering with his feet and balancing with the free hand on the wheel. Boelcke and the other German fliers declined to use anything but regular rifle ammunition fed by the usual web belt and shooting at a speed that is greater than that of the ordinary automatic pistol, sometimes exceeding 500 shots a minute."

There are few reporters today who could have competed with Swope in the meticulous recording of detail—the mark of every truly great newspaperman.

26. A DYING REPORTER RELATES
THE COMING OF WAR IN AFRICA

Will Barber of the Chicago Tribune dictates
his last story in an Ethiopian hospital

Pulitzer Prize for Correspondence, 1936

Will Barber was a New Yorker. When the London office of the Chicago *Tribune* sent him on his first big assignment, he had been married only a year and was thirty-one years old. He became the first American correspondent to reach Ethiopia, the initial victim of armed Axis aggression; the first to sound the alarm to sleeping America.

He cabled stories of Italian troop movements and menacing preparations. He interviewed the alarmed "king of kings," Emperor Haile Selassie. He told of the pathetic, primitive Ethiopian warriors and their spears and drums, preparing to face Mussolini's war planes, tanks and machine guns. He traveled into the Ogaden desert to the potential front lines, and there contracted the malaria that killed him.

This was his last story, dictated just before he died.

WAR DRUMS DEFY AN AIR ATTACK

By Will Barber

From the Chicago Tribune, Oct. 4, 1935

ADDIS ABABA, ETHIOPIA, Oct. 3—To the rolling throb of a five-foot lion's hide war drum, echoing the explosion of Italian bombs which fell on the towns of Adowa and Adigrat in northern Ethiopia, Emperor Haile Selassie today ordered a general mobilization tantamount to a declaration of war upon Italy.

The government announced that fighting is in progress near Adowa in the district of Agame in Tigre province. It was reported that the Italians were retreating under cover of airplanes.

It was also officially announced that women and children were killed in the Italian air attack and that Red Cross hospitals were bombed. The exact number of casualties was not known. The emperor immediately filed a protest and a full report with the League of Nations.

The long-awaited mobilization order sent the crowd of chieftains and warriors gathered in front of the old palace into a frenzy of hatred against the Italians and in a lesser vein against all foreigners.

Foreign newspapermen—heretofore treated with unfailing courtesy on all occasions—were swept off the palace steps by a mob of warriors as they struggled forward to hear the call to arms. . . .

THE DEATH OF A WAR CORRESPONDENT

From the Chicago Tribune, Oct. 7, 1935

(A newspaperman is not often news. But when he is the son, the grandson, the great-grandson, and the great-great grandson of soldier war correspondents; when he is the first on an Ethiopian battle front; when he plunges into a pestilential desert to be first with the news; when he dies of a malignant fever; when a fellow war correspondent cables the report of his death and when his father

"COME ON IN, I'LL TREAT YOU RIGHT, I USED TO KNOW YOUR DADDY," *by C. D. Batchelor*

PULITZER PRIZE, 1937 NEW YORK DAILY NEWS

writes his obituary, the rules are suspended.—Editor, Chicago *Tribune*.)

The following cable dispatch was received yesterday from Robinson Maclean, correspondent of the Toronto (Ont.) *Telegram* in Addis Ababa:

ADDIS ABABA, Oct. 6—Wilfred Courtenay Barber, correspondent of the Chicago *Tribune*, the first American newspaperman to reach Ethiopia to report on the present conflict, died at 12:45 o'clock this afternoon. The cause was heart failure, due to toxemias combined with infected kidneys and malaria. He was thirty-two years old.

Barber scooped the world with his first stories from Ethiopia last June—again by going into the yellow hell of the Ogaden desert to get the story of Ethiopia's front lines. Returning from Ogaden, he wrote that malaria would get the whites who dared its burning sands.

His last story, dictated from his sickbed in the Seventh Day Adventist hospital, told how the war drums called the Ethiopians to mobilize for the war he came to cover.

Yesterday morning, before the doctors had been able to see the malaria in the temperature chart that stayed constantly high because of double infection, he said: "I am going to get better because I have to—I have to cover the war." An hour later the fever surged and he lay unconscious until 11 o'clock this morning, when he rallied briefly. Arrangements had been made for an airplane to bring his wife into Addis Ababa and to take him out. Such permission had never before been granted, but it was immediately ordered by Emperor Haile Selassie, who knew Barber not only as a truthful newsman but as a friend.

An indication of this was added today when the war-torn emperor ordered that all possible be done to show Ethiopia's sorrow over Barber's death. Tomorrow afternoon at 4 o'clock Barber's remains will be buried on a hilltop overlooking Addis Ababa.

There followed, in careful reportorial detail, a story datelined Nyack, N. Y., which told of Will Barber's birth on September 15, 1903, his education at Columbia University, his introduction to newspaper work and his marriage to Miss Josephine Dorothy Sibbald, of Chicago, in Paris on October 2, 1934, and a summation of his work as a war correspondent. It was signed Frederick Courtenay Barber with this footnote appended:

"Note to Editor—Dictating my son's obituary has crucified me, but there is nobody else here to do it. Shall I send carbon to New York *Daily News?* F. C. B."

Will Barber was posthumously voted the Pulitzer Prize for distinguished correspondence for 1936.

27. CARLOS P. ROMULO PENETRATES
THE ORIENT'S WALL OF SILENCE

On the eve of Pearl Harbor, a Filipino
warns that a billion Orientals seek freedom

Pulitzer Prize for Correspondence, 1942

A bedraggled little Filipino turned up in a San Francisco drug store toward the end of World War II. He was dirty and tired. His clothes were ragged. His cap hung about his ears.

"May I have a tube of toothpaste?" he asked.

"If you don't have an old tube to turn in, I can't sell you a fresh tube," a clerk replied. Then he jeered, "Don't you know there's a war on?"

The little Filipino knew there had been a war. Next day, if the clerk had looked sharply enough, he might have recognized his disappointed customer as Brigadier General Carlos P. Romulo. Now cleaned up and fitted out in a fresh uniform, with appropriate insignia of rank and service ribbons, he was being paraded through San Francisco's beflagged streets as a triumphant hero.

He was all of that. Leaving his post as editor of the *Philippines Herald,* the Philippines' only English evening newspaper at the time, he had become a member of the staff of General Douglas MacArthur and fought through the last days of Bataan and Corregidor. He had been the last man off Corregidor before it fell to the Japanese. And throughout the darkest days of World War II, he had served with MacArthur and returned with him to the Philippines at the head of the conquering American forces. He had not even had a chance to change from his makeshift battle uniform before being flown to the United States.

When the United States granted independence to the Philippines, Romulo became his country's ambassador in Washington. Always a persuasive spokesman in the United Nations for the rights of small nations and for Oriental peoples, he was elected president of the United Nations General Assembly. Such was the force of his oratory and his presence that he could hold an audience of 20,000 persons silent and spellbound in New York's Madison Square Garden. He lectured and toured widely throughout this country and the rest of the world.

But somehow, when he wanted to illustrate what was wrong with the American attitude toward the Orient, he would remember the story of the supercilious clerk in San Francisco and tell it with a gentle smile— as if it were a joke. It isn't. In a series of articles which he wrote for the *Philippines Herald* during a 20,000 mile tour in 1941, almost on the eve of Pearl Harbor, he warned that the one billion peoples of the Orient were bidding for freedom and held themselves the equals—not the inferiors— of the West.

"It is entirely within the realm of possibility," he wrote, "that Britain and the Netherlands may, after the war, carry out . . . a program of democratization in their colonies. But if they do not, then the hope of the colonial peoples in this part of the world must lie with the United States of America, which is the one power that can put its shoulder resolutely behind the wheel of progress here and make it turn regardless of the opposing forces of colonial greed and imperialist exploitation."

Much of the series that sent him traveling from Chungking to Indonesia, which was distributed by King Features to 112 newspapers, and which won him the Pulitzer Prize for correspondence in 1942, is of course dated. But the sternness of his warning concerning the foreign policy of the Western world still carries great conviction. Parts of his first article from Hong Kong, and his concluding piece from Baguio, the Philippines, are reprinted here.

"THE LONGING FOR LIBERTY . . . WILL GROW"

By Carlos P. Romulo

From the Philippines Herald (Manila), Sept. 15, 1941

Here in Hong Kong, for the first time outside the Philippines, you sense the forces and tensions at work in their approximate proportions and relations with one another. Here in this last remaining bastion of British power in the Chinese mainland, you begin to see the movement and direction of the new historical epoch upon which the Chinese, and many millions of colonial peoples with them, have entered.

You sense, for the first time, the magnitude of the conflict that

has only begun—on the one hand, the conflict between rival im-
perialisms, and on the other, the conflict between these imperialist
powers and the one billion colored peoples whom they hold under
subjection.

Here, the familiar battle cries of democracy have but a distant
echo amidst the incoherent babble of Asia's dumb and inarticulate
millions. The Filipinos and the Chinese—or, rather, those among
them who are wide awake and articulate, repeat the democratic
slogans of the current war, and perhaps believe sincerely that they
are automatically included in the scope and purpose of these
slogans.

Unfortunately, it is not the few who understand these slogans
(or think they do) and who repeat them as lustily as any true-
born democrat of Britain and America, who will establish the right
of Asia's oppressed millions to the blessings of democracy—when
the war is over and the democratic powers have triumphed. That
right will be established by the collective effort of the peoples of
China, India, Indonesia, Siam, Malaya, Indochina and the Philippines, assisted by the progressive elements in America, Britain, and
perhaps in Soviet Russia as well.

It is in the light of this principle that I view the Far Eastern crisis
or any war into which that crisis may develop in the event all
palliatives and efforts at conciliation should fail.

I believe, to start with, that in a war between Japan and the
democratic front in the Far East, no colony or state in this part of
the world ought ever to hesitate on which side to fight—if it is to
fight at all. Each and all must fight to a man on the side of the de-
mocracies.

Many of them will have to do so, having no choice in the matter.
But a recalcitrant colony can make trouble for the ruling power
in the event of war, and this fact can and should constitute the basis
for a mutually advantageous bargain.

The democratic front in the Far East, impressive in resources
and military strength, though it may have grown in recent months,
cannot fully face the menace of further Japanese aggression without the loyal support of the native peoples. This is true in India,
Burma, the Philippines, and Indonesia.

Hence, it is important for the peoples of all these key countries

"IF I SHOULD DIE BEFORE I WAKE," *by Jacob Burck*

PULITZER PRIZE, 1941   CHICAGO TIMES

to realize the importance of the weapon they hold in their hands. If their loyal cooperation is needed by the democratic front, then let that cooperation be given in the fullest possible measure—but always upon the assurance that the triumph of democracy shall have a practical meaning, in terms of progress, for the benighted and exploited peoples of Asia. . . .

From the Philippines Herald (Manila), Nov. 1, 1941

This trip has brought home to me how completely defenseless subject peoples can be when the facilities for information are not in their hands. There is a steel wall of silence around Burma and around Indonesia and only that which the sovereign powers want known is allowed to escape out of that steel wall to the outside world. Hence, it took a brown-skinned journalist to inform the world of recent developments in the nationalistic movements of Burma and Indonesia, because only he can feel with the Burmese and the Indonesians what is throbbing in the hearts of millions of brown subject peoples of Asia.

I set out on my recent tour determined to see things for myself as a Filipino and to record them primarily for a Filipino audience. Too long have we in the Philippines looked at events around us through the eyes of observers whose interests are frequently alien to our own, and accepted as facts what have been ladled out to us by prejudiced writers who have no sympathy with our ideals and our aspirations. I thought that this was the first chance that our people have had to see their neighboring countries through Filipino eyes, to feel the strivings of the Oriental peoples as a Filipino should feel them.

Thus, through all the handicaps and barriers of censorship and knowing full well that what I had to say would not always be pleasant to other ears, I presented the truth as I saw it. . . .

It is pathetic to see the sense of complete frustration that has taken hold of the nationalists I have talked to because, as they said, "What feeble voice we have is heard only among ourselves and not at all by the outside world." But the spirit of nationalism and the desire for freedom that has been stimulated by the war aims of Roosevelt and Churchill cannot be muffled by censorship no matter how repressive. The longing for liberty that I heard spoken in whispers in a secluded newspaper office in Burma, and in a tumbledown shack in the rice fields of Java will grow more intense with each repressive measure until it shall have become a force too strong to be contained any longer.

If Burma, Thailand, Indochina, and Indonesia have become less alien-sounding to Filipino ears than before, if I have aroused in the hearts of our own people a new and deeper interest in the destiny of the 100,000,000 brown peoples of South Asia, I shall consider the rare opportunity that was mine to have been profitably employed.

Divide et impera, divide and rule, has ever been the major tenet of imperialism from time immemorial. Thus we in the Philippines hear little or nothing of the nationalist movements and the struggles for freedom of the peoples of India, Burma, Indonesia, and Indochina, and you can be sure that they hear nothing absolutely about the Philippines at all. This is the rule of the Gestapo on an international scale: not to let two or three persons get together and know each other's thoughts, for thus the ruler imperils his authority and the seeds of freedom are sown.

I set forth on my trip as a journalist and as a Filipino. As a Filipino I must acknowledge my indebtedness to the benign rule of America for the privilege of believing in democracy and enjoying its manifold blessings. I went forth believing mightily in democracy and I have returned believing more mightily still in democracy. For as a journalist I know that journalism of the highest type cannot be true to its mission unless it can claim that during these dark days for freedom everywhere it has done its share in giving expression to the just and natural aspirations of all peoples regardless of race or creed.

28. WHEN THE JAPANESE WERE CAUGHT
WITH THEIR KIMONOS DOWN

Ira Wolfert of NANA watches the fifth Battle
of the Solomons and writes his story

Pulitzer Prize for International Reporting, 1943

The state of the military art has advanced so fantastically since World War II that it may never again be possible to give an eyewitness account of a naval battle. Supersonic planes, atomic-powered submarines, and the atomic warhead rocket have made close-range naval warfare all but fruitless.

In more than one sense, therefore, Ira Wolfert's account of the fifth battle of the Solomons in 1942 is historic. It was one of the last great sea battles of modern times, and one of the few even in World War II in which a correspondent could see and record the action on both sides. Moreover, the American victory insured the success of the small, desperate beginning of the comeback from disaster at Pearl Harbor—the campaign across that Pacific that ended with Hiroshima and unconditional surrender on the U.S.S. *Missouri* in Tokyo Bay.

Wolfert, then a correspondent for the North American Newspaper Alliance, won the Pulitzer Prize for International Reporting in 1943. A New Yorker born and a 1930 graduate of the Columbia School of Journalism, he covered the Pacific campaigns, was twice wounded, and came home to embark upon a career as a magazine writer and novelist.

Here is an abridged account of his first story from Guadalcanal, as it was published in a number of American newspapers more than a month after the Solomons victory was assured.

"A RECKLESS FIGHT FOR LIFE"

By Ira Wolfert

From North American Newspaper Alliance, Dec. 16, 1942

FROM A BASE IN THE GUADALCANAL SECTOR, Nov. 15—(Delayed)— The fifth battle of the Solomons, which in many ways proved a Japanese disaster unprecedented in the history of the world's great navies, began with a contest over reinforcements of men and supplies for our embattled land forces on Guadalcanal.

Reconnaissance had revealed that the Japanese were building up an extensive force to retake the Solomons, but we threw the first punch, landing the initial wave of our reinforcements on November 11 (Solomons time). We held the initiative that day and on November 12, when the second wave landed.

The reinforcements were sufficient to make Major General Alexander A. Vandegrift of the Marine Corps remark to this reporter, "I now feel it is no longer possible for the Japanese to land enough strength at any one time to take Guadalcanal away from us."

The Japanese were hastily forming convoys behind their first line of fire, an invasion force estimated by intelligence here to be three divisions with full equipment. The sea train formed consisted of eight transports, one an NYK liner, which is the biggest the Japanese have. The other seven ranged downward to 18,000 tons. Accompanying these troopships were four cargo vessels of about 12,000 tons carrying the raiment of the Emperor's divisions, while screening the array were at least four battleships, plus a complement of cruisers and destroyers.

On Friday the 13th, this force, making up the bulk if not all of Japan's South Pacific fleet, moved toward the arena and wrested the initiative from us. This transformed the character of the dispute into a replica, only more so, of all the previous Solomons battles— a skillful, tenacious, heedlessly bloody attempt to reduce permanently our Guadalcanal salient by wiping out its sea armor and obliterating its garrisons, planes, and men.

At 1:40 on Friday morning United States forces here began fighting, not for some future offensive with the Japanese, but for their lives. The result of this desperate, completely reckless fight for life by the Americans that was to continue until Sunday morning was twenty-eight warships sunk, including at least one battleship and probably two battleships, plus ten warships damaged. This reporter, being less conservative than the United States Navy, and more willing to trust the evidence of his own eyes, personally scores more than half of the ten "damaged" as being sunk. Our cost was seven destroyers and two light cruisers.

All the major actions of the battle took place within clear view of the naked eye. This is the first battle in the history of modern war that could be viewed in its entirety by a single man standing

THE LIGHT OF ASIA, *by H. M. Talburt*

PULITZER PRIZE, 1933 WASHINGTON DAILY NEWS

still. Thousands of land-bound Marines, Army, and Navy men had seats so close to the drama that the actors literally spilled from the stage into their laps. Then the spectators joined in the action savagely.

(The opening phases of the battle, the troop landings by the United States Navy, were fiercely but unsuccessfully contested by Japanese aircraft which sustained heavy losses. That set the stage for the main naval action beginning with the advance of the Japanese fleet after nightfall on November 12.)

Those seven hours of darkness, with each moment as silent as held breath, were the blackest our troops have faced since Bataan, but at the end of them our Navy was there, incredibly, like a Tom Mix of old, like the hero of some melodrama. It turned the tide of the whole battle by throwing its steel and flesh into the breach against what may have been the heaviest Japanese force yet engaged by surface ships in this war.

Again the beach had a front-row seat for the devastating action. Rear Admiral Daniel J. Callaghan's force steaming into line dove headlong into a vastly more powerful Japanese fleet which was steaming around tiny Savo Island with guns set for point-blank blasting of Guadalcanal and loaded with high explosive shells instead of armor-piercing shells.

Matching cruisers and destroyers against battleships is like putting a good bantamweight against a good heavyweight, but the Japs unquestionably were caught with their kimonos down around their ankles. They could have stayed out of range and knocked out our ships with impunity and then finished us on the ground.

We opened fire first. The Japanese ships, steaming full speed, were on us, over us, and all around us in the first minute. Torpedoes need several hundred feet in order to arm themselves with their propellers. Our destroyers discharged torpedoes from such close range that they could not wind up enough to explode. The range was so close that the Japanese could not depress their guns to fire at the waterline, which is why so many hits landed on the bridge and two of our admirals were killed.

The action was illuminated by brief, blinding flashes by Japanese searchlights which were shot out as soon as they were turned on by muzzle flashes from big guns, by fantastic stream tracers, and by a huge range of colored explosives as two Japanese destroyers and one of our destroyers blew up within seconds of one another. Two Japanese planes, which were overhead intending to drop flares on the target, were caught like sparrows in a badminton game and blown to bits.

In the glare of three exploding ships the two naval forces could be seen laboring and wallowing in their recoils, throwing up waves in the ordinarily lake-like harbor which hit like rocks against the beach. The sands of the beach were shuddering so much from gunfire that they made the men standing there quiver and tingle from head to foot.

From the beach it looked like a door opening and closing and opening and closing over and over again. The unholy show took place in the area immediately this side of Savo Island. Our ships, in a line of about 3,000 yards, steamed into a circle of Japanese ships which opened at the eastern end like a mouth gaping with surprise. They ran, dodged, and reversed their field, twisted, lurched, and lunged, but progressed generally along the inside of the lip of the Japanese.

Since the Japanese circle was much bigger than our line, the Japanese ships, first at one end and then at the other, fired across the empty space into one another. It took about thirty minutes for our ships to complete the tour of the circle and by the end of the tour the Japanese ships had ceased to exist as an effective force.

29. THE MAN WHO COULDN'T SWIM SURVIVES A TORPEDOED WARSHIP

*Larry Allen of the AP is rescued at sea
and writes how H.M.S. Galatea went down*

Pulitzer Prize for International Reporting, 1942

Laurence Edmund (Larry) Allen is a war correspondent who has roved the world's trouble areas for the Associated Press. He holds the Bronze Star, Croix de Guerre, and the Order of the British Empire. He has been bombed, torpedoed, shot at with rifles, machine guns and assorted other conventional armaments, and knows what it means to be a prisoner of war.

WATER! *by Frank Noel*

SURVIVORS OF A TORPEDOED SHIP, DRIFTING IN A LIFEBOAT IN THE INDIAN
OCEAN, SNAPPED BY FRANK NOEL, A FELLOW PASSENGER.

PULITZER PRIZE, 1943   ASSOCIATED PRESS

TARAWA ISLAND, *by Frank D. Filan*

PULITZER PRIZE, 1944   ASSOCIATED PRESS

Of all his stories written under fire, perhaps the most gripping is his account of his own survival when H.M.S. *Galatea*, a 5,220-ton cruiser, went down December 16, 1942 in a torpedo attack. Allen, assigned to duty with the British Mediterranean fleet, had had a narrow escape January 15, 1941 during a bombing attack on the British Aircraft Carrier *Illustrious*. But on the *Galatea*, covering the movement of a convoy through enemy waters, Allen nearly lost his life. Here is his story, as cleared by censorship and distributed by the Associated Press—one of the file that won him the Pulizer Prize for International Reporting in 1942.

FORTY-FIVE MINUTES OF HELL ON AN OILY SEA

By Larry Allen

From the Associated Press Report, Jan. 10, 1942

ALEXANDRIA, EGYPT, Jan. 10 — (AP) — The British light cruiser *Galatea*, struck by three torpedoes from an Axis submarine, flopped over like a stabbed turtle and went down within three minutes off Egypt's Mediterranean coast in the inky darkness just after midnight on the morning of December 16.

The torpedoes, launched from close range, smashed in swift succession against the *Galatea's* after-portside, amidships, and forward, tearing into her interior with loud blasts and spurting flame.

On the dying cruiser's quarterdeck I clung tenaciously to the starboard rail until the list of the ship flung me into the cold, choppy sea. Then I battled through thick, oily scum for forty-five minutes before being rescued.

We had been dive-bombed for more than seven hours on December 14, while patrolling with a squadron of cruisers and destroyers off Libya, but the *Galatea* successfully beat off those attacks and headed eastward.

At midnight on December 15 the cruiser's announcer system warned: "First-degree readiness heavy armament." Gunners thus were ordered to stand by for expected action.

A Marine sentry aroused me from a nap in the captain's cabin, and I ran to the commander's cabin and informed the Reuters naval correspondent, Alexander Massey Anderson. Adjusting life belts, we stepped out into the inky blackness of the quarter-deck and raced toward the bridge.

We had barely started when the first torpedo smashed into the after-portside with a burst of flame, heavily rocking the *Galatea*. The time was 12:02 a.m.

Torpedoes seemed to chase us along the deck, for the second crashed through amidships with a blinding flash and a third struck forward, just under a six-inch gun turret. The ship shuddered all over.

Then as it dipped quickly and deeply into the sea on the portside I caught hold of the deck rail, dropped my tin helmet, bomb anti-flash gear and raincoat, and with one hand unscrewed the nozzle on the life belt hose hung around my neck. I blew into it with all the breath I could summon, inflating it just as the cruiser flopped completely over.

The sharp keeling over of the ship flung me sliding down the starboard side into the sea. Hundreds of officers and seamen plunged into the water along with me.

Anderson had reached the railing a little to the right of me. I heard him shout something to an officer as I slid into the sea. I never saw him again.

I could not swim and was fearful lest the pressure of a deep submersion collapse the old life belt which I had retrieved after the bombing of the *Illustrious* just one year ago today.

As I slipped under the water the cruiser disappeared with a tremendous suction, leaving a huge lake of oil. There was one muffled blast as she took her death plunge.

I swallowed large quantities of oil scum and water before I bobbed to the surface. The sea all around was dotted with heads of hundreds of sailors.

Several sailors had succeeded in getting a small motor lifeboat launched. Trying to splash toward it I went under again. My lungs felt as if they were bursting, but I came up, and a sailor helped me aboard the boat.

But a score of others had the same idea. The boat's stern rapidly filled with water as the weight of more and more men pushed it down. Finally it tipped over, hurling us all into the sea.

I managed to reach the boat and pull myself into the front cockpit again. Then the boat sank.

With a lone sailor I hung to the very tip of the bow until it

WHAT A PLACE FOR A WASTE PAPER SALVAGE CAMPAIGN
by J. N. ("Ding") Darling

PULITZER PRIZE, 1943   NEW YORK HERALD TRIBUNE

slipped beneath the waves. I even hung on until it pulled me under and I got another large dose of oil and water. I strained every muscle to force my head above the surface. From beneath the waves a pair of hands reached up and pawed at my shoulders, then slipped away.

I collided with a small floating spar. Desperately I tried and succeeded in tucking it under my left arm, still carefully holding up the life belt with the right.

I joined with scores of others in crying for help, hoping in the pitch darkness to attract the attention of the destroyers. No one had a flashlight, so it was difficult for the rescue ships to find us.

At that moment I saw a huge black silhouette of a destroyer about seventy-five yards ahead.

"Help, I'm drowning," gasped a sailor in the water near me.

"Keep going," I called weakly. "Look, there's a destroyer ahead."

That seemed to give him new energy. He swam toward the destroyer. I tried, but couldn't get any closer. The waves seemed to carry me farther away as I screamed for help.

A big wave swamped me again with a mouthful of oil. Then, as if miraculously, another wave pushed me forward almost directly under the propellors of the destroyer *Griffin*.

I called for help until my throat felt burned out. Suddenly a long oily rope was flung over the side. I grasped it but there was no strength left in my hands.

"Hang on!" an officer on the ship shouted. "We'll pull you up."

"Can't!" I called as the rope slipped from my fingers.

"Try to get a little forward," the officer shouted. "We are putting over a rope ladder."

Somehow I managed to propel myself forward and hang onto the ladder, safe, but so spent that I couldn't pull myself up even the first rung unaided.

At that moment a life raft drifted against the destroyer's side. I repeatedly banged my head against the warship and cried out time and again, "Stop it! You're killing me!"

Sailors on the raft grasped the rope ladder and clambered up to safety while I fought desperately to keep from drowning. Several stepped upon my head, pushing me down into the water.

Only half conscious, I hooked my right arm through the rung of the ladder, which helped keep my head above water occasionally, and again I called out for help. A young British sailor aboard the raft saved my life.

"I'll help you!" he shouted. "Get this rope under your arms!"

He passed a thick, heavy rope under my arms, tied it, and flung the end to the quarter-deck of the destroyer. Three sailors slowly pulled me out of the oily mass.

"This fellow's an American," I dimly heard someone say as they read the words "American naval correspondent" on the sleeve of my oil-soaked coat while pressing the water from my lungs.

They cut off all my clothes and carried me to the mess deck below, where nearly one hundred other survivors were getting medical attention.

30. ERNIE PYLE COVERS
THE NORMANDY BREAKTHROUGH

*"It is an unnerving thing to be bombed
by your own planes"*

Pulitzer Prize for Reporting, 1944

Ernie Pyle hated war. Yet, it was his fate to become the greatest war correspondent of his time and to die in battle. When he went to North Africa with the first American troops to see battle there, he left a lifetime of journalism behind him.

The little bald man with the weazened elfin smile could have settled down, as an acknowledged oldster, in the comparative safety of the rear and spun out his war stories. But he couldn't. He was too honest a reporter—and too brave. He had to be up front with the footsloggers, the infantrymen whom he admired and who loved him because he was one of their own.

Pyle was in the vast D-Day armada off the Normandy beaches and landed soon after the first troops. One of his finest stories, reporting war in all its manifold phases, was his account of the Normandy breakthrough on July 25, 1944 in which he was under fire and narrowly escaped injury and death. It is republished here, slightly condensed, as an example of the type of work that won him the Pulitzer Prize for Reporting.

Nine months later, on April 18, 1945, Ernie Pyle was shot and killed by a Japanese sniper on Ie Shima. After the war his body was brought back to Honolulu where it now rests in the National Cemetery.

"THE GI CAN BE MAJESTIC"

By Ernie Pyle

Written for Scripps-Howard Newspaper Alliance

If you don't have July 25 pasted in your hat I would advise you to put it there immediately. At least paste it in your mind. For I have a hunch that July 25 of the year 1944 will be one of the great historic pinnacles of this war. It was the day we began a mighty surge out of our confined Normandy spaces, the day we stopped calling our area the beachhead and knew we were fighting a war across the whole expanse of France.

Our front lines were marked by long strips of colored cloth laid on the ground, and with colored smoke to guide our airmen during the mass bombing. Dive bombers hit it just right. We stood and watched them barrel nearly straight down out of the sky. They were bombing about half a mile ahead of where we stood. They came in groups, diving from every direction, perfectly timed, one right after another. Everywhere we looked separate groups of planes were on the way down, or on the way back up, or slanting over for a dive, or circling, circling, circling over our heads waiting for their turn.

The air was full of sharp and distinct sounds of cracking bombs and the heavy rips of the planes' machine guns and the splitting screams of diving wings. It was all fast and furious, yet distinct. And then a new sound gradually droned into our ears, a sound deep and all-encompassing with no notes in it—just a gigantic faraway surge of doomlike sound. It was the heavies. They came from directly behind us.

At first they were the merest dots in the sky. We could see clots of them against the far heavens, too tiny to count individually. They came on with a terrible slowness. They came in flights of twelve, three flights to a group and in groups stretched out across the sky. They came in "families" of about seventy planes each. Maybe those gigantic waves were two miles apart, maybe ten miles. I don't know. But I do know they came in a constant procession and I thought it would never end. What the Germans must have thought is beyond comprehension. . . .

It is possible to become so enthralled by some of the spectacles of war that a man is momentarily captivated away from his own danger. That's what happened to our little group of soldiers as we stood watching the mighty bombing. But the benign state didn't last long. As we watched there crept into our consciousness a realization that the windrows of exploding bombs were easing back toward us, flight by flight, instead of gradually forward, as the plan called for.

Then we were horrified by the suspicion that those machines, high in the sky and completely detached from us, were aiming their bombs at the smoke line on the ground—and a gentle breeze was drifting the smoke line back over us!

An indescribable kind of panic came over us. We stood tensed in muscle and frozen in intellect, watching each flight approach and pass over, feeling trapped and completely helpless. And then all of an instant the universe became filled with a gigantic rattling as of huge ripe seeds in a mammoth dry gourd. I doubt that any of us had ever heard that sound before, but instinct told us what it was. It was bombs by the hundred, hurtling down through the air above us.

Many times I've heard bombs whistle or swish or rustle, but never before had I heard bombs rattle. I still don't know the explanation of it. But it is an awful sound.

We dived. Some got into a dugout. Others made foxholes and ditches and some got behind a garden wall—although which side would be "behind" was anybody's guess. I was too late for the dugout. The nearest place was a wagon shed which formed one end of the stone house. The rattle was right down upon us. I remember hitting the ground flat, all spread out like the cartoons of people flattened by steam rollers, and then squirming like an eel to get under one of the heavy wagons in the shed.

An officer whom I didn't know was wriggling beside me. We stopped at the same time, simultaneously feeling it was hopeless to move farther. The bombs were already crashing around us. We lay with our heads slightly up—like two snakes—staring at each other. I know it was in both our minds and in our eyes, asking each other what to do. Neither of us knew. We said nothing. We just lay sprawled, gaping at each other in a futile appeal, our faces about a foot apart, until it was over.

I can't record what any of us actually felt or thought during those horrible climaxes. I believe a person's feelings at such times are kaleidoscopic and indefinable. He just waits, that's all—with an inhuman tenseness of muscle and nerves. An hour or so later I began to get sore all over, and by midafternoon my back and shoulders ached as though I'd been beaten with a club. It was simply the result of muscles tensing themselves too tight for too long against anticipated shock. And I remember worrying about War Correspondent Ken Crawford, a friend from back in the old Washington days, who was several hundred yards ahead of me.

As far as I knew, he and I were the only two correspondents with the Fourth Division. I didn't know who might be with the divisions on either side—which also were being hit, as we could see. It was not until three days later, back at camp, that I learned that Lieutenant-General McNair and AP Photographer Bede Irvin had been killed in this same bombing and that Ken was safe.

When we came out of our ignominious sprawling and stood up again to watch, we knew that the error had been caught and checked. The bombs again were falling where they were intended, a mile or so ahead. Even at a mile away a thousand bombs hitting within a few seconds can shake the earth and shatter the air. There was still a dread in our hearts, but it gradually eased as the tumult and destruction moved slowly forward.

Two Mustang fighters, flying like a pair of doves, patrolled back and forth, back and forth, just in front of each oncoming wave of bombers, as if to shout to them by their mere presence that here was not the place to drop—wait a few seconds, wait a few more seconds. And then we could see a flare come out of the belly of one plane in each flight, just after they had passed over our heads.

The flare shot forward, leaving smoke behind it in a vivid line, and then began a graceful, downward curve that was one of the most beautiful things I've ever seen. It was like an invisible crayon drawing a rapid line across the canvas of the sky, saying in a gesture for all to see: "Here! Here is where to drop. Follow me." And each succeeding flight of oncoming bombers obeyed, and in turn dropped its own hurtling marker to guide those behind.

Long before, the German ack-ack had gone out of existence. The ack-ack gunners either took to their holes or were annihilated. How many waves of heavy bombers we put over I have no idea. I had counted well above 400 planes when personal distraction obliterated any capacity or desire to count. I only know that 400 was just the beginning. There were supposed to be 1,800 planes that day, and I believe it was announced later that there were more than 3,000.

It seems incredible to me that any German could have come out of that bombardment with his sanity. When it was over even I was grateful, in a chastened way that I had never experienced before, for just being alive.

I thought an attack by our troops was impossible then, for it is an unnerving thing to be bombed by your own planes. During the bad part a colonel I had known a long time was walking up and down behind the farmhouse, snapping his fingers and saying over and over to himself, "goddamit, goddamit!" As he passed me once he stopped and stared and said, "goddamit!"

And I said, "There can't be any attack now, can there?" And he said, "No," and began walking again, snapping his fingers and tossing his arm as though he were throwing rocks at the ground.

The leading company of our battalion was to spearhead the attack forty minutes after our heavy bombers ceased. The company had been hit directly by our bombs. Their casualties, including casualties in shock, were heavy. Men went to pieces and had to be sent back. The company was shattered and shaken. And yet Company B attacked—and on time to the minute!

They attacked, and within an hour they sent word back that they had advanced 800 yards through German territory and were still going. Around our farmyard men with stars on their shoulders almost wept when the word came over the portable radio. The American soldier can be majestic when he needs to be.

31. THE LIBERATION OF PARIS:

FROM KISSES TO BULLETS

Mark Watson of the Baltimore Sun
tells of a great day during World War II

Pulitzer Prize for International Reporting, 1945

The liberation of Paris was one of the great days of World War II. It was also a great day for General Charles De Gaulle, France's President chosen in 1959. The American war correspondents were so eager to get to Paris that some of them, notably Ernest Hemingway, entered ahead of the liberating armies—and were soundly cheered, hugged, and kissed by a delirious French populace.

The Americans and French came surging in and the Germans went charging out so rapidly that gleaming blue-and-gold August day that it seemed almost like a miracle. Ernie Pyle, riding in with Henry T. Gorrell of the United Press, told how his jeep was blocked by excited Parisians.

"We all got kissed until we were literally red in the face and I must say we enjoyed it," wrote the tough little historian of the trials and triumphs of GI Joe. "Everybody, even beautiful girls, insisted on kissing you on both cheeks. Somehow, I got started kissing babies that were being held up by their parents, and for awhile I looked like a baby-kissing politician."

Pierre J. (Pete) Huss, who had covered the rise of Hitler in Berlin for the old International News Service and was now in uniform as an American correspondent, went to the Hotel Scribe bar for a drink and found the Germans had been there so recently that their half-empty glasses were still standing around. But nothing daunts a French bartender. Those at the Scribe merely doused the German drinks, washed the glasses and presented fresh ones to the incoming Americans.

Mark Watson of the Baltimore *Sun*, who won the 1945 Pulitzer Prize for International Reporting for his war correspondence in that year of 1944, was among those first liberators of Paris. He was then fifty-seven years old, a veteran of the A.E.F. in World War I and had had a very full and distinguished career as both a soldier and a newspaper reporter and editor. He had covered the great campaign from the beaches of Normandy, up through St. Lo and across France to Paris. He was to go on through the Siegfried Line, Aachen, and the last Nazi offensive at the Battle of the Bulge.

But this was one of his great days—that August 25, 1944 when he entered Paris again at the head of an army. "Never," he wrote, "have I seen such exultation in the mass. . . . One of my colleagues says he never was so woman-handled in his life—and the Paris welcome is not yet near exhausted. . . . Perhaps it could not happen, save in Paris."

The following story by Mark Watson—the dramatic last stand of the Germans in Paris on Aug. 26, 1944—is reprinted in essential text from his Pulitzer Prize-winning entry.

"VIVE LA FRANCE! . . . VIVE DE GAULLE"

By Mark S. Watson

From the Baltimore Sun, Aug. 27, 1944

PARIS, Aug. 26 (By Radio—Delayed)—The most enormous and delighted crowd of celebrants which the memory holds was today transformed in an instant into a panic-stricken multitude, fleeing in terror in all directions to escape a snipers' attack from Germans who had hidden in the upper floors of Paris for this very purpose.

It was an astonishing and tragic end to a day which had begun in high enthusiasm and continued to swell into something approaching joyous hysteria.

One purpose of the attack was certainly to assassinate General Charles De Gaulle, who was heading the liberation parade and receiving an exultant reception which was greater than his warmest adherents had expected.

De Gaulle was unhurt. We saw him hurried away from the flying bullets around the Hotel deVille (City Hall) to a place of safety which has not been identified.

In the square of the Hotel deVille, where a speech was to have taken place and which was packed almost solidly with cheering humanity, I counted thirty stretchers carrying wounded men and women. This was only a small section of the city, and the firing was general, as if at a signal, wherever crowds were assembled.

The snipers were hidden in the Cathedral of Notre Dame and in other towers, and on roofs of buildings overlooking miles of crowded streets.

In the square before the Hotel deVille, during twenty minutes

THE OUTSTRETCHED HAND, *by Edmund Duffy*

PULITZER PRIZE, 1940 BALTIMORE SUN

of the wildest fusillade, there was admirable discipline by the French police and militia, who calmly peered aloft, seeking evidence of the snipers, and maintained a steady fire at suspected windows. . . . Helmeted and plumed bandsmen of the Republican Guard stood like rocks to add the influence of their calm.

We had our jeep at the side of the Champs Elysees, exactly where we had been yesterday when snipers took a few shots from the Grand Palais.

Up and down that magnificent boulevard, which is certainly the world's finest for parades, humanity was simply packed. At the far end was the silhouette of the Arc de Triomphe itself, the whole vast height quivering with the waving of the largest flag I ever saw.

At the lower end, the Place de la Concorde, every one of its famous monuments was encrusted with people. The Hotel Crillon, from which yesterday we saw the German garrison expelled, had its windows and cornices loaded, as did the nearby American embassy.

Beside us stood another section of the famous Republican Guard band, its trumpeters whirling their instruments, its drum corps rolling its magnificent drums in a manner in which no other band in the world can approach.

There was a great roar from up the avenue and all else was forgotten in the universal shout of "De Gaulle! De Gaulle!"

Behind an escort of jeeps carrying photographers and a platoon of French tanks came De Gaulle on foot, towering above all those around him. He stepped by the band, saluting as they played the "Marseillaise," then proceeded slowly while the crowd roared happily.

Behind him came a torrent of French paraders mostly in civilian clothes, with armbands to identify them. We fell in with the column and made the long march just behind the general. At the Place de la Concorde, he entered an automobile and was hurried swiftly away through canyons of shouting Parisians.

At the Hotel deVille, he was just about to make his speech when the first shot was fired. Only the most vigilant heard it, and they swiftly hustled De Gaulle into the car. While the loud speakers simply said, "Vive De Gaulle!" the leader himself was spirited away toward the south with a motorcycle escort surrounding him.

Almost immediately the full fusillade began, and in a matter of seconds the whole throng was racing for cover with the loud speaker saying calmly,

"Parisians in the square will evacuate it immediately so that we can restore order."

They were already on the way. We do not know how many crawled under our jeep but the space was so completely filled that there was nothing for the original occupants to do save stay outside and hope that hostile and friendly bullets alike would hit somewhere else, which as usual they did.

A French policeman exchanged compliments with me and we agreed fully about the character of all snipers, particularly German snipers, while he took an occasional pot shot at a likely looking window. The square was cleared in fifteen minutes and firing became only spasmodic there, but on the way back to the hotel we ran into more firing at numerous streets. We learned that the fusillade had been general over an immense range of the city's streets.

Yet crowds are extraordinary things. As soon as the fusillade ended, everyone began to pour back on the streets to talk it over.

H. R. Knickerbocker wrote of his colleague, Mark Watson, on February 2, 1945:

"He literally elevated our profession by his presence. Utterly fearless, and with an infectious calm of manner under fire, Watson's bearing never failed to have an inspiring effect, not only on his colleagues, but on officers and men as well. When you consider also the fact that he was the most scholarly student of war among all the correspondents, it is no wonder that he enjoyed not only the affection of his companions, but the highest esteem of all the Allied senior officers with whom he came in contact. . . . He had more energy than many men twenty years younger than he."

In 1958, Watson, then dean of American war correspondents at seventy-one, was still active for the Baltimore *Sun*, covering the latest in atomic warhead rockets and space missiles.

32. THE END OF WORLD WAR II:
THE LAST RAID—AND PEACE

Homer Bigart writes two classic stories
for the New York Herald Tribune

Pulitzer Prize for International Reporting, 1946

Homer Bigart has covered the wars of this generation beachhead by beachhead, from Anzio to Leyte and Okinawa. He has been under fire from front lines in France to foxholes in Korea. He has flown with bombing missions over enemy territory, analyzed both our victories and defeats with merciless candor and scorned the ease and comparative safety of rear-area rewriting of double-talking communiques. He has always wanted to see for himself.

But Bigart is no Richard Harding Davis or Floyd Gibbons among war correspondents, although his reputation today is more formidable than was theirs in their own day. There is no glamor about him. He is a stolid, thoughtful, careful 190-pounder with a controlled stutter, a magnificent eye and ear for the significant fact and a slow deliberation at the typewriter that can drive an editor crazy on a deadline. He is no easy, carefree TV-type newspaperman who can toss off a 1,000-word story in a few minutes and not bother to read copy on it. He puts great effort into both his reporting and his writing and makes his own breaks by following the story wherever it leads.

There have been morning glories in the field of war correspondence, as in no other in journalism; unskilled, untrained reporters who burst upon the world with one great story because they alone were in the right place at the right time, and then were never heard of again. Bigart's career is directly the opposite. He has been a newspaperman all the way and been able to dodge none of the unpleasant chores, from running coffee as a night copy boy to handling routine obits and doing the drudgery on the church page.

Born in Hawley, Pa., October 25, 1907, he studied at Carnegie Tech and N.Y.U. and did the humblest of chores in the New York *Herald Tribune* city room until he finally made general assignment work as a reporter. But beginning in 1942, when he shoved off to cover the American bombing raids near Wilhelmshaven, there hasn't been a year when he hasn't faced guns leveled in anger somewhere in the world. He covered both the war in Europe and Asia during World War II and the Korean War afterward, achieving distinction in both. When he shifted his activities later to the New York *Times*, he divided his work between domestic crises such as the Little Rock integration dispute and the cold war front in the troubled Middle East in 1958.

He won two Pulitzer Prizes—the first for his Pacific war correspondence in 1946 and the second for his foxhole reporting under fire in the Korean War. The following two stories represent some of the most distinguished pieces in the folder that won him his first prize.

"HOPE THIS IS THE LAST, BABY"

By Homer Bigart

From the New York Herald Tribune, Aug. 16, 1945

IN A B-29 OVER JAPAN, Aug. 15—The radio tells us that the war is over but from where I sit it looks suspiciously like a rumor. A few minutes ago—at 1:32 a.m.—we fire-bombed Kumagaya, a small industrial city behind Tokyo near the northern edge of Kanto Plain. Peace was not official for the Japanese either, for they shot right back at us.

Other fires are raging at Isesaki, another city on the plain, and as we skirt the eastern base of Fujiyama Lieutenant General James Doolittle's B-29s, flying their first mission from the 8th Air Force base on Okinawa, arrive to put the finishing touches on Kumagaya.

I rode in the *City of Saco* (Maine), piloted by First Lieutenant Theodore J. Lamb, twenty-eight, of 103-21 Lefferts Blvd., Richmond Hill, Queens, N. Y. Like all the rest, Lamb's crew showed the strain of the last five days of the uneasy "truce" that kept Superforts grounded.

They had thought the war was over. They had passed most of the time around radios, hoping the President would make it official. They did not see that it made much difference whether Emperor Hirohito stayed in power. Had our propaganda not portrayed him as a puppet? Well, then, we could use him just as the war lords had done.

The 314th Bombardment Wing was alerted yesterday morning. At 2:20 p.m., pilots, bombardiers, navigators, radio men, and gunners trooped into the briefing shack to learn that the war was still on. Their target was to be a pathetically small city of little

HOMECOMING, *by Earle L. Bunker*

PULITZER PRIZE, 1944 OMAHA WORLD-HERALD

FLIGHT OF REFUGEES ACROSS WRECKED BRIDGE IN KOREA
by Max Desfor

PULITZER PRIZE, 1951 ASSOCIATED PRESS

obvious importance, and their commanding officer, Colonel Carl R. Storrie, of Denton, Texas, was at pains to convince them why Kumagaya, with a population of 49,000, had to be burned to the ground.

There were component parts factories of the Nakajima aircraft industry in the town, he said. Moreover, it was an important railway center.

No one wants to die in the closing moments of a war. The wing chaplain, Captain Benjamin Schmidke, of Springfield, Mo., asked the men to pray, and then the group commander jumped on the platform and cried: "This is the last mission. Make it the best we ever ran."

Colonel Storrie was to ride in one of the lead planes, dropping four 1,000-pound high explosives in the hope that the defenders of the town would take cover in buildings or underground and then be trapped by a box pattern of fire bombs to be dumped by eighty planes directly behind.

"We've got 'em on the one yard line. Let's push the ball over," the colonel exhorted his men. "This should be the final knockout blow of the war. Put your bombs on the target so that tomorrow the world will have peace."

Even after they were briefed, most of the crewmen hoped and expected that an official armistice would come before the scheduled 5:30 take-off. They looked at their watches. Two and a half hours to go.

You might expect that the men would be in a sullen, almost mutinous, frame of mind. But morale was surprisingly high.

"Look at the sweat pour off me," cried Major William Marchesi, of 458 Baltic Street, Brooklyn. "I've never sweated out a mission like this one."

A few minutes earlier the Guam radio had interrupted its program with a flash and quoted the Japanese Domei Agency announcement that Emperor Hirohito had accepted the peace terms.

Instantly the whole camp was in an uproar. But then a voice snapped angrily over the squawk box: "What are you trying to do? Smash morale? It's only a rumor."

So the crews drew their equipment—parachutes, Mae Wests, and flak suits—and got on trucks to go out to the line. We reached the

City of Saco at about 4:30 p.m., and there was still nearly an hour to go before our plane, which was to serve as a pathfinder for the raiders, would depart.

We were all very jittery. Radios were blaring in the camp area but they were half a mile from us and all we could catch were the words "Hirohito" and "Truman." For all we knew, the war was over.

Then a headquarters officer came by and told Lieutenant Lamb that the take-off had been postponed thirty minutes in expectation of some announcement from Washington.

By that time none of us expected to reach Japan, but we knew that unless confirmation came soon the mission would have to take off, and then very likely salvo its bombs and come home when the signal "Utah, Utah, Utah," came through. That was the code agreed upon for calling off operations in the event of an announcement of peace by President Truman.

Lamb's crew began turning the plane's props at 5:45, and we got aboard. "Boy, we're going to kill a lot of fish today," said Sergeant Karl L. Braley, of Saco, Maine.

To salvo the bombs at sea is an expensive method of killing fish.

We got San Francisco on the radio. "I hope all you boys out there are as happy as we are at this moment," an announcer was saying. "People are yelling and screaming and whistles are blowing."

"Yeah," said one of the crewmen disgustedly, "they're screaming and we're flying."

We took off at 6:07.

We saw no white flags when we reached Japanese territory. Back of the cockpit Radioman Staff Sergeant Rosendo D. del Valle Jr., of El Paso, Texas, strained his ears for the message, "Utah, Utah, Utah." If it came on time, it might save a crew or two, and perhaps thousands of civilians at Kumagaya.

The message never came. Each hour brought us nearer the enemy coast. We caught every news broadcast, listening to hours of intolerable rot in the hope that the announcer would break in with the news that would send us home.

The empire coast was as dark and repellent as ever. Japan was still at war, and not one light showed in the thickly populated Tokyo plain.

Lamb's course was due north to the Kasumiga Lake, then a right angle, turning west for little Kumagaya. It was too late now. There would be bombs on Kumagaya in a few minutes.

Kumagaya is on featureless flats five miles south of the Tone River. It is terribly hard to pick up by radar. There were only two cues to Kumagaya. Directly north of the town was a wide span across the Tone, and a quarter of a mile south of it was a long bridge across the Ara River.

The radar observer, Lieutenant Harold W. Zeisler, of Kankakee, Ill., picked up both bridges in good time and we started the bomb run.

An undercast hid the city almost completely but through occasional rifts I could see a few small fires catching on from the bombs dropped by the two preceding pathfinders.

The Japanese were alert. Searchlights lit the clouds beneath us and two ack-ack guns sent up weak sporadic fire. Thirty miles to the north we saw Japanese searchlights and ack-ack groping for the bombers of another wing attacking Isesaki.

Leaving our target at the mercy of the eighty Superforts following us, we swerved sharply southward along the eastern base of Fujiyama and reached the sea. At one point we were within ten miles of Tokyo. The capital was dark.

Every one relaxed. We tried to pick up San Francisco on the radio but couldn't. The gunners took out photos of their wives and girl friends and said: "Hope this is the last, baby."

This postscript is written at Guam. It was the last raid of the war. We did not know it until we landed at North Field.

The results of the raid we learned from the pilots who followed us over the target. General conflagrations were devouring both Kumagaya and Isesaki. Japan's tardiness in replying to the peace terms cost her two cities.

Bigart was over Japan again on August 27, this time in a stripped-down B-17 making the first unarmed flight over Japan since the cessation of hostilities. He described what was left of Nagasaki after the atom bomb was dropped on it and he saw an American flag spread out on the ground at a nearby prisoner-of-war camp just before the plane swooped low to drop rations to the pitiful survivors of the Japanese "death march" in which so many Americans died after Bataan and Corregidor.

On August 31, he was in Tokyo:

"The Japanese capital is no longer a city. . . . The 2,000,000 people still living in Tokyo are on the verge of starvation, with practically no food coming in from the fertile surrounding plain. . . . Chickens are available only on the black market and cost $25. . . ."

Unlike the journalistic uproar over the end of World War I, when a premature message from the United Press caused the celebration of the "false armistice," and the end of World War II in Europe, when an Associated Press correspondent broke an agreement and released the story, the end came in Japan almost as an anti-climax. Here is Bigart's story.

THE SILENT PEACE OF TOKYO BAY

By Homer Bigart

From the New York Herald Tribune, Sept. 3, 1945

ABOARD U. S. S. MISSOURI, TOKYO BAY, Sept. 2—Japan, paying for her desperate throw of the dice at Pearl Harbor, passed from the ranks of the major powers at 9:05 a.m. today when Foreign Minister Mamoru Shigemitsu signed the document of unconditional surrender.

If the memories of the bestialities of the Japanese prison camps were not so fresh in mind, one might have felt sorry for Shigemitsu as he hobbled on his wooden leg toward the green baize covering table where the papers lay waiting.

He leaned heavily on his cane and had difficulty seating himself. The cane, which he rested against the table, dropped to the deck of this battleship as he signed.

No word passed between him and General Douglas MacArthur who motioned curtly to the table when he had finished his opening remarks.

Lieutenant-General Jonathan M. Wainwright, who surrendered Corregidor, haggard from his long imprisonment, and Lieutenant-General A. E. Percival, who surrendered Singapore on another black day of the war, stood at MacArthur's side as the Allied Supreme Commander signed for all the powers warring against Japan.

Their presence was a sobering reminder of how desperately close to defeat our nation had fallen during the early months of 1942.

The Japanese delegation of eleven looked appropriately trim and sad. Shigemitsu was wearing morning clothes—frock coat, striped pants, silk hat, and yellow gloves. None of the party exchanged a single word of salute while on board, except the foreign minister's aide, who had to be shown where to place the Japanese texts of the surrender document.

Shigemitsu, however, doffed his silk hat as he reached the top of the starboard gangway and stepped aboard the broad deck of the *Missouri*.

Such was Bigart's first dispatch. There were many others that followed, stretching out to great length, but in its essentials his lead caught and held the spirit of that last day in Tokyo Bay when, for a second time in this generation, the world hoped that war would be no more—and again was bitterly disappointed.

VI. WHEN AMERICAN REPORTERS PIERCED THE IRON CURTAIN

Ivan, the mightiest Russian of them all, has fascinated American correspondents for two generations.

It isn't very easy to get to Ivan. You'll never meet him outside the Iron Curtain. He's not the diplomatic type, and he also isn't the kind who's wanted as an official Soviet propagandist (tourist, that is). Nor is Ivan readily available if you feel a great desire to hunt him up and talk with him at home. He doesn't take to foreigners for reasons that are too distressingly obvious in a police state.

Ivan is the average Russian. He's the little man who goes about his work quietly under the hard rule of a dictatorial, and often cruel, government. When Stalin ruled, Ivan and his wife and children toiled to put over the Five Year Plans. After Hitler's attack, Ivan fought and bled and many of his sons died. Now, under Khrushchev, he is in the factories making Sputniks, rockets, atomic bombs, and all manner of scientific devices that challenge that strange, strange land across the North Pole—the United States.

Just why Ivan supports his masters and puts up with their weird gyrations in the name of Communism is something that Americans have always wondered about. Stories of the average Russian pop up year after year in the Pulitzer Prize files—stories by Paul Ward of the Baltimore *Sun*, Eddy Gilmore of the Associated Press, Harrison Salisbury of the New York *Times* and the many, many others who preceded them and who have since gone behind the Iron Curtain.

There isn't any particular conclusion to be drawn from all this careful reporting and writing, except that the Russians we see in the United States are scarcely typical of Ivan or his kind. For the Russian on tour, like the American at home, is often on his best behavior—friendly, smiling, anxious to please. What happens when the average American goes abroad as a tourist, or the Russian is asked to entertain at home, cannot be quite so accurately forecast.

In any case, it is clear that much of the future of the world depends on the ability of the Americans and the Russians to find some way of living together peacefully. For that reason, all the reporting that has been done behind the Iron Curtain—whether in Russia, or the various satellite states or Yugoslavia—has a central purpose. It is one of the few ways in which Americans can learn something of what to expect from the people of the Soviet Union, if not their rulers of the moment.

The problem of selection of material, therefore, has been particularly difficult in this respect. What follows will provide a rare glimpse of Joseph Stalin and his origins, a candid and still useful appraisal of American-Soviet relationships, and the stories of the downfall of two Russians who bid for great power and failed.

As for Ivan, he remains the greatest mystery of all.

33. WHAT JOSEPH STALIN'S MOTHER
THOUGHT OF HER BOY

"I didn't want him to be anything but a priest,"
she tells H. R. Knickerbocker

Pulitzer Prize for Correspondence, 1931

Hubert Renfro Knickerbocker was discouraged. He had been pounding the sidewalks of New York, which are so friendly in song and story, and so bleak to many a youngster looking for his first job.

Knick was a youthful, red-headed Texan. He had been trying to crash into New York journalism for weeks without success. Finally, because even red-headed Texans are likely to give up, he went back to the Columbia School of Journalism to see a friend and take counsel.

The friend was a shrewd, tough, sharp-voiced little taskmaster—Professor Charles P. Cooper, ex-managing editor of the New York *Sun*. ex-night city editor of the New York *Times*. Coop, as generations of

Columbians called him behind his back, really liked youngsters. When he got a good one, he worked over him with the zeal of a Marine drill instructor. Knick was a good one. He had been graduated in 1921, but now he was ready to go back to Texas.

Coop told him to hold on and grabbed a telephone. To a friend at the *Sun*, he said, "There's a young fella in my office you've got to hire. I'm sending him right down."

In later years, when Coop told the story, he used to grin slyly. "I never did that before, and I never did it again. Had no idea if I could get away with the bluff. But it worked. Knick caught on. And I guess he'll be a newspaperman we'll hear from."

Knick worked for the *Sun*, later for the old New York *Evening Post* and finally for International News Service. He was a war correspondent in Spain, during World War II, and finally in Indonesia during the "police action" of the Dutch that eventually led to Indonesian independence. He wrote many fine stories in his career, often ventured into far places and never feared danger.

But perhaps his most interesting work, even today, is his pioneering series of articles on Russia which he wrote as a comparatively young man for the New York *Evening Post* and the Philadelphia *Public Ledger,* then under the ownership of Cyrus H. K. Curtis. Except for Walter Duranty, no correspondent had done very much to explore Russia's economy in the early 1930s.

Knick decided to make a story out of it, even though it seemed on the surface to be dull stuff. (Today, it is so easy to see that Russia's bid for economic mastery of the world should have been the big foreign story even in its earliest days—but it wasn't!) After patient efforts to persuade the Soviet government, he finally obtained permission and set out on a 10,000-mile trip to survey the progress of the Five Year Plan in 1930. In his 24-part series, he discussed dumping of Soviet products, the use of convict labor, short selling, and many other practices that seemed to him to threaten the West.

The economic news of that Five Year Plan, of course, is old stuff now. But among Knickerbocker's twenty-four stories was one that still retains its interest for it was the first to penetrate the mystery of Joseph Stalin's family, his early life, his motivations, his beginnings on the path to absolute power over Russia and a reign as terrible as that of any ancient despot.

Here is Knickerbocker's interview, in substance, with Stalin's mother as it was published in the New York *Evening Post*. For this story, and the twenty-three others in the series on "The Red Trade Menace," he won the Pulitzer Prize for Correspondence in 1931.

THE BOYHOOD OF SOSO THE GREAT

By H. R. Knickerbocker

From the New York Evening Post and Philadelphia
Public Ledger, Dec. 1, 1930

TIFLIS—A Georgian schoolboy was asked to name the foremost rulers in his country's history.

"Vachtang the Brave," he answered, "David the Restorer, Queen Tamara, and Soso the Great."

"Why Soso the Great?" asked his teacher.

"Because Soso was the first to annex Russia to Georgia."

The anecdote tells volumes, but not of course until one knows who Soso is. He is the ruler of 150,000,000 though his party calls him merely "the most trustworthy interpreter of Lenin's doctrines," and his title is only Secretary General of the Central Committee. His picture hangs in every shop, factory, and office in the Soviet Union. It peers out from newspaper front pages at regular intervals all over the world. He is probably the most powerful political leader in any nation. In Russia his name is a cult, a promise, and a threat.

It is none of these things to his mother. To Ekaterina Djugashvili, Joseph Djugashvili, known as Koba to the Czar's police, as Stalin to the world, is simply Soso, the son whose career, astounding, improbable, has not even yet fully reconciled her to the disappointment she suffered when he failed to become a priest.

No member of Stalin's family except himself had been interviewed until today. His friends will not speak of his private life. There is no man of equal prominence in the world about whose person is woven so impenetrable a veil of secrecy as that which surrounds the chieftain of the All Union Communist Party. Power allures. Power, from a source mysterious, terrifies. Mystery about his person is one of the effective reasons why Stalin in Russia is synonymous with power unlimited.

Stalin's mother was the first of his family to break the spell of silence about him.

It was in the palace of the former Viceroy of Georgia that we met. Not in the drawing room that might have served as a salon for a queen-mother at another age, but in one of her two commodious but simple living rooms.

The palace, luxuriously situated in the midst of a great sub-tropical garden, sprawls at the foot of one of the highest chain of hills that overlook Tiflis. The Viceroys of the Czars had good living here. Assassinations and attempted assassinations on the part of the fiercely independent Georgians kept a succession of incumbents moving in and out of the vice-regal apartments.

At their doors today stand uniformed sentries of the G.P.U. In the reception hall the walls are plastered with announcements pertaining to the business of the Council of People's Commissars of the Trans-Caucasian Republic, whose headquarters are here. Revolutionary posters and the eternal appeal for harder work on the Five-Year Plan remind one that all the way from Siberia to the edge of Persia the Soviet Union is dominated today by a single purpose, and a single will.

It was the maternal source of that will, which today is incorporated fully in the person of Joseph Stalin, that I was seeking. Ten minutes of wandering through leafy courts, winding corridors, up and down stairs, brought me to her rooms, on the first floor.

A middle-aged woman answered our knock, asked what we wanted. She looked mistrustfully at the foreigner but consented to ask Mrs. Djugashvili if she would exchange a few words about her son. Fortunately there are few occupations so entirely agreeable to Ekaterina Djugashvili as that of talking about Joseph Djugashvili.

The mother of Russia's man of steel looked very small when she came through the big double doors leading from her bedroom. Gray-haired, slender, dressed in gray woolen Georgian peasant costume, she peered at us pleasantly through silver-rimmed spectacles. She listened a moment as I explained my desires, her firm smile expanding at the mention of Stalin.

To my Georgian interpreter she said: "I am sorry I speak so little Russian."

Stalin, master of the territories that once were called all the Russias, grew up in a family whose distaste for Russia was too great to admit the Russian language. The son learned it as a necessary instrument for the revolution. Today he uses it in pronouncements that determine the course of the nation, and seventy-two million Russians listen. To his mother, it is still a foreign tongue.

With simple courtesy she asked us to be seated. We drew up chairs to a big table covered with worn red cloth. She apologized for having no coffee or tea to offer us.

Characteristically she began, "Soso was always a good boy."

"Excuse me—who is Soso?"

"Soso? Why that's my son, Joseph. Soso is our Georgian pet name for Joseph. Yes, he was always a good boy. I never had to punish him. He studied hard, was always reading or talking and trying to find out about everything. He started to school when he was eight years, in Gori."

At the mention of the name Gori, a village about three hours from Tiflis, her tone became insistent and with vehemence she declared:

"I want you to correct one thing. They talk a lot about Soso's being born in Lilo, but that's entirely wrong. Lilo was only the place where his grandfather was born. Soso was born in Gori. I could show you the place. I know he was born there. I'm his mother and I ought to know."

She became quite excited about this.

"It was fifty years ago. Soso will be fifty-one eight days after Christmas old style. I don't know what date it would be by this new way of reckoning. I never could learn it. I only know I was twenty years old then and Soso was my fourth son.

"But all the others died before he was born. And Soso was my only son. Of course, I treasured him. Above everything in the world."

"And now," we interceded, "you are very proud of him. But did you ever dream he would become what he is today?"

She smiled a bit nervously, turned and smiled again at the middle-aged woman, a neighbor friend, and said:

"Well, no! You must know that we had planned quite other things for Soso. His father, Vissarion—well, if his father had lived he might have made a cobbler out of Soso. You see, my husband was a cobbler, and his father and his father's father, and as far back as we could remember, all his folks had been cobblers. Peasant cobblers. And his father said he would make a good cobbler out of Soso. But his father died when Soso was eleven years old.

"YOU ALWAYS WERE A GREAT FRIEND OF MINE, JOSEPH"
by Herbert L. Block ("Herblock")

PULITZER PRIZE, 1954   WASHINGTON POST & TIMES-HERALD

"And then,"—she paused and cast another smile at her friend, who smiled back—"and then, you see, I didn't want him to be a cobbler. I didn't want him to be anything but,"—she paused again—"a priest."

"Yes," she declared more firmly, "I did dream that one day Soso would finish his studies and become a priest. That's what I dreamed."

Visions of the anti-religious institute in the Strastnoi Monastery in Moscow, the flamboyant posters of the League of the Godless, numerous church buildings in various stages of dismantlement and of the whole significance of the Communist Party's attitude toward the church came to mind.

"But," we asked, "are you still religious?"

"Well," she hesitated, "I'm afraid—I'm afraid I'm not as religious as I used to be. My son has told me so much." She peered a little harder through her spectacles.

"See!" she exclaimed in a more animated tone, pointing to a picture on the wall. "That's how he looked when he was in the theological seminary."

It was Joseph, an adolescent, in the coarse, straight-collared jacket of a seminarist. Already in the youth, the eyes, mouth and facial expression bore promise of that strength of will that one day was to win him a new and meaningful name.

Another picture, quite recent, showed Stalin in a white roubashka, seated. It was inscribed, "To my mother." A much larger portrait of Lenin hung on the opposite wall, and facing the windows was a reproduction of the scene, famous in Soviet history, of the shooting by White troops of the twenty-six Baku commissars. It, too, was inscribed by the artist, "To Comrade Ekaterina Djugashvili."

"But there's so much to correct," she resumed. "It is not true that Soso was expelled from the Theological Seminary in Tiflis. I took him out on account of his health."

This was news indeed. All the official biographical sketches of Stalin declare that he was a student at the Theological Seminary in Tiflis, that the religious instruction there "did not correspond to the needs of the young Djugashvili," that he became interested in revolutionary ideas and was expelled for being "unreliable."

It is a point that will be recognized as important by any one acquainted with the psychology of the Communist Party. I probed deeper.

"No, I tell you," she insisted, "he was not expelled. I took him out on account of his health. When he went up to Tiflis from Gori and entered the seminary he was fifteen years old and he was one of the strongest boys you ever saw. But then he studied too hard in the seminary and by the time he was nineteen he was so run down that the doctors said he might get tuberculosis. So I took him out of school. He did not want to go. I took him out. He was my only son."

She finished firmly. There was no very effective answer to that. But I risked a last attempt.

"But everybody says, and all the books say, that he was expelled."

"Nonsense," she exclaimed, "I took him out."

Possibly this time the official records are correct. Not only possible, but certain, that Stalin's mother believes she is rendering a correct account of what must have been one of the most painful episodes of her life. To his mother, a devout woman, expulsion was something that simply had to be explained away. One couldn't admit that one's son, so soon to become a priest, had been cast out for "unreliability." To the neighbors, to the family, to everybody who asked, one had to say it was his health.

All that was thirty-two years ago, twenty years before the revolution that put such a new light on expulsion from a theological seminary. Twenty years of repeating the same story imbeds it irretrievably in one's mind. After twenty years it is too late to make amendments. Stalin's mother is positive of her facts—so are the official records.

For Ekaterina Djugashvili those twenty years were too full of worry to be lightly touched upon.

"I am seventy-one," she said, "but I'd be a much younger woman if it hadn't been for those years. The worst of it was when I never knew where he was. Always, in jail, in exile, in Siberia, even at the last in the Arctic."

One could appreciate her feelings. The record of those years is an extraordinary one. It explains a good many things—why they called young Djugashvili hard, why Lenin said of him that he would be a cook who'd brew hot broth, why they say in Moscow now that he is brewing it, and why his mother worried. It is a far more interesting and instructive record than that of most heads of a great state.

The mere table of dates tells the story:

1898—Aged eighteen, joined Social-Democratic organization, Tiflis.

1901—Put under police surveillance, fled to Baku, helped found first illegal Marxist group.

1902—Arrested.

1902-03—Imprisoned, Kutalsk and Batum.

1903—Exiled to Eastern Siberia for three years.

1908—Arrested, exiled to Vologodsky Gubernia for six years.

1909—Escaped.

1909—Arrested, jailed, exiled to Vologodsky Gubernia for three years.

1911—Escaped.

1912—Arrested, exiled to Narimsky Krai, northern Siberia.

1912—Escaped.

1913—Arrested, exiled to Turukhansky Krai, village of Kureyka, within the Arctic Circle.

1917—Released by the Kerensky revolution.

Nothing could hold him but the Arctic Circle. In the nineteen years from 1898 to 1917 he was arrested, jailed, and exiled six times, escaped five times, spent a total of about eight years behind the bars or in confinement camps. They say of Stalin that he of all the exiles was least affected by their hardships. Robust, he thrived under conditions that killed his comrades.

The mere mention of those times sent a shudder of painful memories over his mother. It has been most difficult for her to realize the full significance of the change that has taken place in the status of her son.

"I visited the Kremlin once," she said. "Just once I've been in Moscow. I lived with my son there. I didn't like it. The trip is too far, and it's not like Georgia. But he seldom gets further than Sochi, over there on the coast. I think he is there now. Soso came to see me once in 1921 and once three years ago."

There was a touch of wistfulness in her voice. To his own mother, too, Stalin had elements that were mysterious. She looked around the room and there was a long pause. The room seemed to grow bigger and Mrs. Djugashvili smaller. It was a big room, and it con-

tained a great deal of furniture, seven chairs, all different; two plain
wardrobes, three sofas, a small table in one corner and a big one
where we were sitting. All this furniture seemed scanty. Outside a
breeze stirred the fig tree in the court. The breeze moved a wisp of
Mrs. Djugashvili's gray hair.

"Moscow is very far."

"See," she exclaimed, and hurried over to the corner table piled
high with newspapers and periodicals. She pointed at the pile of
publications, every one of them containing an article, speech or
picture of Stalin. "See how he works. All this he has done. He works
too hard.

"And, too, he has a family of his own, but he's much too busy for
any family. There's my grandson, Yasha, Soso's boy by his first wife.
Yasha is twenty-four. His mother, Katherine, died of pneumonia
before the revolution.

"And now I've two more grandchildren, Soso's boy Vassily. He's
eight. And the little girl, Svetlana. She's five. Both of them are by
Soso's second wife, Nadezhda Alleluja. Alleluja was a great Communist, a friend of Lenin's. Nadezhda is his daughter."

The mention of Lenin reminded her of something. "You know,"
she said, "it was Lenin that gave Soso the name of Stalin. Lenin said
he was like steel. It was a good name."

It was past noon. I asked if we could take her picture. She
demurred. She had a headache. It would be impossible.

"Perhaps later in the day?"

"Well, perhaps. Come about five o'clock and I'll see."

At five we were there. Ekaterina Djugashvili had been ready for
us an hour. This time her costume was not the plain house dress of
the Georgian peasant woman. It was the ceremonial black and
white, the tasteful and effective native dress for state occasions.

We walked in the garden. Around us the magnolias and cape
jessamines, the dark foliage of sub-tropical plants, the flaming red
of late autumn flowers, made Russia fade to a remote memory.
Ekaterina Djugashvili said good-by. In the cordial Georgian manner
she took my hand in both of hers and said: "I want to ask one thing.
Will you send one of those pictures to Soso?"

I promised I would.

Knickerbocker was killed on July 12, 1949 with twenty-three other correspondents when a KLM plane, which was flying them home from the Indonesian war, crashed against a hillside in India. He was fifty-one years old.

34. THIS IS RUSSIA—UNCENSORED:

FREEDOM IS JUST A WORD

Edmund Stevens of the Christian Science Monitor
quits the land behind the Iron Curtain

Pulitzer Prize for International Reporting, 1950

After three years of continuous residence in Moscow and nearly fifteen years of reporting about Russia from both sides of the Iron Curtain, Edmund Stevens wrote a penetrating series for the *Christian Science Monitor* entitled, "This Is Russia—Uncensored."

In it, he described the Russia that he knew intimately as a Russian-speaking foreign correspondent of long experience and a special adviser of the War Department during World War II. In leaving, he told of being harried, spied upon, given little or no cooperation in his work. And yet, in spite of personal abuse and the deep freeze that had settled then over American-Soviet relations, Stevens remained hopeful that a world-wrecking atomic war could be averted.

In the next to the last of his forty-three articles, published on January 28, 1950, he gave the basis for these hopes. The series as a whole won the Pulitzer Prize of 1950 for International Reporting. His article follows.

EAST OF THE IRON CURTAIN

By Edmund Stevens

From the Christian Science Monitor, Jan. 28, 1950

The serflike bondage of the "free" Soviet citizen to his job is one element of an unrelaxing economic stranglehold upon the masses. Equally important is the total state control of the production of food and consumer goods, a control constantly used to coerce and cajole, reward and punish, in the interests of the Communist Party line.

In the past, the government deliberately starved the refractory peasantry into submission to collectivization. Today the Soviets are vigorously wooing the loyalty of urban workers and intellectuals by making more and better foodstuffs available to them at lower prices. This is made possible by the substantial gains in postwar production, plus the economic benefits reaped through control of eastern Europe.

Soviet postwar economic progress is not only a tribute to the country's recuperative powers, but to the effectiveness of large-scale economic planning. This principle, which the Soviets pioneered, has now been accepted and adopted in some measure throughout the civilized world on a national and even international scale. Perhaps the crowning expression is the Economic Cooperation Administration.

In meeting the Communist challenge, the democratic West now seeks to demonstrate that economic planning can succeed in a free society, without the physical and mental compulsions on which the Soviets rely so heavily. This is vital, for one of the greatest dangers to democracy is lest the West, in opposing Communism, resort to the same methods the Communists employ, and lest human liberty succumb to some equally odious brand of totalitarianism.

One saw this happen in Germany, where Nazism largely began and developed as an anti-Communist crusade. Historians long will study the similar methods of the two antithetical systems. Hitler used economic pressure for political ends in the same way Stalin does. He, too, wooed the working class with improved living standards. Ironically, the wealth of eastern Europe, now flowing into the Soviet Union to raise the Russian workers' living standards, ten years back was pouring into Germany, where it helped convince the German workers and intellectuals that it paid to belong to the Herrenvolk (master race).

The common denominator of Nazism and Communism is in the appeal to materialism, in the conviction that violence and coercion can settle any issue, in the belief that power justifies any means. Above all, both inherit from a common philosophic source the rejection of fixed standards of right and wrong, true and false. Without these moral compass points to steer by, no nation can cleave to the course of progress. Technology and organizing efficiency, instead of benefiting mankind, then operate for evil. In the Nazi Weltanschauung (philosophy), it accounts for concentration camps, lethal gas chambers and dreams of "tomorrow the world."

In the Soviet Weltanschauung it has led to forced labor camps, mass purges, police terror and dreams of world Communism—and the end is not yet in sight.

Yet people in the West, who from mental laziness, lapse of memory, or sheer exasperation advocate a preventive war as the only way out at present should be reminded that the recent war generated problems fully as serious as those it solved, plus the tremendous senseless destruction. Even in vanquished Germany, final victory over Nazism still hinges on whether the German people can be won over to democratic ideals.

The notion that Communism can be disposed of effectively by military means is even more absurd. Not only is such a war likely to result in universal ruin, visited on victors and vanquished alike, but the decisive battle would still remain to be fought in the realm of ideas—and for the possession not of territory but of men's minds.

In the coming years the strongest, most determined foes of the police state are likely to develop East of the Iron Curtain, where not even forcible indoctrination can neutralize the lessons of immediate knowledge and experience. There are in Russia today legions of thinking, intelligent people who chafe under the omnipotent police state and long with their whole being for freedom.

The Russians as a race are neither domineering nor aggressive nor xenophobe. They are warmly human, gregarious, and endowed with an avid and friendly curiosity about other peoples. All these qualities instinctively tend to alienate them, if not from the Soviet system, at least from its present policies at home and abroad.

Moreover, thousands upon thousands of people in all walks of life have at some time sustained some deep personal hurt from the police regime. Each new purge or "ideological campaign" adds new contingents of malcontents. While all open criticism of the regime is effectively prevented and the ears and eyes of the M.V.D. (secret police) are omnipresent, such is human nature that every individual has at least one person he fully trusts, and thus an endless chain extends, even though it lacks organized form.

The mental outlook of the average Soviet citizen passes through three main stages, according to age groups:

1. Below twenty-five years of age, most susceptible to intense indoctrination—the glowing visions conjured up by propaganda ap-

peal to the youthful imagination, unsullied as yet by worldly experience.

2. From twenty-five to thirty-five, gradual frustration of hopes destroyed by contact with daily life and conditions.

3. After thirty-five, final disillusionment. This breeds hard, selfish cynicism, resigned routine-conditioned apathy, or intense inner rebellion, depending on the status and makeup of the individual. The men who staff the party and state apparatus come under the first category (cynicism). The majority of citizens fall in the second (apathy). But many, at the least sign of hope, would gravitate toward the third (rebellion).

The opening months of the Nazi invasion disclosed how deeply disaffection had eaten into the fabric of Soviet society—before Hitler's political blunders and cruelties repelled even those who at first looked upon the Kremlin as the greater evil.

It is essential that the West learn to distinguish between the police state and the Soviet people, for if the former are implacable foes, the latter, unless stupidly antagonized, are potential friends and allies.

And it is they who eventually will decide their country's destiny.

Eight years after Stevens predicted the rise of resistance east of the Iron Curtain, Boris Pasternak challenged the power of Communist rule in Soviet Russia in his powerful novel, *Dr. Zhivago*. But the regime forced him to refuse a Nobel Prize for his work. The first test of strength pitted the whole authority of the Soviet government against an elderly novelist. The novelist lost.

35. HARRISON SALISBURY REVEALS
HOW BERIA SEALED HIS OWN FATE

The man who might have been a Soviet dictator
hesitated and paid with his life

Pulitzer Prize for International Correspondence, 1955

Harrison Evans Salisbury spent eighteen years with the United Press (now United Press International) and acquired habits of work that have remained with him ever since.

Beginning with his graduation from the University of Minnesota in 1930, he was trained first as a wire service reporter, then as a political writer in Washington, bureau manager in London and Moscow, and finally as foreign editor. He became known in his profession as one of the most thorough and reliable correspondents in foreign service, and also one of the fastest anywhere. At the UPI, even today, there are executives who remember his rewrite jobs at national political conventions with a glow of admiration, or his decisiveness at Big Four conferences with respect for his accuracy.

In 1949, Salisbury shifted to the New York *Times* to become its Moscow correspondent and for six years thereafter was one of the few American reporters in Moscow.

What he saw of life in the world's largest police state at once depressed him and gave a deep thoughtfulness to his dispatches. He covered the last days of Stalin and gave both currency and credibility to reports that they had been shortened by the design of his plotting colleagues in the Kremlin. He saw Georgi M. Malenkov at the outset of his brief reign in Stalin's place, and noted the quick passage of such power-seekers as Lavrenti P. Beria. He was one of the first to sense that Nikita S. Khrushchev was the man to watch.

For his series, "Russia Re-Viewed," Salisbury was awarded the Pulitzer Prize for International Reporting in 1955. This is one of his articles, a condensed version of the end of Beria.

AN IRON COLLAR AROUND MOSCOW
By Harrison E. Salisbury
From the New York Times, Sept. 21, 1954

For about seventy-eight hours in March of last year, Lavrenti Pavlovich Beria held Russia in the hollow of his pudgy hand. He was supreme. There was no one who could challenge him—not Malenkov, not Khrushchev, not Molotov, not the Army.

At any moment within those fateful hours, Beria might have proclaimed himself dictator, all-supreme ruler of Russia, heir of Stalin.

He did not do so, and in that failure to act he sealed his own fate. The life that came to an end last Christmas Eve, probably in the blood-stained cellars of the Lubyanka Prison, was doomed from that moment when Beria did not act.

The story of the March days of 1953, just before and just after the death of Stalin, has never been publicly told. Much of it was con-

cealed and suppressed by the Moscow censorship. Many details are
not yet and possibly never will be known outside the tight little
circle of men in the Kremlin who were the chief actors in one of the
great dramas of modern times.

Enough is known, however, so that the factors that led to Beria's
removal and execution can be traced with almost crystal clarity, in
an otherwise Florentine labyrinth of intrigue and counterintrigue,
plot and counterplot.

These factors were so obvious at the time that this correspondent
could confidently note in his private correspondence that a showdown over Beria's power was inevitable.

To see why this was so it is necessary to turn back to the story of
the events of Stalin's death in March, 1953—the real story, not the
emasculated one that was all that fearful censors permitted correspondents to cable at the time.

The first announcement of Stalin's fatal illness was made in
Moscow about 8 a.m. on March 4, 1953. It was said the General-
issimo had suffered a massive cerebral hemorrhage early Monday
morning, March 2, two days previously. It was apparent to everyone in Moscow that this was the end for Stalin. The only question
was how long the end would be in coming. It did not seem likely
to be long.

This anticipation proved correct. At 4 a.m. on March 6, the
Moscow radio, in its short-wave broadcasts overseas and to pro-
vincial newspapers within Russia, announced that Stalin had died
at 9:50 the previous evening. . . .

Around 7:30 a.m., the censorship on Stalin's death was lifted and
it was about 9 o'clock before I again emerged from the telegraph
office. Vast changes met my eyes. By that time there were thousands
of troops in the central part of the city and great lines of trucks.
Columns of tanks had also made their appearance on upper Gorky
Street. All the trucks, all the tanks, all the troops bore the familiar
red-and-blue insignia of the Ministry of Internal Affairs (M.V.D.).
They were Beria's forces.

There was an iron collar around Moscow's heart and from about
10 or 11 a.m. of March 6, 1953 until 4 p.m. on March 9 it was not
removed.

During those hours not one person entered or left the center of

Moscow without leave of the M.V.D. command, Beria's command.

It was not likely that the men in the Kremlin had failed to note that they were, in effect, prisoners of the M.V.D. They were men trained to think in military terms and, particularly, in terms of civil war and street fighting. To the military leaders the realization of their position must have been even more forcible.

Because the M.V.D. was not just a group of initials. It was not just a department of the government. It was an individual. A powerful, ruthless man of extraordinary ability named Lavrenti Pavlovich Beria. And it was Beria's troops and Beria's tanks and Beria's trucks that had accomplished this small miracle and taken over the city of Moscow while the radios were still blaring out the news of Stalin's death to the startled citizenry.

Using the basic movement plans that twice a year had been employed on May Day and on Nov. 7 to control traffic movement in the center of the city, and simply extending the plan back to control the whole city and its environs, Beria had with the smoothness of clockwork put Moscow into his grasp.

It was too smooth and too complete and too good.

No military man could see that exhibition and feel a moment's safety—unless he trusted Beria completely or unless Beria was the top boss. It was too plain and too obvious that Beria had a machine that, before dawn any morning, could take over the Kremlin, take over Moscow, and, having done this, have a crack at making Beria master of all Russia.

There is not much doubt that Beria himself was fully aware of his power at that moment. It is also likely that he had only in the final hours of Stalin's life regained full and unchallenged control over the M.V.D. He and his command of this vast police army had been one of the targets of machinations that generally are described as the so-called "doctor's plot" which had a vital role in the events leading up to Stalin's death.

But in the coalition of forces that occurred at or about the time of Stalin's death, Beria got back his M.V.D. Perhaps that is why he overplayed his hand so badly at a moment when he was not prepared to strike for full mastery of Russia. Perhaps he did not fully realize the impression he could make on his colleagues.

TIME TO BRIDGE THAT GULCH, *by Bruce Russell*

PULITZER PRIZE, 1946   LOS ANGELES TIMES

Whatever the explanation, on the next day, Monday, when Stalin was formally laid to rest beside Lenin, Beria spoke at the funeral bier along with Georgi M. Malenkov and Vyacheslav M. Molotov. There was an undercurrent in Beria's speech that could have flowed only from his own knowledge of his power.

He sounded just a little condescending toward Mr. Molotov and Mr. Malenkov—perhaps more in his delivery than in his language. What was more interesting, he sought to convey without exactly saying so that he spoke for the Army as well as the police.

It took only three and a half months to demonstrate that condescension was not exactly called for on Beria's part and that he had shown the Army, only too plainly, the power and danger of his position. There can be no doubt that, from the moment Beria sealed off the Kremlin and Moscow with his troops, he signed his own death warrant.

He was not strong enough to rule. But he was too dangerous to any other ruler or rulers. In the unstable coalition of party, police, and Army, Beria had too much sheer military power that could be too quickly applied at the center. He was too big for the triumvirate, but not big enough to be dictator.

The only real surprise about Beria's end was that it came so soon. It was a measure of the real weakness of his position (once his troops were out of Moscow) that his colleagues were able to deliver the coup de grace so quickly and with hardly a ripple on the surface of the Moscow waters.

36. ZHUKOV GREETS THE HEARST TEAM: "I HOPE TO VISIT THE U.S."

An exclusive interview with Russia's military hero of World War II before the Khrushchev purge

Pulitzer Prize for International Reporting, 1956

The Soviet Union was on the verge of a momentous change in government early in 1955. All unknown to the world outside the Iron Curtain, Premier Georgi Malenkov, Stalin's successor, was tottering. From his key role as First Secretary of the Communist Party, Nikita S. Khrushchev was about to bid for supreme power.

Into snowy, freezing Moscow that winter came William Randolph Hearst Jr., publisher of the New York *Journal-American;* Frank Conniff, whom he had taken from the *Journal-American's* staff as his editorial assistant, and Kingsbury Smith, the European manager of International News Service. This was what Bill Hearst liked to call the Hearst team.

The visit to Moscow had been Hearst's own idea. He had decided it would be a good time to size up the Soviet government and talk to its leading men, that it might make a first-rate series for the Hearst papers. He and the big, affable Conniff, who had come up the hard way from night rewrite, got together with Smith, the suave veteran foreign correspondent known to newspapermen as Joe.

Now Joe Smith was no stranger at handling a major story in Moscow. It was his questionnaire to Stalin during the Berlin blockade that had given the United States the first tip that the Russians were ready to call the whole thing off; for in answering it, Stalin had casually dropped out all reference to one of his major demands, an accommodation on currency. Smith, moreover, had covered Big Four conferences and knew what could be expected from the Russians—and what could not. He therefore set about carefully arranging interviews in advance for the visit of the Hearst team to Moscow and succeeded beyond his wildest dreams. The Russians seemingly liked the idea of talking to the Hearst chain, with its record of three decades of bitter opposition to both the Soviet and Communism.

Accordingly, the Hearst team made world-wide news with its interviews with Khrushchev, Marshal Nikolai Bulganin, Marshal Georgi Zhukov, and Foreign Minister Vyacheslav M. Molotov. For on February 8, 1955, the day of the Zhukov interview, Premier Malenkov fell and the ebullient Khrushchev boosted the elderly Bulganin into the premiership. Molotov and Zhukov were spared for the time being, but they also were to go later before Khrushchev shouldered Bulganin aside and became premier himself.

Much of the interview material dealt with the Tachen Islands evacuation, which the U. S. Navy then was about to undertake to remove 15,000 Chinese Nationalist troops. Both Molotov and Khrushchev gave assurances that they didn't want the conflict between Red China and the Nationalist Chinese to develop into a major war. Moreover, Bulganin, in his first exclusive interview as premier, said he wanted to improve relations with the United States. The Tachen evacuation seemingly was guaranteed against interference.

Perhaps the least newsworthy interview at the time, but historically the one that may be the most significant, was the talk of the Hearst team with Marshal Zhukov, Russian hero of World War II and deputy defense minister at the time. Shortly after Khrushchev made himself secure, Zhukov was removed from power and he later fell under the accusation of being a "revisionist," the deadly charge that preceded the execution of Imre Nagy of Hungary.

Here, in its essential text, is the Zhukov interview.

THE END OF A DREAM

By Kingsbury Smith

From International News Service, Feb. 8, 1955

MOSCOW, Feb. 8—Soviet Marshal Georgi Zhukov, first deputy defense minister and commander of the Red armies in the final Allied defeat of Nazi Germany, told William Randolph Hearst Jr. today it was his "dream" to visit the United States some day. Zhukov said the time was not ripe for such a visit now.

In the first exclusive interview he has ever granted, Zhukov spoke warmly of his friendship for General Dwight D. Eisenhower.

Zhukov parried the question whether, if he were the supreme allied commander in Europe, he would consider a German military contribution essential to make Western Europe defensible. He also complained about American military bases around Russia and expounded Soviet policy concerning the prohibition of nuclear weapons.

Describing Eisenhower as a "very fine person," the 66-year-old Russian military leader said:

"In 1945, I had a talk with General Eisenhower before he left Germany for the United States.

"We exchanged best wishes and General Eisenhower said the United States would never attack the Soviet Union.

"I said the Soviet Union would never attack the United States. I consider I was not wrong in what I said and I hope General Eisenhower was right in what he said. We spoke as soldiers and saw no grounds for war between our countries. My sincere wish is to see an improvement in the relations between our two countries.

"I know our relations will get better. Then I hope to be able to visit the United States."

Zhukov, who was commander in the battle of Moscow when Hitler's armies suffered their first staggering setback and who formulated the plan for the defense of Stalingrad, received Mr. Hearst at his office in the Soviet Defense Ministry in the center of Moscow. Zhukov was alone.

The American publisher was accompanied by Frank Conniff, his editorial assistant, and this correspondent. A Soviet Intourist official, who has acted as our guide during our visit to Moscow, also accompanied us to interpret the conversation.

Zhukov's chest was bedecked with eight rows of medals, topped by three stars representing a triple award of Hero of the Soviet Union. He came forward with a smile and greeted Mr. Hearst warmly.

During the opening part of the conversation, Zhukov said he often remembers his friendly meetings with General Eisenhower. He said:

"I was invited twice by General Eisenhower to visit the United States. I was very grateful for those invitations. It has always been my dream to visit the United States. But unfortunately conditions of health and last-minute developments prevented me from going at the time I received the invitations.

"I fear that relations between our two countries presently are not quite suitable for such a visit, but I certainly hope to go some day. We must establish relations of good neighbors. An exchange of military missions just now would be useless."

We called Zhukov's attention to the belief expressed by Marshal of the Royal Air Force Sir John Slessor that there was no chance of another great war being waged without recourse to nuclear weapons, and asked whether the Soviet marshal shared this view. Zhukov replied:

"I think contrarily. We must prohibit the use of these weapons. We must do so in the interests of humanity."

Asked whether he did not think the prohibition of these nuclear weapons would tip the balance of military power in favor of the Soviet bloc, Zhukov cautiously answered:

"First of all, we do not think we have any great superiority of conventional weapons. If one does not wish to launch new wars, there is no need for these [atomic] weapons."

Mr. Hearst said might not the possession of these weapons by both sides serve as a guarantee of peace and as assurance against anyone starting anything?

Zhukov replied that so long as nuclear weapons exist, "somebody, some crazy person or people might use such weapons. The existence of these weapons is very dangerous for both parties. Possession of these weapons by both sides will simply lead to an arms race."

This correspondent recalled that General Alfred M. Gruenther, Atlantic Pact Supreme Commander, was authorized at the last meeting of the Atlantic Pact Council to base defense plans on the assumption that atomic weapons would be used if there should be a major war.

Asked whether Soviet defense plans were based on the same assumption, Zhukov said:

"It is better that we think less about war plans and more about avoiding war."

Revealing that he is a member of the all-powerful Central Committee of the Russian Communist Party, Zhukov said his view on desirability of improving Russo-American relations represented not only his personal opinion, but also that of the government and party.

We recalled that Nikita S. Khrushchev, First Secretary of the Soviet Communist Party, in an interview with Mr. Hearst last Saturday, had recognized the right of America to do what it felt necessary for its own security.

Zhukov said he did not think American bases in Europe were necessary for the defense of the United States.

We pointed out that the United States, under the Atlantic Pact, was committed to defend its European allies as well as itself. Zhukov replied:

"You are bound to justify your point of view. We are bound to justify ours. We must not simply look for justification of our respective viewpoints. We must try to make a new war impossible."

This correspondent said Western diplomats and others felt that during the years of military weakness in the West, America's possession of the atomic bomb had a bearing on the maintenance of peace. Zhukov said:

"You had too few bombs then to have had any bearing on the military situation. You had only five or six atomic bombs in the United States at that time."

Conniff said: "You have better information than we do about how many atomic bombs we had then."

We thanked the Marshal for the time he had given us and for his frankness and friendliness.

Zhukov smiled broadly and shook each of us by the hand.

He said: "This meeting has reminded me of our wartime victory days."

The Hearst team won the Pulitzer Prize in International Reporting for 1956. President Eisenhower personally expressed his appreciation for the journalistic enterprise that had made the four interviews possible. Sir Winston Churchill said to the team members: "You did nothing but good."

There is a postscript to the adventure. Kingsbury Smith became publisher of the New York *Journal-American* in 1959.

VII. COLD WAR AND HOT: FROM KOREA TO HUNGARY

It is fashionable to call the Korean War the worst-reported conflict in American history. It wasn't.

Anybody who was there knows what incredible feats war correspondents performed to get news to the American people. If many editors chose to bury it, or cut it to ribbons; if people didn't like to read about it, that was obviously not the fault of the men and women who risked their necks at the battle fronts.

The reporters told the story, hour by hour, day by day, whether the news was of qualified victories or stunning defeats. Prize-winners or not, they stuck out the war that couldn't be won and couldn't be lost. Consider just one example:

Quite by accident on the morning of Sunday, June 25, 1950, Jack James of the United Press ran into an American intelligence officer at the Embassy in Seoul. It was raining and James, remembering he had left his raincoat at the Embassy, had gone there to retrieve it. But the intelligence officer didn't know that.

"What have you heard from the border?" he asked.

James didn't know what the officer was talking about but he played it dead-pan. "Not much. What have you heard?"

"Hell, I've heard nothing since the report that the North Koreans had crossed the 38th Parallel everywhere except in the area of the 8th Division."

James checked. It didn't take him long to find out that the invasion was on. The first UP bulletins went out. Before noon the first reporters were at the front lines sending back eyewitness stories of the disaster.

On July 5, when the first American troops went into action under the United Nations banner, Peter Kalischer of the UP was trapped in a foxhole 100 yards from enemy troops but managed to slog back through the paddy fields with the story while enemy broadcasts were listing him as a prisoner-of-war.

Nor were United Press men alone, by any means, in their devotion to duty. Marvin Stone and Bob Elegant of International News Service, Don Whitehead and Relman Morin of the Associated Press, and many more in the wire service corps gave extraordinary service over many months.

Of the newspaper specials, the work of Homer Bigart and Marguerite Higgins, both of the New York *Herald Tribune*, became the talk of the press corps and the military as well. They seemed to rival each other in daring, wherever they went. The somewhat more friendly team of Keyes Beech and Fred Sparks, both veterans of the Chicago *Daily News* Foreign Service, rivaled their contemporaries in every respect.

In 1951, the Trustees of Columbia University and the Advisory Board on the Pulitzer Prizes were so impressed with the Korean War reporting that they broke precedent to give six Pulitzer Prizes for International Reporting to Miss Higgins, Beech, Bigart, Morin, Sparks and Whitehead. Scripps-Howard correspondent Jim Lucas was added to that list in 1954. The United Press was recognized in 1957 for Russell Jones's brilliant reporting of the Russian attack on the Budapest rebels. Between these two events came the ups and downs of the cold war—the Korean peace, the visit of a Russian delegation to Iowa, and—most important of all—the conduct of American foreign policy by President Eisenhower and Secretary of State Dulles.

All these facets of the post-World War II civilization, and many more, brought an era of new responsibility to American journalism. If people didn't want to listen to unpleasant news, if people didn't want to read of small wars and large defeats, could the American newspaper afford to play them down? The answer is that no responsible newspaper did so. Here is a part of the record, as it is

written in the files of the Pulitzer Prizes, to show that newspapermen and women did their part—as they always will.

37. MARGUERITE HIGGINS SEES
THE MARINES LAND AT INCHON

She goes in with the fifth wave to cover
the United Nations' comeback in Korea

Pulitzer Prize for International Reporting, 1951

"It's impossible . . ."

Marguerite Higgins applied to the Graduate School of Journalism at
Columbia University for admission on the opening day in September,
1941, and that was what she was told. She put up a spirited argument.
Even though the class was full, she was admitted and was graduated in
1942 with her M.S. in Journalism.

"It's impossible . . ."

She wanted to begin work immediately for a New York newspaper
but of course everyone told her nobody would take on a green cub, and
a girl at that, even if she did happen to be blonde, pert, and pretty. So
she became a campus correspondent for the New York *Herald Tribune*
and made the staff upon graduation.

"It's impossible . . ."

She wanted to become a war correspondent, but naturally women
simply couldn't compete with men in such a rough field, and besides it
was dangerous. She was in Berlin at the end of World War II, covering
the entry of American troops into the ruined German capital and was
one of the first correspondents into the concentration camp at Dachau.

"It's impossible . . ."

She wanted to cover the Korean War although General Douglas Mac-
Arthur himself was against women front-line war correspondents, even
competent ones. She covered the long retreat from Seoul, was in the fifth
wave of the Marines' landing at Inchon, reported the disheartening trail
back from North Korea after the Chinese intervention, and was often
under fire at total disregard of her safety.

"It's impossible . . ."

She was nominated by the New York *Herald Tribune* for a Pulitzer

Prize for her Korean War correspondence, but no woman had ever captured a prize for war correspondence and very few had ever been given a Pulitzer award for anything. With five of her colleagues, she won a Pulitzer Prize for International Reporting in 1951.

Such, in brief, is the story of Marguerite Higgins, born in Hong Kong in 1920 of an American father and French mother; schooled in France, the University of California, and Columbia; war correspondent and competitor extraordinary on the news fronts of the world. The following story is part of the material that won her a Pulitzer Prize.

"EVERYBODY GET DOWN. HERE WE GO"

By Marguerite Higgins

From the New York Herald Tribune, Sept. 18, 1950

WITH THE U.S. MARINES AT INCHON, KOREA, Sept. 15 (Delayed)— Heavily laden U.S. Marines, in one of the most technically difficult amphibious landings in history, stormed at sunset today over a ten-foot sea wall in the heart of the port of Inchon and within an hour had taken three commanding hills in the city.

I was in the fifth wave that hit "Red Beach," which in reality was a rough, vertical pile of stones over which the first assault troops had to scramble with the aid of improvised landing ladders topped with steel hooks.

Despite a deadly and steady pounding from naval guns and airplanes, enough North Koreans remained alive close to the beach to harass us with small-arms and mortar fire. They even hurled hand grenades down at us as we crouched in trenches which unfortunately ran behind the sea wall in the inland side.

It was far from the "virtually unopposed" landing for which the troops had hoped after hearing of the quick capture of Wolmi Island in the morning by an earlier Marine assault. Wolmi is inside Inchon harbor and just off "Red Beach." At H-hour minus seventy, confident, joking Marines started climbing down from the transport ship on cargo nets and dropping into small assault boats. Our wave commander, Lieutenant R. J. Schening, a veteran of five amphibious assaults, including Guadalcanal, hailed me with the comment, "This has a good chance of being a pushover."

Because of tricky tides, our transport had to stand down the channel and it was more than nine miles to the rendezvous point where our assault waves formed up.

The channel reverberated with the ear-splitting boom of warship guns and rockets. Blue and orange flame spurted from the "Red Beach" area and a huge oil tank, on fire, sent great black rings of smoke over the shore. Then the fire from the big guns lifted and the planes that had been circling overhead swooped low to rake their fire deep into the sea wall.

The first wave of our assault troops was speeding toward the shore by now. It would be H-hour (5:30 p.m.) in two minutes. Suddenly, bright orange tracer bullets spun out from the hill in our direction.

"My God! There are still some left," Lieutenant Schening said. "Everybody get down. Here we go!"

It was H-hour plus fifteen minutes as we sped the last 2,000 yards to the beach. About half way there the bright tracers started cutting across the top of our little boat. "Look at their faces now," said John Davies of the Newark *News*. I turned and saw that the men around me had expressions contorted with anxiety.

We struck the sea wall hard at a place where it had crumbled into a canyon. The bullets were whining persistently, spattering the water around us. We clambered over the high steel sides of the boat, dropping into the water and, taking shelter beside the boat as long as we could, snaked on our stomachs up into a rock-strewn dip in the sea wall.

In the sky there was good news. A bright, white star shell from the high ground to our left and an amber cluster told us that the first wave had taken their initial objective, Observatory Hill. But whatever the luck of the first four waves, we were relentlessly pinned down by rifle and automatic weapon fire coming down on us from another rise on the right.

There were some thirty Marines and two correspondents crouched in the gouged-out sea wall. Then another assault boat swept up, disgorging about thirty more Marines. This went on for two more waves until our hole was filled and Marines lying on their stomachs were strung out all across the top of the sea wall.

An eerie colored light flooded the area as the sun went down with a glow that a newsreel audience would have thought a fake. As the dusk settled the glare of burning buildings all around lit the sky.

Suddenly, as we lay there intent on the firing ahead, a sudden rush of water came up into the dip in the wall and we saw a huge LST (Landing Ship, Tank) rushing at us with the great plank door half down. Six more yards and the ship would have crushed twenty men. Warning shouts sent every one speeding from the sea wall, searching for escape from the LST and cover from the gunfire. The LST's huge bulk sent a rush of water pouring over the sea wall as it crunched in, soaking most of us.

The Marines ducked and zigzagged as they raced across the open but enemy bullets caught a good many in the semi-darkness. The wounded were pulled aboard the LSTs, six of which appeared within sixty-five minutes after H-hour.

As nightfall closed in, the Marine commanders ordered their troops forward with increasing urgency, for they wanted to assure a defensible perimeter for the night.

In this remarkable amphibious operation, where tides played such an important part, the Marines were completely isolated from outside supply lines for exactly four hours after H-hour. At this time the out-rushing tides—they fluctuate thirty-one feet in twelve-hour periods—made mud flats of the approaches to "Red Beach." The LSTs bringing supplies simply settled on the flats, helpless until the morning tides would float them again.

At the battalion command post the news that the three high-ground objectives—the British Consulate, Cemetery Hill, and Observation Hill—had been taken arrived at about H-hour plus sixty-one minutes. Now the important items of business became debarking tanks, guns, and ammunition from the LSTs.

Every cook, clerk, driver, and administrative officer in the vicinity was rounded up to help in the unloading. It was exciting to see the huge M-26 tanks rumble across big planks onto the beach, which only a few minutes before had been protected only by riflemen and machine gunners. Then came the bulldozers, trucks, and jeeps.

It was very dark in the shadow of the ships and the unloaders had a hazardous time dodging bullets, mortar fire, and their own vehicles.

North Koreans began giving up by the dozens by this time and we could see them, hands up, marching across the open fields toward the LSTs. They were taken charge of with considerable glee by a Korean Marine policeman, Captain Woo, himself a native of Inchon, who had made the landing with several squads of men who were also natives of the city. They learned of the plan to invade their home town only after they had boarded their ship.

Tonight, Captain Woo was in a state of elation beyond even that of the American Marines who had secured the beachhead. "When the Koreans see your power," he said, "they will come in droves to our side."

As we left the beach and headed back to the Navy flagship, naval guns were booming again in support of the Marines. "This time," said a battalion commander, "they are preparing the road to Seoul."

38. WITH THE MARINES IN KOREA:
A TRIAL BY BLOOD AND ICE

Keyes Beech of the Chicago Daily News relates
how they came out of Changjin Reservoir

Pulitzer Prize for International Reporting, 1951

Keyes Beech, a seasoned war correspondent and Marine combat correspondent in World War II, cabled the Chicago *Daily News* from Suwon, Korea, three days after Red armies surged south across the 38th Parallel on June 25, 1950:

"I have a feeling that I have just witnessed the beginning of World War III."

Critical, daring, reckless of his own safety, Beech was all over the Korean front. He fell back with the United States forces from Seoul in the disheartening long retreat at the outset of the war. When the counterattack came, he was up in the front lines and flew deep into North Korea after the Chinese "volunteers" intervened to cover the Marine breakout from Changjin Reservoir, one of his most brilliant stories.

With five other war correspondents, including his Chicago *Daily News* colleague, Fred Sparks, he was awarded a Pulitzer Prize in International Reporting for 1951. Here is his story of the Marine breakout.

FORTY MILES OF ICY HELL IN NORTH KOREA

By Keyes Beech

From the Chicago Daily News, Dec. 11, 1950

YONPO AIRSTRIP, KOREA—"Remember," drawled Colonel Lewis B. "Chesty" Puller, "whatever you write, that this was no retreat. All that happened was we found more Chinese behind us than in front of us. So we about-faced and attacked."

I said "so-long" to Puller after three snowbound days with the 1st Marine Division, 4,000 feet above sea level in the sub-zero weather of Changjin Reservoir. I climbed aboard a waiting C-47 at Koto Airstrip and looked around.

Sixteen shivering Marine casualties—noses and eyes dripping from cold—huddled in their bucket seats. They were the last of more than 2,500 Marine casualties to be evacuated by the U.S. Air Force under conditions considered flatly impossible.

Whatever this campaign was—retreat, withdrawal, or defeat—one thing can be said with certainty. Not in the Marine Corps' long and bloody history has there been anything like it. And if you'll pardon a personal recollection, not at Tarawa or Iwo Jima, where casualties were much greater, did I see men suffer as much.

The wonder isn't that they fought their way out against overwhelming odds but that they were able to survive the cold and fight at all. So far as the Marines themselves are concerned, they ask that two things be recorded:

1. They didn't break. They came out of Changjin Reservoir as an organized unit with most of their equipment.

2. They brought out all their wounded. They brought out many of their dead. And most of those they didn't bring out they buried.

It was not always easy to separate dead from wounded among the frozen figures that lay strapped to radiators of jeeps and trucks. I know because I watched them come in from Yudam to Hagaru, 18 miles of icy hell, five days ago.

That same day I stood in the darkened corner of a wind-whipped tent and listened to a Marine officer brief his men for the march to Koto the following day. I have known him for a long time but in the semidarkness, with my face half-covered by my parka, he didn't recognize me. When he did the meeting broke up. When we were alone, he cried. After that he was all right.

I hope he won't mind my reporting he cried, because he's a very large Marine and a very tough guy.

He cried because he had to have some sort of emotional release; because all his men were heroes and wonderful people; because the next day he was going to have to submit them to another phase in the trial by blood and ice. Besides, he wasn't the only one who cried.

In the Marines' twelve-day, forty-mile trek from Yudam to the "bottom of the hill," strange and terrible things happened.

Thousands of Chinese troops—the Marines identified at least six divisions totalling 60,000 men—boiled from every canyon and rained fire from every ridge. Sometimes they came close enough to throw grenades into trucks, jeeps, and ambulances.

Whistles sounded and Chinese ran up to throw grenades into Marine foxholes. Another whistle and the Chinese ran back.

Then mortar shells began to fall. The 3d Battalion of the 5th Marine Regiment was reduced to less than two companies but still was ordered to attack "regardless of cost."

"We had to do it," said Lieutenant Colonel Joe Stewart, of Montgomery, Ala. "It was the only way out."

Fox Company, 7th Regiment, was isolated for three or four days—nobody seems to remember dates or days—but held at terrible cost.

One company killed so many Chinese the Marines used their frozen bodies as a parapet. But for every Chinese they killed there were five, ten, or twenty to take his place.

"What'n hell's the use in killing them," said one Marine. "They breed faster 'n we can knock 'em off."

The Chinese had blown bridges and culverts behind the Americans. The Marines rebuilt them or established bypasses under fire.

No part of a division escaped, including headquarters sections composed of file clerks, cooks, and bakers. Bullets plowed through a Korean house in Hagaru occupied by General O. H. P. Smith.

Always the infantry had to take high ground on each side of the road to protect the train of vehicles that sometimes stretched ten miles.

When the Chinese attacked a train the artillerymen unhooked their guns from their vehicles and fired muzzle bursts from between trucks at the onrushing foe. This was effective, but rather rough on Marine machine gunners who had set up their guns on the railroad tracks fifteen or twenty yards in front of the artillery.

If there was an occasional respite from the enemy there was none from the cold. It numbed fingers, froze feet, sifted through layers of clothing, and crept into the marrow of your bones. Feet sweated by day and froze in their socks by night. Men peeled off their socks —and the soles of their feet with them.

Among the men of the 5th Marines, Lieutenant Commander Chester M. Lessenden Jr., of Lawrence, Kansas, a Navy doctor, became a hero.

"Lessenden is the most saintly, Godlike man I've ever known," said Stewart. "He never seemed to sleep. He was always on his feet. He never said it can't be done. And yet he was suffering from frostbite worse than most of the men he treated."

In their struggle to keep from freezing, the Marines wrapped their feet in gunnysacks or pieces of old cloth scrounged from the countryside. When they could, they built fires but this wasn't often because fire gave away their positions.

When they came at Koto before the final breakthrough to the sea they made tents of varicolored parachutes used by the Air Force to drop supplies. The red, white, and green chute tents looked like Indian wigwams.

Some covered themselves with Japanese quilts dropped from the air. But they were warmest when they were fighting. Combat was almost welcome because they forgot about the cold.

The cold did strange things to their equipment. Because of sub-zero temperatures artillery rounds landed as much as 2,000 yards short. Machine guns froze up. Men tugged frantically at their frozen bolts. The M-1 rifle generally held up but the Marines cursed the lighter carbine.

Communications gear broke down because equipment, like men, can stand only so much. Canteens burst as water froze inside them.

Despite all these things, the Marines who walked down from Changjin Reservoir still could laugh.

"It was impossible for us to get out because we were surrounded, encircled, and cut off," said one lieutenant. "But we never got the word so we came on out. That's us—we never get the word."

39. *THIS, TOO, WAS WAR IN KOREA:*
A HOME ON PORK CHOP HILL

Jim Lucas writes of life and death
in "Our Town" and "His Town"

Pulitzer Prize for International Reporting, 1954

Jim Lucas covered the Korean war for twenty-six of its thirty-six months. Like Ernie Pyle, he wrote of war from up front where the hard-bitten infantrymen were doing the fighting and the dying.

It was typical of Lucas to move up to the Imjin River in North Korea and report, "This is such a miserable country to die in. It's not that it's Korea. It would be miserable country if it were Ohio, Texas, Indiana, or Pennsylvania. War is universal and battlefields are the same . . ."

Lucas, like Pyle, caught some of the feelings of the soldiers at the front and was able to communicate them vividly to the American public. Here was no glory, no heroics, no victorious army to cheer—only the mud in the valleys and the freezing cold in the mountains, the frustrations of a war that couldn't be won and couldn't be lost.

Much more than the bulletin-type bang-bang news leads that were ground out at headquarters, Lucas's stories caught the attention of the public back home. And although he wrote primarily as a correspondent for the Scripps-Howard newspapers, many of his pieces were run in others as well. The following account, from the scene of one of the bloodiest battles the Americans fought with the Communists, is typical of his work.

"OUR TOWN" ON PORK CHOP HILL

By Jim Lucas

From the Scripps-Howard newspapers, Jan. 3, 1953

PORK CHOP HILL, KOREA, Jan. 3—Our Town atop Pork Chop Hill is in a world of its own.

Its contacts with the outside world are few—but imperative. Its immediate concern is the enemy on the next ridge. That's "His Town." To "His Town" Our Town gives grudging respect. But if possible, "His Town" is going to be wiped out.

Our Town's business is war. It produces nothing but death. To exist, therefore, it must rely on others. Food, mail, clothing—even the weapons of destruction—are shipped in.

These items are sent in from that part of the outside world which the men of Our Town call "rear." As often—and far more passionately—they are at war with "rear" as they are with the enemy. "Rear," which includes anything beyond the foot of Pork Chop, is populated, Our Town is convinced, by idiots and stumblebums.

Physically, Our Town—while hardly attractive—is not uncomfortable. Much municipal planning went into it.

The streets are six to eight feet deep. At times after dark, Our Town's streets are invaded by men from His Town. The citizens of Our Town invariably expel these interlopers. To assist in maintaining law and order on such occasions, the shelves along the streets of Our Town are liberally stocked with hand grenades.

There are thirty to fifty houses in Our Town. They are referred to as bunkers. Each street and each bunker is numbered. After a few days it's comparatively easy to find one's way.

Half of Our Town's bunkers are living quarters. The others are stores—storage bunkers, that is. From these you can obtain a wide assortment of ammunition, sandbags, candles, charcoal, or canned rations.

Our Town's buildings are sturdy. The typical building is at least six feet underground. It is made of four-by-ten-inch logs to which are added many sandbags. It's almost impervious to enemy shelling.

Our Town is not without its social life. I went visiting this morning at 19 Third Street in Our Town. Entering No. 19, one gets down on his hands and knees. The front door is low.

My hosts were First Lieutenant Pat Smith of Hollywood, Calif., Corporal Joe Siena of Portland, Conn., Private First Class Eddie Williams of Brooklyn, and Private Don Coan of Anadarko, Okla.

Don had coffee brewing in an old ration can. He opened a can of sardines. Eddie was heading for the rear on a shopping trip. His list included candles, a coffee pot (which he'd had on order for a month already), and a reel of communications wire. He also was taking a field telephone for repairs.

Our Town, like others, enjoys small talk. Over coffee, the group discussed what a man should do if a grenade-wielding Chinese suddenly appeared at the door. There was no unanimous decision.

Our Town has its own banker—Warrant Officer James W. Cherry of Jackson, Tenn. He came up the other afternoon. Within 300 yards of the enemy, he distributed $23,411.

Many men didn't want their money really. Money is an almost valueless commodity up here. Three days from now, the postal officer will come up the hill, selling money orders.

If money has no value, other things do. Things like candles, fuel, toilet tissue. There's never enough charcoal for the stoves which heat the bunkers. To stay warm you can climb into your sleeping bag—if you're a fool. The men refer to sleeping bags as "coffins." Too many soldiers have been killed before they could unzip their sleeping bags.

Our Town's Mayor is a tall, gangling Texan—Captain Jack Conn of Houston. He's company commander. The Vice Mayor is his executive officer—First Lieutenant Bill Gerald, also of Houston. Bill Gerald is a Negro.

The Battalion Commander, Lieutenant Colonel Seymour Goldberg of Washington, D.C., is convinced Our Town is a pigsty. Our Town's residents think Colonel Goldberg is a martinet.

Colonel Goldberg always arrives in a foul mood, to be expected, since high-up officials usually are blind to local problems. The Colonel expects miracles overnight. (Privately, he concedes this is an act—"If I didn't raise hell, they wouldn't take me seriously.")

Our Town endures this outsider stoically. The Colonel says the men need haircuts. "When would they have time to get haircuts?" says Our Town's citizens. He says the bunkers need cleaning. "They look all right to us," fume Our Towners. "We live here." He says ammunition isn't stored properly. "Let up on these all-night patrols and we'll store it right," retorts Our Town—not to the Colonel's face, of course.

Invariably the Colonel corrals a hapless private and demands he be court-martialed for one thing or another. Our Town's Mayor dutifully notes the boy's name and then throws away the notes when the Colonel leaves.

But the Colonel expects this.

There was much glee the other day when the Colonel issued an order that any man found outside a bunker without bullet-proof vest on be punished. A moment later, the Colonel left the bunker—and forgot his vest.

There's method in the Colonel's madness. He deliberately sets out to make Our Town hate him. "If I didn't," he says, "it would go to pot."

You see, the Colonel once was a company commander who hated "rear." But on Bloody Triangle Hill, he won a promotion. Now he's part of "rear." He knows he must prod the men up front, so that their outfit will remain—despite the presence of death itself—a proud, disciplined, organized Army fighting unit.

After lengthy negotiations, an armistice for Korea was signed by United Nations and Communist delegates at Panmunjon on July 27, 1953 and the fighting ceased. Jim Lucas was awarded the Pulitzer Prize for International Reporting for 1954 as the climax to his two years and two months of distinguished service as a war correspondent.

40. "THE GREAT DECEPTION" PRODUCES A GREAT STORY

Don Whitehead writes the story of President-elect Eisenhower's secret trip to Korea

Pulitzer Prize for National Reporting, 1953

Secrecy is one of the unhappy by-products of the search for security in this deepening age of space-piercing missiles and atomic power.

There are increasing demands on the press for restraints of all kinds. In the military, some would withhold more information from the American people. In the field of statecraft, tender-skinned diplomats think they could do more with the Russians if the press only wouldn't cover conferences. Some in the world of business wish talk of recessions could be kept out of the papers. And even at the local school-board level, one can find officials who would like to keep their activities under cover.

Small wonder, then, that newspapers generally are suspicious of anything that smacks of official secrecy—of the kind of pressure and behind-the-scenes regulation that would reduce a free press to the level of an official gazette. To the timid, this represents a spirit of anarchy which would put self-interest above all else.

And yet, the American press has kept secrets even when they seemed of doubtful value. It was demonstrated time and again during World War II and, perhaps even more spectacularly, during President-elect Dwight D. Eisenhower's six-day trip to the Korean battlefront in the late fall of 1952 in fulfillment of a campaign promise.

Hundreds, perhaps thousands, of American newspapermen and journalists of the other mass media knew of the trip. Thousands of Koreans knew about it, for Seoul was gay with banners of welcome for the distinguished visitor. Yet, not a word was published in the American press or broadcast by TV or radio during the period when General Eisenhower was in danger of a sneak enemy attack. If the Chinese or North Korean Communist armies knew of his presence, they gave no sign. And the first the world at large knew that the President-elect had been in Korea was when he already had left.

Of the three wire service correspondents who were selected by their organizations to make the trip, Don Whitehead won nation-wide recognition for his 4,400-word account of "The Great Deception" for the Associated Press. A tall, soft-spoken Kentuckian, he had distinguished himself as a war correspondent both in World War II and Korea and already held a Pulitzer Prize for his Korean coverage in 1951. He also had covered the 1952 Presidential campaign, and therefore was known to General Eisenhower as a political reporter as well.

Whitehead wrote no bulletin leads. He didn't attempt to jam the last-minute news in the first sentence. Slowly, carefully, calmly, he developed his story in chronological fashion so that it still stands the test of time.

Here it is, a moment in history, when the American press for six days maintained complete silence about the whereabouts of the President-elect of the United States.

THREE FATEFUL DAYS IN KOREA

By Don Whitehead

From the Associated Press, Dec. 5, 1952

WITH EISENHOWER IN KOREA, Dec. 5—It was 5:30 a.m. (EST) on Saturday, November 29, when two men stepped quickly through the doorway of the residence at 60 Morningside Drive in New York City into the cold, star-lit night.

Their overcoat collars were turned up as though against the chill. They strode swiftly to the limousine that had pulled up at the curb a few feet from the doorway, ducked into the car, and it drove away. The street was bare and silent once again.

One of the men was United States Secret Service Agent Edward Green and the other was President-elect Eisenhower. This was the beginning of the Eisenhower mission to Korea where he hoped—as millions of Americans did—that a way could be found to bring an honorable end to the bloody fighting which in two and a half years had claimed 126,000 American dead, wounded, and missing.

As the Eisenhower car drove toward Mitchel Field, the Air Force base on Long Island, other automobiles in other parts of the city moved in a precision pattern, also converging on Mitchel Field. There two big Air Force Constellations waited in the darkness.

A few minutes before Eisenhower had left his Morningside Heights residence, Defense Secretary-designate Charles E. Wilson had strolled out of the Waldorf-Astoria Hotel and entered a cab. He told the driver to drop him off at the southeast corner of 58th Street and Fifth Avenue.

This gray-haired, distinguished industrialist—president of the General Motors Corp.—stepped out at the designated spot, paid the driver, and then stood on the street corner for a moment.

The sounds of the city were muted at this hour. A few cruising cabs drove by and a few pedestrians walked quickly in the cold streets. A car drew up beside Mr. Wilson, the door opened, and he stepped inside. It drove off into the pattern that was forming.

From a half dozen different points, six reporters and photographers quietly left their lodgings and converged on Pennsylvania Station, which sounds like an improbable place for secrecy in movements.

But the six were lost among the other early travelers waiting for their trains, lounging in doorways and trying to kill time.

A black limousine drove down the ramp to the unloading platform and the six news men strolled one by one to the car driven by Secret Service Agent Ed Sweeney. The group was joined by Eisenhower's press secretary, James C. Hagerty.

Mr. Sweeney moved out quickly toward the East River, across the big Triborough Bridge over the East River and out on Long Island to a back road paralleling Mitchel Field. The car stopped at a gate, a light was flashed, some one said the magic words, "Secret

Service," to a major who then identified the occupants by name.

The gate opened and we followed a car that swung suddenly into the gate to guide us. Then the big Constellation loomed ahead. We stepped out into the sharp, chill wind.

"I'm sorry we don't have coffee," an Air Force general said, "but security cuts down the number of people we can use at this hour."

There were two Constellations, one for General Eisenhower and his party of seven. They included General Eisenhower's old friend, General Omar N. Bradley, chairman of the Joint Chiefs of Staff, who had flown up from Washington; Major General Wilton B. Persons (retired), his close friend and White House assistant-to-be; Herbert Brownell of New York, who will be the Attorney General in the Republican administration; Mr. Wilson; James Rowley, Secret Service Agent in charge of the White House detail; and Lieutenant John Davies, who was to act as General Eisenhower's secretary.

The second plane carried the newspaper men; Colonel Paul T. Carroll of Woonsocket, R.I., temporarily assigned to the party; Mr. Hagerty, and Secret Service Agent Richard Flohr.

In addition, both planes carried double crews of twenty-two men. This was a total of thirty-nine on board the ships.

The Eisenhower plane took off at 5:55 a.m., just as the blackness was turning to gray. The second plane followed ten minutes later. At 2:55 p.m. and 2,641 miles later the planes set down at Travis Field near San Francisco to refuel. An hour later they were off for the long overseas flight to Hickam Field, Hawaii.

No one left the planes at Travis. The ships paused just long enough to take on the fuel and then they roared westward again.

It was just after midnight when the lights of Honolulu showed on the horizon, sparkling in the dark sea like jewels reflecting the brightness of the round moon. The planes swept out of the darkness onto the Hickam Field runway and taxied to a secluded part of the field. Again no one left the planes as crews swarmed into the wings to fill the tanks. Minutes later we were air-borne again.

Midway Island was next—1,320 miles and 4 hours and 50 minutes later. Gulls, terns, and those ridiculous members of the albatross family known as gooney birds wheeled overhead or gathered in conclaves near the apron of the field.

The gooney birds—some with wingspreads up to nine feet—

appeared to be putting on a show just for the amusement of the
General and his party. They waddled toward each other, touched
bills, bowed, curtsied, and then danced about in solemn and absurd
tribal rites.

Our ships were traveling under false identifications and numbers,
but there was tight security across the whole Pacific from San Francisco to Korea to guard against any leak that General Eisenhower
was en route.

It was Sunday, November 30, when we left Midway on the longest
oversea hop of the trip—the 2,695 miles to Iwo Jima. But a few
minutes after leaving the island it was Monday. Our ships had
crossed the International Dateline.

Our press plane was less than halfway to Iwo Jima when the
No. 1 engine began losing power. Major Thomas E. Dye, of Somer-
set, Ky., was forced to feather the prop and we flew with only three
engines. A fuel pump had gone bad.

Major Dye headed for Wake Island for emergency repairs and
radioed his decision to the Eisenhower plane. "Message received,"
was the only reply, a curt reminder that security even prohibited
any talking back and forth between the planes. But we learned
later that General Eisenhower and his group were concerned over
our safety until they learned we had limped into Wake Island safely.

It seemed to us that the whole population of Wake Island had
turned out to see our plane land and we wondered if the news of
General Eisenhower's trip hadn't already swept around the world.

But Richard Fisher, United States Commissioner on the island
and Pan American Airways manager, came aboard and assured us
that the island had been "secured" and communications were being
watched so that inter-island traffic would reveal nothing unusual.

With this assurance, the Secret Service and security guard permitted us to leave the plane for the first time since we had left
New York.

Three hours later the faulty fuel injector had been repaired and
we were roaring off Wake Island toward Iwo Jima.

The Eisenhower ship landed on Iwo Jima at 3:30 p.m. and we
landed five hours later.

One of General Eisenhower's first acts on Iwo Jima was to visit
the Marine memorial on Mount Suribachi—that knob of a hill where

a gallant little band of warriors in February, 1945, raised the American flag in defiance of the Japanese making a fanatical defense of this island.

There the General stood looking out across the black beaches where 21,000 men were killed or wounded in trying to storm the stronghold. And he was told the story of Iwo Jima by Colonel W. W. Buchanan, of Athens, Ga., who was the assistant operations officer for the 4th Marine Division, and by M/Sergeant Robert T. Fox of Honolulu and Long Beach, Calif., who had been with the 2d Battalion of the 24th Marine Regiment on the assault.

The General turned in early—before 8 p.m.—to get a good night's rest. He hadn't been off his ship until Iwo, and most of this time he had spent in getting briefings from General Bradley and reports from the Korean war zone.

The General had just gone to bed when Captain Wayne Melvin, of Los Angeles, rang his telephone—thinking it was the number for the base commander.

Telling the story later, Captain Melvin said:

"I rang No. 10 and after a while somebody answered and I asked if Major Weldon was there.

"This guy said, no, Weldon wasn't there and I asked if he knew where I could reach Weldon.

"He said: 'No, I'm just a visitor here.' And then I knew I was talking to Eisenhower."

The island had begun to buzz with excitement the day before when planes began landing and depositing V.I.P.s, a staff car, and six brand-new refrigerators for the officers' quarters.

Second Lieutenant Eugene G. Hobbie, of Red Level, Ala., said he figured it had to be General Eisenhower who was coming to Iwo.

"When they brought those refrigerators in from Japan and then a staff car," he said, "I couldn't see them doing it for anybody but Eisenhower. So I went around making bets with the guys on who was coming in.

"Most of them figured it was a command staff meeting and I got $60 bet that it would be Ike."

Then another plane came in to Iwo carrying security police, special cooks and waiters, and service personnel to handle the influx of visitors.

These men had received only an hour's notice to pack and get ready to move to an unknown destination.

Second Lieutenant William H. Thompson, of Chicago, said he was told to get ready for an emergency assignment. He was the food supply officer at the Air Force base at Tachikawa, Japan.

"I said I had a day off coming to me and I wasn't supposed to work that day," Lieutenant Thompson said with a grin. "The man said, 'That's just too bad, because you are leaving in an hour.'"

The Eisenhower party was billeted in spanking clean Quonset huts just a few yards from the beach where the Americans stormed Iwo Jima in one of the bloodiest battles of World War II. Sentries patrolled the huts throughout the night and Secret Service agents kept watch with them.

A young officer said to me:

"They told us to give you everything you wanted—and if you asked for the battleship *Missouri,* then I was to call for the island commander and he would see what he could do about that."

The first time reporters saw General Eisenhower on the trip was at breakfast next day, December 2. He came into the officers' mess about 7:30 a.m., looking rested and in top condition. He grinned and waved to those in the room.

"By golly," he said, "I got into bed at 7 o'clock last night and then I woke up at 4 o'clock this morning and had a devil of a time going back to sleep."

After breakfast, the General agreed to go back up to Suribachi so that cameramen could get the picture they had missed the day before. He rode in a Chevrolet sedan to the foot of Suribachi, and then climbed out to transfer to a jeep for the steep climb up a dusty trail cut out of the side of the hill.

Mr. Wilson asked the driver why the change was being made from the sedan to the jeep.

"That hill's too steep for the Chevrolet to make it," the driver said.

"Are you sure?" Mr. Wilson asked.

"I'm damned sure, Sir," the youth replied.

Later, the driver was told he had been talking to the next Secretary of Defense and the man whose company makes Chevrolets.

"Oh, lordy," he exclaimed. "I put my foot in my mouth, didn't I?" He was assured he had—both feet.

General Eisenhower's plane took off at 2 p.m. from Iwo for the 1,700-mile flight to Seoul. The overnight stop at Iwo had been planned so that he would arrive in Korea after nightfall.

It was 7:57 p.m., Korea time (5:57 a.m., Tuesday, in New York City) when the General's plane touched down on the icy runway near Seoul. It had spanned the 10,836 miles between New York and Korea in 47 hours 15 minutes' flying time. The temperature was 10 degrees above zero.

Armed guards and Secret Service agents waited on the field— but there was no welcoming committee. General Mark Clark, Supreme Allied Commander in the Far East, had remained at the United States 8th Army headquarters in Seoul with General James Van Fleet, 8th Army commander. The only newspapermen present were those in the Eisenhower party. Their plane had landed twenty minutes ahead of the General's.

General Eisenhower stepped from his plane wearing civilian clothes and only a medium-weight brown camel's hair overcoat to shield him from Korea's wintry winds, the coldest of the season.

The General quickly climbed into a waiting sedan with General Bradley and Mr. Wilson. Two Secret Service agents—Messrs. Rowley and Flohr—were in the front seat. Then the heavily guarded caravan moved quickly across a land of frozen rice paddies into the war-battered city of Seoul.

Only President Syngman Rhee of the Republic of Korea had any notice of the General's arrival. But there was plenty of evidence that the President-elect was expected. Banners and arches across the streets carried messages of welcome—and appeal.

They said, "Welcome President-elect Eisenhower." Others read: "Drive away the Chinese Reds"—"Strengthen R.O.K. Forces"—"We Oppose Withdrawal Of United Nations Forces."

At 8th Army headquarters, General Eisenhower was warmly welcomed by Generals Clark and Van Fleet—and the first thing he asked for was hot chocolate. He retired shortly after dinner.

The General was up early on Dec. 3 and spent the morning being briefed on the Korean situation by Generals Clark and Van Fleet and others.

General Clark later told this reporter: "We gave him the whole story including the problems that lie ahead for us." He didn't say what the problems were.

After lunch, General Eisenhower was flown in an L-19 "puddle-jumper" plane to an air field where he visited a fighter interceptor squadron and the 67th Tactical Reconnaissance Wing headquarters.

This time he wore regular Army issue winter clothing—with no insignia. The winter clothing had been issued to the General and those in his party during the morning. He was accompanied by the entire group which had traveled with him from New York—and by his son, Major John Eisenhower, who is stationed in Korea as an assistant operations officer for the 3d Infantry Division.

Major Eisenhower had flown from the front early in the morning to see his father and to stay with him during his Korean visit. It was the first time he had seen his father since July.

Outside the squadron headquarters, General Eisenhower stopped to shake hands with Captain Herbert Weber, of Brattleboro, Vt., a jet pilot just back from a mission along the Yalu River.

"Did you get any MiGs?" General Eisenhower asked.

"We saw some," Captain Weber said, "but we didn't get into any fights."

On the apron of the field, General Eisenhower stopped to chat for a moment with Lieutenant Ira M. Porter, of Fort Worth, Tex., a 23-year-old jet pilot with two MiGs to his credit—and a Silver Star for heroism in action.

A few minutes later, he was flying from the air field toward the 1st Marine Division headquarters on the fighting front while F-86 Sabre jets swept the skies on the lookout for any enemy planes trying a sneak attack from the north.

The frozen land below—white with ice and snow—showed the scars of old battles.

The little planes carrying the Eisenhower party set down on an air strip six miles from the actual battle line. But in this area a sniper had shot a Marine two nights before.

The Marine band—waiting in 8-above-zero weather—played "Ruffles and Flourishes" for the President-elect. Just as the echoes faded into the bleak hills there was the sound of sharp explosions.

"What are they dropping in here?" General Eisenhower snapped.

The officers near by laughed and explained that a pilot had just fired four rockets into enemy positions—the sound carrying for miles in the sharp, cold mountain air.

General Eisenhower was given a secret briefing of the situation along the Marines' front. And when he was ready to visit another unit his son couldn't be found. He had wandered away for a moment.

When he returned, General Van Fleet said: "You're the General's aide. That's your job. Stick with him." But the rebuke was given with a smile.

In mid-afternoon the General arrived at 1st Corps headquarters where units of fighting men from fifteen nations stood stiffly at attention in the bitter cold. General Eisenhower had changed his G.I. hat for an overseas cap. He "trooped the line" and then stood on a platform at the edge of the air strip while the troops marched in review with a color guard carrying the American and United Nations flags.

The Australians came first—tall men with wide-brimmed hats— and then the British, Belgians, Canadians, Colombians and Ethiopians. There were Frenchmen, Greeks, Koreans, and Dutchmen, New Zealanders, Filipinos, Thailanders, and Turks, and finally units of the United States Army and Marines.

Loud speakers had been set up with a microphone on the stand— and every one expected the General to make a talk to the troops who symbolized the effort of the free world to resist aggression. But General Eisenhower remained silent.

From the reviewing stand, he went to corps headquarters, where he received another briefing on the battle situation in this zone of the front. Then he flew back to Seoul for an hour-long talk with President Rhee, who came to 8th Army headquarters.

One source said Mr. Rhee had proposed a seven-point program calling, in part, for a free and unified Korea; strengthening of the R.O.K. forces, and U. N. aid for the reconstruction of Korea.

But there was no report that the General had made any promises on what he might do—although he has advocated building up the military strength of South Korea in order to lift some or all of the burden of fighting from American troops in Korea.

General Eisenhower's second day in Korea—Thursday, Dec. 4—was a whirlwind visit of United Nations combat units in the snow-covered valleys near the front.

I asked soldier after soldier how he felt about the President-elect's visit—and there was not one who did not say he was glad the General had made the trip and that he had hopes General Eisenhower would find a way to end the war.

Sergeant Joseph Kililea, of County Roscommon, Ireland—in the British Commonwealth Division—put it this way: "If anybody can end it, General Eisenhower can. He's the man to do it, sir."

Lieutenant John Condit, of Baltimore, said: "The boys all hope Ike can do something. But they aren't expecting miracles."

Captain Paul Morrissey, of 43 Kelsey Avenue, Trenton, N. J., said: "We feel at least he might come up with something to end this thing."

And so it went—a feeling that somewhere, somehow, the General would find a way out for them in this stalemated war.

General Eisenhower traveled from unit to unit by plane—an L-19 —hopping over the frozen mountains from valley to valley sometimes in sight of the front, where Air Force and Navy planes were hitting the enemy positions with napalm and bombs.

During the day, the General visited the Commonwealth Division, the R.O.K. 1st Division, a surgical hospital, a R.O.K. cavalry unit, and the United States 2d and 3d Divisions. After more than thirty-four hours, only a few of the front-line troops knew he was in Korea.

At the 3d Division command post, General Eisenhower ate lunch with members of the 15th Regiment—the battalion which he commanded only twelve years ago as a lieutenant colonel. The soldiers didn't know they were to lunch with General Eisenhower until they saw him climb from a jeep.

While General Clark, General Van Fleet, and the other generals and V.I.P.s went into a mess tent for lunch, General Eisenhower sat on a pine box in the near-zero weather to eat and chat with Sergeant Jack R. Hutcherson, of Frankford, Mo., Corporal James A. Murray, of Muskogee, Okla., and Private First Class Casper Skudlarck, of Avon, Minn.

The social atmosphere was a bit strained as newspapermen and photographers crowded around them to watch every bite and to picture every move. The General—again wearing no insignia—cleaned his tray of pork chops, mashed potatoes, gravy, sauerkraut, peas, and apple pie.

Later, he watched a R.O.K. unit assault a hill in realistic training maneuvers. Mr. Wilson, General Bradley, General Clark, General Van Fleet, Mr. Brownell, and President Rhee were among the spectators.

When it was over, Mr. Rhee presented General Eisenhower with a big silk Republic of Korea flag and the General said, "I assure you, Mr. President, that it will hang in a suitable place where people will see it and not forget it."

Mr. Rhee and the South Korean generals have made it clear to General Eisenhower during his visit that they favor his plan to build up the strength of the South Korean Army.

General Eisenhower returned to 8th Army headquarters in midafternoon and one of his visitors was Major General William Chase, who heads the United States military mission in Formosa. This conference was a hint that General Eisenhower also was getting a fill-in on Chiang Kai-shek's Nationalist Chinese Army and its capabilities.

The General's third day in Korea was reserved for a news conference and further talks with General Chase and other military men. He refused to talk politics and concentrated on the problems of peace.

These were three fateful days for Korea—and the world.

The American press broke its six-day voluntary silence about the President-elect's trip just an hour after his departure from Korea on December 5, 1952. In addition to the stories written by Whitehead and the two other wire service correspondents who had been with the Eisenhower party, many thousands of words also were filed by correspondents regularly stationed with the troops in Korea and by the stay-at-home Washington correspondents.

Out of this tremendous flood of words, the Whitehead story—which was not written to capture the top headlines on Page 1—captured the imaginations of most American editors and their readers. It was awarded the Pulitzer Prize for National Reporting for 1953—Whitehead's second Pulitzer recognition. He is now chief of the New York *Herald Tribune's* Washington bureau.

41. THE DES MOINES REGISTER BRINGS
THE RUSSIANS TO IOWA'S TALL CORN

Lauren K. Soth writes a simple invitation
with enormous impact on a bi-polar world

Pulitzer Prize for Editorial Writing, 1956

Iowans are direct and friendly people. And Lauren K. Soth, editorial page editor of the Des Moines *Register* and *Tribune,* speaks for a lot of them.

On February 10, 1955, he casually wrote an editorial in the *Register* inviting the Russians to come to Iowa. He really didn't think anything would come of it. But, he insisted, it *was* a good idea.

From this beginning, the United States and Russia cautiously developed a program of cultural and scientific exchange visits. If Lauren Soth had not acted on his idea, who can say if Pianist Van Cliburn would have had quite so easy a time getting to Moscow for his now-historic triumph, or if the State Department would have been quite so ready to admit the Moiseyev dancers for a tour that was climaxed by a one-hour national TV show?

There is, moreover, no way of measuring the effect of the cultural exchange, nor of predicting whether it will grow or collapse. But for the uncertain period of its duration, the cold war has seemed at times to be a trifle less menacing.

Soth himself would be the last to forecast what the future will bring. But for his key role in trying to bring two peoples closer together and thus attempting to relax international tension, he won the Pulitzer Prize for Editorial Writing in 1956. Here is his prize-winning editorial.

IF THE RUSSIANS WANT MORE MEAT . . .

By Lauren K. Soth

From the Des Moines Register, Feb. 10, 1955

Nikita Khrushchev, who seems to be the real boss of the Soviet Union now, signaled his emergence to power by a well-publicized speech before the Central Committee last month, lambasting the performance of the Soviet economic managers. In this speech

Khrushchev especially attacked the management of agriculture. And in doing so, he took the rare line of praising the United States.

Khrushchev advocated the development of feed-livestock agriculture as in the United States. "Americans have succeeded in achieving a high level of animal husbandry," he said. He urged Soviet collective and state farms to plant hybrid corn to provide more feed for livestock. And he demanded an eightfold increase in corn production by 1960.

Speaking as an Iowan, living in the heart of the greatest feed-livestock area of the world, we wish to say that, for once, the Soviet leader is talking sense. That's just what the Russian economy needs—more and better livestock so the Russian people can eat better.

We have no diplomatic authority of any kind, but we hereby extend an invitation to any delegation Khrushchev wants to select to come to Iowa to get the lowdown on raising high quality cattle, hogs, sheep, and chickens. We promise to hide none of our "secrets." We will take the visiting delegation to Iowa's great agricultural experiment station at Ames, to some of the leading farmers of Iowa, to our livestock breeders, soil conservation experts, and seed companies. Let the Russians see how we do it.

Furthermore, we would be glad to go to Russia with a delegation of Iowa farmers, agronomists, livestock specialists, and other technical authorities. Everything we Iowans know about corn, other feed grains, forage crops, meat animals, and the dairy and poultry industries will be available to the Russians for the asking.

We ask nothing in return. We figure that more knowledge about the means to a good life in Russia can only benefit the world and us. It might even shake the Soviet leaders in their conviction that the United States wants war; it might even persuade them that there is a happier future in developing a high level of living than in this paralyzing race for more and more armaments.

Of course the Russians wouldn't do it. And we doubt that even our own government would dare to permit an adventure in human understanding of this sort. But it *would* make sense.

Somewhat to Lauren Soth's surprise, both the United States and Russia went for his idea. And on July 18, 1955, a Russian farm delegation of twelve headed by V. V. Matskevich, later to become the Soviet Minister of Agriculture, flew to Des Moines.

The Russians took full advantage of every part of the invitation extended so unofficially by an American newspaper which thought merely that it would be a good idea. When they returned to their own country, they proceeded to introduce Iowa methods to Soviet agriculture with results that obviously pleased both Matskevich and his boss, Khrushchev.

Soth, in return, toured Russian farm lands with an American delegation and wrote articles for his newspaper poking some very large holes into the Soviet agricultural system as compared with operations conducted in the American midlands.

"We did not see everything we wanted to see, as was to be expected," he concluded. "The Kremlin cannot get over its fears of observation from the outside, for it well knows that the Soviet system cannot stand comparison with the West.

"Nevertheless, the freedom we had was a far cry from the way foreigners have been treated in Russia during most of the last ten years."

42. "A FIGHT TO THE DEATH":
RUSSELL JONES COVERS BUDAPEST

A United Press correspondent reports
a hopeless battle for freedom

Pulitzer Prize for International Reporting, 1957

"It is 10 minutes past 2 a.m. in Budapest."

Russell Jones, who had just arrived in the stricken Hungarian capital that October 29, 1956, was dictating to the United Press bureau in Vienna by telephone.

"The roar of tanks on the move thunders across this aching city. But in the darkness before dawn only the Russian commanders know if the rumbling of armor means more death or peace at last.

"Is the Soviet army withdrawing? Here in the Hotel Duna—the word means Danube—you can't tell the direction of the grinding gears and the groaning engines."

Soon Jones knew. And he and the handful of correspondents remaining in the city told a shocked, incredulous world that the Russians were mowing down the rebellious Hungarians without remorse, without pity, without shame. Already, 3,000 persons had been killed in that vain bid for freedom—bare hands against tanks.

How many more were to die? What was Budapest's fate?

In the thirty-seven bloody, terror-stricken days and nights that followed, Russell Jones covered Budapest. Often he was under fire. Many times he couldn't get through censorship. And when he did, sometimes he could say but a few hasty, cryptic words and leave it to his associates to do the best they could.

That was reporting.

In the Jones file which was awarded the Pulitzer Prize for International Reporting for 1957, there are many stories that crept through censorship. Some had to be combined with events elsewhere, so that Jones's stuff frequently was woven into the news pattern of a great wire service— day leads, night leads, bulletins, overnites, and all the rest.

Yet the stamp of his reporting from the scene was on every piece of United Press copy datelined Budapest. Here are some of his own stories from the file of the United Press (now United Press International) during the period from October 29 to December 3 while he was on the job in Budapest.

A REPORTER WEEPS FOR BUDAPEST

By Russell Jones

From the United Press file, Oct. 29-Dec. 3, 1956

BUDAPEST, Nov. 15 (UP)—Life as the only American correspondent left in shattered Budapest is sometimes frightening, sometimes amusing. But mostly it is a continuous feeling of inadequacy both as an American and a reporter who helplessly watched the murder of a people.

For the first time since I was a boy I wept.

I saw a former British soldier break down completely. The situation was worse than the Warsaw uprising into which he was parachuted in 1944.

None of us are Hemingways and it needs a Hemingway to tell this story adequately.

Since a convoy of other newsmen left Budapest under Russian guard last week-end there have been five Western journalists left to tell the world what happens here. There are two British reporters, a Frenchman, a stateless person, and myself.

Except for the stateless person, who has continued to live in the shelter of the British legation, all of us are gathered in the Duna Hotel on the East bank of the Danube.

In the last few days our life has settled down to a routine struggle —checking with Western diplomats for their reports on the situation, futile attempts to interview the puppet regime of Janos Kadar, endless wandering through the city to find out what is going on, and hours-long struggles for telephone connections with the outside world.

Our average day: Sleeping in hotel rooms—unheated in near freezing weather—then rushing for a bath before the hot water supply is cut off at 9 a.m. Then down to the hotel lobby where everyone is sitting family-style at two long tables. The dining room itself is unusable since Russian shells have knocked out two of the huge windows.

The food—bread and bad coffee for breakfast—comes from the basement as the kitchen was destroyed by a Soviet attack.

After a quick check of the situation we start our morning struggle to telephone. Sometimes we find ourself with a story written but no telephone, and other times with a connection but no news.

Our tours of the town are punctuated by frequent checks by Soviet soldiers or Hungarian AVO—secret police.

Treatment at the check points can vary from a polite salute and waving hands to the suspicious examination of all papers by an AVO man apparently unable to read. As the evening curfew at 7 p.m. local time nears, the checks become more rigorous—and more frightening. One correspondent was killed and three others wounded in the early stages of the revolt and none of us is anxious to join the casualty list.

Walking through the city is made more difficult by masses of Hungarians streaming along in their search for food and wandering aimlessly through the wreckage, determined to continue their general strike until the Russians leave. They have nothing else to do.

Our meals are shared by a handful of prostitutes, elderly "class enemies" who returned from deportation after the revolt, a Swiss Red Cross man, a Czech businessman whose faith in Communism has been shaken, and a few ordinary Hungarians bombed out of their homes.

A strange multilingual community has been established with the Hungarians watching for news, the prostitutes washing the correspondents' laundry, and correspondents completing less eagerly the normal work of the newsman.

One of the few bright spots in the city is the Grand Hotel on Margaret Island, isolated from the rest of the city by the Danube River. The Island might be a thousand miles away from the scene of death and destruction.

Yesterday I lunched there with Mrs. Tanya Rahmann, wife of the Indian Charge D'Affaires in Budapest, and rarely have had a more pleasant meal. But it was a brief interlude.

On leaving, as on entering the Island, I made a sharp right turn literally under the guns of a huge Soviet tank, which stood at a Soviet check point on Margaret Island, and drove back to the tangle of fallen street car wires, piles of rubble, and crowds of hopeless, desperate people.

A NOTE FOR LOUIS IN AMERICA

BUDAPEST, Nov. 21 (UP)—They ask the same whispered questions in the hurried conversations that spring up wherever the only American goes in search of news in Budapest.

"How do I get out? . . . What are the borders like?"

"How many times do the Russians check you before the borders?"

The news has come to this battle-torn city that President Eisenhower will allow 5,000 Hungarian refugees to enter the United States. Hungarians want to know how to get out and this reporter is a busy man.

Already the U. S. legation has been besieged by dozens of Hungarians seeking visas under the "Eisenhower Plan."

While the fighting was going on, many a newspaperman received tearful pleas for help, for moral support from the freedom fighters—both men and women. Now there are the whispers, and the notes. Dozens and dozens of times, in three weeks in Budapest, you have found the notes.

You come back to your car and find a note stuck under the windshield wiper. You find them under your plate at lunch. They are slipped into your hand as you pass by.

Sometimes they want you to get word to relatives in America. At the Csepel Island Steelworks south of Budapest yesterday, a hand reached out of the crowd and pressed a dirty scrap of paper into my hand.

"To Louis Menyhert, 34-54 89th St., Jackson Heights (New York City)," a scratchy pencil had written. "We are all living. I also have uncles in San Diego and Detroit. We miss them."

It was signed "Louis."

To the Louis in Long Island, I can only say: Your friend or relative is safe. I did not see him, only the hand, but there is his message and God bless him.

After Jones's expulsion from Budapest, he wrote as follows about the battle of Budapest.

WHY BUDAPEST FOUGHT

LONDON, Dec. 10—The greatest shock to the Hungarian Communists and their Russian masters must have been the type of people who fought the hardest.

Believe none of the stories that this was a misguided uprising fomented to restore the great estate owners of the Horthy regency or the industrial magnates. I saw with my own eyes who was fighting and heard with my ears why they fought.

The first armed resistance came from students of the schools and universities, the youth who had been so carefully selected as the party elite of the future.

The fiercest fighters were the workers, the proletarians in whose name Communism had ruled. Even the Hungarian army, purged and repurged a dozen times, joined the battle for freedom or sat on the sidelines.

The two big names that came out of the revolt were Communist— Imre Nagy, a lifelong party member, and Lieutenant Colonel Pal Maleter, who had deserted to the Russians in World War II and returned as a Red partisan.

Wherever came the spark, it found its tinder among the common people.

The areas of destruction, the buildings most desperately defended and the dead themselves are the most eloquent proof of this. It was the workers' tenements that Soviet siege guns smashed, factory buildings that became forts and the tired shabby men with broken shoes and horny hands of the laborer who died by the thousands. The women with their hair bound with kerchiefs and the cheap and tawdry dresses of working people.

A seventeen-year-old girl, twice wounded at Corvin Theatre, told me she fought because "it isn't right that my father with four children to feed should get only 900 florints ($80) a month."

The chairman of the Workers' Council at the Csepel Iron and Steel plant with 38,000 workers, biggest in the country, said, "These are our factories. We will fight to the death to hold them. But we will continue plant maintenance because we want to work here again."

In Dorog, one of the coal centers, miners continued to work despite the general strike. But not to produce coal. They didn't want *their* mines ruined by flooding.

The same attitude is true in the country. The farmers want to get out of the collectives but they do not want the restoration of the landlords. They think everyone should have the right to own and till his own land. Something like 100 acres a family would be fair, they think.

It was for these simple, basic things that the Hungarian people fought. These and the right to speak and think freely, to elect men of their own choice, and to raise their children in their own way.

They will go on fighting for them.

About 30,000 Hungarians are estimated to have died in Budapest, according to some observers. The Hungarian Communist regime puts the figure far lower. How many rebels were executed and deported may not be known for a long time. The Soviet Union lifted the curtain with the announcement in 1958 that Imre Nagy and General Pal Maleter had been executed. Thus, a fight for freedom behind the Iron Curtain was lost.

43. EISENHOWER AND DULLES,

AS JAMES RESTON SAW THEM

*Two pieces for the Sunday side of the New York Times
help win him a Pulitzer Prize*

Pulitzer Prize for National Reporting, 1957

From Homer to Ernie Pyle, reporters in all ages have brought a compelling fascination to the story of war. "Scotty" Reston's greatest contribution to American journalism is that he has brought the same vitality and excitement to the faltering story of the peacemakers.

Born in Scotland in 1909 and graduated from the University of Illinois in 1932, James Barrett Reston traveled a roundabout path to achieve eminence as the chief Washington correspondent of the New York *Times* and winner of two Pulitzer Prizes. He broke in with the Springfield (Ohio) *Daily News,* worked as a publicity man for Ohio State University and the Cincinnati Reds (now patriotically renamed the Redlegs) and became an Associated Press reporter. In 1939, he shifted to the London bureau of the New York *Times,* for two years covered the "blitz" that failed, and then turned up in the Washington bureau.

In 1944 he carried off top journalistic honors at the Dumbarton Oaks conference to prepare the way for the founding of the United Nations, breaking one exclusive story after another by Restonian boldness and guile. No one had done that well at a quasi-peace talk since Herbert Bayard Swope at Versailles.

It was only the beginning of Reston's adventures. After winning the Pulitzer Prize for National Reporting in 1945 for giving the world the first news of American, British, and Russian peace plans, he embarked on many other exploits. A rather slight, mild, inoffensive-looking man with a bland smile and a deceptively open approach, he established a reputation among both diplomats and newspapermen for being able to judge the point of origin of a big story as unerringly as Willie Mays ever went back for a fly ball. When reporters gathered impatiently to await the arrival of the Secretary of State or some other diplomatic potentate, it sometimes happened that Reston would drive up with the news source a willing captive.

Some of this, of course, was due to the reputation of the New York *Times* for printing textual and other formal material at lengths economically barred to most competing newspapers. But often Reston was able to get material on his own. He broke the text of the Japanese peace treaty, got the Yalta papers out of the State Department but had to share them with an indignant Chicago *Tribune*, presented Dr. J. Robert Oppenheimer's defense to security charges, and had a three-hour exclusive interview with Nikita S. Khrushchev in Moscow at a time when such interviews were still news.

Reston's second Pulitzer Prize, awarded for his National Reporting in 1957, saluted his all-around ability as an interpreter of national affairs. The following two pieces, selected from his 1956 Pulitzer file, were published as columns on the editorial page of the Sunday edition of the *Times*. This was at a time when President Eisenhower, having recovered from his heart attack, was trying to decide whether to run for a second term and establishing a reputation for devastating honesty in connection with his health problems. It was a time, too, when Secretary of State Dulles was somewhat more on the defensive than usual in the ups-and-downs of the cold war. Reston's 1956 estimates of Eisenhower and Dulles follow.

EISENHOWER: A GOOD MAN IN A BAD TRADE

By James Reston

From the New York Times, Jan. 15, 1956

WASHINGTON, Jan. 21—The Republicans did everything but canonize President Eisenhower this week at the start of his fourth year in the White House but, in a way, they forgot their best point.

He is not another Washington or Lincoln, as the party orators proclaimed Friday night, but an honest man who has proved that simple goodness is still a great force in national and world politics.

In a city and a world that have lately been rewarding men for their bad qualities rather than their good qualities—for slickness rather than genuineness, for glibness rather than sincerity, for appearance rather than for substance and character—this just happens to be about the most important contribution a public man can make.

To puff him up into a genius, as his well-meaning partisan colleagues have been doing this week, blurs his true quality and denies him the satisfaction he would treasure the most.

This is his realization that the American system of government will work under the leadership of a man who is faithful to the ordinary decencies and durable principles of American life and that the people will instinctively prefer such a man to more brilliant and profound competitors.

The success of his simple honesty is startling, and overwhelms numerous other obvious defects. The events of this week illustrate the point.

He was involved in three controversies all at once: Secretary of State Dulles' interview in *Life* magazine; General Matthew B. Ridgway's charge that the President had misled the country by implying that the 1954 defense program was supported by Ridgway; and the internal White House controversy about what the President should say to the voters of New Hampshire about putting his name in the state primary election.

The President was ill-informed about the *Life* article. Every Ambassador in the capital was waiting to hear whether he actually had "decided" to order a limited atomic war under certain circumstances in Manchuria and South China without informing Congress or his allies. He didn't answer the question. In fact, he admitted that he hadn't even read the article. This made him probably the only world statesman who hadn't read it, but at least it was an honest answer. Same with the Ridgway charges. He didn't know the facts. The issue was over one of his own State of the Union messages, but he referred the whole thing to the Pentagon.

He took the New Hampshire controversy head on. He invited other candidates to get into the primary. He urged the voters to consider all personalities. He stated with astonishing candor that his health would never be as good as it was before his heart attack, and that his future life "must be carefully regulated to avoid excessive fatigue."

So what did the Republicans do? They treated him to the biggest dinner party on record, raised a whopping big sum to re-elect him in 1956, and put the Citizens for Eisenhower organization back in business.

What is in back of all this? Why did the President make such a damaging and unnecessary confession about his health? Having made it, why is he still in doubt? And having heard it, why do the other Republican leaders refuse even to discuss another candidate?

The President made the statement because it is true, and he is an honest man. Having made it, he still delays because delay permits him to keep control of the political situation in the party, gives him more time to ponder the alternatives, and postpones the terrible choice between going on and giving up.

Finally, the other Republican politicians refuse to think about alternatives, because the alternatives are so difficult or unpleasant. Also, they know their man. Eisenhower has often said one thing in politics and done another. He wasn't going to get into politics originally, but he did. He wasn't going to wage a pre-convention fight for the nomination in 1952, but he did. He wasn't going to get into a rough and tumble with Stevenson (Adlai E. Stevenson, Democratic nominee for President), but he ended by clubbing him all over the country.

This encourages the Republican leaders to wait and hope. They like Ike and believe in him, and they will do anything for him except to listen to what he says.

They have read his New Hampshire statement, of course, but they have spent most of the week looking for the hooker. This is the way with Washington. It reads so much between the lines that it forgets about the print. It can deal with the half-true, half-false partisan politician. It can handle frauds or boobs or political twisters, but the dead-level, candid, spontaneous character puts it in a spin.

THE STRANGE CASE OF JOHN FOSTER DULLES

From the New York Times, Jan. 22, 1956

WASHINGTON, Jan. 14—Like every Secretary of State since the war, John Foster Dulles has pulled some lovely boners, but, unlike his predecessors, Mr. Dulles has added something new to the art of diplomatic blundering.

This is the planned mistake. He doesn't stumble into booby traps; he digs them to size, studies them carefully, and then jumps.

The common diplomatic bloomer is usually the result of ignorance, haste, imprecision, bad temper, or having to choose between hard and difficult courses of action.

Mr. Dulles has not made this kind of mistake very often. He is well-informed. He is the hardest-working man in Washington. He is patient and precise in extemporaneous speech, and he has not yet got into trouble playing question and answer with the reporters.

His mistakes are of a different variety. They are usually avoidable. They are almost always obvious, and they are usually made in carefully prepared statements or speeches.

He wrote into the President's first State of the Union Message the passage construed as "unleashing" Chiang Kai-shek to invade the China mainland.

He "liberated" the Communist satellites first in the Republican party's 1952 foreign affairs platform at the Chicago convention, which he drafted, and later in several other prepared speeches.

He announced that he was going to make an "agonizing reappraisal" of American foreign policy if France did not join the European Defense Community—this in a formal statement to the North Atlantic Treaty Council in Paris.

He put into a formal speech before the New York Council on Foreign Relations his threat of "massive retaliation" against the Communist world—a threat which required a 2,000-word clarification and has plagued him ever since.

He issued last month a formal statement describing Goa on the fringe of India as a "province" of Portugal—just at the time when he was planning a trip to India to patch up our ragged relations with Prime Minister Nehru.

And now this week he has been involved in another controversy because he claimed that he had three times carried the nation to the "brink" of war and scared the Communists off two of the three times by threats of atomic retaliation.

The common denominator of all these things is that the Secretary of State was under no compulsion to say them and that, having decided to say them, he overstated the case.

He has since been forced to qualify the liberation statements to make clear that he meant "peaceful liberation"; to put Chiang Kai-shek back on the leash; to swallow France's rejection of the E.D.C. without any "agonizing reappraisal"; and to make clear that there would be "massive retaliation" only in response to some momentous Communist move that threatened the security of the nation.

He is still standing on his boast that he avoided war three times by threatening atomic retaliation against Manchuria and South

HATS, *by Reginald W. ("Reg") Manning*

PULITZER PRIZE, 1951   ARIZONA REPUBLIC & MCNAUGHT SYNDICATE

China, though this capital is full of well-informed men who regard this as a combination of bad history, bad diplomacy, and bad manners.

He has made a life-long study of the arts of diplomacy, and has turned Assistant Secretary of State Carl McCardle into a personal press agent—yet the effect of his latest flight into print has been to emphasize his weaknesses rather than to clarify his strength.

This is unfortunate for two reasons: It blurs Mr. Dulles' real achievements, and it diverts attention from the remarkably solid front that has been built up in both parties for the policy of collective security.

There are differences of opinion between the parties about how much emphasis to put on foreign economic aid, and whether to proceed with the chain of military agreements in the Middle East, but the area of agreement is far larger than the area of disagreement, and Mr. Dulles is entitled to a great deal of credit for this extremely important development.

In fact, one could almost say that the biggest foreign policy issue between Mr. Dulles and the Democrats today is Mr. Dulles himself. The Democrats have produced no clear alternative to his policies, even in the Middle East. Nor do they complain so much about what he does. But what he says drives them nuts, and gives the impression of great division where very little fundamental policy division exists.

This, of course, is the way things usually go in Washington. The really big story here is that the Republicans are offering a program and a budget that are so New Dealish and internationalist that Bob Taft, if he were here, would feel betrayed.

There is probably not another capital in the world today where the party in power has offered a program which meets with such widespread approval from one end of the political spectrum to the other.

Nevertheless, politicians must fight, and if they don't have big things to fight about, they will fight just as hard about small things.

VIII. NEW SUNS AND NEW MOONS: SPACE AND THE ATOM

"A new method of exploiting atoms, and thus transmuting or disintegrating elements . . . was laid today before the American Association for the Advancement of Science . . ."

The story was from the New York *Times*. The reporter: Alva Johnston. The place: Cambridge, Mass. The date: December 30, 1922.

It is curious, in the light of today's world when any bright schoolboy knows the basic importance of the hydrogen atom, to read Johnston's pioneering story on the subject. He wrote that S. A. Mitchell, vice president of the AAAS Astronomical Section, had said the fundamental element of matter is probably hydrogen, "all others being made up out of hydrogen . . ."

Discussing Dr. Louis Bell's experiments in smashing carbon atoms into helium under great electrical temperatures, Dr. Mitchell was quoted as follows in the Johnston story:

"These results suggest the view that the nuclei of all atoms are made up of multiples of hydrogen nuclei, each carrying a unit positive charge, the combination being bound together by external electrons."

Without really knowing it, man stood on the threshhold of the atomic age in 1922. Johnston's report was the first science story to win a Pulitzer Prize for Reporting.

There was much more about atomic energy in the coverage of science at the tercentenary of Harvard University, for which five reporters including William L. Laurence of the New York *Times* were awarded Pulitzer Prizes in 1937. Laurence and another of the 1937 winners, John J. O'Neill of the New York *Herald Tribune,* had an even more significant story in 1939. This was the splitting of a uranium atom, with a tremendous release of energy, by the Columbia University Physics Department on January 30 of that year.

It is therefore all the more remarkable that the United States was able to keep secret the making of the atomic bomb, its first test explosion in New Mexico, and the takeoff of the bomber *Enola Gay* with the first atomic bomb that was dropped on Hiroshima. But with the destruction of Hiroshima, the birth of the atomic age became known to man in its most destructive aspects. Homer Bigart's visit to Hiroshima made that frighteningly clear.

The shock of that first blast has never quite been equaled by anything since—not by the bombing of Nagasaki nor the testing of the hydrogen bomb nor even the launching of the first Sputnik and the first Explorer moons to circle the earth at 18,000 miles an hour. Man does not absorb new sensations easily, and cannot readily believe what he does not understand. To the atomic reporters and the correspondents from outer space will go the most difficult assignments of all. They must make sure first of all that they are believed.

Some of the wonder and the terror of the reports that follow—the forerunners and pioneers of the darkening age of fantasy—will show why this inevitably must be so.

44. THE BIRTH OF THE ATOMIC AGE:
"A FIREBALL LIT THE DESERT"

How the first atomic bomb rocked the earth,
as told by William L. Laurence, who saw it

Pulitzer Prize for Reporting, 1946

A small, intense man with the serene gaze of a scholar and the pressed-in nose of an unsuccessful prize-fighter vanished from The New York *Times* city room in the spring of 1945. He was William L. Laurence, science reporter, whose rumpled clothes and unruly mop of tangled gray hair had become a trademark in his business. He was one of five science writers who had won a Pulitzer Prize for Reporting in 1937. All Publisher Arthur

Hays Sulzberger knew was that the government secretly had "borrowed" his most knowledgeable science man at less pay than his *Times* salary, and The *Times* was obligingly making up the difference.

The nature of Bill's assignment did not become public knowledge until after the first atomic bomb had been dropped on Hiroshima. Then, and then only, did his associates at The *Times* learn that he had been the only reporter to witness the birth of the atomic age with the explosion of the first atomic bomb at Alamagordo Air Base in the New Mexico desert on July 16, 1945, that he had prepared reports covering every conceivable angle of the initial atomic bomb test and the first atomic bombing of Japan, and that the world of journalism was forever in his debt.

For Bill Laurence's stuff was the only authentic material, outside the formal announcements from President Truman and the War Department, that gave the world the awesome details of what an atomic bomb blast meant. It was rewritten, or used as is, by newspapers all over the world as soon as the government released it on the day the first bomb blasted Hiroshima, August 6, 1945.

Actually, even if the government had not taken Bill Laurence into its confidence, he would have known what was going on. He had known the background for a long time. In The *Times* of January 31, 1939, he had written a story beginning:

"The splitting of a uranium atom into two parts, each consisting of a gigantic 'cannon-ball' of the tremendous energy of 100,000,000 electron volts, the greatest amount of atomic energy so far liberated on earth, was announced here yesterday by the Columbia University Department of Physics . . ."

On May 5, 1940, The *Times* had published his story disclosing that a uranium isotope called U-235 could be the source of enormous atomic energy and that German as well as American physicists were working to develop it. Before the month was out, on May 30, there was another Laurence story in The *Times* disclosing fantastic progress in unlocking the energy of U-235. In September of the same year, the *Saturday Evening Post* published Laurence's story entitled, "The Atom Gives Up." It was so touchy that within a short time, as Meyer Berger wrote in his *The Story of The New York Times,* the FBI was snapping up every copy of the Post it could find, warning the Post to issue no more and asking to be notified whenever a request was made for a copy.

That was how Laurence got the inside track, and he kept it to himself until the government released him from at least a part of his pledge. He recalled rather wistfully, "I had seen things no human eye had ever seen before—that no human mind before our time could have conceived possible. I had watched in constant fascination as men worked with heaps of uranium and plutonium great enough to blow major cities out of existence. I had prepared scores of reports on what I had observed and I couldn't help but dream of what sensations they would have been in The *Times*. They never saw a copy desk. Each went into a strong safe marked 'Top Secret.' Some eventually got into print, but many have never been made public."

Laurence's first story of the New Mexico atom bomb blast, released by the government on August 6, 1945, began:

"Mankind's successful transition to a new age, the Atomic Age, was ushered in July 16, 1945, before the eyes of a tense group of renowned scientists and military men gathered in the desertlands of New Mexico to witness the first end results of their $2,000,000,000 effort . . ."

It was September 26, 1945 before he could do the same story, under his own by-line for his own newspaper. With the publication of that ten-article series, the first of which is reproduced here in condensed form, he became forever known as "Atomic Bill" Laurence (and William H. Lawrence of The *Times* became "Non-Atomic Bill"). For that series and his eyewitness report of the atomic bombing of Nagasaki, an official War Department release, he won his second Pulitzer Prize for Reporting in 1946.

"THE NEAREST THING TO DOOMSDAY"

By William L. Laurence

From the New York Times, Sept. 26, 1945

The Atomic Age began at exactly 5:30 Mountain War Time on the morning of July 16, 1945 on a stretch of semi-desert land about fifty airline miles from Alamagordo, N. M., just a few minutes before the dawn of a new day on that part of the earth.

At that great moment in history, ranking with the moment long ago when man first put fire to work for him and started on his march to civilization, the vast energy locked within the hearts of the atoms of matter was released for the first time in a burst of flame such as had never before been seen on this planet, illuminating earth and sky for a brief span that seemed eternal with the light of many super-suns.

The elemental flame, first fire ever made on earth that did not have its origin in the sun, came from the explosion of the first atomic bomb. It was a full-dress rehearsal preparatory to use of the bomb over Hiroshima and Nagasaki—and other Japanese military targets had Japan refused to accept the Potsdam Declaration for her surrender.

I watched the birth of the Era of Atomic Power from the slope of a hill in the desert land of New Mexico, on the northwestern corner of the Alamagordo Air Base, about 125 miles southwest of Albuquerque. The hill, named Compania Hill for the occasion, was twenty miles to the northwest of Zero, the code name given to the spot chosen for lighting the first atomic fire on this planet.

The bomb was set on a structural steel tower 100 feet high. Nine miles away to the southwest was the base camp. This was G.H.Q. for the scientific high command, of which Professor Kenneth T. Bainbridge of Harvard University was field commander.

At a command over the radio at zero minus one minute all observers at the Base Camp, about 150 of the "Who's Who" in science and the armed forces, lay down "prone on the ground" in their preassigned trenches, "face and eyes directed toward the ground and with head away from Zero."

Three other posts had been established south, north, and west of Zero, each at a distance of 10,000 yards (5.7 miles). These were known, respectively, as South-10,000, North-10,000 and West-10,000, or S-10, N-10 and W-10.

Here the shelters were much more elaborate wooden structures, their walls reinforced by cement, and buried under a massive layer of earth.

S-10 was the control center. Here, Professor J. Robert Oppenheimer, as scientific commander in chief, and his field commander, Professor Bainbridge, issued orders and synchronized the activities of other sites.

Here the signal was given and a complex of mechanisms was set in motion that resulted in the greatest burst of energy ever released by man on earth up till that time. No switch was pulled, no button pressed, to light this first cosmic fire on this planet.

At forty-five seconds to zero, set for 5:30 o'clock, young Dr. Joseph L. McKibben of the University of California, at a signal from Professor Bainbridge, activated a master robot that set off a series of other robots. Moving "electronic fingers" writ and moved on until, at last, strategically spaced electrons moved to the proper place at the proper split second.

Suddenly, at 5:29.50, as we stood huddled around our radio, we heard a voice ringing through the darkness, sounding as though it had come from above the clouds:

"Zero minus ten seconds!"

A green flare flashed out through the clouds, descended slowly, opened, grew dim and vanished into the darkness.

The voice from the clouds boomed out again:

"Zero minus three seconds!"

Another green flare came down. Silence reigned over the desert. We kept moving in small groups in the direction of Zero. From the east came the first faint signs of dawn.

And just at that instant there rose from the bowels of the earth a light not of this world, the light of many suns in one.

It was a sunrise such as the world had never seen, a great green super-sun climbing in a fraction of a second to a height of more than 8,000 feet, rising ever higher until it touched the clouds, lighting up earth and sky all around with a dazzling luminosity.

Up it went, a great ball of fire about a mile in diameter, changing colors as it kept shooting upward, from deep purple to orange, expanding, grower bigger, rising as it was expanding, an elemental force freed from its bonds after being chained for billions of years.

For a fleeting instant the color was unearthly green, such as one sees only in the corona of the sun during a total eclipse.

It was as though the earth had opened and the skies had split. One felt as though he had been privileged to witness the Birth of the World—to be present at the moment of Creation when the Lord said: Let There Be Light.

On that moment hung eternity. Time stood still. Space contracted into a pinpoint.

To another observer, Professor George B. Kistiakowsky of Harvard, the spectacle was "the nearest thing to Doomsday that one could possibly imagine."

"I am sure," he said, "that at the end of the world—in the last milli-second of the earth's existence—the last man will see what we saw!"

A great cloud rose from the ground and followed the trail of the Great Sun.

At first it was a giant column that soon took the shape of a supramundane mushroom. For a fleeting instant it took the form of the Statue of Liberty magnified many times.

Up it went, higher, higher, a giant mountain born in a few seconds instead of millions of years, quivering convulsively.

It touched the multi-colored clouds, pushing its summit through them, kept rising until it reached a height of 41,000 feet, 12,000 feet higher than the earth's highest mountain.

All through this very short but extremely long time-interval not a sound was heard. I could see the silhouettes of human forms motionless in little groups, like desert plants in the dark.

The new-born mountain in the distance, a giant among pigmies against the background of the Sierra Oscuro range, stood leaning at an angle against the clouds, a vibrant volcano spouting fire to the sky.

Then out of the great silence came a mighty thunder. For a brief interval the phenomenon we had seen as light repeated itself in terms of sound.

It was a blast from thousands of blockbusters going off simultaneously at one spot.

The thunder reverberated all through the desert, bounced back and forth from the Sierra Oscuros, echo upon echo. The ground trembled under our feet as in an earthquake.

A wave of hot wind was felt by many of us just before the blast and warned us of its coming.

The Big Boom came about 100 seconds after the Great Flash—the first cry of a new-born world. It brought the silent, motionless silhouette to life, gave them a voice.

A loud cry filled the air. The little groups that hitherto had stood rooted to the earth like desert plants broke into a dance, the rhythm of primitive man dancing at one of his fire festivals at the coming of spring.

They clapped their hands as they leaped from the ground—earthbound man symbolizing a new birth in freedom—the birth of a new force that for the first time gives man means to free himself from the gravitational pull of the earth that holds him down.

The dance of the primitive man lasted but a few seconds, during which an evolutionary period of about 10,000 years had been telescoped. Primitive man was metamorphosed into modern man—shaking hands, slapping his fellow on the back, all laughing like happy children.

The sun was just rising above the horizon as our caravan started on its way back to Albuquerque and Los Alamos. It rose to see a new thing under the sun, a new era in the life of man.

We looked at it through our dark lenses to compare it with what we had seen.

"The sun can't hold a candle to it," one of us remarked.

45. HOMER BIGART AT HIROSHIMA:

"THEY ARE STILL DYING"

A month after the atom bomb blasted the city,
people still couldn't believe it

Pulitzer Prize for International Reporting, 1946

The power to destroy civilization, if not life itself, lies naked within the grasp of mankind today. The unlocking of the atomic secrets of uranium and plutonium, and of hydrogen that followed so swiftly afterward, have changed the world beyond recall. Moon shots and rockets now explore outer space. The issue, however, is still the same as it was on June 14, 1946 when tall, white-haired Bernard M. Baruch called upon the United Nations to "choose between the quick and the dead."

It seems so very long ago, and yet it is only a little more than a decade, since a lumbering B-29 Superfortress called the *Enola Gay* groped through the mists over Japan to drop the first atomic bomb devoted to military use on Hiroshima. President Harry S. Truman made the disclosure to an astonished, and even unbelieving, world within a few hours after the blast on August 6, 1945.

The War Department, asked to estimate the results of that first bomb with a force equal to 20,000 tons of TNT, said it "as yet was unable to make an accurate report" because "an impenetrable cloud of dust and smoke" obscured the target area.

A United Press dispatch reported from Washington: "The Osaka radio, without referring to the atomic bomb dropped on Hiroshima, hinted tonight at the terrific damage it must have caused by announcing that train service in the Hiroshima and other areas had been canceled."

Japan formally surrendered on September 2, 1945. The following day, the first party of American newspapermen traveled to Hiroshima and recorded for the world what had happened that morning when the *Enola Gay* flew over it. This is, in its essentials, the story Homer Bigart filed from Hiroshima to the New York *Herald Tribune,* part of the superb achievement in the Pacific that won for him the Pulitzer Prize for International Reporting in 1946.

"THEY DIDN'T LOOK LIKE HUMAN BEINGS"

By Homer Bigart

From the New York Herald Tribune—dispatch dated Sept. 3, 1945

HIROSHIMA, JAPAN, Sept. 3 (Delayed)—We walked today through Hiroshima, where survivors of the first atomic bomb explosion four weeks ago are still dying at the rate of about one hundred daily from burns and infections which the Japanese doctors seem unable to cure.

The toll from the most terrible weapon ever devised now stands at 53,000 counted dead, 30,000 missing and presumed dead, 13,960 severely wounded and likely to die, and 43,000 wounded. The figures come from Hirokuni Dadai, who, as "chief of thought control" for Hiroshima Prefecture, is supposed to police subversive thinking.

On the morning of August 6 the 340,000 inhabitants of Hiroshima were awakened by the familiar howl of air-raid sirens. The city had never been bombed—it had little industrial importance. The Kure naval base lay only twelve miles to the southeast and American bombers had often gone there to blast the remnants of the imperial navy, or had flown mine-laying or strafing missions over Shimonoseki Strait to the west. Almost daily enemy planes had flown over Hiroshima, but so far the city had been spared.

At 8 a.m. the "all clear" sounded. Crowds emerged from the shallow raid shelters in Military Park and hurried to their jobs in the score of tall, modern, earthquake-proof buildings along the broad Hattchobori, the main business street of the city. Breakfast fires still smoldered in thousands of tiny ovens—presently they were to help to kindle a conflagration.

Very few persons saw the Superfortress when it first appeared more than five miles above the city. Some thought they saw a black object swinging down on a parachute from the plane, but for the most part Hiroshima never knew what hit it.

A Japanese naval officer, Vice-Admiral Masao Kanazawa, at the Kure base said the concussion from the blast twelve miles away was "like the great wind that made the trees sway." His aide, a senior lieutenant who was to accompany us into the city, volunteered that the flash was so bright even in Kure that he was awakened from his sleep. So loud was the explosion that many thought the bomb had landed in Kure.

When Lieutenant Taira Ake, a naval surgeon, reached the city at 2:30 p.m. he found hundreds of wounded still dying unattended in the wrecks and fields on the northern edge of the city. "They didn't look like human beings," he said. "The flesh was burned from their faces and hands and many were blinded and deaf."

Dadai was standing in the doorway of his house nearly two miles from the center of impact. He had just returned from Tokyo.

"The first thing I saw was a brilliant flash," he said. "Then after a second or two came a shock like an earthquake. I knew immediately it was a new type of bomb. The house capsized on top of us and I was hit by falling timbers.

"I found my wife lying unconscious in the debris, and I dragged her to safety. My two children suffered cuts, and for the next hour or so I was too busy to think of what was happening in the city."

Doctors rushed from the Kure naval base—including Lieutenant Ake—were prevented from entering the city until six hours after the blast because of the searing heat of the explosion. City officials said that many indoors who were buried under collapsing walls and roofs subsequently were burned to death in the fires that broke out within a few minutes after the blast.

The first impression in the minds of survivors was that a great fleet of Superfortresses flying at great height somehow had sneaked past the defenses and dropped thousands of fire bombs. Even today there are many who refuse to believe that a single bomb wiped out the city.

A party of newspapermen led by Colonel John McCrary was the first group of Americans to reach Hiroshima. We flew in today in a

B-17, our pilot, Captain Mark Magnan, finding a hole in the clouds over Kure and setting the plane down on the tiny runway of the naval air base there with about seventy feet to spare.

The admiral in charge of the base, after telling us what he knew of the bombing, gave us two sedans and a truck and we drove down a mountain, through ruined Kure and past the navy yard.

Three miles outside Hiroshima we saw the first signs of blast damage—loose tiles torn from roofs and an occasional broken window. At the edge of town there were houses with the roofs blown off, while the walls facing the center of the city had caved inward.

Finally we came to the river and saw the Island of Hiro, which holds, or rather held, the main districts of Hiroshima, which means "Hiro Island."

In the part of town east of the river the destruction had looked no different from a typical bomb-torn city in Europe. Many buildings were only partly demolished, and the streets were still choked with debris.

But across the river there was only flat, appalling desolation, the starkness accentuated by bare, blackened tree trunks and the occasional shell of a reinforced concrete building.

We drove to Military Park and made a walking tour of the ruins.

By all accounts the bomb seemed to have exploded directly over Military Park. We saw no crater there. Apparently the full force of the explosion was expended laterally.

Aerial photographs had shown no evidence of rubble, leading to the belief that everything in the immediate area of impact had been literally pulverized into dust. But on the ground we saw this was not true. There was rubble everywhere, but much smaller in size than normal.

Approaching the Hattchobori, we passed what had been a block of small shops. We could tell that only because of office safes that lay at regular intervals on sites that retained little else except small bits of iron and tin. Sometimes the safes were blown in.

The steel door of a huge vault in the four-story Geibi Bank was flung open, and the management had installed a temporary padlocked door. All three banking houses—Geibi, Mitsubishi, and the Bank of Japan—were conducting business in the sturdy concrete building of the Bank of Japan, which was less damaged than the rest.

Since the bank and the police station were the only buildings open for business, we asked our naval lieutenant guide if we could enter. He disappeared and was gone for several minutes.

We stood uneasily at the corner of the bank building, feeling very much like a youth walking down Main Street in his first long pants. There weren't many people abroad—a thin trickle of shabbily dressed men and women—but all of them stared at us.

There was hatred in some glances, but generally more curiosity than hatred. We were representatives of an enemy power that had employed a weapon far more terrible and deadly than poison gas, yet in the four hours we spent in Hiroshima none so much as spat at us, nor threw a stone.

We later asked the naval lieutenant, who once lived in Sacramento, to halt some pedestrians and obtain eyewitness accounts of the blast. He was very reluctant to do so.

"They may not want to talk to you," he said. But finally he stopped an old man, who bared his gold teeth in an apparent gesture of friendship.

"I am a Christian," said the old man, making the sign of the cross. He pointed to his ears, indicating deafness, and the lieutenant, after futile attempts to make him hear, told us that the old man, like many others, apparently had suffered permanent loss of his hearing when the crashing blast of the atomic bomb shattered his ear drums.

The lieutenant stopped a few more middle-aged civilians, but they backed off, bowing and grinning. They said they were not in Hiroshima August 6.

Two boys walking barefoot through the rubble displayed no fear of infection, although no doctor could say positively that the danger had ended. The boys said they had been brought in from the countryside to help clean up the city.

The cloying stench of death was still very noticeable in the street, and we were glad when the lieutenant finally motioned us inside the bank.

Those who entered Hiroshima and stayed only a few hours showed no ill effects, doctors said, but many who attempted to live in the ruins developed infections that reacted on the blood cells as destructively as leukemia, except that the white blood corpuscles and not the red were consumed. Victims became completely bald; they lost all appetite; they vomited blood.

A few of the main streets of Hiroshima have been cleared. Trolleys ran through the blighted areas down to the waterfront. But the public is forbidden to drink from wells, and water has to be brought in from the countryside.

One of the first questions asked by Japanese newspapermen was: "What effect will the bomb have on future wars?" They also asked whether Hiroshima "would be dangerous for seventy years." We told them we didn't know.

Bigart's figures, and his estimates of the final count, were not too far off. Out of a population of 343,969 the bomb killed 78,150 at Hiroshima, injured 37,425, and 13,083 were accounted missing.

46. "I SAW THE ATOMIC BOMB
DROPPED ON NAGASAKI"

Bill Laurence of the New York Times writes
the first eyewitness story of the raid

Pulitzer Prize for Reporting, 1946

William L. Laurence was at Tinian Island on August 5, 1945 when perspiring scientists put together the first atomic bomb destined for military use. Always the reporter, although he could not now publish anything he had learned in The New York *Times,* he tried to wangle a ride on the first atomic bomber over Hiroshima in order to write the story for the War Department—and presumably for release to the world at large.

Chunky, good-humored Brigadier General Thomas F. Farrell shook his head. General Farrell's word was final, since he was deputy to Major General Leslie R. Groves, commander of the Manhattan project. "Filled up for this one," Farrell said. "You're going on the second flight."

So it happened that Bill Laurence rode in a pathfinder B-29 Superfortress that guided the atomic bomber *The Great Artiste* over Nagasaki on August 9, 1945 as the official reporter for the War Department. His eyewitness story wasn't released for a month, and by that time World War II was over. The toll at Nagasaki, a city of 252,630, was 73,884 dead. Laurence's story, in condensed form, follows.

DESTINY CHOSE NAGASAKI

By William L. Laurence

From the New York Times, Sept. 9, 1945

WITH THE ATOMIC-BOMB MISSION TO JAPAN, Aug. 9 (Delayed)—We are on our way to bomb the mainland of Japan. Our flying contingent consists of three specially designed B-29 Superforts, and two of these carry no bombs. But our lead plane is on its way with another atomic bomb, the second in three days, concentrating in its active substance an explosive energy equivalent to twenty thousand and, under favorable conditions, forty thousand tons of TNT.

We have several chosen targets. One of these is the great industrial and shipping center of Nagasaki, on the western shore of Kyushu, one of the main islands of the Japanese homeland.

This atomic bomb is different from the bomb used three days ago with such devastating results on Hiroshima.

In command of our mission is Major Charles W. Sweeney, 25, of 124 Hamilton Avenue, North Quincy, Mass. His flagship, carrying the atomic bomb, is named *The Great Artiste*, but the name does not appear on the body of the great silver ship, with its unusually long, four-bladed, orange-tipped propellers. Instead, it carries the number 77, and someone remarks that it was "Red" Grange's winning number on the gridiron.

We took off at 3:50 this morning and headed northwest on a straight line for the Empire. The night was cloudy and threatening, with only a few stars here and there breaking through the overcast. The weather report had predicted storms ahead part of the way but clear sailing for the final and climactic stages of our odyssey.

We were about an hour away from our base when the storm broke. Our great ship took some heavy dips through the abysmal darkness around us, but it took these dips much more gracefully than a large commercial air liner, producing a sensation more in the nature of a glide than a bump, like a great ocean liner riding the waves, except that in this case the air waves were much higher and the rhythmic tempo of the glide was much faster.

We reached Yakushima at 9:12 and there, about four thousand feet ahead of us, was *The Great Artiste* with its precious load. I saw

Lieutenant Leonard A. Godfrey (the navigator) and Sergeant Ralph D. Curry (radio operator) strap on their parachutes and I decided to do likewise.

We started circling. We saw little towns on the coastline, heedless of our presence. Our weather scouts had sent us code messages, deciphered by Sergeant Curry, informing us that both the primary target as well as the secondary were clearly visible.

The winds of destiny seemed to favor certain Japanese cities that must remain nameless. We circled about them again and again and found no opening in the thick umbrella of clouds that covered them. Destiny chose Nagasaki as the ultimate target.

We had been circling for some time when we noticed black puffs of smoke coming through the white clouds directly at us. There were fifteen bursts of flak in rapid succession, all too low. Captain Frederick C. Bock (commander of the Superfort) changed his course. There soon followed eight more bursts of flak, right up to our altitude, but by this time were too far to the left.

We flew southward down the channel and at 11:33 crossed the coastline and headed straight for Nagasaki, about one hundred miles to the west. Here again we circled until we found an opening in the clouds. It was 12:01 and the goal of our mission had arrived.

We heard the prearranged signal on our radio, put on our arc welder's glasses, and watched tensely the maneuverings of the strike ship about half a mile in front of us.

"There she goes!" someone said.

Out of the belly of *The Great Artiste* what looked like a black object went downward.

Captain Bock swung around to get out of range; but even though we were turning away in the opposite direction, and despite the fact that it was broad daylight in our cabin, all of us became aware of a giant flash that broke through the dark barrier of our arc welder's lenses and flooded our cabin with intense light.

We removed our glasses after the first flash, but the light still lingered on, a bluish-green light that illuminated the entire sky all around. A tremendous blast wave struck our ship and made it tremble from nose to tail. This was followed by four more blasts in rapid succession, each resounding like the boom of cannon fire hitting our plane from all directions.

Observers in the tail of our ship saw a giant ball of fire rise as though from the bowels of the earth, belching forth enormous white smoke rings. Next, they saw a giant pillar of purple fire, ten thousand feet high, shooting skyward with enormous speed.

By the time our ship had made another turn in the direction of the atomic explosion the pillar of purple fire had reached the level of our altitude. Only about forty-five seconds had passed. Awestruck, we watched it shoot upward like a meteor coming from the earth instead of from outer space, becoming ever more alive as it climbed skyward through the white clouds. It was no longer smoke, or dust, or even a cloud of fire. It was a living thing, a new species of being, born right before our incredulous eyes.

At one stage of its evolution, covering millions of years in terms of seconds, the entity assumed the form of a giant square totem pole, with its base about three miles long, tapering off to about a mile at the top. Its bottom was brown, its center was amber, its top white. But it was a living totem pole, carved with many grotesque masks grimacing at the earth.

Then, just as it appeared as though the thing had settled down into a state of permanence, there came shooting out of the top a giant mushroom that increased the height of the pillar to a total of forty-five thousand feet. The mushroom top was even more alive than the pillar, seething and boiling in a white fury of creamy foam, sizzling upward and then descending earthward, a thousand Old Faithful geysers rolled into one.

It kept struggling in an elemental fury, like a creature in the act of breaking the bonds that held it down. In a few seconds it had freed itself from its gigantic stem and floated upwards with tremendous speed, its momentum carrying it into the stratosphere at a height of sixty thousand feet.

But no sooner did this happen when another mushroom, smaller than the first one, began emerging out of the pillar. It was as though the decapitated monster was growing a new head.

As the first mushroom floated off into the blue it changed its shape into a flowerlike form, its giant petals curving downward, creamy white outside, rose-colored inside. It still retained that shape when we last gazed at it from a distance of about two hundred miles.

The Trustees of Columbia University, on the recommendation of the Advisory Board on the Pulitzer Prizes, voted the 1946 Pulitzer Prize for Reporting to William Leonard Laurence with these words:

"For a distinguished example of reporting:

"William Leonard Laurence, New York *Times,* for his eye-witness account of the atom-bombing of Nagasaki and his subsequent ten articles on the development, production, and significance of the atomic bomb."

As the science editor of the New York *Times,* "Atomic Bill" Laurence is still following the story in which he pioneered.

47. THE NEW YORK TIMES REPORTS
THE DAWN OF THE SPACE AGE

Sputnik I is fired at 18,000 miles an hour
—part of a prize-winning staff file

Pulitzer Prize for International Reporting, 1958

In a corner of The New York *Times's* editorial page, there will occasionally be a short, sharp piece on some topic or personality in the news. That is the only written contribution known to be the work of its publisher, Arthur Hays Sulzberger.

Yet, in the years since the death of his father-in-law, the honorable titan, Adolph S. Ochs, Sulzberger has worked in his own quiet and unassuming way to develop The *Times* into something far more than a good gray record of all the news that's fit to print. The result has been a gain of 100,000 in circulation over the past ten years, a record unique in the nation for a paper of The *Times's* caliber.

The most significant part of The *Times's* newsgathering network is its foreign service of more than fifty regular foreign correspondents, many additional stringers, and the various local and national staff members and editorial writers who go abroad on special missions.

It is no wonder, then, much to Publisher Sulzberger's satisfaction, that his newspaper on two occasions in the history of the Pulitzer Prizes has achieved special recognition for staff efforts in foreign correspondence. In 1941, the newspaper was awarded a special citation in this field. In 1958, it won the Pulitzer Prize for International Reporting—the only newspaper staff thus far to be so honored in this particular category.

While no particular staff member was cited for outstanding work, it was without doubt a banner year for the desk presided over by Foreign

Editor Emanuel R. Freedman. Dispatches from behind the Iron Curtain led the way with Managing Editor Turner Catledge and James Reston interviewing Nikita S. Khrushchev; Harrison E. Salisbury penetrating into rarely visited Albania, Bulgaria, and Rumania; Sidney L. Gruson reporting from Warsaw on developments in far-off Red China; and youthful William J. Jorden and Max Frankel regularly working in Moscow. But there was much other significant work, including Herbert L. Matthews' exclusive interview with the Cuban rebel leader, Fidel Castro; the dispatches of Elie Abel and the late John MacCormac from central Europe, those of A. M. Rosenthal in Southeast Asia and Thomas J. Hamilton's United Nations reporting.

Here is a representative report from the *Times* 1957 file—Bill Jorden's story in essential part on the launching of Sputnik I.

THE EARTH GAINS AN ARTIFICIAL MOON

By William J. Jorden

From the New York Times, Oct. 5, 1957

MOSCOW, Saturday, Oct. 5—The Soviet Union announced this morning that it had successfully launched a man-made earth satellite into space yesterday.

The Russians calculated the satellite orbit at a maximum of 560 miles above the earth and its speed at 18,000 miles an hour.

The official Soviet news agency Tass said the artificial moon, with a diameter of twenty-two inches and a weight of 184 pounds, was circling the earth once every hour and thirty-five minutes. This means more than fifteen times a day.

Two radio transmitters, Tass said, are sending signals continuously on frequencies of 20.005 and 40.002 megacycles. These signals were said to be strong enough to be picked up by amateur radio operators. The trajectory of the satellite is being tracked by numerous scientific stations.

Tass said the satellite was moving at an angle of 65 degrees to the equatorial plane and would pass over the Moscow area at 1:46 a.m. and 6:42 a.m., Moscow time, today.

"Its flight," the announcement added, "will be observed in the rays of the rising and setting sun with the aid of the simplest optical instruments, such as binoculars and spyglasses."

The Soviet Union said the satellite was "successfully launched"

yesterday. Thus is claimed victory over the United States in the race
to put such a scientific instrument into space.

The announcement said the Soviet Union planned to send up
more and bigger and heavier artificial satellites during the International Geophysical Year, an eighteen-month period of study of
the earth, its crust, and the space surrounding it.

The rocket that carried the satellite into space left the earth at
the rate of five miles a second, the Tass announcement said. Nothing was revealed, however, concerning the material of which the
man-made moon was constructed.

The United States has announced its intention of putting one or
more earth satellites into space, probably next spring. The Soviet
Union said its sphere circling the earth had opened the way to
interplanetary travel.

It did not pass up the opportunity to use the launching for propaganda purposes. It said in its announcement that people now could
see how "the new socialist society" had turned the boldest dreams
of mankind into reality.

The Soviet announcement said that as a result of the tremendous
speed at which the satellite was moving it would burn up as soon
as it reached the denser layers of the atmosphere. It gave no indication of how soon that would be.

When the United States government made known its plans for
an earth-circling satellite, it said that the American model would be
about the size of a basketball and that it would move around the
earth at a speed of 18,000 miles an hour in a path 200 to 300 miles
above the earth.

Military experts have said that the satellites would have no prac-
ticable military application in the foreseeable future. . . . Their real
significance would be in providing scientists with important new
information concerning the nature of the sun, cosmic radiation,
solar radio interference, and static-producing phenomena radiating
from the north and south magnetic poles. All this information would
be of inestimable value for those who are working on the problem
of sending missiles and eventually men into the vast reaches of the
solar system.

From his Moscow vantage point, Bill Jorden went on to report the orbiting of more Sputniks. After the 184-pound Sputnik I, he wrote a colorful account of the 1,120-pound Sputnik II with its little dog passenger when they went up on November 3, 1957. On May 15, 1958, after the United States had put two 30-pound Explorers and a 3-pound Vanguard into orbit, Jorden told of the flight of the 3,000-pound Sputnik III on May 15, 1958. The youthful Moscow bureau chief was in a fair way to become a veteran reporter of flights into outer space when his tour of duty ended and he returned to New York.

48. WALTER LIPPMANN AND SPUTNIK: A WARNING FOR THE U.S.

A distinguished editorial writer and columnist looks at America in the space age

Special Pulitzer Prize Citation for 1958

Walter Lippmann's career is one of the most useful guideposts in modern American journalism. From the era of the Fourteen Points to the age of outer space, he has written with clarity and wisdom of the perplexities in a changing world. From the day of the muckrakers of 1910 to that of the vicuna coat investigators of 1958, he has never failed to speak out with courage and conviction.

It is, of course, awesome in itself to consider the many-sided facets of a journalistic career that has spanned well-nigh fifty years. He was assistant to Lincoln Steffens, associate editor of the *New Republic,* an aide in World War I and later at Versailles to both President Wilson and Colonel E. M. House, editor of the New York *World* and eventually the syndicated editorial columnist of the New York *Herald Tribune.*

But neither length nor variety of themselves have made Lippmann one of the acknowledged leaders of American journalism. In the generations that have known two world wars and the cold war, a great depression and several recessions, and finally a daring scientific plunge into the unknown world of the atom and outer space, he has had something of importance to say to the American people of his time. No mere cheer leader, or perennial optimist, or even a constant prophet of doom could have attracted the following that has been Lippmann's. His honesty and sincerity alone would have prevented him from taking one attitude toward all developments, in any case.

Typical of his work was his piece in the New York *Herald Tribune* of

October 10, 1957 after the Soviet Union's ton and a half Sputnik had orbited into space and thereby shocked the United States into an all-too-brief period of self-examination. It follows.

THE PORTENT OF THE MOON

By Walter Lippmann

From the New York Herald Tribune, Oct. 10, 1957

The few who are allowed to know about such things, and are able to understand them, are saying that the launching of so big a satellite signifies that the Soviets are much ahead of this country in the development of rocket missiles. Their being so much ahead cannot be the result of some kind of lucky guess in inventing a gadget. It must be that there is a large body of Soviet scientists, engineers, and production men, plus many highly developed subsidiary industries, all successfully directed and coordinated, and bountifully financed.

In short, the fact that we have lost the race to launch the satellite means that we are losing the race to produce ballistic missiles. This in turn means that the United States and the Western World may be falling behind in the progress of science and technology.

This is a grim business. It is grim, in my mind at least, not because I think the Soviets have such a lead in the race of armaments that we may soon be at their mercy. Not at all. It is a grim business because a society cannot stand still. If it loses the momentum of its own progress, it will deteriorate and decline, lacking purpose and losing confidence in itself.

The critical question is how we as a people, from the President down, will respond to what is a profound challenge to our cultural values—not to the ideal of the American way of life but—to the way in fact we have been living our life. Our response could be to think of it all in terms of propaganda, and to look around for some device for doing something spectacular to outmatch what the Russians have done. The other response would be to look inward upon ourselves primarily with our own failings, and to be determined not so much to beat the Russians as to cure ourselves.

The question then might be defined in this way: why is it that in the twelve years that have passed since the end of World War II, the United States which was so far in the lead has been losing its lead to the Russians who at the end of the war were so nearly prostrate? Mr. Khrushchev would say, no doubt, that this is because communism is superior to capitalism. But that answer really begs the question, which is not why the Soviets have moved ahead so fast but why we, who had moved very fast, have not been moving fast enough. For while our society is undoubtedly progressive, it has not in the postwar years been progressive enough.

I do not pretend to know the whole answer to what is for us and for our future so fateful a question. But I venture to think that even now we can discern certain trends that since the world war have appeared in American life and must be taken into account.

We must put first, I think, the enormous prosperity in which, as the politicians have put it to the voters, the private standard of life is paramount as against the public standard of life. By the public standard of life I mean such necessities as defense, education, science, technology, the arts. Our people have been led to believe in the enormous fallacy that the highest purpose of the American social order is to multiply the enjoyment of consumer goods. As a result, our public institutions, particularly those having to do with education and research, have been, as compared with the growth of our population, scandalously starved.

We must put second, I think, a general popular disrespect for, and even suspicion of, brains and originality of thought. In other countries, in Germany and in most of Europe and Russia, it is an honor, universally recognized, to be a professor. Here it is something to put a man on the defensive, requiring him to show that he is not a highbrow and that he is not subversive.

What McCarthyism did to the inner confidence of American scientists and thinkers has constituted one of the great national tragedies of the postwar era. It is impossible to measure the damage. But the damage that was done was very great. It was done in the kind of thinking where the difference between creation and routine lies in the special courage to follow the truth wherever it leads.

With prosperity acting as a narcotic, with Philistinism and McCarthyism rampant, our public life has been increasingly doped and without purpose. With the President in a kind of partial retirement, there is no standard raised to which the people can repair.

QUO VADIS? *by Bruce M. Shanks*

FROM THE PRIZEWINNING FILE OF 1958   BUFFALO EVENING NEWS

Thus we drift with no one to state our purposes and to make policy, into a chronic disaster like Little Rock. We find ourselves then without a chart in very troubled waters.

Out of respect for Lippmann's career and his editorial achievements, he was awarded a special citation on recommendation of the Advisory Board on the Pulitzer Prizes in 1958. Perhaps the honor, and the prize itself, might have come to him far earlier had he not adopted the attitude that, as the editor of Pulitzer's *World*, he should not be considered for a Pulitzer Prize. He felt so strongly about it that once he wrote a letter to the then Advisory Board secretary requesting that his work should not be placed before the committee of judges. Lippmann's wisdom has been matched only by his modesty and his integrity.

IX. THE LONELY STRUGGLE: MAN AGAINST HIS FATE

Hundreds of persons die in automobile accidents over summer week-ends in America. Yet, signs of public alarm are rare.

Thousands may be exposed to radioactive fallout; millions all over the earth may be facing starvation. Still, it is difficult if not impossible to make an impression on the public unless a person or a group, caught in a net of circumstance, arouses sympathy.

But let a seven-year-old boy like Benny Hooper tumble into a Long Island well and the whole country becomes avidly interested in the effort to save him. When Benny was rescued from the well at Manorville on May 17, 1957, he was king of American boys—for at least a day.

This public feeling for the drama of man's struggle against the elements, against disaster, disease, and death, has been familiar to storytellers throughout the ages. It is one of the basic ingredients of news, as we know it. Philosophers may deplore it, welfare workers and others may condemn this singling out of the individual rather than the mass of unfortunates, but there is precious little that any newspaper editor can do about it. Or, even if by some chance he could do something, I would suspect the average editor would print the story first and philosophize about it afterward. The editor doesn't live, regardless of what restrictions may be imposed on him, who doesn't love a good story.

This instinctive public interest in the plight of the individual has made many a hero in the past and will create many more. The captain striving to save his ship during a storm at sea . . . the pilot coming in for a landing with only one engine out of four turning over . . . the helpless community braced for a flood or perhaps a tornado . . . the stricken child whom doctors are trying to save . . . all these and many more are ingredients of the lonely struggle.

Many such accounts are in the files of the Pulitzer Prizes. From them, the following have been selected as examples of what reporters have done to tell the story of man's struggle against his fate.

49. A 21-YEAR-OLD REPORTER SEES
THE ORDEAL OF FLOYD COLLINS

"Skeets" Miller of the Louisville Courier-Journal
stirs the nation with his stories

Pulitzer Prize for Reporting, 1926

The memory of Floyd Collins is dim now, but once he dominated the news of a nation. For eighteen days in 1925, while this unremarkable mountain youth lay trapped in Sand Cave, Kentucky, America was interested in little else.

William Burke Miller, night executive officer of the National Broadcasting Company, was a red-headed, 21-year-old reporter then for the Louisville *Courier-Journal*. He pleaded with his city editor for the assignment out-of-town once a stringer sent the tip.

"All right," he was told grudgingly. "But we're not paying you $25 a week to risk your neck in that cave. Don't go in it."

"Skeets" Miller disobeyed orders.

As he later recalled, he was ashamed not to go into the cave to try to help Floyd Collins. Because "Skeets" was only five feet two and weighed but 120 pounds, he could wriggle through a narrow tunnel 100 feet long to the spot 60 feet below the earth's surface where Collins lay.

The youth had been trapped January 29, 1925 while searching on his father's farm for a cavern that would draw tourists like the famous Mammoth Cave five miles away.

Now the tourists came, thousands of them. They could not see Collins, lying on his side with a boulder pinning his left foot so that he could barely move. They couldn't see the drip of water on his face, but they could and did watch the rescue efforts for 18 days until, on February 17, 1925, Collins died. Every newspaper in the land played the story. The

GIRL LEAPS TO DEATH IN HOTEL FIRE
by Arnold Hardy, amateur photographer

PULITZER PRIZE, 1947   ASSOCIATED PRESS

NEAR COLLISION AT AIR SHOW, *by Bill Crouch*

PULITZER PRIZE, 1950   OAKLAND (CALIF.) TRIBUNE

New York *Times* alone gave it eight columns, which is somewhat more than all but the most critical exchanges of notes with Moscow now receives.

Miller's stories were the first to arouse national attention. He made five trips to try to help Collins at the risk of his own life, and reported his findings in fascinating detail. Once Collins told him:

"Now, fellow, you better go out and get warm. But come back. You're small and I believe you're going to get me out."

One of Miller's stories, as published in the Louisville *Courier-Journal*, follows in condensed form. It was part of the file that won him the Pulitzer Prize for Reporting in 1926.

JOURNEY INTO A TOMB

By William Burke Miller

From the Louisville Courier-Journal, Feb. 2, 1925

CAVE CITY, KY., Feb. 2—Floyd Collins is suffering torture almost beyond description, but he is still hopeful he will be taken out alive, he told me at 6:20 o'clock tonight on my last visit to him.

Until I went inside myself I could not understand exactly what the situation was. I wondered why someone couldn't do something quick, but I found out why.

I was lowered by my heels into the entrance of Sand Cave. The passageway is about five feet in diameter. After reaching the end of an eighty-foot drop I reached fairly level ground for a moment.

From here on I had to squirm like a snake. Water covers almost every inch of the ground, and after the first few feet I was wet through and through. Every moment it got colder. It seemed that I would crawl forever, but after going about ninety feet I reached a very small compartment, slightly larger than the remainder of the channel.

This afforded a breathing spell before I started on again toward the prisoner. The dirty water splashed in my face and numbed my body, but I couldn't stop.

Finally I slid down an eight-foot drop and, a moment later, saw Collins and called to him. He mumbled an answer.

My flashlight revealed a face on which is written suffering of many long hours, because Collins has been in agony every conscious moment since he was trapped at 10 o'clock Friday morning.

I saw the purple of his lips, the pallor on the face, and realized that something must be done before long if this man is to live.

Before I could see his face, however, I was forced to raise a small piece of oil cloth covering it.

"Put it back," he said. "Put it back—the water!"

Then I noticed a small drip-drip-drip from above. Each drop struck Collins' face. The first few hours he didn't mind, but the constant dripping almost drove him insane. His brother had taken the oil cloth to him earlier in the day.

This reminded me of the old water torture used in ages past. I shuddered.

Here I was at the end of the journey, and I saw quickly why it was that workmen who had penetrated as far as I had accomplished but little. I was exhausted, as they had been. I was numb from head to foot. Chills raced through my body. I missed the fresh air. I came to know in this brief time what Collins had suffered, but I could not comprehend fully. I felt certain I would get out. Collins has hopes, nothing more. I was in no physical pain. Collins' foot, held by a six-ton rock in a natural crevice, is never without pain.

I tried to squirm over Collins' body to reach the rock, but his body takes up nearly all the space. I squeezed in, hunting for some way to help, until he begged me to get off.

"It hurts—hurts awful," he said.

Collins is lying on his back, resting more on the left side, so that his left cheek rests on the ground. His two arms are held fast in the crevice beside his body, so that he really is in a natural straitjacket.

I was behind Lieut. Robert Burdon of the Louisville Fire Department and followed by Homer Collins, brother of the victim, and Guy Turner. Homer Collins had brought with him some body harness to place around his brother and we finally succeeded in putting it on him.

The prisoner helped as best he could by squirming and turning as much as possible, and finally we were ready to haul away on the rope attached to Collins. We pulled as much as we could and it seemed as though we made headway. It was estimated we moved the prisoner five inches.

Perhaps we did, but I can hardly realize it. All of us were on the point of collapse and after a short time our strength failed. We couldn't do any more.

We saw that the blankets and covering which Collins' brother had brought to him were in place and that he was resting as comfortably as we could make him.

Then we left near his head a lantern well filled with oil. It isn't much, but the tiny light it throws means much in that relentless trap and it may bring some bit of consolation to a daring underground explorer whose chance for life is small.

We said farewell and the last man started backward. I found soon that the trip out is worse than the one in. I encountered difficulty in crawling backward for a time, but practice soon enabled me to make progress.

Every foot it seemed the dirty water would splash in my face. I didn't mind it on my body any more, because I was numb to it. Frequently I had to back up in an incline, and the water would flow down to my neck, but as I said, I already was as cold as I could get.

It was with the utmost relief that I came to the small compartment about midway from the entrance which affords to the rescuer his only resting place. I found that by working my head down to my feet and by easing my feet backward, that I could face about.

This aided a great deal and within twenty minutes I came in sight of lights at the entrance. But, before reaching it, I discovered that two members of our party were unable to proceed farther. I spent what little strength remained in me to get them out.

The struggle went on for fifteen more days. And at last, on February 17, "Skeets" Miller wrote for his paper:

"In death, as in the last week or more of his life, Floyd Collins must remain entrapped in Sand Cave. . . . The tomb is sealing itself in collapse. . . . Soon Floyd Collins will be lost forever in a cave he died to explore."

Miller, too, has often wondered why Collins caught and held national attention. As he pointed out, less than six weeks after the Sand Cave tragedy, twenty or more miners died in a West Virginia coal field but the story raised hardly a ripple.

"In the ensuing years," Miller wrote to me, "I've decided it was the 'aloneness' of Floyd in his suffering and eventual death that held public sympathy. All of us as children fear the dark and being enclosed even for a moment in a closet. The darkness, the closed-in area of his imprisonment, must have been magnified by every human who heard of his plight. That's the only suggestion I have deduced since 1925."

50. THE SUBMARINE OPERATION
THAT SAVED A BOY'S LIFE

*George Weller of the Chicago Daily News tells
how amateurs did the job in enemy waters*

Pulitzer Prize for Reporting, 1943

George Anthony Weller, born in Boston in 1907, once was deeply interested in dramatic art. After receiving his A.B. from Harvard, he was serious enough about it to become a student at the Max Reinhardt School in Vienna, and later an actor in the Max Reinhardt Theater.

But, like most young Americans of the day in Vienna, he drifted into the orbit of the foreign correspondents who gathered in the dusty old Haupttelegrafen Amt and the friendly, cheerful Cafe Louvre where the talk was gay and the *schlagobers* thick. It was no great surprise, therefore, when he became one himself and roved the Balkans.

At the outset of World War II, he joined the staff of the Chicago *Daily News*. Throughout the early days of the Pacific campaign, he was often under fire and his early interest in the drama stood him in good stead. Some of his dispatches were vivid and flashing with life. An excellent example of his work was the reconstruction of the celebrated operation performed by a pharmacist's mate in a submarine under enemy waters, published in the Chicago *Daily News* and awarded the Pulitzer Prize for Reporting in 1943. While it wasn't the first story on the operation, it was by far the most effective and years later became a TV thriller in the series known as Pulitzer Prize Playhouse.

Weller went back to Harvard after World War II as a Nieman Fellow and has continued to roam the world for the Chicago *Daily News*. This is his Pulitzer Prize story.

"I'M STILL IN THERE PITCHING"

By George Weller

From the Chicago Daily News, Dec. 14, 1942

SOMEWHERE IN AUSTRALIA—"They are giving him ether now," was what they said back in the aft torpedo rooms.

"He's gone under and they're ready to cut him open," the crew whispered, sitting on their pipe bunks cramped between torpedoes.

One man went forward and put his arm quietly around the shoulder of another man who was handling the bow diving planes.

"Keep her steady, Jake," he said. "They've just made the first cut. They're feeling around for it now."

"They" were a little group of anxious-faced men with their arms thrust into reversed white pajama coats. Gauze bandages hid all their expressions except the tensity in their eyes.

"It" was an acute appendix inside Dean Rector of Chautauqua, Kansas. The stabbing pains had become unendurable the day before, which was Rector's first birthday at sea. He was nineteen years old.

The big depth gauge that looks like a factory clock and stands beside the "Christmas tree" of red and green gauges regulating the flooding chambers showed where they were. They were below the surface. And above them were enemy waters crossed and re-crossed by whirring propellers of Japanese destroyers and transports.

The nearest naval surgeon competent to operate on the nineteen-year-old seaman was thousands of miles and many days away. There was just one way to prevent the appendix from bursting, and that was for the crew to operate upon their shipmate themselves.

And that's what they did; they operated upon him. It was probably one of the largest operations in number of participants that ever occurred.

"He says he's ready to take his chance," the gobs whispered from bulkhead to bulkhead.

"That guy's regular"—the word traveled from bow planes to propeller and back again.

They "kept her steady."

The chief surgeon was a 23-year-old pharmacist's mate wearing a blue blouse with white-taped collar and squashy white duck cap. His name was Wheeler B. Lipes. He came from Newcastle, near Roanoke, Va., and had taken the Navy hospital course in San Diego, thereafter serving three years in the naval hospital at Philadelphia, where his wife lives.

Lipes' specialty as laboratory technician was in operating a machine that registers heartbeats. He was classified as an electro-cardiographer. But he had seen Navy doctors take out one or two appendixes and thought he could do it. Under the sea, he was given his first chance to operate.

There was difficulty about the ether. When below the surface the pressure inside a boat is above atmospheric pressure. More ether is absorbed under pressure. The submariners did not know how long their operation would last.

They did not know how long it would take to find the appendix. They did not know whether there would be enough ether to keep the patient under throughout the operation.

They didn't want the patient waking up before they were finished.

They decided to operate on the table in the officers' wardroom. In the newest and roomiest American submarine the wardroom is approximately the size of a Pullman car drawing room. It is flanked by bench seats attached to the wall, and a table occupies the whole room. You enter with knees already crooked to sit down. The only way any one can be upright in the wardrooms is by kneeling.

The operating table was just long enough so that the patient's head and feet reached the two ends without hanging over.

First they got out a medical book and read up on the appendix, while Rector, his face pale with pain, lay in the narrow bunk. It was probably the most democratic surgical operation ever performed. Everybody from boxplane man to the cook in the galley knew his role.

The cook provided the ether mask. It was an inverted tea strainer. They covered it with gauze.

The 23-year-old "surgeon" had as his staff of fellow "physicians" all men his senior in age and rank. His anaesthetist was Communications Officer Lieutenant Franz Hoskins of Tacoma, Wash.

Before they carried Rector to the wardroom, the submarine captain, Lieutenant Commander W. B. Ferrall of Pittsburgh, asked Lipes as the "surgeon" to have a talk with the patient.

"Look, Dean, I never did anything like this before," Lipes said. "You didn't have much chance to pull through, anyhow. What do you say?"

"I know just how it is, Doc," said Rector. "Let's get going."

It was the first time in his life that anybody had called Lipes "Doc." But there was in him, added to the steadiness that goes with the submariner's profession, a new calmness.

The operating staff adjusted gauze masks while members of the engine room crew pulled tight their reversed pajama coats over their extended arms. The tools were laid out. They were far from perfect or complete for a major operation. The scalpel had no handle.

But submariners are used to "rigging" things. The medicine chest had plenty of hemostats, which are small pincers used for closing blood vessels. The machinist "rigged" a handle for the scalpel from a hemostat.

When you are going to have an operation, you must have some kind of an antiseptic agent. Rummaging in the medicine chest, they found sulfanilamide tablets and ground them to powder. One thing was lacking: there was no means of holding open the wound after the incision had been made. Surgical tools used for this are called "muscular retractors." What would they use for retractors? There was nothing in the medicine chest that gave the answer, so they went as usual to the cook's galley.

In the galley they found tablespoons made of Monel metal. They bent these at right angles and had their retractors.

Sterilizers? They went to one of the greasy copper-colored torpedoes waiting beside the tubes. They milked alcohol from the torpedo mechanism and used it as well as boiling water.

The light in the wardroom seemed insufficient; operating rooms always have big lamps. So they brought one of the big flood lamps used for night loadings and rigged it inside the wardroom's sloping ceiling.

The moment for the operation had come. Rector, very pale and stripped, stretched himself out on the wardroom table under the glare of the lamps.

Rubber gloves dipped in torpedo alcohol were drawn upon the youthful "Doc's" hands. The fingers were too long. The rubber ends dribbled over limply.

"You look like Mickey Mouse, Doc," said one onlooker.

Lipes grinned behind the gauze.

Rector on the wardroom table wet his lips, glancing a side look at the tea strainer ether mask.

With his superior officers as his subordinates, Lipes looked into their eyes, nodded, and Hoskins put the tea mask down over Rector's face. No words were spoken; Hoskins already knew from the book that he should watch Rector's eye pupils dilate.

The 23-year-old surgeon, following the ancient hand rule, put his little finger on Rector's subsiding umbilicus, his thumb on the point of the hip bone, and, by dropping his index finger straight down, found the point where he intended to cut. At his side stood Lieutenant Norvell Ward of Indian Head, Maryland, who was his assistant surgeon.

"I chose him for his coolness and dependability," said the Doc afterward of his superior officer. "He acted as my third and fourth hands."

Lieutenant Ward's job was to place the tablespoons in Rector's side as Lipes cut through successive layers of muscles.

Engineering Officer Lieutenant S. Manning of Cheraw, S. C., took the job which in a normal operating room is known as "circulating nurse." His job was to see that packets of sterile dressings kept coming and that the torpedo alcohol and boiling water arrived regularly from the galley.

They had what is called an "instrument passer" in Chief Yeoman H. F. Wieg of Sheldon, N. D., whose job was to keep the tablespoons coming and coming clean. Submarine Skipper Ferrall too had his part. They made him "recorder." It was his job to keep count of the sponges that went into Rector. A double count of the tablespoons used as retractors was kept: one by the Skipper and one by the cook, who was himself passing them out from the galley.

It took Lipes in his flap-finger rubber gloves nearly twenty minutes to find the appendix.

"I have tried one side of the caecum," he whispered after the first minutes. "Now, I'm trying the other side."

Whispered bulletins seeped back into the engine room and the crew's quarters. "The Doc has tried one side of something and now is trying the other side."

After more search, Lipes finally whispered, "I think I've got it. It's curled way up into the blind gut."

Lipes was using the classical McBurney's incision. Now was the time when his shipmate's life was completely in his hands.

"Two more spoons." They passed the word to Lieutenant Ward.

"Two spoons at 1445 hours (2:45 p.m.)," wrote Skipper Ferrall on his note pad.

"More flashlights. And another battle lantern," demanded Lipes.

The patient's face, lathered with white petrolatum, began to grimace.

"Give him more ether," ordered the Doc.

Hoskins looked doubtfully at the original five pounds of ether now shrunk to hardly three-quarters of one can, but once again the tea strainer was soaked in ether. The fumes mounted up, thickening the wardroom air and making the operating staff giddy.

"Want those blowers speeded up?" the captain asked the Doc.

The blowers began to whirr louder.

Suddenly came the moment when the Doc reached out his hand, pointing toward the needle threaded with twenty-day chromic catgut.

One by one the sponges came out. One by one the tablespoons, bent into right angles, were withdrawn and returned to the galley. At the end it was the skipper who nudged Lipes and pointed to the tally of bent tablespoons. One was missing. Lipes reached in the incision for the last time and withdrew the wishboned spoon and closed the incision.

They even had the tool ready to cut off the thread. It was a pair of fingernail scissors, well scalded in water and torpedo juice.

At that moment the last can of ether went dry. They lifted up Rector and carried him into the bunk of Lieutenant Charles K. Miller of Williamsport, Pa. Lieutenant Miller alone had control of the ship as diving officer during the operation.

It was half an hour after the last tablespoon had been withdrawn that Rector opened his eyes. His first words were, "I'm still in there pitching."

The first appendix ever known to have been removed below enemy water vibrated in a bottle on the submarine's shelves as the craft went on patrol. Thirteen days later, Rector was back on the job manning the battle phones. And sixteen years later, the hero of the operation was Lieutenant Wheeler B. Lipes, Medical Service Corps, U. S. Navy.

"Lieutenant Lipes," wrote Admiral C. C. Kirkpatrick, the Navy's Chief of Information, "did not receive a specific decoration for his performance of the appendectomy. He of course did receive much praise and world-wide acclaim for what appears to be a first major operation performed in a submarine—submerged in the China Sea."

51. A CITY EDITOR PROVES
HE HAS A HEART

Paul Schoenstein of the New York Journal-American
leads an attempt to save a baby's life

Pulitzer Prize for Reporting, 1944

There is an ancient journalistic myth, spread largely by the unknowing, that city editors are mean and thoughtless men. Their detractors would have you believe they are all heartless taskmasters, intent only on the gathering of the news; that they would mortgage their souls for a big local story to spread across Page 1; and that they drive their staffs relentlessly with whips and scorpions.

The indictment is worth only the briefest examination, for it has no basis today.

Once, of course, it could have been documented with a few grains of fact. It was, unhappily, true that in the dark past a city editor once lived who fired a reporter on Christmas Eve and delighted to relate the deed. But he has long since become a managing editor and a pillar of the community who would shudder at such crass goings-on.

There was a city editor also who, upon hearing that his star rewrite man was ill in a remote village, sent ambulances tearing to the rescue from various parts of the state and then gaily forwarded the bill to the victim. And there was another wretch who broke into happy tears of laughter across the city desk when he learned that one of his reporters, sent to expose an insane asylum, had been adjudged a dangerous case and refused release.

It was, moreover, not merely an amusing short story at the time but the bitter truth that a city editor dispatched undertakers complete with black wreath and coffin to call upon the girl of his dreams on the night when she married another man. And it is still a matter of record that a city editor many years ago murdered his wife and then spent his declining years watering the beautiful flowers at Sing Sing Prison.

Such city editors are out of another age. For today, the city editor is a home-loving husband and doting father, a mortgage-holder and suburban country club member, a cheery disciple of wholesome living and to-getherness. He smiles and says good-morning to the copy boy, or good evening to the receptionist; worries about the untidiness of the city room, and even has been known to pass the time of day by having a drink with a copyreader. Some city editors unashamedly display Phi Beta Kappa keys and one made history of a kind by dancing gallantly with his star lady reporter even though she was on strike and he wasn't.

All of which makes it pertinent to consider the distinguished career of Paul Schoenstein of the New York *Journal-American,* the only city editor who ever won a Pulitzer Prize for reporting.

Like all able city editors, he was a victim of the ancient journalistic myth which has already been analyzed. It had been said that he, like some other city editors, was likely to assign a reporter to find the hottest place in town on a day when the mercury officially went over 100 degrees; also, that he was capable of sending a man to cover a murder at far-off Throgg's Neck and then demand a complete story ten minutes later.

To these canards, Schoenstein gave a full and complete answer on August 12, 1943, when the paper was full of war news and a city editor could scarcely hope to make Page 1 even by dropping dead.

But here in essential part is the story that ran on Page 1 of the *Journal-American* that Thursday.

"ONLY SEVEN HOURS TO LIVE"

From the New York Journal-American, Aug. 12, 1943

A tiny white light flashed a summons on the New York *Journal-American* city desk switchboard. The time was 3:40 p.m. yesterday.

The city editor who answered the telephone heard these words:

"My little girl is in Lutheran Hospital. The doctors say she has only seven hours to live, unless she gets the new drug penicillin. It is her only hope. The doctors have used sulfa drugs and everything else. I must find someone with enough authority to help her. Can you help me?"

"WONDER WHY MY PARENTS DIDN'T GIVE ME SALK SHOTS?"
by Tom Little

PULITZER PRIZE, 1957   NASHVILLE TENNESSEAN

The caller identified himself as Lawrence J. Malone, of 83-11 34th Avenue, Jackson Heights, a clerk. The child who lay near death in Lutheran Hospital, at 144th Street and Convent Avenue, Manhattan, was his daughter, Patricia, 2.

The search for penicillin was not an easy one. For this drug, hailed by medical science as a miracle worker, was so scarce as to be almost unobtainable. Even the armed forces were able to obtain only a small percentage of the penicillin they needed.

Yet, two minutes after the father had appealed for help, the *Journal-American* city desk set to work on the job with determination. It was a grim fight. "Only seven hours to live unless . . ."

A call to Lutheran Hospital verified that the child barely was alive, that she suffered from a rare blood disease, the staphylococci type of septicemia, a type of blood poisoning. Sulfa drugs had been used. Two blood transfusions had been given. They had not helped. Penicillin was held out as the only hope.

A call was put in for U. S. Surgeon General Thomas Parran in Washington. New York drug firms were canvassed and it was learned that E. R. Squibb & Sons manufactured penicillin.

The call to Dr. Parran was referred to Dr. A. N. Richards, in charge of research at the Office of Scientific Development in Washington. "The Squibb laboratory at New Brunswick, N. J., has a supply of penicillin," said Dr. Richards. "I'll wire them a release order immediately."

In the meantime it was learned that Dr. Chester Keefer, Boston surgeon and War Production Board member, had direct authority to order release of the precious drug for civilian use. He was called and communicated with Dr. Dante Collitti, staff surgeon at Lutheran Hospital.

"You will get the penicillin," Dr. Keefer promised Dr. Collitti.

That was at 4 p.m. Doctors were amazed at the speed with which a source of penicillin had been discovered and the red tape binding its release cut.

Now plans were set in motion to arrange for police of two states to escort the mercy shipment of penicillin from New Brunswick to the bedside of the dying girl. At 6:30 p.m., Dr. Collitti met an anxious group of reporters at the entrance to the Holland Tunnel.

It was 7:30 p.m. when the car of mercy drew to a stop before the Squibb laboratories.

Three guards waited there. One of them stepped to the car. "Dr. Collitti? Here is the penicillin."

Dr. Collitti held the cardboard carton, inside of which lay the penicillin packed in dry ice. "Now," he remarked, "we have a fighting chance."

The last stage of the trip was covered in record time—from Holland Tunnel to Lutheran Hospital in eight minutes. The speedometer registered a steady 65 miles an hour in the race up the West Side Highway. Just before the car pulled up at the hospital entrance, Dr. Collitti said,

"You fellows have done something today that all the doctors in the world couldn't have done."

"Maybe," one of the reporters said, "but from now on, Doc, it's up to you."

Afterwards reporters tiptoed into the fourth-floor room of the unconscious child. She breathed in labor but her tiny features beneath a silky mop of brown hair showed no evidence of pain. "She's a pretty sick girl," one nurse whispered.

At their Jackson Heights home, Patricia Malone's parents wept.

"Thank God," murmured Lawrence Malone.

"At least," said Katherine Malone, "my little girl will have a chance."

It would be pleasant to report that the story had a happy ending, but it didn't turn out that way. Patricia Malone surmounted the crisis, following the injection of penicillin, and the story spread throughout the nation's press. But two months later, she died. Her heart had been weakened by the infection. For their work, Paul Schoenstein and the staff of the New York *Journal-American* were awarded the Pulitzer Prize for reporting for 1944. Having proved that a city editor could have a heart, he became an assistant managing editor and a pillar of New York journalism.

52. DEATH OVER GRAND CANYON: HOW 128 PERSONS DIED

*The Salt Lake Tribune local staff covers
an air crash 400 miles away*

Pulitzer Prize for Local Reporting, 1957

When two great air liners crashed over the Grand Canyon on June 30, 1956, taking a toll of 128 lives, the wreckage fell in one of the most difficult and inaccessible regions on earth. Yet, some 400 miles away in Salt Lake City, the local staff of the Salt Lake *Tribune* got on the job at once.

For news knows no boundaries. When a big story breaks, no matter where, a responsible newspaper covers it.

This was one of the biggest stories of that year, or any other, for that matter. There had been perhaps a one in a million chance that two commercial aircraft, taking off minutes apart from Los Angeles for an eastbound transcontinental trip, would crash over Grand Canyon. Yet, it had happened, with the highest death toll yet recorded in the history of commercial aviation.

The Salt Lake *Tribune's* job was memorable. In a chartered airplane, Reporter Robert F. Alkire and Photographer Jack White explored the vast gash in the earth worn by the muddy Colorado River, searching for the wreckage. They found the United Air Lines' DC 7, which had carried 58 persons to death, on bleak Chuar Butte. A half mile south, on Temple Butte, they spotted the remains of the TWA Super-Constellation which had gone down with 70 persons. They dropped off at Cedar City, in southwestern Utah, to write the story and get the pictures in.

As Executive Editor Arthur C. Deck said, "The coverage of this tragic news event was so broad, and involved so many obstacles which our staff overcame, that we felt the entire staff should be named in preference to individuals."

When the Pulitzer Prizes were awarded for 1957, that was why one went to the staff of the Salt Lake *Tribune*. In recognition of the ever-broadening concept of what is local news, the prize was for local reporting under edition deadline pressure. Alkire's story of his flight over Grand Canyon was an excellent example of the quality of the *Tribune's* coverage.

FLIGHT INTO GRAND CANYON

By Robert F. Alkire

From the Salt Lake Tribune, July 2, 1956

CEDAR CITY, UTAH, July 1—I have just come from the scene of the world's worst commercial air disaster. There isn't much left.

Bits of torn metal and blackened fire-burned areas mark the only trace of two giant airliners—a DC-7 owned by United Airlines and a TWA Super-Constellation—that Saturday carried 128 persons to death.

The site of the crashes is about 22 miles northeast of Grand Canyon, Ariz. Men who live and work in this country call it "the most rugged in the world."

Near the confluence of the Little Colorado and Colorado Rivers in Grand Canyon there stands a 6,500-foot bluff—Chuar Butte. On a 700-foot knoll extending east from the butte there is a black drape. That possibly will be the final resting place of the 58 passengers and crewmen who rode the tumbling United Airlines DC-7 to destruction.

A half-mile south of the butte, in a narrow canyon, a bit of metal glints in the sun. And at this spot—designated as Temple Butte—another 70 persons riding a Trans World Airliner plunged to death.

Even a trained observer could be fooled by the lack of evidence at the site. No large chunks of aircraft. No broken, twisted seats. No bodies visible from a plane 220 feet above the scene.

Where the DC-7 thudded into the knoll, it looks as though a giant had carefully mixed small bits of metal and black paint and dumped it neatly over the top of the huge rock. The burn area drains down both sides of the knoll, indicating the DC-7 struck with such force on the very edge of the rock that about half of it was flung 50 feet or more up over the top.

In the region of the Constellation wreckage there are bigger chunks of metal, but again no signs of bodies or even the definite outlines of a fuselage in the burn patch. Even if a ground party were to reach the area, chances of climbing the vertical 700-foot knoll to the UAL liner are dim, indeed.

BOMBER CRASHES IN STREET

FROM THE FILE THAT WON THE PULITZER PRIZE, 1956, FOR
THE ENTIRE PICTURE STAFF OF THE NEW YORK DAILY NEWS.

SINKING OF THE LINER ANDREA DORIA, *by Harry A. Trask*

PULITZER PRIZE, 1957 BOSTON TRAVELER

As you approach the area by air from the northwest, you understand the frustrating difficulty of locating even a huge airliner in the maze of side-canyons that stretch away from the mighty Colorado River and its containing Grand Canyon.

From 4,000 feet overhead, all canyons look hauntingly alike and rivers flow together in a muddle of twists and turns that make it difficult to separate the Colorado from its feeder streams. Faint paths of small animals wander aimlessly over the red sand among the low, green-hued sagebrush. Here, a man afoot must be careful of his path as death is only the next step away.

The sun has no mercy and nature no shade for 120-degree temperatures fire the sand and the careless or foolish can die fast. As you come abreast of the canyon rim, the sand breaks away and 2,000 feet below the raging Colorado is only a trickle, twisting through jagged walls of rock.

Where is the Little Colorado that pinpoints the site of the crashes?

A dozen meandering 2,000-foot high canyons pour into the area, but only one is the smaller river. Still, it isn't necessary to look at the ground. Straight ahead in the mist above the chasm, several planes wheel like cautious buzzards. Now and then one dips from the pattern over the crash and zips past the black scar on the knoll, rising again to circle again—futilely.

Several of the circling aircraft are seaplanes, members of rescue services, but out of their element here, and others are private and military planes. They are not there to look for survivors for almost certainly there are none. But they serve to guide other craft into the area and to advise ground directors.

Perhaps the strangest thing about the crashes is that both planes are a mere mile or two from the east side of the canyon (the river flows north and south at the site).

Had the tumbling airliners fallen that distance further east, they would have struck a broad plateau and been spotted immediately. Ground parties and helicopters would have had no difficulty reaching them.

But in their locations amid the rugged canyon walls, even experienced pilots wonder whether a 'copter could reach the site. Perhaps the most terrible thing about the scene is the lack of evidence.

You wonder how two giant four-engine airlines with tremendous wing spans and carrying tons of metal and equipment could so obliterate themselves along with their human cargoes.

It is with a flood of relief that after several passes within 220 feet of the blackened knoll, you climb back above the river mist and into the sunlight, leaving 128 victims of the world's bloodiest commercial aviation disaster to what is in all probability their final rest.

53. JOHN PAULSON AND STAFF
COVER A DAKOTA TORNADO

The editor of the Fargo (N.D.) Forum finds
his basement is the safest spot

Pulitzer Prize for Local Reporting, 1958

"A tornado's hitting! It's on West Main Avenue headed for downtown!"

That news burst upon the Fargo (N. D.) *Forum* at 7:40 p.m. June 20, 1957. John D. Paulson, the editor, was at his home with his family when the *Forum's* night editor phoned him. Even then, the devastating wind funnel was sweeping through Fargo and he and his family headed for the basement.

Some of the *Forum's* staff were caught in the open. Others huddled in the city room. But as quickly as they could, once the danger was over, they got on the job and told the story. The tornado had destroyed or damaged sixty-six blocks in Fargo, killed ten persons, and injured scores of others.

Less than six hours after the tornado, the *Forum* hit the streets of the stunned city with twenty-four columns of tornado news and fourteen pictures. John Paulson and his staff had done a job. The *Forum* was awarded the Pulitzer Prize for Local Reporting under edition deadline pressure for 1958. Some of the personal stories from that edition follow.

"THE WINDS SWELLED TO A BLAST"

By John D. Paulson

From the Fargo (N. D.) Forum, June 21, 1957

When a newspaperman is caught directly in the path of a tornado, he acts just like everybody else. He gets his family into the southwest corner of the basement, stays there himself, and prays that no one is hurt.

At least, that is what I did.

Minutes before the tornado struck, I was sitting in the kitchen after dinner telling the youngsters that a tornado warning didn't necessarily mean that it would hit our house. Then came a phone call from the Fargo *Forum* office with Night Editor James Acton reporting that a terrific tornado had hit West Main Street and was heading for downtown Fargo.

As I talked, I looked out of the west window of our home and saw the trees beginning to shake as the winds swelled to a blast. I told Zoe and the four youngsters to head for the basement. The lights went out. In another half minute I told Acton that I, too, was headed for the basement.

Down there in the southwest corner we just sat and waited for what was going to happen. I peeked upward out of the small basement window and saw all kinds of debris sailing through the air in a northerly direction.

Then the debris began to swirl and I knew we were in the virtual center of the tornado's funnel. There were sounds of windows popping upstairs and some more solid thuds.

Then in a minute or two it was all over.

On the way upstairs for a look, the first thing we saw was a back door smashed in. The kitchen was a mess, with dishes, utensils, food, and broken glass scattered all around. Throughout the downstairs more windows were smashed and rain came spitting in.

A glance at the backyard showed that our two car garage had disappeared. On the roof of the car that had been inside the garage was a two-foot-square chunk of brick chimney.

There was nothing to do but get the family into the car and take them over to my parents, and report for tornado duty at the Fargo *Forum.*

This was the way the tornado came to Fargo. Tom Lucier, a reporter for the *Forum,* tried to evacuate his wife and baby by car and was caught under the death-dealing black cloud. He lived to write this story:

"LIGHTNING RIPPED THE SKY"

By Tom Lucier

As though threatened by an A-bomb attack, hundreds—perhaps thousands—of Fargo-Moorhead residents evacuated the two cities as tornado funnels appeared over the western horizon Thursday night.

With my wife and baby, I joined a stream of nervous motorists that sped north out of Moorhead along Highway 75. There were scores of cars parked along the highway and congested knots of vehicles at every crossroad and intersection.

Shortly after 7:30 p.m., we left our south Moorhead home. To the west, seemingly directly over Fargo, we saw the massive funnel forming and revolving. Great gulps of ragged clouds were being sucked from all directions into the vortex as the gigantic funnel moved toward us.

From under the terrible blue-black storm head, small funnels dangled like teats from an udder. Then two solid, almost perpendicular funnel columns formed side by side, seemingly reaching to the ground. We said a silent prayer for anyone who might be under these black brooms of potential sudden death and moved on to the north.

By this time traffic was converging onto Highway 75 from all avenues and we joined the caravan. Many of the evacuees had stopped along the highway and gotten out of their cars to watch the huge formation move over the city with deadly majesty.

The wind seemed to be coming from all directions and as we watched with the rest, the great column began to veer toward the northeast—straight in our direction.

With a chill sensation of danger, I joined the cars that began now to move north at increasing speed.

Now the great black cloud was directly over us—we could no longer determine the location of the funnel, if it was still active.

Suddenly the countryside was swept with a pounding, blinding rain. The wind howled, lightning ripped the sky and hailstones—some nearly as big as ping-pong balls—pelted the car. Traffic came to a stop.

When it was over, we saw the thunderhead moving west over Dilworth. Although still funnel-shaped, it did not look so dangerous as before and did not touch down. It seemed to be breaking up.

As we waited to start back to Moorhead, a long gray-white tube snaked down from the swirling skies and touched down on the momentarily flooded fields east of the highway about 500 yards away.

This tube, of relatively small diameter, seemed to curl thousands of feet into the air. Moments later, it was sucked up into the atmosphere and disintegrated.

No ball game, no story. Or so Eugene Fitzgerald would have thought on an ordinary night. But that night, at the baseball field when the Fargo-Moorhead game with Duluth-Superior was called off, the sports editor of the *Forum* ran head-on into one of the biggest stories of his life. He wrote, in a quiet, matter-of-fact way:

"A SICKENING SIGHT"

By Eugene Fitzgerald

About 100 of us were at Barnett Field Thursday evening awaiting the start of the Fargo-Moorhead Twins baseball game with Duluth-Superior.

We watched the tornado form in the west. We had no idea the thing was only four blocks away. We went into the clubhouse to get out of the rain. At about 8:15, assured that there would be no game, I left, heading for home.

Traffic on Broadway was blocked at Fifteenth Avenue N. I was directed to go east on Fifteenth Avenue. At John D. Paulson's home at Fourteenth Avenue and Second Street N., we noticed the first damage. Gerald Redmond's garage at 1363 Second Street was gone.

Then we saw the Ken Collins home, facing El Zagal Bowl on Fourteenth Avenue and First Street. It looked like it had been shelled. That was the first intimation we had that my home might have been in the path of the wind.

What had been a normal home at 1301 Second Street N only a little more than an hour earlier when we left for the game was a shambles. My garage, attached to the house, was completely gone.

In the front room, which runs the length of the house facing the street, the floor was bare. Two big chairs, the davenport, a piano, the television set and even the rug had been swept through the north side of the house, where the wall had been blown off.

The piano was on the television set just outside the house. The rest of the furniture wasn't in sight. Your home, almost totally destroyed, is a sickening sight.

But I had a more serious worry. I forgot it quickly enough when I saw my fifteen-year-old son, Phil, left at home alone when we went to the baseball game, in the street with a flashlight. He had spent the period of the storm in the basement.

We had just finished spring cleaning Tuesday. I don't believe we'll call the cleaning woman back right away.

X. OF PEOPLE AND PLACES:
GOLDEN THREADS
OF HUMAN INTEREST

The United Nations was very young. Russian misconduct in the Security Council was very new. And the reporters' gallery in what had been the girls' gym at Hunter College in New York City was very full of experts. If you looked hard, you could even find a few working reporters.

When old Jimmy Byrnes began his big speech, the floodlights glinting on his balding white head and fingering the silver on the spectacles that made him look like a country judge, it was as if a sigh had rustled through the building. Everybody knew the United States would insist on asking the Security Council to demand why Russian troops had invaded Iran. Nearly everybody suspected the Russians wouldn't want to talk about it. Byrnes, for the U.S., did the expected.

The clock ticked on. The Russians gathered up their papers. And Andrei Gromyko, much younger then and immaculate in a capital-istic-looking double-breasted suit, said a few words in Russian and walked out. But as quickly as the Security Council door swung shut behind him, Frank Begley, a Connecticut Irishman, was at his side. In those days, he was what amounted to the United Nations' chief of police and guarding the delegates was his job.

"Mr. Ambassador," said Begley. "The photographers are waiting downstairs for you."

"Tell them to go away," Gromyko said peevishly.

Begley murmured politely that it was a free country, and the Ambassador would have to run the photographic gauntlet. But he suggested that perhaps the Ambassador would want to button up his overcoat.

Gromyko, suspicious over such solicitude, snapped, "Button up my overcoat? Why? Why should I button up my overcoat?"

"Because, Mr. Ambassador," said the discreet Begley, "you are unzipped and your shirttail is showing."

Which explains why the angry-looking Gromyko that March day clutched his overcoat about him although the weather was mild. It also illustrates the journalistic thesis that even the stuffiest of mortals remembers occasionally to act like a human being. It is of such incidents that the golden texture of human interest reporting is woven, whether at great events or small.

But just as there is no way to cover a story with a stop-watch or get out a paper with a slide rule, no one yet has been able to discover a way of predicting when or where such incidents will occur. The only certainty is that they attach themselves, in an uncanny way, to people and places at particular moments that are most fitting. So, when Edward VIII began his famous abdication speech, his first thoughts were not of the passing of empire but of "the woman I love."

And when John J. Leary went into the West Virginia coal fields for the New York *World* in 1919 to write a Pulitzer Prize-winning series, his most interesting story was not about the striking coal miners at all but about a college-bred gunman.

"The number of notches in his gun are not less than half a dozen and perhaps in excess of a dozen," Leary wrote. "Only once is he known to have lost a fight. On that occasion he made the mistake of carrying the war on the United Mine Workers into their own district headquarters. When he emerged, it was to go to the local hospital with a bullet wound through both lungs . . . According to the miner who shot him, he was beaten to the draw."

The examples of human interest reporting in the Pulitzer Prize files are varied. They range from Kirke L. Simpson's classic "Warrior's Requiem" to some of the lighter columns of James Reston and the somber mourning of Ernie Pyle for a fallen soldier. These and others follow—some of the human stories of the era.

BABE RUTH BOWS OUT, *by Nathaniel Fein*

PULITZER PRIZE, 1949   NEW YORK HERALD TRIBUNE

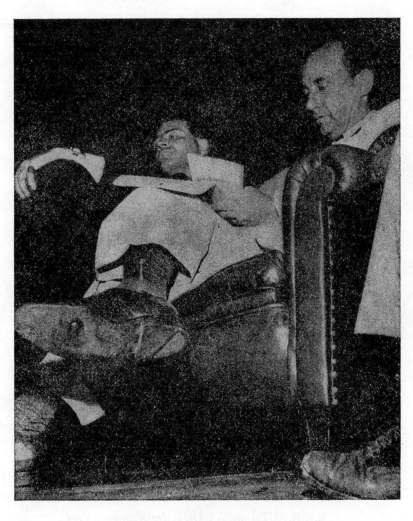

HOLE IN ADLAI'S SHOE, *by William M. Gallagher*

PULITZER PRIZE, 1953 FLINT (MICH.) JOURNAL

TRAGEDY BY THE SEA, *by John L. Gaunt*

A YOUNG COUPLE STANDS BESIDE AN ANGRY SEA IN WHICH ONLY
A FEW MINUTES EARLIER THEIR YEAR-OLD SON HAD PERISHED.

PULITZER PRIZE, 1955   LOS ANGELES TIMES

FAITH AND CONFIDENCE, *by William C. Beall*

PULITZER PRIZE, 1958   WASHINGTON DAILY NEWS

54. "HE WAS HOME, THE UNKNOWN"
KIRKE SIMPSON'S GREAT STORY

An Associated Press reporter writes a classic
about the Unknown Soldier for the night wire

Pulitzer Prize for Reporting, 1922

In these days of chopped-up "readability" journalism, Kirke Larue Simpson's account of the burial of the Unknown Soldier remains one of the enduring classics of American newspaper work. Emotional writing may be somewhat less than fashionable now. Yet, Simpson's stories stand the test of time.

From the moment the old cruiser *Olympia* nosed out of the Potomac River mists on an Indian summer morning in 1921, bearing the coffin of the nameless hero, Simpson was on the job for the Associated Press. He wrote out of a full heart. The AP, which is somewhat less than demonstrative as a rule, used every word.

Simpson wrote story after story. It was, after all, what is known as a running story and it changed hour by hour. Moreover, AP morning papers wanted stories different from AP evening papers. The reporter obliged. He did one piece for the AP night report of November 9, and four more for the day and night reports of November 10 and 11. In addition, for evening papers of November 11, he sent what is known in the business as a "past-tensed" story by mail. In this, the Unknown Soldier already was entombed and various speeches that could be obtained in advance were used, the whole being released by wire as soon as the event officially occurred.

After complying with all these wire service requirements, Simpson at last sat in the AP Washington bureau and did his great "live" story— the final one—for the night wire of the AP on November 11. It is republished here. For it, and his others, he was awarded the Pulitzer Prize for Reporting in 1922. It was the finest story of his thirty-seven years for the AP, and one of the greatest that ever sped over the "A" wire.

THE WARRIOR'S REQUIEM

By Kirke L. Simpson

From the Associated Press night wire, Nov. 11, 1921

WASHINGTON, Nov. 11 (AP)—Under the wide and starry skies of his own homeland America's unknown dead from France sleeps tonight, a soldier home from the wars.

Alone, he lies in the narrow cell of stone that guards his body; but his soul has entered into the spirit that is America. Wherever liberty is held close in men's hearts, the honor and the glory and the pledge of high endeavor poured out over this nameless one of fame will be told and sung by Americans for all time.

Scrolled across the marble arch of the memorial raised to American soldier and sailor dead, everywhere, which stands like a monument behind his tomb, runs this legend: "We here highly resolve that these dead shall not have died in vain."

The words were spoken by the martyred Lincoln over the dead at Gettysburg. And today with voice strong with determination and ringing with deep emotion, another President echoed that high resolve over the coffin of the soldier who died for the flag in France.

Great men in the world's affairs heard that high purpose reiterated by the man who stands at the head of the American people. Tomorrow they will gather in the city that stands almost in the shadow of the new American shrine of liberty dedicated today. They will talk of peace; of the curbing of the havoc of war.

They will speak of the war in France, that robbed this soldier of life and name and brought death to comrades of all nations by the hundreds of thousands. And in their ears when they meet must ring President Harding's declaration today beside that flag-wrapped, honor-laden bier:

"There must be, there shall be, the commanding voice of a conscious civilization against armed warfare."

Far across the seas, other unknown dead, hallowed in memory by their countrymen, as this American soldier is enshrined in the heart of America, sleep their last. He, in whose veins ran the blood of British forbears, lies beneath a great stone in ancient Westminster

Abbey; he of France, beneath the Arc de Triomphe, and he of Italy under the altar of the Fatherland in Rome.

And it seemed today that they, too, must be here among the Potomac hills to greet an American comrade come to join their glorious company, to testify their approval of the high words of hope spoken by America's President. All day long the nation poured out its heart in pride and glory for the nameless American. Before the first crash of the minute guns roared its knell for the dead from the shadow of Washington Monument, the people who claim him as their own were trooping out to do him honor. They lined the long road from the Capitol to the hillside where he sleeps tonight; they flowed like a tide over the slopes about his burial place; they choked the bridges that lead across the river to the field of the brave, in which he is the last comer.

As he was carried past through the banks of humanity that lined Pennsylvania Avenue a solemn, reverent hush held the living walls. Yet there was not so much of sorrow as of high pride in it all, a pride beyond the reach of shouting and the clamor that marks less sacred moments in life.

Out there in the broad avenue was a simple soldier, dead for honor of the flag. He was nameless. No man knew what part in the great life of the nation he had filled when last he passed over his home soil. But in France he had died as Americans always have been ready to die, for the flag and what it means. They read the message of the pageant clear, these silent thousands along the way. They stood in almost holy awe to take their own part in what was theirs, the glory of the American people, honored here in the honors showered on America's nameless son from France.

Soldiers, sailors, and marines—all played their part in the thrilling spectacles as the cortege rolled along. And just behind the casket, with its faded French flowers on the draped flag, walked the President, the chosen leader of a hundred million, in whose name he was chief mourner at his bier. Beside him strode the man under whom the fallen hero had lived and died in France, General Pershing, wearing only the single medal of Victory that every American soldier might wear as his only decoration.

Then, row on row, came the men who lead the nation today or

have guided its destinies before. They were all there, walking proudly with age and frailties of the flesh forgotten. Judges, senators, representatives, highest officers of every military arm of government and a trudging little group of the nation's most valorous sons, the Medal of Honor men. Some were gray and bent and drooping with old wounds; some trim and erect as the day they won their way to fame. All walked gladly in this nameless comrade's last parade.

Behind these came the carriage in which rode Woodrow Wilson, also stricken down by infirmities as he served in the highest place of the nation, just as the humble private riding in such state ahead had gone down before a shell or a bullet. For that dead man's sake, the former President had put aside his dread of seeming to parade his physical weakness and risked health, perhaps life, to appear among the mourners for the fallen.

There was handclapping and a cheer here and there for the man in the carriage, a tribute to the spirit that brought him to honor the nation's nameless hero, whose commander-in-chief he had been.

After President Harding and most of the high dignitaries of the government had turned aside at the White House, the procession, headed by its solid blocks of soldiery and the battalions of sailor comrades, moved on with Pershing, now flanked by Secretaries Weeks and Denby, for the long road to the tomb. It marched on, always between the human borders of the way of victory the nation had made for itself of the great avenue; on over the old bridge that spans the Potomac, on up the long hill to Fort Myer, and at last to the great cemetery beyond, where soldier and sailor folk sleep by the thousands. There the lumbering guns of the artillery swung aside, the cavalry drew their horses out of the long line and left to the foot soldiers and the sailors and marines the last stage of the journey.

Ahead, the white marble of the amphitheater gleamed through the trees. It stands crowning the slope of the hills that sweep upward from the river and just across was Washington, its clustered buildings and monuments to great dead who have gone before, a moving picture in the autumn haze.

People in thousands were moving about the great circle of the amphitheater. The great ones to whom places had been given in the sacred enclosure and the plain folk who trudged the long way just to glimpse the pageant from afar were finding their places. Everywhere within the pillared enclosure bright uniforms of foreign soldiers appeared. They were laden with the jeweled order of rank to honor an American private soldier, great in the majesty of his sacrifices, in the tribute his honors paid to all Americans who died.

Down below the platform placed for the casket, in a stone vault, lay wreaths and garlands brought from England's king and guarded by British soldiers. To them came the British Ambassador in the full uniform of his rank to bid them keep these tributes from overseas safe against that hour.

Above the platform gathered men whose names ring through history—Briand, Foch, Beatty, Balfour, Jacques, Diaz, and others— a brilliant array of place and power. They were followed by others, Baron Kato from Japan, the Italian statesmen and officers, by the notables from all countries gathered here for tomorrow's conference and by some of the older figures in American life too old to walk beside the approaching funeral train.

Down around the circling pillars the marbled box filled with distinguished men and women, with a cluster of shattered men from army hospitals accompanied by uniformed nurses. A surpliced choir took its place to wait the dead.

Faint and distant, the silvery strains of a military band stole into the big white bowl of the amphitheater. The slow cadences and mourning notes of a funeral march grew clearer amid the roll and mutter of the muffled drums.

At the arch where the choir waited the heroic dead, comrades lifted his casket down and, followed by the generals and the admirals, who had walked beside him from the Capitol, he was carried to the place of honor. Ahead moved the white-robed singers, chanting solemnly. Carefully, the casket was placed above the banked flowers and the Marine Band played sacred melodies until the moment the President and Mrs. Harding stepped to their places beside the casket; then the crashing, triumphant chords of "The Star-Spangled Banner" swept the gathering to its feet again.

A prayer, carried out over the crowd by amplifiers so that no word was missed, took a moment or two, then the sharp, clear call of the bugle rang "Attention!" and for two minutes the nation stood at pause for the dead, just at high noon. No sound broke the quiet as all stood with bowed heads. It was much as though a mighty hand had checked the world in full course. Then the band sounded and in a mighty chorus rolled up the words of "America" from the hosts within and without the great open hall of valor.

President Harding stepped forward beside the coffin to say for America the thing that today was nearest to the nation's heart, that sacrifices such as this nameless man, fallen in battle, might perhaps be made unnecessary down through the coming years. Every word that President Harding spoke reached every person through the amplifiers and reached other thousands upon thousands in New York and San Francisco.

Mr. Harding showed strong emotion as his lips formed the last words of the address. He paused, then with raised hand and head bowed, went on in the measured, rolling period of the Lord's Prayer. The response that came back to him from the thousands he faced, from the other thousands out over the slopes beyond, perhaps from still other thousands away near the Pacific, or close packed in the heart of the nation's greatest city, arose like a chant. The marble arches hummed with the solemn sound.

Then the foreign officers who stand highest among the soldiers or sailors of their flags came one by one to the bier to place gold and jeweled emblems for the brave above the breast of the sleeper. Already, as the great prayer ended, the President had set the American seal of admiration for the valiant, the nation's love for brave deeds and the courage that defies death, upon the casket.

Side by side he laid the Medal of Honor and the Distinguished Service Cross. And below, set in place with reverent hands, grew the long line of foreign honors, the Victoria Cross, never before laid on the breast of any but those who had served the British flag; all the highest honors of France and Belgium and Italy and Rumania and Czechoslovakia and Poland.

To General Jacques of Belgium it remained to add this own touch to these honors. He tore from the breast of his own tunic the medal of valor pinned there by the Belgian king, tore it with a sweeping gesture, and tenderly bestowed it on the unknown American warrior.

Through the religious services that followed, and prayers, the swelling crowd sat motionless until it rose to join in the old, consoling "Rock of Ages," and the last rite for the dead was at hand. Lifted by his hero bearers from the stage, the unknown was carried in his flag-wrapped, simple coffin out to the wide sweep of the terrace. The bearers laid the sleeper down above the crypt on which had been placed a little of the soil of France. The dust his blood helped redeem from alien hands will mingle with his dust as time marches by.

The simple words of the burial ritual were said by Bishop Brent, flowers from war mothers of America and England were laid in place.

For the Indians of America Chief Plenty Coos came to call upon the Great Spirit of the Red Men, with gesture and chant and tribal tongue that the dead should not have died in vain, that war might end, peace be purchased by such blood as this. Upon the casket he laid the coup stick of his tribal office and the feathered war bonnet from his own head. Then the casket, with its weight of honors, was lowered into the crypt.

A rocking blast of gunfire rang from the woods. The glittering circle of bayonets stiffened to a salute to the dead. Again the guns shouted their message of honor and farewell. Again they boomed out; a loyal comrade was being laid to his last, long rest.

High and clear and true in the echoes of the guns, a bugle lifted the old, old notes of Taps, the lullaby for the living soldier, in death his requiem. Long ago some forgotten soldier poet caught its meaning clear and set it down that soldiers everywhere might know its message as they sink to rest:

"Fades the light;
And afar
Goeth day, cometh night,
And a star,
Leadeth all, speedeth all,
To their rest."

The guns roared out again in the national salute. He was home, The Unknown, to sleep forever among his own.

Simpson retired from the Washington staff of the Associated Press in 1945, at the age of sixty-five. In 1958 he was living quietly in San Francisco.

55. ANNE O'HARE McCORMICK
VISITS VATICAN CITY

The New York Times's foreign specialist writes
a colorful account of the life of Pius XI

Pulitzer Prize for Correspondence, 1937

Anne O'Hare McCormick was the foremost woman journalist of her day. Her reporting from Europe immediately after World War I sounded a warning for America of the rise of Fascism. She predicted the emergence of Mussolini, traced Hitler's rise to power, and bitterly expressed the conviction that war would follow.

"Nothing better or more stable can be established by more war," she wrote in 1935, "but in the long view it is equally certain that there must be war—not all the sanctions in the world can stop it—until there is a league not only to enforce but to create peace . . ."

Mrs. McCormick became a member of The New York *Times* editorial board in 1937, after having written for that newspaper as a free lance and special correspondent from 1921 on. Her area of operation was the world. Her column on the *Times* editorial page was called "Abroad." Of course she also worked in the United States when the occasion was opportune.

"Your field," Publisher Arthur Hays Sulzberger told her, "will be the freedoms. It will be your job to guard against encroachments on them anywhere."

That was Mrs. McCormick's mission until her dying day. In 1937, having established an enviable reputation for foreign reporting over a period of years, she was awarded the Pulitzer Prize for Correspondence. While it is technically outside the span of the calendar year of 1936 for which the prize was awarded, her visit to Vatican City as published in the *Times Magazine* is typical of her best work in many respects.

In its topical purpose, the piece is dated. It was written at a time when Pope Pius XI was striving to end the Italian aggression in Ethiopia without issuing a moral condemnation of Mussolini, from whom the Pontiff had just won a hard territorial settlement. Aside from its sympathetic analysis of these political difficulties, however, Mrs. McCormick drew an unforgettable word picture of the life of a Pope in his tiny state. That portion of her report follows.

"A BORN POPE"

By Anne O'Hare McCormick

From the New York Times, Dec. 15, 1935

ROME—Pope Pius XI assisted recently at the memorial mass celebrated annually in the Sistine Chapel for the Cardinals who have died during the year. Around him that morning were grouped most of the living Cardinals of the Curia. Beyond the lovely marble screen of Mino da Fiesole they sat in two rows facing one another, their bent white heads and crimson capes overshadowed by Michelangelo's "Last Judgment"—in a world of dark signs perhaps still the greatest handwriting on the wall. The Pope himself sat apart, on a throne beside the altar, a hieratic figure that nothing overshadowed. In his stiff, bell-like cope, his tall miter, he looked rigid and symbolic as the rock of Peter.

At public functions Pius XI has this quality of immobility that makes every one around him appear fidgety and nervous. His vigor is extraordinary for a man of seventy-eight. His strong-featured face is still bronzed after a summer spent on the terraced hills above Lake Albano. His black hair is only sprinkled with gray. As he intones the benediction his voice is firm and resonant. His step is heavier but as decisive as on the June day in 1921 when he entered the nearby Hall of the Consistory to receive the red hat.

Even more extraordinary than the Pope's vigor is his quietness. It is not the quiet of serenity; there is too much iron in it for that. In the Vatican they speak of him as "a born Pope," meaning that his character is as papal as his office. In a period so overwhelmed by shouting rulers, he is the only one I have seen who suggests force in repose. . . .

Pius XI is intensely interested in the events and movements of his time. He reads widely, catechizes all his visitors, dips into thousands of letters. You would not believe how many people write directly to the Pope if you did not see the baskets of letters carried into his study every morning, there to be opened in his presence by four secretaries. Still less would you imagine the scope and character of these epistles.

Obviously, it occurs to people of all persuasions, all over the world, to confide to the Supreme Pontiff their family difficulties, their spiritual problems, their material needs. As many advise him what to do as ask his advice. A large proportion ask for money. The Pope does not answer these letters personally, but on hundreds he draws a line in red pencil opposite the main point of the letter and sends it off to be dealt with by his Nuncio in the country whence it comes or the Bishop of some distant diocese.

A recent visitor found him with a pile of letters from England on one hand, a book describing the new political tendencies of France on the other, and in front of him the London *Times*, which he reads every morning. After a perfunctory inquiry as to the visitor's health —and Pius XI has little concern for the ills of the flesh, in himself or others—he plunged without preliminaries into a keen discussion of world affairs.

In character he is not so much austere as habitually serious. He seldom smiles or relaxes. His thoroughness and tirelessness are proverbial at the Vatican. He knows the dioceses under his charge as well as he knew the books on his shelves when he was librarian of two of the great libraries of Italy. He has organized his handker-chief-size kingdom to the last detail with the most business-like precision.

The Vatican has been completely modernized during his reign, and many of its great art collections have been rehoused. He has built enormously, for use rather than beauty, in the space at his disposal since Vatican City became the smallest independent state in the world. It is due to him that it is so small; he deliberately cut out of the final settlement the adjoining Villa Doria and its park which Mussolini wished to cede. "The Church wants independence," he said, "not territory."

"Everything this Pope touches he tidies up," remarked an old Monsignore rather somberly, and you can see his passion for order and system in the arrangements of Vatican City and in the model dairy farm he has constructed at his country villa at Castel Gandolfo where the scrubbed "papal briefs," as the dairymen call the newest calves, swagger in blue-tiled stalls that are the marvel of the countryside.

Stronger still is his passion for order in the world. Political order, social order, moral order. The Pope is terribly anxious as he looks out upon the gloomy confusion of the secular scene.

56. ERNIE PYLE WRITES AN OBIT:
THE DEATH OF CAPTAIN WASKOW

A war correspondent turns aside from battle
to record a soldier's tribute

Pulitzer Prize for Correspondence, 1944

Nobody ever called him Ernest Taylor Pyle, but that was his name. He did everything there was to do in the newspaper business. Reporter . . . desk man . . . managing editor . . . war correspondent. He was even a copyreader in New York for awhile. The battered wooden horseshoe where he ground out headlines may still be seen at the Columbia Graduate School of Journalism.

Pick up any collection of Ernie Pyle's pieces, from bound volumes to the faded and crumbling scrapbook in the Pulitzer Prize files at Butler Library, Columbia University. Open it at random and you'll find something worth reading. There is no single piece of his that is remembered above all others. He never wrote a really bad one.

This one is an obit, after a fashion. He wrote it while serving in Italy as a war correspondent for Scripps-Howard Newspaper Alliance in 1943. It was in the collection that won for him the Pulitzer Prize for Correspondence in 1944.

"I SURE AM SORRY, SIR"

By Ernie Pyle

Written for Scripps-Howard Newspaper Alliance

In this war I have known a lot of officers who were loved and respected by the soldiers under them. But never have I crossed the trail of any man as beloved as Captain Henry T. Waskow, of Belton, Texas.

Captain Waskow was a company commander in the Thirty-sixth Division. He had led his company since long before it left the States. He was very young, only in his middle twenties, but he carried in

him a sincerity and a gentleness that made people want to be guided
by him.

"After my father, he came next," a sergeant told me.

"He always looked after us," a soldier said. "He'd go to bat for us
every time."

"I've never knowed him to do anything unfair," another said.

I was at the foot of the mule trail the night they brought Captain
Waskow down. The moon was nearly full, and you could see far up
the trail, and even part way across the valley below.

Dead men had been coming down the mountain all evening,
lashed onto the backs of mules. They came lying belly-down across
the wooden pack-saddles, their heads hanging down on one side,
their stiffened legs sticking out awkwardly from the other, bobbing
up and down as the mules walked.

The Italian mule skinners were afraid to walk beside the dead
men, so Americans had to lead the mules down that night.

Even the Americans were reluctant to unlash and lift off the
bodies when they got to the bottom, so an officer had to do it himself and ask others to help.

I don't know who that first one was. You feel small in the presence
of dead men, and you don't ask silly questions. They slid him down
from the mule, and stood him on his feet for a moment. In the half-
light he might have been merely a sick man standing there leaning
on the others. Then they laid him on the ground in the shadow of
the low stone wall beside the road. We left him there beside the
road, that first one, and we all went back into the cowshed and sat
on water cans or lay on the straw, waiting for the next batch of
mules.

Somebody said the dead soldier had been dead for four days, and
then nobody said anything more about it. We talked soldier talk for
an hour or more; the dead man lay all alone, outside in the shadow
of the wall.

Then a soldier came into the cowshed and said there were some
more bodies outside. We went out into the road. Four mules stood
there in the moonlight, in the road where the trail came down off
the mountain. The soldiers who led them stood there waiting.

"This one is Captain Waskow," one of them said quietly.

Two men unlashed his body from the mule and lifted it off and laid it in the shadow beside the stone wall. Other men took the other bodies off. Finally, there were five lying end to end in a long row. You don't cover up dead men in the combat zones. They just lie there in the shadows until somebody comes after them.

The unburdened mules moved off to their olive grove. The men in the road seemed reluctant to leave. They stood around, and gradually I could sense them moving, one by one, close to Captain Waskow's body. Not so much to look, I think, as to say something in finality to him, and to themselves. I stood close by and I could hear.

One soldier came and looked down, and he said out loud, "God damn it!" That's all he said, and then he walked away.

Another one came, and he said, "God damn it, to hell, anyway!" He looked down for a few last moments and then turned and left.

Another man came. I think he was an officer. It was hard to tell officers from men in the dim light, for everybody was bearded and grimy. The man looked down into the dead captain's face and then spoke directly to him, as though he were alive, "I'm sorry, old man."

Then a soldier came and stood beside the officer and bent over, and he too spoke to his dead captain, not in a whisper but awfully tenderly, and he said, "I sure am sorry, sir."

Then the first man squatted down, and he reached down and took the captain's hand, and he sat there for a full five minutes holding the dead hand in his own and looking intently into the dead face. And he never uttered a sound all the time he sat there.

Finally he put the hand down. He reached over and gently straightened the points of the captain's shirt collar, and then he sort of rearranged the tattered edges of the uniform around the wound, and then he got up and walked away down the road in the moonlight, all alone.

The rest of us went back into the cowshed, leaving the five dead men lying in a line, end to end, in the shadow of the low stone wall. We lay down on the straw in the cowshed, and pretty soon we were all asleep.

57. HOW THEY RAISED THE FLAG
ON MOUNT SURIBACHI

The story of the greatest picture of World War II,
as told by Joe Rosenthal, who took it

Pulitzer Prize for Photography, 1945

Joe Rosenthal was on assignment for the Associated Press in the Pacific during World War II. He was a photographer. His business was to spot the picture, point the camera, focus, and snap the shutter. He wasn't supposed to write.

But when he took the most famous picture of World War II—the raising of the flag on Mount Suribachi at Iwo Jima—the Associated Press asked him to do a piece about it. Here it is, from the Pulitzer Prize files.

"I HOPE THIS WAS WORTH THE EFFORT . . ."

By Joe Rosenthal

From the Associated Press file, March 7, 1945

GUAM, March 7 (AP)—"See that spot of red on the mountainside?" the bos'n shouted above the noise of our landing craft nearing the shore at the base of Suribachi Yama.

"A group of Marines is climbing up to plant our flag up there. I heard it from the radioman."

He was plenty excited—and so was I.

The fall of this 560-foot fortress in four days of gallant Marine fighting was a great thing. A good story and we should have good pictures.

So in I went, back to more of that slogging through the deep volcanic sand, warily sidestepping the numerous Japanese mines. On past the culverts where the Japanese dead lay among the wreckage of their own gun positions and up the steep, winding, always sandy trail.

Marine Private Bob Campbell, a San Francisco buddy of mine, and Sergeant Bill Janausk, of Tacoma, Wash., were with me and carried firearms for protection (which is disallowed to correspondents).

There was still an occasional sharp crack of rifle fire close by and the mountainside had a porcupine appearance of bristling all over, what with machine and anti-aircraft guns peering from the dugouts, foxholes and caves. There was little sign of life from these enemy spots, however. Our men were systematically blowing out these places and we had to keep clear of our own demolition squads.

As the trail became steeper, our panting progress slowed to a few yards at a time. I began to wonder and hope that this was worth the effort when suddenly over the brow of the topmost ridge we could spy men working with the flagpole they had so laboriously brought up about three-quarters of an hour ahead of us.

I came up and stood by a few minutes until they were ready to swing the flag-bearing pole into position.

I crowded back on the inner edge of the volcano's rim, back as far as I could, in order to include all I could in the scene within the angle covered by my camera lens.

I rolled up a couple of large stones and a Japanese sandbag to raise my short height clear of an intervening obstruction. I followed up this shot with another group of cheering Marines and then I tried to find the four men I heard were the actual instigators of the grand adventure. But they had scattered to their units and I finally gave it up and descended the mountain to get the pictures out and on their way to possible publication.

The way down was quite a bit easier, the path becoming well worn and men were carrying ammunition supplies, food, and rations necessary for complete occupation of this stronghold.

The Marine history will record Iwo Jima as high as any in their many gallant actions in the Pacific.

I have two vivid memories: The fury of their D-Day assault and the thrill of that lofty flag-raising episode.

It is hard now in the quiet atmosphere of this advance camp to find words for it. The Marines at Iwo Jima were magnificent.

As will be seen, Rosenthal did not realize even when he turned out this story that his picture was destined to be famous. Long afterward, he recalled that he was so late getting to the spot where the flagpole was being raised that he had to take a desperation shot in the hope of getting some kind of a picture. He didn't know whether he'd gotten anything or not.

It was only when the AP let him know of the truly overwhelming reception that had been given to his magnificent picture that he finally knew he'd done it—taken *the* great war photograph. He received the Pulitzer Prize for Photography in 1945. His picture served as the model for a heroic Marine statue that honors the 4,590 Marines who were killed in action at Iwo Jima.

He was taking pictures for the San Francisco Chronicle in 1958.

58. GANDHI SPINS THE THREAD
OF INDIAN HISTORY

Price Day of the Baltimore Sun obtains
one of the last interviews with the Mahatma

Pulitzer Prize for International Reporting, 1949

When the British announced on February 20, 1947 that they were withdrawing from India, Mohandas K. Gandhi achieved his life's purpose. India was to be free.

The Mahatma, as India's holy man was known, had led the campaign of civil disobedience against British rule—a concept based on Thoreau's famous essay. He had known great hardship and had often been imprisoned for his beliefs. Now, perhaps, it seemed to some that his labors were almost over.

But to Gandhi it was as if they had just begun. For with the British withdrawal from India and Pakistan came the dreadful communal rioting that cost so many Hindu, Moslem, and Sikh lives. The Hindus and Sikhs fled in fear of their lives from Moslem Pakistan. Moslems got out of India as quickly as they could.

It was Gandhi's last task to try to halt the slaughter. In Calcutta, he fasted to show the people his disapproval of the rioting. And after that he came to New Delhi to try to arrange matters by statecraft after his appeal to the emotions apparently had failed.

Price Day, a correspondent for the Baltimore *Sun,* was in New Delhi at that time gathering material for a series of articles on India. Joining forces with Robert Stimson of the British Broadcasting Company, he decided to try for an interview with the Mahatma. They waited for several days. Then, to their surprise, the call came. One of Gandhi's followers led them to the house in New Delhi where he was staying. Day's interview, published in the Baltimore *Sun*, was the result. It was one of the last Gandhi granted to any reporter for only eleven days later, on January 30, he was shot and killed by a Hindu fanatic in India's capital.

Day was awarded the Pulitzer Prize in International Reporting for 1949 for his work in India. His Gandhi interview, slightly condensed, follows.

"I MAY NOT BE ALIVE"

By Price Day

From the Baltimore Sun, Jan. 19, 1948

NEW DELHI—"A good thread," said the Mahatma, "is a thing of beauty and a joy forever."

With the fingers of one hand he maintained the proper delicate tension on the cotton thread he was spinning. With the other hand he turned the small, flat *charkha*—spinning wheel—at his side on the white mattress.

Broken threads, he explained, could be repaired but should not be. He held up a little ball of broken threads. They were valuable as lamp wicks, he said, and in many other ways, such as for stuffing pin-cushions like the one on the low table in front of his mattress.

Also on the table sat a porcelain group of three monkeys: hear, see, speak no evil.

A few papers, a bottle of ink, a penpoint in a stained holder, a quart bottle two-thirds full of water and his famous dollar watch made up the rest of the homely furnishings of his immediate establishment.

At the moment he was staying in one of the richest houses in New Delhi, though normally he lives there in the colony of the sweepers, among the lowest of untouchables. In either place, the mattress and the objects on and before it are the same.

Hand-spinning, of course, is a token of Mohandas Karamchand Gandhi's identification of himself with the depressed millions of India, and of his belief in village industries. It also appears to assist him in his processes of thought.

Furthermore, at this particular time, the thin white thread, held out in his fingers, seemed to symbolize India.

The time was that of the Delhi riots, when fear had arisen that the least bit too much strain might snap the new thread of government in the Indian Dominion and prevent the fabrication of the potentially strong *khadi,* home-woven cloth of full and effective Indian self-rule.

Gandhi, after his 73-hour fast in Calcutta, had arrived in Delhi on the worst day of the riots, and had at once announced his intention of remaining until they ended.

His real task, however, was much wider than the stopping of the Delhi troubles. By the time of his arrival in New Delhi, it had become plain that the mass flight of Hindus and Sikhs from Pakistan and of Moslems from India threatened both dominions with economic disaster unless it was halted.

Less dramatically than by fasting, but with no less concentration, he went to work on a campaign which, if successful, might well be recorded by history as the greatest of all his achievements.

In brief, innumerable conferences, in his evening talks, in writing, he pursued his task hour by hour, changing his approach with each change in the situation.

"I no longer have plans," he said when interviewed. "I may hold a prayer meeting tonight—but I may not be alive.

"Whenever I make plans, something—call it God, call it Nature—intervenes. I had planned to go to the Punjab at once, but now I must stay in Delhi.

"A man going to a fire with a bucket of water must put out any fires he finds along his way. If I do this here, I will still have water to spare for the conflagration ahead."

Despite his age—by Hindu reckoning he is seventy-nine, by Western seventy-eight—Gandhi recovered quickly from the Calcutta fast.

He is in fact not a frail man, rather, a wiry one. When he walks he supports himself with one hand on the shoulder of one of his followers, often his granddaughter Manu, but in his step there is a definite, if deliberate, spring.

Also, he is tall rather than short, although when seated on his mattress the thin, naked torso, the squarish bald skull and the large ears make him appear smaller than he is.

His voice is no longer strong, but is quiet and definite. His hands are small and steady.

Surrounded by adoration, he is still relaxed, at times drily witty, occasionally almost gay. Behind his glasses—or over their upper rims—his eyes are alert and lively.

His personal needs go little beyond pen, paper, transportation, umbrella, sandals, enough *khadi* for a peasant loincloth, and the rice, vegetables, goat's cheese and curds on which he exists.

His entourage, however, consisting as it does of secretaries, cooks, physicians, and followers, is elaborate enough to have elicited the remark from an admirer that no one would ever know how much it had cost to keep the Mahatmaji in poverty.

Busy as he is, the atmosphere around Gandhi is one of calm and cleanliness—a rare atmosphere in India in the stormy weeks after independence.

59. FOR MARGARET TRUMAN:
ADVICE TO A BRIDE

James Reston of the New York Times writes
on the care and feeding of a husband

From the Pulitzer Prize National Reporting File for 1957

Among Mrs. Clifton Daniel's souvenirs of her wedding day, unless she has mislaid it, is a column of good advice published on the austere editorial page of The New York *Times* and signed by no less an authority on romance than James Reston, The *Times's* chief Washington correspondent. Any newspaperman who has ever been a husband—and perhaps a lot who haven't—will agree with his findings.

It is, of course, a matter of record that Clifton Daniel, an editor of The *Times,* and former President Truman's daughter, Margaret, were married on April 21, 1956 despite whatever small doubts Scotty Reston may have raised. His advice to a bride, dated that same day, is republished here for two reasons. It happened somehow to creep into the

formidable exhibit that won him the Pulitzer Prize for National Reporting
in 1957. It also makes good reading.

A NOTE TO MISS TRUMAN

By James Reston

From the New York Times, April 22, 1956

WASHINGTON, April 21—Clifton Daniel, the poor man's Prince
Rainier, told the reporters in Independence, Mo., yesterday that
his working hours at The New York *Times* were from 9:30 a.m. to
5:30 p.m., but his bride had better not be deceived.

It is not a reporter's working hours that count, but the hours he
works. These are regulated by the news, and the news is regulated
by a very simple mathematical rule.

This is that the news of the day, no matter how trivial or un-
important, always takes up more time than a married man has.

It makes no difference how many hours a man has to write a story
or fix up a story for publication. That story, late or soon, momentous
or frivolous, will develop a life of its own. It will kill time. It will
refuse to go down on the paper. It will develop inaccuracies, and
it will suggest historical parallels which the writer will not be able
to run down in the library.

This is known, or will hereafter be known, as O'Neill's Law of
Time Saturation. (Why?—Why not!)* It is infallible, and can be
reduced to a simple formula: News stories expand and time con-
tracts, meeting inexorably each day precisely twenty minutes after
a man is supposed to be home for dinner.

It is not difficult to understand why this is so. Anybody who has
ever watched a careful reporter agonizing in the labors of composition knows that this cannot be done without a certain ritual.

A man cannot sit down and bash things out unless he is already
banging up against deadline and long past dinnertime. He must pay
attention to the important things of life. Style is everything. He
must, for example, be free to look out the window, go get himself
a ham sandwich, find and light his tobacco, check on the progress
of the ball games, dig out a fact, contribute to the topical banter that

---

* A reminder that Ray O'Neill, National Affairs Editor of the *Times*, meets
deadlines.

is always in progress in a newspaper office, find himself a vivid active verb, and if he happens to be the assistant to the foreign editor (or even if he isn't), visit with the latest correspondent back from the wars.

Also this 5:30 business is preposterous. John Foster Dulles never ends the cold war until well after 6 each day, and now that the politicians are on the loose in the Presidential campaign, the Republic is seldom saved before 10:30 or 11 o'clock at night.

If Miss Margaret will just think about this for a minute, the facts of newspaper life will soon be apparent. Suppose a government official decides that he wishes to awaken an indifferent world with a vast pronunciamento, or stun the opposition with some verbal thunderbolt? What does he do?

He has somebody else write a speech and polish it. He gets it cleared by thirty-eight other officials, and when all the facts are arranged to suit his convenience, he issues it to the press.

He then goes home—at 5:30. His hoax for the day is finished, but when *his* day is over, the reporter's day is just beginning. Some inky wretch then has to take the spin out of the official announcement, and set it straight and in perspective.

When the Honorable Harry S. Truman retired as President of the United States and returned home to Independence, Mo., a reporter asked him what he did on his first day home. Mr. Truman replied, in a statement that touched a responsive note in every husband's heart: "I took the suitcases up to the attic."

This illustrates the great difference between life with a politician and life with a newspaperman. No newspaperman ever has time to take the suitcases up to the attic. Few New York newspapermen ever manage to get a house with an attic, and those who do are almost always on the run and therefore leave their suitcases in the front hall.

Nevertheless, it will be fun. Daniel will not work from 9:30 a.m. to 5:30 p.m., and there isn't a man in the newspaper business less likely to be good at taking suitcases up to the attic. But when he does get home, eventually, he will have something to say, and, after all, few men who arrive home on the 6:22 train can do that.

XI. ON CIVIL LIBERTIES:
THE HUMAN RIGHTS ISSUE

Mr. Blank was fired by the State Department in 1947. The reason: security.

What followed was a nightmare.

Mr. Blank was refused knowledge of the charges against him. He was told none of his questions would be answered. He was denied an appeal. He was denied the right to be confronted by his accusers. Finally, he was told he just had to be fired. He couldn't resign.

This was the story Bert Andrews broke in the New York *Herald Tribune* on November 2, 1947, being careful not to identify either Mr. Blank or six others discharged with him. Andrews did not criticize or defend the State Department. Nor did he attack or defend the records of the persons involved, or presume to judge them innocent or guilty.

What interested him was the shocking procedure that was used in what had been, up to that time at least, a democratic government. He got together documented evidence, including this quote from Mr. Blank at a "hearing" before his superiors at the State Department:

"I'm not blaming you gentlemen: you are held within certain rules and regulations, but I'd like to know what to talk about and what to say. It's extremely difficult in such a situation. I don't know who said anything about me or what has been said about me, and the press release makes it even worse; I mean, the kind of a statement where nothing has been developed. I mean, I am not trying to get mad or anything, I appreciate the situation, but I am involved in a very disastrous way in this."

Hamilton Robinson, chairman of the four-man State Department "hearing" committee, told Mr. Blank there was a "very definite difference between the word security and the word loyalty." "I think," said Robinson, "loyalty must necessarily be a conscious proposition. Security or the lack of it might be conscious or unconscious."

Mr. Blank, bewildered at this semantic rationale, begged to know: "What have I done? What shall I tell employers? . . ."

It is seldom that a story has cut so deeply in Washington. After Andrews' stories, Mr. Blank was allowed to resign as were six other discharged employees. Moreover, State Department procedures were changed to permit appeals to the Loyalty Review Board. For his work, Andrews was awarded the Pulitzer Prize for National Reporting in 1948.

Two other reporters, Anthony Lewis and Edwin O. Guthman, have won Pulitzer Prizes for similar stories—the clearing of persons unjustly accused during the wave of fright set in motion by the late Senator Joseph R. McCarthy. But as far back as William Allen White, the record of the Pulitzer Prizes on civil liberties shows the consideration that has been given to such efforts by newspapermen. Some of the work of editors and reporters in this field follows. It is a matter of regret that such pieces as that of Bert Andrews are so long and so difficult to cut that they cannot be fairly presented here.

60. WILLIAM ALLEN WHITE WRITES
TO AN ANXIOUS FRIEND

The publisher of the Emporia Gazette explains
a creed that alone can banish fear

Pulitzer Prize for Editorial Writing, 1923

William Allen White was a symbol of America.

He was born in Emporia, Kansas, in 1868 and died there in 1944. As the editor of the Emporia *Gazette*, he placed his personal concept of journalism on a level as high as that of the greatest newspapers in any metropolis. He loved his town, his state and his country and, equal to the sum of all these, he loved his profession.

People believed in him—not only the people of Emporia but the people of America. He had something to say to them, and they usually understood and they usually agreed. But even when they did not, they respected him. He was one of them, and never forgot it.

Some of his writings survive him. There is the piece in praise of conservatism, "What's the Matter with Kansas?" which brought him the first flush of fame. And "Mary White," the editorial written on the death of his teen-age daughter. And of course his autobiography.

But the piece, brief though it is, which has the most to say to troubled America today is the one for which he received the Pulitzer Prize for Editorial Writing in 1924. To all those who would hobble and stifle and snuff out the independence of a newspaperman and the freedom of the press because they fear the consequences of liberty of thought and liberty of publication, this is William Allen White's answer.

It is still the best answer.

TO AN ANXIOUS FRIEND

By William Allen White

From the Emporia (Kansas) Gazette, July 27, 1922

You tell me that law is above freedom of utterance. And I reply that you can have no wise laws nor free enforcement of wise laws unless there is free expression of the wisdom of the people—and, alas, their folly with it. But if there is freedom, folly will die of its own poison, and the wisdom will survive. That is the history of the race. It is the proof of man's kinship with God. You say that freedom of utterance is not for time of stress, and I reply with the sad truth that only in time of stress is freedom of utterance in danger. No one questions it in calm days because it is not needed. And the reverse is true also; only when free utterance is suppressed is it needed, and when it is needed, it is most vital to justice. Peace is good. But if you are interested in peace through force and without free discussion, that is to say, free utterance decently and in order—your interest in justice is slight. And peace without justice is tyranny, no matter how you may sugar-coat it with expediency. This state today is in more danger from suppression than from violence, because in the end, suppression leads to violence. Violence, indeed, is the child of suppression. Whoever pleads for justice helps to keep the peace; and whoever tramples upon the plea for justice, temperately made in the name of peace, only outrages peace and kills something fine in the heart of man which God put there when we got our manhood. When that is killed, brute meets brute on each side of the line.

So, dear friend, put fear out of your heart. This nation will survive, this state will prosper, the orderly business of life will go forward if only men can speak in whatever way given to them to utter what their hearts hold—by voice, by posted card, by letter or by press. Reason never has failed men. Only force and repression have made the wrecks in the world.

61. "WHO KNOWS WHAT EFFECT
SUCH AN EDITORIAL WOULD HAVE?"

*The Los Angeles Times fights a lawyers' attempt
to limit its right of fair comment*

Pulitzer Prize for Public Service, 1942

In times of crisis, individual liberties are in constant danger of erosion. The tide of totalitarian thought comes sweeping in on a nation that is indifferent or supine, and washes away at the precious supports of free speech and a free press until the whole structure of freedom collapses. The threat exists today, as never before, in a world rent by cold war. In varying forms, it has been present throughout history.

Nor are the enemies of democracy alone in their attack on the privileges of a free people. Sometimes, in a misguided moment, the friends and supporters of democratic government are themselves led into an attempt at suppression from the very highest of motives. There were those who did not want newspapers to comment fairly and honestly on news of a recession, when everyone knew that it existed. There are others who would not want material published on such scientific advances as rocket experiments, when tens of thousands of persons near a rocket base can see and hear whenever such a test takes place. And there are special groups, such as a minority of doctors or lawyers and sometimes even educators, who feel that full publication in some way infringes on or even injures them in some way for which a rationalization is always provided.

Such an effort by a special group of lawyers acting in the name of the Los Angeles Bar Association caused the Los Angeles *Times* to be held in contempt of court in 1938 for routine editorial comment on three cases and for publishing two editorials in its own defense. It was one of the most extraordinary proceedings of its kind since John Peter Zenger won the basic battle for a free press in colonial America.

The Bar Committee obviously had "saved up" its ammunition to take the *Times* into court and try to limit its right of free and fair comment. The editorials cited praised the conviction of sit-down strikers by a jury, upheld a manslaughter verdict in a case of some prominence at the time, approved the conviction of a woman politician as a bribe-seeker, commented on the disposition of Jackie Coogan's earnings as a child actor, and attacked a plea for probation for Teamsters' Union members who had been convicted of assaulting nonunion truck drivers.

Arguing that appeals were pending in some cases, and that judges could be influenced in others, the counsel for the Bar group pleaded: "Who knows what effect such an editorial would have . . . upon the mind of the average judge or upon the mind of a weak judge or a spineless judge? . . . If such publications are permitted, it would not be long before the general public will come to believe that judgments can be dictated by such newspaper articles or by pressure from one group or another, or from a newspaper . . ."

To this the *Times* replied with the following editorial, which was one of the two published in its own defense that were originally held a part of its crime.

CURIOUS REASONING

From the Los Angeles Times, June 7, 1938

The extraordinary "contempt of court" action brought in the name of the Los Angeles Bar Association against the *Times* is an attempt to reduce to such narrow limits the right and duty of newspapers to analyze public questions as practically to destroy their usefulness in that respect.

The theory which the Bar Association's five-man Contempt Committee appears hastily to have embraced is that no case which is before the courts may be so analyzed or commented upon until the courts have said their last word upon it. For example, four of the five *Times* editorials cited by the committee are classified by it as being "in contempt of court" because, while they were published after jury verdicts had been returned, the publication occurred before the judges' disposition of the cases, which were criminal ones, by sentence or otherwise. The idea seems to be that such comment is calculated to sway a judge one way or the other so that, as a result, the disposition of the case might thereby be made different from that dictated by its own intrinsic merits.

This notion is itself scarcely complimentary to the courts which are supposed to, and usually do, function on the basis of their own best judgment and knowledge of the law, independent of any extraneous influence. It further fails to take into account the fact that, with few exceptions, the penalties for all classes and degrees of crime are fixed by law within such limits as to allow judges comparatively small latitude in which such extraneous influence, were it actually effective, could operate.

In the fifth editorial complained of by the Bar Association's committee, the *Times,* in common with some hundreds of other newspapers over the country, expressed its views on the question raised by the litigation over Jackie Coogan's earnings. In the apparent view of the committee, it was "contempt" to say that, in this paper's opinion, children ought to have some rights to and share in the products of their own labor. The expression of this opinion, the committee seems to think, should be punished as willful effort to influence the court—notwithstanding that the law in the case is perfectly clear and that it presumably will be decided according to what the law says and not according to anyone's opinion as to what it ought to say.

However, the biggest of the several obvious holes in the committee's contentions is the fact that no legal case is ever finally disposed of until it has been passed upon by the highest court of jurisdiction to which it is permitted to be taken. The process of appeal upon appeal often occupies years; the Tom Mooney case, for example, is not legally settled yet, since the United States Supreme Court has not yet ruled upon it. This case is more than twenty years old. Mooney has grown gray in prison, thousands upon thousands of newspaper editorials, books, pamphlets, and argumentative articles have been published for and against his cause. And according to the logical projection of the Bar Association committee's curious reasoning, every one of them is in contempt of court!

Nearly every great public question is at some time or other the subject of litigation. Are we to be prohibited from discussing and analyzing such questions until after the Supreme Court has ruled thereon? Millions of words for and against the National Recovery and Agricultural Adjustment Acts—the most important statutes in a generation—were published between the time of the first court attacks on them in 1933 and the time the Supreme Court invalidated them finally some two years later. In that interval they were in the status of unadjudicated legal cases and, therefore, in the conception of this committee, published argument regarding them must have been in contempt of court and should have been prevented or punished!

Free discussion of public questions is one of our greatest safeguards; efforts to suppress it one of our gravest perils. Wise decisions are hammered out on the anvils of debate. Facts are essential but only thoughtful study and analysis make them useful. The editorial columns of newspapers are natural leaders of public discussion. Though the views they express may at times be biased or erroneous, they are still the stimuli of thought and argument through which just public judgments are finally arrived at. Their privileges can be and sometimes are abused, but the principle for which they stand is not one lightly to be tampered with.

The case was carried to the Supreme Court of the United States which, on December 8, 1941, upheld the *Times*. The court held that there must be a "clear and present danger" to the administration of justice before there is contempt.

"The likelihood, however great, that a substantive evil will result cannot alone justify restriction upon the freedom of speech or the press," the court ruled. "The assumption that respect for the judiciary can be won by shielding judges from published criticism wrongly appraises the character of American public opinion. . . . An enforced silence, however limited, solely in the name of preserving the dignity of the bench, would probably engender resentment, suspicion, and contempt much more than it would enhance respect."

For its campaign to uphold freedom of the press, the Los Angeles *Times* accordingly was awarded the Pulitzer Prize for Public Service for 1942 at a time when the American press voluntarily had placed itself under wartime censorship restrictions.

62. WHAT IT TOOK TO CLEAR
AN ACCUSED PROFESSOR

A reporter for the Seattle Times
disproves charges of Communist activity

Pulitzer Prize for National Reporting, 1950

Professor Melvin Rader was in trouble. A Communist had accused him of studying at a Communist Party training school near Kingston, N. Y., in the summer of 1938.

Professor Rader had denied it. The University of Washington records in Seattle had shown that he had taught there up to July 20, 1938. Then, he and his wife had spent the rest of the summer at Canyon Creek Lodge in western Washington.

But, the Washington State Un-American Activities Committee chose not to believe the liberal-minded philosophy professor. It stood by its witness, George Hewitt, a Communist, even though Hewitt had been charged with perjury in Seattle and New York courts had refused extradition.

That was the almost unbelievable situation in the summer of 1948 when the Seattle *Times* and a keen, impartial reporter, Edwin O. Guthman, decided to investigate to find out who was lying.

Rader cooperated. But it was difficult after ten years to find proof to support his alibi. He remembered having gone to a dentist near Canyon Creek during his 1938 holiday, but the dentist had destroyed the records. He recalled staying at a hotel with his wife on the way to Canyon Creek that summer, but the hotel had gone out of business and its records were unavailable.

Chairman Albert F. Canwell, of the Un-American Activities Committee, had the Canyon Creek Lodge register pages, disclosing when the Raders had been there, but refused at the time to give them up or let either the reporter or the professor look at them.

And to cap the nightmare of doubt and suspicion, an innocent-looking white card showing that the Canyon Creek proprietor had written to the Raders in 1940 was misinterpreted as "proof" that the professor had stayed at the Lodge that year, and not 1938 as he had claimed.

But for five months Guthman followed a cold trail and succeeded in clearing Rader. Here are essential parts of the Seattle *Times's* stories telling how the job was done.

"THERE IT IS—RADER—'38!"

By Edwin O. Guthman

From the Seattle Times, Oct. 21, 1949

Professor Melvin Rader, who was accused before the Legislature's Un-American Activities Committee in July, 1948, of having attended a secret Communist school in New York in 1938, was cleared today by Dr. Raymond B. Allen, University of Washington president.

The university administration is convinced that the charge against Rader, 45-year-old philosophy professor, has been refuted and that Rader was accused falsely, Dr. Allen announced.

Dr. Allen issued a statement absolving Rader after studying evidence uncovered by Rader and the Seattle *Times,* and after former Representative Albert F. Canwell of Spokane, who had headed the Un-American Activities Committee, failed to keep an appointment with Dr. Allen yesterday. . . .

The *Times* checked Rader's story and found it could be corroborated by documentary evidence and testimony of reputable citizens.

Dr. Carl Jensen, a prominent Seattle eye specialist, had tested Rader's eyes and given him a prescription for new glasses on August 15, 1938.

Rader voted in the primary election of September 13, 1938, city records disclosed.

The two dates, plus university records showing that Rader taught summer school until July 20, and had signed for a book at the university library July 29, made it highly improbable that Rader had traveled to New York that summer.

The Communist school was reported to have lasted six weeks. . . . Rader said he and Mrs. Rader and their daughter went to Canyon Creek July 30 or 31 and stayed until about September 5.

Weighing most heavily against Rader was the small typewritten card which Canwell Committee investigators took from the files of Canyon Creek Lodge two days after George Hewitt, the Communist, testified before the committee.

The card bore Mrs. Rader's name and listed her address as 6017 30th Avenue, N.E. A date "8-16-40" and "(40)" had been penned on the card plus the notation, "Prof. at U. of Washington, guest for 1 month."

The Canwell Committee assumed that the card meant the Raders had been at Canyon Creek in 1940, not 1938. The address was the tip-off that the committee was wrong.

An examination of the 1938, '39 and '40 telephone books and city directories showed that the Raders lived at the address on the card in 1938, had moved to 1402 E. 63d Street in 1939 and were living at 1750 E. 62d Street in 1940.

Mrs. Quincy Mueller, elderly former owner of the Canyon Creek resort, told this reporter that the card did not indicate when the Raders stayed at the lodge, but was from an index she had used for correspondence purposes.

Shown a photostatic copy of the card, Mrs. Mueller declared that the notation, "8-16-40," referred to the date when she last wrote to the Raders. At that time, she recalled, she offered to sell them a lot near the resort.

Further indication that the Raders had been at the lodge in 1938 came from Mrs. Ida Kirby, who had been housekeeper at Canyon Creek.

Mrs. Kirby remembered that after the Raders' vacation was over, she drove them to their home in Seattle. It was on 30th Avenue, their 1938 address. . . .

Both women believed that Rader or Mrs. Rader had signed the lodge's loose-leaf register. According to Thomas J. Grant, present owner of the lodge, pages from the register were given to the Canwell Committee's investigators.

The committee has never disclosed whether Rader's signature was or was not on the register.

Mrs. Kirby said she accompanied the committee investigators to the lodge to help them find old records which Mrs. Mueller left when she sold the lodge to Grant in 1942.

"We found pages from the register," Mrs. Kirby declared. "As one of the men ran his fingers over the pages, I overheard him say: 'There it is—Rader—'38!' "

After it was all over, Professor Rader wondered:

"But suppose we had not gone to Canyon Creek Lodge that summer? What if I never had my eyes checked, or if I had not taken out the book from the university library? What if Ed Guthman had not helped track down these circumstances? Suppose we had all gone boating on Puget Sound with no one along to verify the voyage? Would I be a ruined man today, my career at an end?"

At least a part of the answer came from Richard L. Neuberger, a reporter at the time and in 1958 a United States Senator from Oregon. Reviewing the strange case, Neuberger wrote in a special piece for the St. Louis *Post-Dispatch:*

"Many residents of the Pacific Northwest are still wondering how far injustice can go, when hysterical witch-hunting gets official backing. Public opinion appears to have gone against the witch-hunters as a result of the Rader case, and legal steps are being considered to prevent a repetition of this near-tragic situation."

Edwin O. Guthman was awarded the Pulitzer Prize for National Reporting in 1950 "for his series on the clearing . . . of Professor Melvin Rader."

63. THE NAVY RIGHTS A WRONG
BECAUSE A REPORTER PERSISTED

Anthony Lewis and the Washington Daily News
help clear Abraham Chasanow

Pulitzer Prize for National Reporting, 1955

There were two highly publicized security cases in 1954. One involved Dr. J. Robert Oppenheimer, the wartime director of the project that gave the United States the atomic bomb and victory over Japan. The other had as its central figure John Paton Davies of the State Department.

There was a third case, that of an obscure Navy employee named Abraham Chasanow who was neither famous nor distinguished and without great resources for his defense. Only Anthony Lewis, then a 28-year-old reporter for the Washington *Daily News,* took Chasanow's part after he had been dismissed as a security risk on April 7, 1954.

Joseph A. Fanelli, attorney for Chasanow, knew Lewis had been following the case from its inception in 1953 and appealed for help. Lewis asked the Navy Department why Chasanow had been dismissed, was refused an answer, and promptly brought the case to public attention.

With the full support of the Washington *Daily News,* the young reporter wrote nine news stories and three editorials about the Chasanow case.

At length, in September 1, 1954, Chasanow was cleared. He wrote: "I do not believe I would have been cleared and restored to my position had it not been for Tony Lewis and the Washington *Daily News.*" For his work, Lewis won the Pulitzer Prize for National Reporting in 1955. His story, reporting Chasanow's victory, follows.

"I AWOKE . . . FROM A BAD DREAM"

By Anthony Lewis

From the Washington (D. C.) Daily News, Sept. 1, 1954

Abraham Chasanow, Navy employee who has been fighting security charges for more than a year while suspended from his job, today won his battle.

The Navy officially and finally dismissed all its charges against him, ordered him reinstated at his old job at the Hydrographic Office and publicly acknowledged that a "grave injustice" had been done him.

Assistant Secretary of the Navy James H. Smith Jr. at a press conference attended also by Mr. Chasanow, said the case already had resulted in some changes of procedure in the Navy security program and further action is being contemplated.

Mr. Chasanow will receive all pay and allowance for the period he was suspended less what he managed to earn on the outside.

The press conference was a dramatic and entirely unprecedented occasion. No one could recall another time when government and officials called reporters in to admit a mistake.

"We want to see what we can do to restore him not only in his job in the Navy but in his reputation with the public," Secretary Smith said.

He said the case revealed the following flaws in the security program procedure:

The case took too long to handle—"a great disadvantage to both the government and the employee." He said procedures have been considerably speeded up, "but we don't want to hurry the jury."

A hearing board fully cleared Mr. Chasanow, but an appeal board overruled that finding without giving Mr. Chasanow or his lawyer a chance to appear before it in person. Mr. Smith said personal appearance is now guaranteed in any case in which an appeal board is planning to make an unfavorable finding.

Anonymous informants, who made derogatory statements about Mr. Chasanow originally, failed to back up their charges when questioned about them.

Mr. Smith put great emphasis on this problem of anonymous accusers.

He said he is now "looking into ways and means of preventing delivery of evidence which people are unwilling to stand up and back."

He said he personally would favor requiring all such derogatory statements to be given under oath. (General government policy on security matters bars such a procedure, however.)

Mr. Chasanow, 43, of 11-T Ridge Road, Greenbelt, Md., was charged and suspended on July 29, 1953. He had worked in the Hydrographic Office almost twenty-three years and at the time of his suspension was making $8,000 a year as director of the supply office for Navy charts.

The charges against him involved his entire community, Greenbelt. He was accused of belonging to a powerful "radical group" in the town. Various Greenbelt leaders said they thought this accusation might have originated with disgruntled residents critical of some of the town housing plans.

Town leaders also said Navy investigators tried to force them to make unfavorable statements about Mr. Chasanow and then falsely reported the friendly comments they actually made.

When the anonymous informants were requestioned, Mr. Smith said, their new statements made only two conclusions possible—they had changed their minds since the first interview or the original investigators had not reported their statements correctly.

Mr. Smith said he will look into the possibility of taking some punitive action against either the informants or the investigators.

The *News* first brought the Chasanow case to public attention last December. Two articles in a *News* series about the security program described the case, although Mr. Chasanow's name was not used.

Another series of articles last April discussed the case by name.

Mr. Chasanow is a small man who is best described by the words

"American middle-class." He has been an official of the Citizens' Association and the Parent-Teacher Association in Greenbelt; in his lapel he wears a Lions Club pin. His wife, Helen, has led Greenbelt's Red Cross and Community Chest drives.

The Chasanows have four children. Phyllis, 15, won the county Fourth of July essay contest just before her father was suspended.

The Navy originally filed eight charges against Mr. Chasanow, all of them related to alleged Communist associations and most of them centered on Greenbelt.

At a three-day hearing last September, Mr. Chasanow produced affidavits from 97 friends and associates who described him as conservative and violently anti-Communist.

Several persons swore they had heard Mr. Chasanow propose, at a town meeting, a loyalty oath for all Greenbelt home-owners. A postman volunteered this affidavit:

"I am familiar with the type of literature the Communists mail to their sympathizers . . . and I cannot recall his receiving any at all. With all the love in his heart for his family, his God, and America, I know there could be no room for Communism."

The three-man hearing board found on October 9 that the various associations charged to Mr. Chasanow were all nonexistent or innocent. The board said it didn't believe there was a "radical group" at Greenbelt and described Mr. Chasanow specifically as a "moderating, constructive, and conservative influence."

For seven months Mr. Chasanow heard nothing. Then, on April 7, Assistant Secretary Smith—on the advice of the Hydrographer and Navy Security Appeals Board—ordered Mr. Chasanow fired. No reason was given for overruling the hearing board.

Mr. Chasanow and his lawyer, Joseph A. Fanelli, felt they had no alternative except to take the case to the public. On April 15 they held an extraordinary press conference at which Greenbelt's mayor, city manager, clerk, minister, and rabbi spoke up for Mr. Chasanow.

Mr. Fanelli petitioned Secretary Smith to reconsider his decision, which had been issued as "final." On May 4—in an action observers called unprecedented—Mr. Smith ordered the case reopened and considered from scratch again.

Mr. Fanelli was on vacation and could not be present at the press conference today. His partner, Joseph Freehill, pointed out that Mr.

Smith was not required by the rules even to reconsider the case once the "final" decision had been made.

He praised Mr. Smith as "a man of courage and integrity" and thanked the press for performing a "public service" by its interest in the case.

The Navy said it wished to emphasize that the new hearing board found Mr. Chasanow "an above-average loyal American citizen . . . [with] long creditable service for the government . . . civic and patriotic activities, exemplary family life" and other factors.

Mr. Chasanow made only two comments during the conference. He said he would definitely return to his Navy job after a brief vacation.

He was asked how he felt.

"I woke this morning from a bad dream," he said. "The sun is shining. Flowers are blooming. Birds are singing."

There is an epilogue. Tony Lewis, a New Yorker born and bred, had worked on the New York *Times* before going to the Washington *Daily News*. On a bright Monday in May, when the Pulitzer Prizes were about to be announced, he wandered into the *Times* office on his day off to see if he could come back. While he was talking with a Times executive in a glass-enclosed office, a piece of copy paper was flattened against the glass behind his back with this message to the executive:

"Better grab this guy. He's just won the Pulitzer Prize."

That was how Lewis learned the news. He was welcomed back to the *Times* and assigned to the Washington bureau. Early in 1955, Chasanow's job in the Navy Hydrographic Office was abolished and he declined another Navy post. He was permitted to resign with full pension and announced he intended to practice law.

64. "WE'VE GOT TO SHOOT THE WORKS
IN A FIGHT FOR TOLERANCE"

*Hodding Carter, of Greenville, Miss., writes
an editorial about a Nisei combat regiment*

Pulitzer Prize for Editorial Writing, 1946

Down where Main Street meets the Mississippi River below the Mason-

Dixon Line, you'll find Hodding Carter publishing his newspaper, the *Delta Democrat-Times* of Greenville, Miss.

Generally, you'll also find the sturdy, soft-spoken Carter with a glint of battle in his eyes for he insists on fighting the South's battles on his own home grounds. That is, primarily, because he believes in the South; also, he's never been one to run away from a fight.

From the day he left the Columbia School of Journalism on the brink of the Great Depression and began newspaper work in New Orleans, close to his native Hammond, La., where he was born in 1907, he has known much more discouragement than the average newspaperman.

But he has never given up a story or gone back on a cause. Once, when the Mississippi House of Representatives voted by 89-19 to condemn him as a "writer of falsehoods" about his state during one of many integration arguments, Carter roundly adopted his own resolution by a vote of 1-0 to call his opponents liars.

His newspaper, his friendly presence, his outspoken editorials, and his championship of tolerance all have won for him a unique position in journalism and many awards.

After the editorial that brought him the Pulitzer Prize for Editorial Writing in 1946, he was invited to become a member of the fourteen-man Advisory Board on the Pulitzer Prizes and accepted. He has been a Guggenheim Fellow, Nieman Fellow, and a holder of the Southern Literary Award. His Pulitzer Prize editorial, published in the *Delta Democrat-Times*, August 27, 1945, after his return from World War II, typifies his best work.

"GO FOR BROKE"

By Hodding Carter

From the Delta Democrat Times, Greenville, Miss., Aug. 27, 1945

Company D of the 168th Regiment which is stationed in Leghorn, Italy, is composed altogether of white troops, some from the East, some from the South, some from the Midwest and West Coast.

Company D made an unusual promise earlier this month. The promise was in the form of a communication to their fellow Americans of the 442d Infantry Regiment and the 100th Infantry Battalion, whose motto is "Go For Broke," and it was subscribed to unanimously by the officers and men of Company D.

In brief, the communication pledged the help of Company D in convincing "the folks back home that you are fully deserving of all the privileges with which we ourselves are bestowed."

The soldiers to whom that promise was made are Japanese-Americans. In all of the United States Army, no troops have chalked up a better combat record. Their record is so good that these Nisei were selected by General Francis H. Oxx, commander of the military area in which they are stationed, to lead the final victory parade. So they marched, 3,000 strong, at the head of thousands of other Americans, their battle flag with three Presidential unit citationed streamers floating above them, their commander, a Wisconsin white colonel, leading them.

Some of those Nisei must have been thinking of the soul-shaking days of last October, when they spearheaded the attacks that opened the Vosges Mountain doorway to Strasbourg. Some of them were probably remembering how they, on another bloody day, had snatched the Thirty-six Division's lost battalion of Texans from the encircling Germans. And many of them were bearing scars from those two engagements which alone had cost the Nisei boys from Hawaii and the West Coast 2,300 casualties.

Perhaps these yellow-skinned Americans, to whose Japanese kinsmen we have administered a terrific and long overdue defeat, were holding their heads a little higher because of the pledge of their white fellow-soldiers and fellow-Americans of Company D. Perhaps, when they gazed at their combat flag, the motto "Go For Broke" emblazoned thereon took on a different meaning. "Go For Broke" is the Hawaiian-Japanese slang expression for shooting the works in a dice game.

The loyal Nisei have shot the works. From the beginning of the war, they have been on trial, in and out of uniform, in army camps and relocation centers, as combat troops in Europe and as front-line interrogators, propagandists, and combat intelligence personnel in the Pacific where their capture meant prolonged and hideous torture. And even yet they have not satisfied their critics.

It is so easy for a dominant race to explain good or evil, patriotism or treachery, courage or cowardice in terms of skin color. So easy and so tragically wrong. Too many have committed that wrong against the loyal Nisei, who by the thousands have proved themselves good Americans, even while others of us, by our actions against them, have shown ourselves to be bad Americans. Nor is the end of this misconception in sight. Those Japanese-American soldiers who paraded at Leghorn in commemoration of the defeat of the nation from which their fathers came, will meet other enemies, other obstacles as forbidding as those of war. A lot of people will begin saying, as soon as these boys take off their uniforms, that "a Jap is a Jap," and that the Nisei deserve no consideration. A majority won't say or believe this, but an active minority can have its way against an apathetic majority.

It seems to us that the Nisei slogan of "Go For Broke" could be adopted by all Americans of good will in the days ahead. We've got to shoot the works in a fight for tolerance. Those boys of Company D point the way.

APPENDIXES

I. THE PULITZER PRIZES:
A BRIEF HISTORY

NOTE: *The following was adapted from an article in the quarterly publication,* Columbia Library Columns, *Vol. VI, No. 3, and is reprinted with the permission of the publishers.*

Late in August, 1902, Joseph Pulitzer somewhat impulsively dictated a confidential memorandum roughing out his "germ of an idea" for a School of Journalism at Columbia University. Toward the end of this rambling, highly personal document, he said:

"Incidentally, I strongly wish the College to pay from the large income I am providing, a sum of [   ] in annual prizes to particular journalists or writers for various accomplishments, achievements and forms of excellence."

This was the genesis of the Pulitzer Prizes. That he thought well of the idea from the first is evident in the suggestion he attached to the memorandum, setting the annual sum to be provided for the prizes at $20,000 or more. It was a sizeable way to fill in a blank in a rough draft. Under the terms of agreement reached April 10, 1903 with the Trustees of Columbia University (not Columbia College, as contemplated in the memorandum), it turned out that the prize idea and prize sum estimate were both practical and durable. The influence which the Pulitzer Prizes have exerted on American letters and journalism is the best evidence of that.

At the time he concluded the first agreement with the university, Mr. Pulitzer was at the height of his fame as publisher of the New York *World* and the St. Louis *Post-Dispatch*. As was evident from his memorandum, his first concern was the school and the prizes came second. But not for long. He was soon writing to a member of the Columbia trustees:

"To the plan of the prizes I am much attached, and believe in the future it will be of the greatest possible benefit and renown to the University, possibly greater than the school itself."

Of his total benefaction of $2,000,000 proposed in the 1903 agreement, Mr. Pulitzer specified that the income of $500,000 of the total was to be "applied to prizes or scholarships for the encouragement of public service, public morals, American literature, and the advancement of education." But he also directed that prizes should not be awarded until the school had been in successful operation for three years, and that the university trustees then should act on the recommendation of an advisory board. He did not, as a result, preside over the award of the first Pulitzer Prizes. He died on October 29, 1911, the School of Journalism was opened September 30, 1912, and it was Commencement, 1917, before the glamorous procession of the Pulitzer Prizes began moving across the mottled landscape of American culture.

The rules laid down for the awards in the 1903 agreement and elaborated on in the Pulitzer will of 1904 are still basic policy. All changes have been made within this framework, including shifts in the type and number of prizes and the method of judging.

What the founder of the Pulitzer Prizes intended is quite clear. While he requested the university's trustees to bestow the awards, he rested in the Advisory Board the principal authority for recommendations to the trustees. In his will, he decreed: "It is my wish . . . that the Advisory Board shall be continued in existence without limitation of time, and I direct that the selection of the persons who shall receive said prizes or scholarships shall be under its control so long as it continues in existence."

He gave the Advisory Board the power to withhold prizes or scholarships in any category if it found competitors below the standard of excellence fixed by the Board, and he made this sweeping statement in addition:

"The Advisory Board shall have the power in its discretion to suspend or to change any subject or subjects; substituting, however, others in their places, if in the judgment of the Board such suspension, changes or substitutions shall be conducive to the public good or rendered advisable by public necessities, or by reason of change of time."

There were thirteen members of the Advisory Board, then called the Advisory Board of the School of Journalism, when it was created in 1912 to make the detailed arrangements for the work of the school and the handling of the prizes. There are fourteen today, the addition being a member of the Journalism faculty as secretary. The Board, on April 18, 1950, became the Advisory Board on the Pulitzer Prizes. In 1954, the

Board limited its members to three consecutive terms of four years each, as a result of which it substantially altered its composition by 1958. The Board elects its own new members.

The Advisory Board became the key to the award of the Pulitzer Prizes under the Plan of Award, adopted in 1915. Its verdicts have been upheld by the trustees of Columbia University. Its deliberations are secret, as they were in the beginning. Its policy has been to announce the awards, not to explain them, defend them, or answer critics. There has always been a Pulitzer on the Board—Ralph, in 1912, son of the first Joseph Pulitzer; Ralph's younger brother, the second Joseph Pulitzer, from 1920 until his death in 1955, and now the son of the second Joseph Pulitzer, Joseph Pulitzer Jr., like his father and grandfather the editor and publisher of the St. Louis *Post-Dispatch*. He presides at the Board's annual session, being elected each time by the membership.

The president of Columbia University also has been a Board member throughout—Nicholas Murray Butler from 1912 to 1945, then Frank D. Fackenthal, General Dwight David Eisenhower, and, since 1953, Grayson Kirk. The remainder of the Board has always been composed of distinguished editors and publishers from papers of all areas and representing small, medium and metropolitan dailies as well as rather widely varying shades of political opinion. It has been traditional that whenever a Board member was considered to be involved either directly or indirectly in the discussion of a particular prize category, he retired from the room and took no part in the voting. Nobody, in other words, has ever been able to vote himself a prize.

There was a provision in the original Plan of Award for membership on the Board by persons not directly connected with newspapers but this has been inoperative, except for the Board secretary.

The Board has always been deeply interested in developing representative juries. For that reason the Letters and other non-journalism juries, although they have operated anonymously throughout the life of the Pulitzer Prizes, have consisted of some of the most distinguished persons in the field of arts and letters. Journalism juries, which before World War II often consisted of the Journalism faculty with the addition of distinguished outsiders from time to time, have usually been made public.

The difference between Letters and Journalism juries—one secret and the other public—has been determined by the Board largely on the basis of the preference of the jurors over four decades. It was always deemed more likely that Letters jurors would be subjected to pressure if their identities were known. But in one basic procedure, all juries have been treated alike—their reports have always been secret.

In the matter of entries for the prizes, nominations have been received very widely from wire services, newspapers, book publishers, dramatists, poets, and a surprisingly large number of suggestions have come from the public. The widest latitude always has been permitted to nominators. Nominating forms and copies of the Plan of Award have always been available at the Secretary's office at Columbia upon request, so that public participation in the awards has steadily increased.

In recent years, several entries submitted by enthusiastic readers have won journalism prizes. Consequently, without any particular stimulus from the university, Board or Jurors, the number of entries in the journalism field reached a record of 761 in 1957, the fortieth year of the prizes. In book categories, where publishers usually try to submit only the top of their lists, the range of entries also has climbed, standing at 278 in 1957, a figure exceeded only by the 336 books that were submitted in 1948.

II. PLAN FOR THE AWARD
OF THE PULITZER PRIZES

The following provisions govern the award of the Pulitzer Prizes and Scholarships established in Columbia University by the will of the first Joseph Pulitzer:

1. The award of prizes and traveling scholarships is made by the trustees of Columbia University on the recommendation of the Advisory Board on the Pulitzer Prizes.

Juries are appointed by the university in each category. They are invited to exercise their independent and collective judgment and to submit from two to five recommendations, without necessarily indicating their order of preference. The jurors are advised that their recommendations are for the information and advice of the Advisory Board only inasmuch as the Advisory Board is charged with the responsibility and authority under the will of Joseph Pulitzer to select, accept, or reject the recommendations of the jurors.

2. Nominations must be made in writing on or before February 1 of a given year. They must be addressed to the Secretary of the Advisory Board, Professor John Hohenberg of the Columbia Graduate School of Journalism, 518 Journalism Building, Columbia University, New York 27, N. Y.

3. Nominations for journalism awards may be made at any time during the calendar year. Printed copies of editorials, articles, cartoons, photo-

graphs, and a biography and a photograph of the individual nominated must accompany all nominations.

For the prizes in letters, three copies of each book must be mailed to the Secretary of the Advisory Board. In the case of a musical composition, performing organizations (orchestras, theaters, etc.) are requested to send nominations accompanied by a recording of the work and one copy of the score. The Advisory Board, at its discretion, may waive the requirement of submission of the score of a musical work if warranted by special circumstances; for example, if there is only one existing score, indispensable for performance. Nomination of a play, opera, or ballet should be made while it is being performed.

4. Competition for prizes is limited to work done during the calendar year ending December 31, except in drama and music. For these prizes, works produced during the twelve months from April 1 through March 31 are considered. Nominations for the music award must be received on or before March 15.

5. If in any one year no book, play, or musical composition nominated for a prize shall be of sufficient excellence in the opinion of the Advisory Board, or if in any other subject of competition all the competitors shall fall below the standard of excellence fixed by the Advisory Board, then in that case the amount of such prize or prizes may be withheld in such year.

6. Nothing in this plan shall be deemed to limit in any way the authority and control of the Advisory Board.

7. Any author, composer, or journalist is eligible for consideration each year for any award, irrespective of the fact that he may have received a prize in any previous year.

8. The Advisory Board meets annually at Columbia University in April. [The prizes are awarded on the first Monday in May.]

A. PRIZES IN JOURNALISM

The following awards will be made annually as Prizes in Journalism:

1. For disinterested and meritorious public service rendered by a United States newspaper, published daily, Sunday, or at least once a week, during the year, a gold medal.

2. For a distinguished example of local reporting in a United States newspaper, published daily, Sunday, or at least once a week, during the year, the test being the quality of local news stories written under the pressure of edition time, one thousand dollars ($1,000).

3. For a distinguished example of local reporting in a United States

newspaper, published daily, Sunday, or at least once a week, during the year, in which the pressure of edition time is not a factor, written in the form of a single article or a series, due consideration being given to the initiative and resourcefulness and to the constructive purpose of the writer, one thousand dollars ($1,000).

4. For a distinguished example of reporting on national affairs, in a United States newspaper, published daily, Sunday, or at least once a week, during the year, one thousand dollars ($1,000).

5. For a distinguished example of reporting of international affairs, including United Nations correspondence, in a United States newspaper, published daily, Sunday, or at least once a week, during the year, one thousand dollars ($1,000).

6. For distinguished editorial writing in a United States newspaper, published daily, Sunday, or at least once a week, during the year, the test of excellence being clearness of style, moral purpose, sound reasoning, and power to influence public opinion in what the writer conceives to be the right direction, due account being taken of the whole volume of the editorial writer's work during the year, one thousand dollars ($1,000).

7. For a distinguished example of a cartoonist's work in a United States newspaper, published daily, Sunday, or at least once a week, during the year, the determining qualities being that the cartoon shall embody an idea made clearly apparent, shall show good drawing and striking pictorial effect, and shall be intended to be helpful to some commendable cause of public importance, due account being taken of the whole volume of the artist's work during the year, one thousand dollars ($1,000).

8. For an outstanding example of news photography as exemplified by a news photograph or photographs in a United States newspaper, published daily, Sunday, or at least once a week, during the year, one thousand dollars ($1,000). (This prize is open to amateurs as well as to photographers regularly employed by newspapers, press associations, or syndicates.)

B. PRIZES IN LETTERS

The following awards will be made annually as Prizes in Letters:

1. For distinguished fiction published in book form during the year by an American author, preferably dealing with American life, five hundred dollars ($500).

2. For the American play, preferably original in its source and dealing with American life, which shall represent in marked fashion the educational value and power of the stage, five hundred dollars ($500).

3. For a distinguished book of the year upon the history of the United States, five hundred dollars ($500).

4. For a distinguished American biography or autobiography teaching patriotic and unselfish services to the people, illustrated by an eminent example, five hundred dollars ($500).

5. For a distinguished volume of verse published during the year by an American author, five hundred dollars ($500).

C. PRIZE IN MUSIC

The following award will be made annually as a Prize in Music:

For distinguished musical composition in the larger forms of chamber, orchestral, or choral music, or for an operatic work (including ballet), performed or published during the year by a composer of established residence in the United States, five hundred dollars ($500).

D. TRAVELING SCHOLARSHIPS

The following traveling scholarships will be awarded annually as follows:

1. On the nomination of the faculty of the Graduate School of Journalism, three traveling scholarships having a value of $1,500 each to graduates of the School of Journalism who shall have passed their examinations with the highest honor and are otherwise most deserving, to enable each of them to spend a year abroad to study the social, political, and moral conditions of the people and the character and principles of the foreign press.

Competition for these scholarships is not necessarily restricted to those who are graduated from the School of Journalism in the year when the award is made.

2. An annual scholarship having a value of $1,500 to an art student in America, who shall be certified as the most promising and deserving by the National Academy of Design, with which the Society of American Artists has been merged.

III. PULITZER PRIZE AWARDS, 1917-1958

JOURNALISM

MERITORIOUS PUBLIC SERVICE

1917   No award.
1918   NEW YORK TIMES for its public service in publishing in full so

many official reports, documents, and speeches by European statesmen relating to the progress and conduct of the war.

1919   MILWAUKEE JOURNAL for its strong and courageous campaign for Americanism in a constituency where foreign elements made such a policy hazardous from a business point of view.

1920   No award.

1921   BOSTON POST for its exposure of the operations of Charles Ponzi by a series of articles which finally led to his arrest.

1922   NEW YORK WORLD for articles exposing the operations of the Ku Klux Klan, published during September and October, 1921.

1923   MEMPHIS COMMERCIAL APPEAL for its courageous attitude in the publication of cartoons and the handling of news in reference to the operations of the Ku Klux Klan.

1924   NEW YORK WORLD for its work in connection with the exposure of the Florida peonage evil.

1925.   No award.

1926   COLUMBUS (Ga.) ENQUIRER SUN for the service which it rendered in its brave and energetic fight against the Ku Klux Klan; against the enactment of a law barring the teaching of evolution; against dishonest and incompetent public officials and for justice to the Negro; and against lynching.

1927   CANTON (Ohio) DAILY NEWS for its brave, patriotic, and effective fight for the ending of a vicious state of affairs brought about by collusion between city authorities and the criminal element, a fight which had a tragic result in the assassination of the editor of the paper, Mr. Don R. Mellett.

1928   INDIANAPOLIS TIMES for its work in exposing political corruption in Indiana, prosecuting the guilty and bringing about a more wholesome state of affairs in civil government.

1929   NEW YORK EVENING WORLD for its effective campaign to correct evils in the administration of justice, including the fight to curb "ambulance-chasers," support of the "fence" bill, and measures to simplify procedure, prevent perjury, and eliminate politics from municipal courts; a campaign which has been instrumental in securing remedial action.

1930   No award.

1931   ATLANTA CONSTITUTION for a successful municipal graft exposure and consequent convictions.

1932   INDIANAPOLIS NEWS for its successful campaign to eliminate waste in city management and to reduce the tax levy.

1933   NEW YORK WORLD-TELEGRAM for its series of articles on veterans' relief, on the real estate bond evil, the campaign urging voters in the late New York City municipal election to "write in" the name of Joseph V. McKee, and the articles exposing the lottery schemes of various fraternal organizations.

1934　MEDFORD (Ore.) MAIL TRIBUNE for its campaign against unscrupulous politicians in Jackson County, Oregon.

1935　THE SACRAMENTO (Calif.) BEE for its campaign against political machine influence in the appointment of two federal judges in Nevada.

1936　THE CEDAR RAPIDS (Iowa) GAZETTE for its crusade against corruption and misgovernment in the state of Iowa.

1937　ST. LOUIS POST-DISPATCH for its exposure of wholesale fraudulent registration in St. Louis. By a coordinated news, editorial, and cartoon campaign this newspaper succeeded in invalidating upwards of 40,000 fraudulent ballots in November and brought about the appointment of a new election board.

1938　THE BISMARCK (N.D.) TRIBUNE for its news reports and editorials entitled, "Self Help in the Dust Bowl."

1939　THE MIAMI DAILY NEWS for its campaign for the recall of the Miami City Commission.

1940　WATERBURY (Conn.) REPUBLICAN & AMERICAN for its campaign exposing municipal graft.

1941　ST. LOUIS POST-DISPATCH for its successful campaign against the city smoke nuisance.

1942　LOS ANGELES TIMES for its successful campaign which resulted in the clarification and confirmation for all American newspapers of the right of free press as guaranteed under the Constitution.

1943　OMAHA (Neb.) WORLD-HERALD for its initiative and originality in planning a state-wide campaign for the collection of scrap metal for the war effort. The Nebraska plan was adopted on a national scale by the daily newspapers, resulting in a united effort which succeeded in supplying our war industries with necessary scrap material.

1944　NEW YORK TIMES for its survey of the teaching of American history.

1945　DETROIT FREE PRESS for its investigation of legislative graft and corruption at Lansing, Michigan.

1946　SCRANTON TIMES for its fifteen-year investigation of judicial practices in the United States District Court for the middle district of Pennsylvania, resulting in removal of the district judge and indictment of many others.

1947   BALTIMORE SUN for its series of articles by Howard M. Norton dealing with the administration of unemployment compensation in Maryland, resulting in convictions and pleas of guilty in criminal court of ninety-three persons.

1948   ST. LOUIS POST-DISPATCH for the coverage of the Centralia, Illinois, mine disaster and the follow-up which resulted in impressive reforms in mine safety laws and regulations.

1949   NEBRASKA STATE JOURNAL for the campaign establishing the "Nebraska All-Star Primary" presidential preference primary which spotlighted, through a bi-partisan committee, issues early in the presidential campaign.

1950   CHICAGO DAILY NEWS AND ST. LOUIS POST-DISPATCH for the work of George Thiem and Roy J. Harris, respectively, in exposing the presence of thirty-seven Illinois newspapermen on an Illinois State payroll.

1951   THE MIAMI HERALD AND BROOKLYN EAGLE for their crime reporting during the year.

1952   ST. LOUIS POST-DISPATCH for its investigation and disclosures of widespread corruption in the Internal Revenue Bureau and other departments of the government.

1953   WHITEVILLE (N.C.) NEWS REPORTER AND TABOR CITY (N.C.) TRIBUNE, two weeky newspapers, for their successful campaign against the Ku Klux Klan, waged on their own doorstep at the risk of economic loss and personal danger, culminating in the conviction of over one hundred Klansmen and an end to terrorism in their communities.

1954   NEWSDAY (Garden City, L. I.) for its exposé of New York State's race track scandals and labor racketeering, which led to the extortion indictment, guilty plea, and imprisonment of William C. DeKoning Sr., New York labor racketeer.

1955   COLUMBUS (Ga.) LEDGER AND SUNDAY LEDGER-ENQUIRER for its complete news coverage and fearless editorial attack on widespread corruption in neighboring Phenix City, Alabama, which were effective in destroying a corrupt and racket-ridden city government. The newspaper exhibited an early awareness of the evils of lax law enforcement before the situation in Phenix City erupted into murder. It covered the whole unfolding story of the final prosecution of the wrong-doers with skill, perception, force, and courage.

1956   WATSONVILLE (Calif.) REGISTER-PAJARONIAN for courageous exposure of corruption in public office, which led to resignation of a district attorney and the conviction of one of his associates.

1957 CHICAGO DAILY NEWS for determined and courageous public service in exposing a $2,500,000 fraud centering in the office of the State Auditor of Illinois, resulting in the indictment and conviction of the State Auditor and others. This led to the reorganization of state procedures to prevent a recurrence of the fraud.

1958 ARKANSAS GAZETTE (Little Rock) for demonstrating the highest qualities of civic leadership, journalistic responsibility, and moral courage in the face of mounting public tension during the school integration crisis of 1957. The newspaper's fearless and completely objective news coverage, plus its reasoned and moderate policy, did much to restore calmness and order to an overwrought community, reflecting great credit on its editors and its management.

REPORTING

NOTE: *The Reporting category originally embraced all fields—local, national, and international. This was how it was developed into the present four separate categories:*

In 1929, a separate category called Correspondence was set up which, until 1947, gave recognition to Washington and Foreign Correspondence.

In 1942, two other separate categories were created called, respectively, Telegraphic Reporting (National) and Telegraphic Reporting (International).

In 1948, the three categories called Correspondence, Telegraphic Reporting (National), and Telegraphic Reporting (International) were merged into two new categories, which were, respectively, National Reporting and International Reporting.

In 1953, there was a further division of the original Reporting category into Reporting, under pressure of edition deadlines, and Reporting, not under pressure of edition deadlines.

The following listing retains the prizes as awarded in the original categories, but an effort is made to list them in the order of development.

1917 HERBERT BAYARD SWOPE, *New York World,* for articles which appeared October 10, October 15, and from November 4 daily to November 22, 1916, inclusive, entitled, "Inside the German Empire."

1918 HAROLD A. LITTLEDALE, *New York Evening Post,* for series of articles exposing abuses in and leading to the reform of the New Jersey State prison.

1919 No award.

1920　JOHN J. LEARY JR., *New York World,* for the series of articles written during the national coal strike in the winter of 1919.

1921　LOUIS SEIBOLD, *New York World,* for an interview with President Wilson.

1922　KIRKE L. SIMPSON, *Associated Press,* for articles on the burial of "The Unknown Soldier."

1923　ALVA JOHNSTON, *New York Times,* for his reports of the proceedings of the convention of the American Association for the Advancement of Science held in Cambridge, Massachusetts, in December, 1922.

1924　MAGNER WHITE, *San Diego Sun,* for his story of the eclipse of the sun.

1925　JAMES W. MULROY AND ALVIN H. GOLDSTEIN, *Chicago Daily News,* for their service toward the solution of the murder of Robert Franks Jr., in Chicago on May 22, 1924, and the bringing to justice of Nathan F. Leopold and Richard Loeb.

1926　WILLIAM BURKE MILLER, *Louisville Courier-Journal,* for his work in connection with the story of the trapping in Sand Cave, Kentucky, of Floyd Collins.

1927　JOHN T. ROGERS, *St. Louis Post-Dispatch,* for the inquiry leading to the impeachment of Judge George W. English of the U. S. Court for the Eastern District of Illinois.

1928　No award.

1929　PAUL Y. ANDERSON, *St. Louis Post-Dispatch,* for his highly effective work in bringing to light a situation which resulted in revealing the disposition of Liberty Bonds purchased and distributed by the Continental Trading Company in connection with naval oil leases.

1930　RUSSELL D. OWEN, *New York Times,* for his reports by radio of the Byrd Antarctic Expedition.

1931　A. B. MACDONALD, *Kansas City* (Mo.) *Star,* for his work in connection with a murder in Amarillo, Texas.

1932　W. C. RICHARDS, D. D. MARTIN, J. S. POOLER, F. D. WEBB AND J. N. W. SLOAN, *Detroit Free Press,* for their account of the parade of the American Legion during the 1931 convention in Detroit.

1933　FRANCIS A. JAMIESON, *Associated Press,* for his prompt, full, skillful, and prolonged coverage of news of the kidnaping of the infant son of Charles A. Lindbergh on March 1, 1932, from the first announcement of the kidnaping until after the discovery of the baby's body nearby the Lindbergh home on May 12.

1934　ROYCE BRIER, *San Francisco Chronicle,* for his account of the lynching of the kidnapers, John M. Holmes and Thomas H. Thurmond in San Jose, California, on Nov. 26, 1933 after they had been jailed for abducting Brooke Hart, a merchant's son.

1935 WILLIAM H. TAYLOR, *New York Herald Tribune,* for his series of articles on the international yacht races.

1936 LAUREN D. LYMAN, *New York Times,* for his exclusive story revealing that the Charles A. Lindbergh family was leaving the United States to live in England.

1937 JOHN J. O'NEILL *(New York Herald Tribune),* WILLIAM L. LAURENCE *(New York Times),* HOWARD W. BLAKESLEE *(AP),* GOBIND BEHARI LAL *(Universal Service)* and DAVID DIETZ *(Scripps-Howard)* for their coverage of science at the tercentenary of Harvard University.

1938 RAYMOND SPRIGLE, *Pittsburgh Post-Gazette,* for his series of articles, supported by photostats of the essential documents, exposing the one-time membership of Mr. Justice Hugo L. Black in the Ku Klux Klan.

1939 THOMAS LUNSFORD STOKES, *Scripps-Howard Newspaper Alliance,* for his series of articles on alleged intimidation of workers for the Works Progress Administration in Pennsylvania and Kentucky during an election. The articles were published in the *New York World-Telegram.*

1940 S. BURTON HEATH, *New York World-Telegram,* for his exposé of the frauds perpetrated by Federal Judge Martin T. Manton, who resigned and later was tried and imprisoned.

1941 WESTBROOK PEGLER, *New York World-Telegram,* for his articles on scandals in the ranks of organized labor, which led to the exposure and conviction of George Scalise, a labor racketeer.

1942 STANTON DELAPLANE, *San Francisco Chronicle,* for his articles on the movement of several California and Oregon counties to secede to form a forty-ninth state.

1943 GEORGE WELLER, *Chicago Daily News,* for his graphic story of how a U. S. Navy Pharmacist's Mate under enemy waters in a submarine performed an operation for appendicitis saving a sailor's life.

1944 PAUL SCHOENSTEIN and Associates, *New York Journal-American,* who cooperated in the development and publication of a news story on August 12, 1943, which saved the life of a two-year-old girl in the Lutheran Hospital of New York City by obtaining penicillin.

1945 JACK S. McDOWELL, *San Francisco Call-Bulletin,* for his campaign to encourage blood donations.

1946 WILLIAM LEONARD LAURENCE, *New York Times*, for his eye-witness account of the atom-bombing of Nagasaki and his subsequent ten articles on the development, production, and significance of the atomic bomb.

1947 FREDERICK WOLTMAN, *New York World-Telegram*, for his articles during 1946 on the infiltration of Communism in the U. S.

1948 GEORGE E. GOODWIN, *Atlanta Journal*, for his story of the Telfair County vote fraud, published in 1947.

1949 MALCOLM JOHNSON, *New York Sun*, for his series of twenty-four articles entitled "Crime on the Waterfront" in New York City.

1950 MEYER BERGER, *New York Times*, for his 4,000 word story on the mass killings by Howard Unruh in Camden, N. J.

1951 EDWARD S. MONTGOMERY, *San Francisco Examiner*, for his series of articles on tax frauds which culminated in an exposé within the Bureau of Internal Revenue.

1952 GEORGE DE CARVALHO, *San Francisco Chronicle*, for his stories of a "ransom racket" extorting money from Chinese in the United States for relations held in Red China.

REPORTING UNDER DEADLINE PRESSURE

1953 PROVIDENCE JOURNAL AND EVENING BULLETIN editorial staff for their spontaneous and cooperative coverage of a bank robbery and police chase leading to the capture of the bandit.

1954 VICKSBURG (Miss.) SUNDAY POST-HERALD for its outstanding coverage of the tornado of December 5, 1953, under extraordinary difficulties.

1955 MRS. CARO BROWN, *Alice* (Tex.) *Daily Echo*, for a series of news stories dealing with the successful attack on one-man political rule in neighboring Duval County, written under unusual pressure both of edition time and difficult, even dangerous, circumstances. Mrs. Brown dug into the facts behind the dramatic daily events, as well, and obtained her stories in spite of the bitterest political opposition, showing professional skill and courage.

1956 LEE HILLS, *Detroit Free Press*, for his aggressive, resourceful, and comprehensive front page reporting of the United Automobile Workers' negotiations with Ford and General Motors for a guaranteed annual wage.

1957 SALT LAKE (Utah) TRIBUNE for its prompt and efficient coverage of the crash of two air liners over the Grand Canyon, in which 128 persons were killed. This was a team job that surmounted great difficulties in distance, time, and terrain.

1958 FARGO (N. D.) FORUM for its swift, vivid and detailed news and picture coverage of a tornado which struck Fargo on June 20. Proceeding under considerable difficulty and overcoming many handicaps, a small but skilled staff put out a complete tornado edition within five hours after the disaster.

REPORTING NOT UNDER DEADLINE PRESSURE

1953 EDWARD J. MOWERY, *New York World-Telegram & Sun,* for his reporting of the facts which brought vindication and freedom to Louis Hoffner.

1954 ALVIN SCOTT MCCOY, *Kansas City* (Mo.) *Star,* for a series of exclusive stories which led to the resignation under fire of C. Wesley Roberts as Republican National Chairman.

1955 ROLAND KENNETH TOWERY, *Cuero* (Tex.) *Record,* for his series of articles exclusively exposing a scandal in the administration of the Veterans' Land Program in Texas. This 32-year-old World War II veteran, a former prisoner of the Japanese, made these irregularities a state-wide and subsequently a national issue, and stimulated state action to rectify conditions in the land program.

1956 ARTHUR DALEY, *New York Times,* for his outstanding coverage and commentary on the world of sports in his daily column, "Sports of the Times."

1957 WALLACE TURNER AND WILLIAM LAMBERT, *Portland Oregonian,* $1,000 each, for their exposé of vice and corruption in Portland involving some municipal officials and officers of the International Brotherhood of Teamsters, Chauffeurs, Warehousemen, and Helpers of America, Western Conference. They fulfilled their assignments despite great handicaps and the risk of reprisal from lawless elements.

1958 GEORGE BEVERIDGE, the *Evening Star* (Washington, D.C.), for his excellent and thought-provoking series, "Metro, City of Tomorrow," describing in depth the urban problems of Washington, D.C., which stimulated widespread public consideration of these problems and encouraged further studies by both public and private agencies.

CORRESPONDENCE

1929 PAUL SCOTT MOWRER, *Chicago Daily News,* for his coverage of international affairs including the Franco-British Naval Pact and Germany's campaign for revision of the Dawes Plan.

1930 LELAND STOWE, *New York Herald Tribune,* for the series of articles covering the conferences on reparations and the establishment of the international bank.

1931 H. R. KNICKERBOCKER, *Philadelphia Public Ledger* and *New York Evening Post,* for a series of articles on the practical operation of the Five Year Plan in Russia.

1932 WALTER DURANTY, *New York Times,* for his series of dispatches on Russia, especially the working out of the Five Year Plan.
      CHARLES G. ROSS, *St. Louis Post-Dispatch,* for his article entitled, "The Country's Plight—What Can Be Done About It?"—a discussion of the economic situation of the United States.

1933 EDGAR ANSEL MOWRER, *Chicago Daily News,* for his day-by-day coverage and his interpretation of the series of German political crises in 1932, beginning with the presidential election and the struggle of Adolf Hitler for public office.

1934 FREDERICK T. BIRCHALL, *New York Times,* for his correspondence from Europe.

1935 ARTHUR KROCK, *New York Times,* for his Washington dispatches.

1936 WILFRED C. BARBER, *Chicago Tribune,* for his reports of the war in Ethiopia.

1937 ANNE O'HARE MCCORMICK, *New York Times,* for her dispatches and feature articles from Europe in 1936.

1938 ARTHUR KROCK, *New York Times,* for his exclusive authorized interview with the President of the United States on February 27, 1937.

1939 LOUIS P. LOCHNER, *Associated Press,* for his dispatches from Berlin.

1940 OTTO D. TOLISCHUS, *New York Times,* for his dispatches from Berlin.

1941 GROUP AWARD—In place of an individual Pulitzer Prize for foreign correspondence, the trustees approved the recommendation of the Advisory Board that a bronze plaque or scroll be designed and executed to recognize and symbolize the public services and the individual achievements of American news reporters in the war zones of Europe, Asia, and Africa from the beginning of the present war.

1942 CARLOS P. ROMULO, *Philippines Herald,* for his observations and forecasts of Far Eastern developments during a tour of the trouble centers from Hongkong to Batavia.

1943 HANSON W. BALDWIN, *New York Times,* for his report of his wartime tour of the Southwest Pacific.

1944 ERNEST TAYLOR PYLE, *Scripps-Howard Newspaper Alliance,* for distinguished war correspondence during the year 1943.

1945 HAROLD V. (HAL) BOYLE, *Associated Press,* for distinguished war correspondence during the year 1944.

1946 ARNALDO CORTESI, *New York Times,* for distinguished correspondence during the year 1945, as exemplified by his reports from Buenos Aires, Argentina.

1947 BROOKS ATKINSON, *New York Times,* for distinguished correspondence during 1946, as exemplified by his series of articles on Russia.

TELEGRAPHIC REPORTING (NATIONAL)

1942 LOUIS STARK, *New York Times,* for his distinguished reporting of important labor stories during the year.

1943 No award.

1944 DEWEY L. FLEMING, *Baltimore Sun,* for his distinguished reporting during the year 1943.

1945 JAMES B. RESTON, *New York Times,* for his news dispatches and interpretive articles on the Dumbarton Oaks security conference.

1946 EDWARD A. HARRIS, *St. Louis Post-Dispatch,* for his articles on the Tidewater Oil situation which contributed to the national-wide opposition to the appointment and confirmation of Edwin W. Pauley as Undersecretary of the Navy.

1947 EDWARD T. FOLLIARD, *Washington* (D.C.) *Post,* for his series of articles published during 1946 on the Columbians, Inc.

NATIONAL REPORTING

1948 BERT ANDREWS, *New York Herald Tribune,* for his articles on "A State Department Security Case" published in 1947.
NAT S. FINNEY, *Minneapolis Tribune,* for his stories on the plan of the Truman administration to impose secrecy about the ordinary affairs of federal civilian agencies in peacetime.

1949 C. P. TRUSSELL, *New York Times,* for consistent excellence covering the national scene from Washington.

1950 EDWIN O. GUTHMAN, *Seattle Times,* for his series on the clearing of Communist charges of Professor Melvin Rader, who had been accused of attending a secret Communist school.

1951 No award.

1952 ANTHONY LEVIERO, *New York Times,* for his exclusive article of April 21, 1951, disclosing the record of conversations between

President Truman and General of the Army Douglas MacArthur at Wake Island in their conference of October, 1950.

1953 DON WHITEHEAD, *Associated Press,* for his article called "The Great Deception," dealing with the intricate arrangements by which the safety of President-elect Eisenhower was guarded enroute from Morningside Heights in New York to Korea.

1954 RICHARD WILSON, *Cowles Newspapers,* for his exclusive publication of the FBI Report to the White House in the Harry Dexter White case before it was laid before the Senate by J. Edgar Hoover.

1955 ANTHONY LEWIS, *Washington* (D.C.) *Daily News,* for publishing a series of articles which were adjudged directly responsible for clearing Abraham Chasanow, an employee of the U. S. Navy Department, and bringing about his restoration to duty with an acknowledgment by the Navy Department that it had committed a grave injustice in dismissing him as a security risk. Mr. Lewis received the full support of his newspaper in championing an American citizen, without adequate funds or resources for his defense, against an unjust act by a government department. This is in the best tradition of American journalism.

1956 CHARLES L. BARTLETT, *Chattanooga Times,* for his original disclosures that led to the resignation of Harold E. Talbott as Secretary of the Air Force.

1957 JAMES RESTON, *New York Times,* for his distinguished national correspondence, including both news dispatches and interpretive reporting, an outstanding example of which was his five-part analysis of the effect of President Eisenhower's illness on the functioning of the executive branch of the federal government.

1958 RELMAN MORIN, *Associated Press,* for his dramatic and incisive eyewitness report of mob violence on September 23, 1957, during the integration crisis at the Central High School in Little Rock, Arkansas.

CLARK MOLLENHOFF, *Des Moines Register* and *Tribune,* for his persistent inquiry into labor racketeering, which included investigatory reporting of wide significance.

TELEGRAPHIC REPORTING (INTERNATIONAL)

1942 LAURENCE EDMUND ALLEN, *Associated Press,* for his stories of the activities of the British Mediterranean Fleet, written as an accredited correspondent attached to the fleet.

1943 IRA WOLFERT, *North American Newspaper Alliance, Inc.*, for his series of three articles on the fifth battle of the Solomons.

1944 DANIEL DE LUCE, *Associated Press*, for his distinguished reporting during the year 1943.

1945 MARK S. WATSON, *Baltimore Sun*, for his distinguished reporting during the year 1944 from Washington, London, and the fronts in Sicily, Italy, and France.

1946 HOMER WILLIAM BIGART, *New York Herald Tribune*, for his distinguished reporting during the year 1945 from the Pacific war theatre.

1947 EDDY GILMORE, *Associated Press*, for his correspondence from Moscow in 1946.

INTERNATIONAL REPORTING

1948 PAUL W. WARD, *Baltimore Sun*, for his series of articles published in 1947 on "Life in the Soviet Union."

1949 PRICE DAY, *Baltimore Sun*, for his series of twelve articles entitled, "Experiment in Freedom—India and Its First Year of Independence."

1950 EDMUND STEVENS, *Christian Science Monitor*, for his series of forty-three articles written over a three-year residence in Moscow entitled, "This Is Russia—Uncensored."

1951 KEYES BEECH, *Chicago Daily News;* HOMER BIGART, *New York Herald Tribune;* MARGUERITE HIGGINS, *New York Herald Tribune;* RELMAN MORIN, *AP;* FRED SPARKS, *Chicago Daily News;* and DON WHITEHEAD, *AP* for their reporting of the Korean War.

1952 JOHN M. HIGHTOWER, *Associated Press*, for the sustained quality of his coverage of news of international affairs during the year.

1953 AUSTIN WEHRWEIN, *Milwaukee Journal*, for a series of articles on Canada.

1954 JIM G. LUCAS, *Scripps-Howard Newspapers*, for his notable front-line human interest reporting of the Korean War, the cease-fire, and the prisoner-of-war exchanges, climaxing twenty-six months of distinguished service as a war correspondent.

1955 HARRISON E. SALISBURY, *New York Times*, for his distinguished series of articles, "Russia Re-Viewed," based on his six years as a *Times* correspondent in Russia. The perceptive and well-written Salisbury articles made a valuable contribution to American understanding of what is going on inside Russia. This was principally due to the writer's wide range of subject matter and depth of background, plus a number of illuminating photographs which he took.

1956 WILLIAM RANDOLPH HEARST JR., KINGSBURY SMITH and FRANK CONNIFF, *International News Service,* for a series of exclusive interviews with the leaders of the Soviet Union.

1957 RUSSELL JONES, *United Press,* for his excellent and sustained coverage of the Hungarian revolt against Communist domination, during which he worked at great personal risk within Russian-held Budapest and gave front-line eyewitness reports of the ruthless Soviet repression of the Hungarian people.

1958 NEW YORK TIMES for its distinguished coverage of foreign news, which was characterized by admirable initiative, continuity, and high quality during the year.

EDITORIALS

1917 NEW YORK TRIBUNE, for an editorial article on the first anniversary of the sinking of the Lusitania.

1918 LOUISVILLE COURIER JOURNAL for the editorial article, "Vae Victis!" and the editorial, "War Has Its Compensation."

1919 No award.

1920 HARVEY E. NEWBRANCH, *Omaha Evening World Herald,* for an editorial entitled, "Law and the Jungle."

1921 No award.

1922 FRANK M. O'BRIEN, *New York Herald,* for an article entitled, "The Unknown Soldier."

1923 WILLIAM ALLEN WHITE, *Emporia* (Kan.) *Gazette,* for an editorial entitled, "To An Anxious Friend."

1924 BOSTON HERALD for an editorial entitled, "Who Made Coolidge?" Special prize of $1,000 was awarded to the widow of the late FRANK I. COBB, *New York World,* in recognition of the distinction of her husband's editorial writing and service.

1925 CHARLESTON (S.C.) NEWS AND COURIER for the editorial entitled, "The Plight of the South."

1926 NEW YORK TIMES, for the editorial by *Edward M. Kingsbury,* entitled "The House of a Hundred Sorrows."

1927 BOSTON HERALD, for the editorial by *F. Lauriston Bullard,* entitled, "We Submit."

1928 GROVER CLEVELAND HALL, *Montgomery* (Ala.) *Advertiser,* for his editorials against gangsterism, floggings, and racial and religious intolerance.

1929 Louis Isaac Jaffe, *Norfolk Virginian-Pilot,* for his editorial entitled, "An Unspeakable Act of Savagery," which is typical of a series of articles written on the lynching evil and in successful advocacy of legislation to prevent it.

1930 No award.

1931 Charles S. Ryckman, *Fremont* (Neb.) *Tribune,* for the editorial entitled, "The Gentlemen from Nebraska."

1932 No award.

1933 Kansas City (Mo.) Star, for its series of editorials on national and international topics.

1934 E. P. Chase, *Atlantic* (Iowa) *News-Telegraph,* for an editorial entitled, "Where Is Our Money?"

1935 No award.

1936 Felix Morley, *Washington Post,* and George B. Parker, *Scripps-Howard Newspapers,* for distinguished editorial writing during the year.

1937 John W. Owens, *Baltimore Sun,* for distinguished editorial writing during the year.

1938 William Wesley Waymack, *Des Moines Register and Tribune,* for his distinguished editorial writing during the year.

1939 Ronald G. Callvert, *Portland Oregonian,* for his distinguished editorial writing during the year, as exemplified by the editorial entitled, "My Country 'Tis of Thee."

1940 Bart Howard, *St. Louis Post-Dispatch,* for his distinguished editorial writing during the year.

1941 Reuben Maury, *New York Daily News,* for his distinguished editorial writing during the year.

1942 Geoffrey Parsons, *New York Herald Tribune,* for his distinguished editorial writing during the year.

1943 Forrest W. Seymour, *Des Moines Register and Tribune,* for his editorials published during the calendar year, 1942.

1944 Kansas City (Mo.) Star, by *Henry J. Haskell,* for editorials written during the calendar year, 1943.

1945 George W. Potter, *Providence Journal-Bulletin,* for his editorials published during the calendar year, 1944, especially for his editorials on the subject of freedom of the press.

1946 Hodding Carter, *Delta Democrat-Times* (Greenville, Miss.), for a group of editorial published during the year 1945 on the subject of racial, religious, and economic intolerance, as exemplified by the editorial "Go for Broke."

1947 WILLIAM H. GRIMES, *Wall Street Journal,* for distinguished editorial writing during the year.

1948 VIRGINIUS DABNEY, *Richmond Times Dispatch,* for distinguished editorial writing during the year.

1949 JOHN H. CRIDER, *Boston Herald,* and HERBERT ELLISTON, *Washington Post,* for distinguished editorial writing during the year.

1950 CARL M. SAUNDERS, *Jackson* (Mich.) *Citizen Patriot,* for distinguished editorial writing during the year.

1951 WILLIAM HARRY FITZPATRICK, *New Orleans States,* for his series of editorials analyzing and clarifying a very important constitutional issue, which is described by the general heading of the series, "Government by Treaty."

1952 LOUIS LACOSS, *St. Louis Globe Democrat,* for his editorial entitled, "The Low Estate of Public Morals."

1953 VERMONT CONNECTICUT ROYSTER, *Wall Street Journal,* for distinguished editorial writing during the year.

1954 BOSTON HERALD, for a series of editorials by *Don Murray,* on the "New Look" in National Defense which won wide attention for their analysis of changes in American military policy.

1955 DETROIT FREE PRESS, for an editorial by *Royce Howes,* on "The Cause of a Strike," impartially and clearly analyzing the responsibility of both labor and management for local union's unauthorized strike in July, 1954, which rendered 45,000 Chrysler Corporation workers idle and unpaid. By pointing out how and why the parent United Automobile Workers' Union ordered the local strike called off and stating that management let dissatisfaction get out of hand, the editorial made a notable contribution to public understanding of the whole program of the respective responsibilities and relationships of labor and management in this field.

1956 LAUREN K. SOTH, *Des Moines Register and Tribune,* for the editorial inviting a farm delegation from the Soviet Union to visit Iowa, which led directly to the Russian farm visit to the U.S.

1957 BUFORD BOONE, *Tuscaloosa* (Ala.) *News,* for his fearless and reasoned editorials in a community inflamed by a segregation issue, an outstanding example of his work being the editorial entitled, "What a Price for Peace," published on February 7, 1956.

1958 HARRY S. ASHMORE, *Arkansas Gazette* (Little Rock) for the forcefulness, dispassionate analysis, and clarity of his editorials on the school integration conflict in Little Rock.

CARTOONS

1922 ROLLIN KIRBY, *New York World,* for the cartoon "On the Road to Moscow."

1923 No award.

1924 JAY NORWOOD DARLING, *New York Tribune,* for the cartoon "In Good Old U.S.A."

1925 ROLLIN KIRBY, *New York World,* for the cartoon "News from the Outside World."

1926 D. R. FITZPATRICK, *St. Louis Post-Dispatch,* for the cartoon "The Laws of Moses and the Laws of Today."

1927 NELSON HARDING, *Brooklyn Daily Eagle,* for the cartoon "Toppling the Idol."

1928 NELSON HARDING, *Brooklyn Daily Eagle,* for the cartoon "May His Shadow Never Grow Less."

1929 ROLLIN KIRBY, *New York World,* for the cartoon "Tammany."

1930 CHARLES R. MACAULEY, *Brooklyn Daily Eagle,* for the cartoon "Paying for a Dead Horse."

1931 EDMUND DUFFY, *Baltimore Sun,* for the cartoon "An Old Struggle Still Going On."

1932 JOHN T. McCUTCHEON, *Chicago Tribune,* for the cartoon "A Wise Economist Asks a Question."

1933 H. M. TALBURT, *Washington* (D.C.) *Daily News,* for the cartoon "The Light of Asia."

1934 EDMUND DUFFY, *Baltimore Sun,* for the cartoon "California Points with Pride—!"

1935 Ross A. LEWIS, *Milwaukee Journal,* for the cartoon "Sure, I'll Work for Both Sides."

1936 No award.

1937 C. D. BATCHELOR, *New York Daily News,* for the cartoon "Come on in, I'll treat you right. I used to know your Daddy."

1938 VAUGHN SHOEMAKER, *Chicago Daily News,* for distinguished service as a cartoonist, as exemplified by the cartoon "The Road Back."

1939 CHARLES G. WERNER, *Daily Oklahoman,* Oklahoma City, for distinguished service as a cartoonist, as exemplified by the cartoon "Nomination for 1938."

1940 EDMUND DUFFY, *Baltimore Sun,* for distinguished service as a cartoonist, as exemplified by the cartoon "The Outstretched Hand."

1941 JACOB BURCK, *Chicago Times,* for distinguished service as a cartoonist, as exemplified by the cartoon "If I Should Die before I Wake."

1942 HERBERT LAWRENCE BLOCK (Herblock), *NEA Service*, for distinguished service as a cartoonist, as exemplified by the cartoon "British Plane," published in various newspapers.

1943 JAY NORWOOD DARLING, *New York Herald Tribune*, for distinguished service as a cartoonist, as exemplified by the cartoon "What a Place for a Waste Paper Salvage Campaign."

1944 CLIFFORD K. BERRYMAN, *Washington* (D. C.) *Evening Star*, for distinguished service as a cartoonist, as exemplified by the cartoon "But Where Is the Boat Going?"

1945 SERGEANT BILL MAULDIN, *United Feature Syndicate*, Inc., for distinguished service as a cartoonist, as exemplified by the cartoon "Fresh, spirited American troops, flushed with victory, are bringing in thousands of hungry, ragged, battle-weary prisoners," in the series entitled, "Up Front With Mauldin."

1946 BRUCE ALEXANDER RUSSELL, *Los Angeles Times*, for distinguished work as a cartoonist during the year 1945, as exemplified by the cartoon "Time to Bridge That Gulch."

1947 VAUGHN SHOEMAKER, *Chicago Daily News*, for the cartoon "Still Racing His Shadow."

1948 REUBEN L. GOLDBERG, *New York Sun*, for the cartoon "Peace Today."

1949 LUTE PEASE, *Newark Evening News*, for the cartoon "Who, Me?"

1950 JAMES T. BERRYMAN, *Washington* (D. C.) *Evening Star*, for the cartoon "All Set for a Super-Secret Session in Washington."

1951 REG (REGINALD W.) MANNING, *Arizona Republic*, for the cartoon "Hats."

1952 FRED L. PACKER, *New York Mirror*, for the cartoon "Your Editors Ought To Have More Sense Than To Print What I Say!"

1953 EDWARD D. KUEKES, *Cleveland Plain Dealer*, for the cartoon "Aftermath."

1954 HERBERT L. BLOCK (Herblock), *Washington* (D. C.) *Post & Times-Herald*, for a cartoon depicting the robed figure of Death saying to Stalin after he died, "You Were Always a Great Friend of Mine, Joseph."

1955 DANIEL R. FITZPATRICK, *St. Louis Post-Dispatch*, for a cartoon published on June 8, 1954 entitled, "How Would Another Mistake Help?" showing Uncle Sam, bayoneted rifle in hand, pondering whether to wade into a black marsh bearing the legend, "French Mistakes in Indo-China." The award is also given for the distinguished body of the work of Mr. Fitzpatrick in both 1954 and his entire career.

1956 ROBERT YORK, *Louisville* (Ky.) *Times,* for the cartoon "Achilles," showing a bulging figure of American prosperity tapering to a weak heel labeled "Farm Prices."

1957 TOM LITTLE, *Nashville Tennessean,* for the cartoon "Wonder Why My Parents Didn't Give Me Salk Shots?" published on January 12, 1956.

1958 BRUCE M. SHANKS, *Buffalo* (N. Y.) *Evening News,* for the cartoon "The Thinker," published on August 10, 1957, depicting the dilemma of union membership when confronted by racketeering leaders in some labor unions.

PHOTOGRAPHY

1942 MILTON BROOKS, *Detroit News,* for the photograph "Ford Strikers Riot."

1943 FRANK NOEL, *Associated Press,* for the photograph "Water!" serviced by the AP.

1944 FRANK FILAN, *Associated Press,* for the photograph "Tarawa Island," serviced by the AP.

EARLE L. BUNKER, *Omaha World-Herald,* for the photograph "Homecoming."

1945 JOE ROSENTHAL, *Associated Press,* for the photograph of the Marines planting the American flag on Mount Suribachi on Iwo Jima.

1946 No award.

1947 ARNOLD HARDY, amateur photographer of Atlanta, Ga., for his photograph of a girl leaping to death in hotel fire, distributed by the AP.

1948 FRANK CUSHING, *Boston Traveler,* for the photograph "Boy Gunman and Hostage."

1949 NATHANIEL FEIN, *New York Herald Tribune,* for the photograph "Babe Ruth Bows Out."

1950 BILL CROUCH, *Oakland* (Cal.) *Tribune* for the photograph "Near Collision at Air Show."

1951 MAX DESFOR, *Associated Press,* for his photographic coverage of the Korean War, an outstanding example of which is "Flight of Refugees across Wrecked Bridge in Korea."

1952 JOHN ROBINSON AND DON ULTANG, *Des Moines Register and Tribune,* for their sequence of six pictures of the Drake-Oklahoma A & M football game of October 20, 1951, in which player Johnny Bright's jaw was broken.

1953   WILLIAM M. GALLAGHER, *Flint* (Mich.) *Journal,* for a photograph of ex-Governor Adlai E. Stevenson with a hole in his shoe, taken during the 1952 Presidential campaign.

1954   MRS. WALTER M. SCHAU of San Anselmo, California, an amateur, for snapping a thrilling rescue at Redding, Calif., the picture being published in the *Akron* (Ohio) *Beacon Journal* and other newspapers and nationally distributed by the AP.

1955   JOHN L. GAUNT JR., *Los Angeles Times,* for a photograph that is poignant and profoundly moving, entitled, "Tragedy by the Sea," showing a young couple standing together beside an angry sea in which only a few minutes earlier their year-old son had perished.

1956   NEW YORK DAILY NEWS for its consistently excellent news picture coverage in 1955, an outstanding example of which is its photo "Bomber Crashes in Street."

1957   HARRY A. TRASK, *Boston Traveler,* for his dramatic and outstanding photographic sequence of the sinking of the liner *Andrea Doria,* the pictures being taken from an airplane flying at a height of 75 feet only nine minutes before the ship plunged to the bottom. (The second picture in the sequence is cited as the key photograph.)

1958   WILLIAM C. BEALL, *Washington* (D. C.) *Daily News* for the photograph "Faith and Confidence," showing a policeman patiently reasoning with a two-year-old boy trying to get closer to a parade.

NEWSPAPER HISTORY AWARD

In 1918, Minna Lewinson and Henry Beetle Hough were awarded a prize for their history of the services rendered to the public by the American Press during the preceding year. It was the only year in which this particular award was given.

SPECIAL CITATIONS

1938   EDMONTON (Alberta) JOURNAL, a special bronze plaque for its editorial leadership in defense of the freedom of the press in Alberta, Canada.

1941   THE NEW YORK TIMES for the public educational value of its foreign news report, exemplified by its scope, by excellence of writing and presentation, and supplementary background information, illustration, and interpretation.

1944   BYRON PRICE, Director of the Office of Censorship, for the creation and administration of the newspaper and radio codes.

MRS. WILLIAM ALLEN WHITE, a scroll indicating appreciation of Mr. White's interest and services during the past seven years as a member of the Advisory Board of the Graduate School of Journalism, Columbia University.

1945 The cartographers of the American press whose maps of the war fronts have helped notably to clarify and increase public information on the progress of the Armies and Navies engaged.

1947 (Pulitzer centennial year.) Columbia University and the Graduate School of Journalism, for their efforts to maintain and advance the high standards governing the Pulitzer Prize awards. The *St. Louis Post-Dispatch,* for its unswerving adherence to the public and professional ideals of its founder and its constructive leadership in the field of American journalism.

1948 DR. FRANK DIEHL FACKENTHAL, a scroll indicating appreciation of Dr. Fackenthal's interest and service during the past years.

1951 CYRUS L. SULZBERGER, *New York Times,* for his exclusive interview with Archbishop Stepinac.

The Advisory Board on the Pulitzer Prizes as a policy does not make any award to an individual member of the Board, and whereas, the outstanding instance of National Reporting in 1950 was the achievement of Mr. Arthur Krock of the *New York Times* in obtaining an exclusive interview with the President of the United States, Be it resolved that the Board make no award in the National Reporting category.

1952 MAX KASE, *New York Journal-American,* for his exclusive exposures of bribery and other forms of corruption in the popular American sport of basketball, which exposures tended to restore confidence in the game's integrity.

KANSAS CITY (Mo.) STAR for the news coverage of the great regional flood of 1951 in Kansas and northwestern Missouri—a distinguished example of editing and reporting that also gave the advance information that achieved the maximum of public protection.

1953 THE NEW YORK TIMES for the section of its Sunday edition headed, "Review of the Week," which for seventeen years has brought enlightenment and intelligent commentary to its readers.

1958 WALTER LIPPMANN, nationally syndicated columnist of the New York *Herald Tribune,* for the wisdom, perception, and high sense of responsibility with which he has commented for many years on national and international affairs.

LETTERS

NOVEL

1917 No award.
1918 *His Family.* By ERNEST POOLE
1919 *The Magnificent Ambersons.* By BOOTH TARKINGTON
1920 No award.
1921 *The Age of Innocence.* By EDITH WHARTON
1922 *Alice Adams.* By BOOTH TARKINGTON
1923 *One of Ours.* By WILLA CATHER
1924 *The Able McLaughlins.* By MARGARET WILSON
1925 *So Big.* By EDNA FERBER
1926 *Arrowsmith.* By SINCLAIR LEWIS
1927 *Early Autumn.* By LOUIS BROMFIELD
1928 *The Bridge of San Luis Rey.* By THORNTON WILDER
1929 *Scarlet Sister Mary.* By JULIA PETERKIN
1930 *Laughing Boy.* By OLIVER LaFARGE
1931 *Years of Grace.* By MARGARET AYER BARNES
1932 *The Good Earth.* By PEARL S. BUCK
1933 *The Store.* By T. S. STRIBLING
1934 *Lamb in His Bosom.* By CAROLINE MILLER
1935 *Now in November.* By JOSEPHINE WINSLOW JOHNSON
1936 *Honey in the Horn.* By HAROLD L. DAVIS
1937 *Gone With The Wind.* By MARGARET MITCHELL
1938 *The Late George Apley.* By JOHN PHILLIPS MARQUAND
1939 *The Yearling.* By MARJORIE KINNAN RAWLINGS
1940 *The Grapes of Wrath.* By JOHN STEINBECK
1941 No award.
1942 *In This Our Life.* By ELLEN GLASGOW
1943 *Dragon's Teeth.* By UPTON SINCLAIR
1944 *Journey in the Dark.* By MARTIN FLAVIN
1945 *A Bell for Adano.* By JOHN HERSEY
1946 No award.
1947 *All the King's Men.* By ROBERT PENN WARREN
[NOTE: *The name of this category was changed to Fiction for 1948 and thereafter.*]

FICTION

1948 *Tales of the South Pacific.* By JAMES A. MICHENER

1949   *Guard of Honor.* By JAMES GOULD COZZENS
1950   *The Way West.* By A. B. GUTHRIE, JR.
1951   *The Town.* By CONRAD RICHTER
1952   *The Caine Mutiny.* By HERMAN WOUK
1953   *The Old Man and the Sea.* By ERNEST HEMINGWAY
1954   No award.
1955   *A Fable.* By WILLIAM FAULKNER
1956   *Andersonville.* By MACKINLAY KANTOR
1957   No award.
1958   *A Death in the Family.* By JAMES AGEE

DRAMA

1917   No award.
1918   *Why Marry?* By JESSE LYNCH WILLIAMS
1919   No award.
1920   *Beyond the Horizon.* By EUGENE O'NEILL
1921   *Miss Lulu Bett.* By ZONA GALE
1922   *Anna Christie.* By EUGENE O'NEILL
1923   *Icebound.* By OWEN DAVIS
1924   *Hell-Bent Fer Heaven.* By HATCHER HUGHES
1925   *They Knew What They Wanted.* By SIDNEY HOWARD
1926   *Craig's Wife.* By GEORGE KELLY
1927   *In Abraham's Bosom.* By PAUL GREEN
1928   *Strange Interlude.* By EUGENE O'NEILL
1929   *Street Scene.* By ELMER L. RICE
1930   *The Green Pastures.* By MARC CONNELLY
1931   *Alison's House.* By SUSAN GLASPELL
1932   *Of Thee I Sing.* By GEORGE S. KAUFMAN, MORRIE RYSKIND, and
       IRA GERSHWIN (with music by GEORGE GERSHWIN)
1933   *Both Your Houses.* By MAXWELL ANDERSON
1934   *Men In White.* By SIDNEY KINGSLEY
1935   *The Old Maid.* By ZOE AKINS
1936   *Idiot's Delight.* By ROBERT E. SHERWOOD
1937   *You Can't Take It With You.* By MOSS HART and GEORGE S.
       KAUFMAN
1938   *Our Town.* By THORNTON WILDER
1939   *Abe Lincoln in Illinois.* By ROBERT E. SHERWOOD
1940   *The Time of Your Life.* By WILLIAM SAROYAN
1941   *There Shall Be No Night.* By ROBERT E. SHERWOOD
1942   No award.

1943 *The Skin of Our Teeth.* By THORNTON WILDER
1944 No award.
1945 *Harvey.* By MARY CHASE
1946 *State of the Union.* By RUSSEL CROUSE and HOWARD LINDSAY
1947 No award.
1948 *A Streetcar Named Desire.* By TENNESSEE WILLIAMS
1949 *Death of a Salesman.* By ARTHUR MILLER
1950 *South Pacific.* By RICHARD RODGERS, OSCAR HAMMERSTEIN, 2ND and JOSHUA LOGAN
1951 No award.
1952 *The Shrike.* By JOSEPH KRAMM
1953 *Picnic.* By WILLIAM INGE
1954 *The Teahouse of the August Moon.* By JOHN PATRICK
1955 *Cat on a Hot Tin Roof.* By TENNESSEE WILLIAMS
1956 *Diary of Anne Frank.* By ALBERT HACKETT and FRANCES GOODRICH
1957 *Long Day's Journey Into Night.* By EUGENE O'NEILL
1958 *Look Homeward, Angel.* By KETTI FRINGS. (This play was adapted from the novel of the same name by Thomas Wolfe.)

HISTORY

1917 *With Americans of Past and Present Days.* By His Excellency J. J. JUSSERAND, Ambassador of France to the United States
1918 *A History of the Civil War, 1861-1865.* By JAMES FORD RHODES
1919 No award.
1920 *The War with Mexico,* 2 vols. By JUSTIN H. SMITH
1921 *The Victory at Sea.* By WILLIAM SOWDEN SIMS in collaboration with BURTON J. HENDRICK
1922 *The Founding of New England.* By JAMES TRUSLOW ADAMS
1923 *The Supreme Court in United States History.* By CHARLES WARREN
1924 *The American Revolution—A Constitutional Interpretation.* By CHARLES HOWARD MCILWAIN
1925 *A History of the American Frontier.* By FREDERIC L. PAXSON
1926 *The History of the United States.* By EDWARD CHANNING
1927 *Pinckney's Treaty.* By SAMUEL FLAGG BEMIS
1928 *Main Currents in American Thoughts,* 2 vols. By VERNON LOUIS PARRINGTON
1929 *The Organization and Administration of the Union Army,* 1861-1865. By FRED ALBERT SHANNON
1930 *The War of Independence.* By CLAUDE H. VAN TYNE

1931   The Coming of the War: 1914. By BERNADOTTE E. SCHMITT
1932   My Experiences in the World War. By JOHN J. PERSHING
1933   The Significance of Sections in American History. By FREDERICK
        J. TURNER
1934   The People's Choice. By HERBERT AGAR
1935   The Colonial Period of American History. By CHARLES MCLEAN
        ANDREWS
1936   The Constitutional History of the United States. By ANDREW C.
        MCLAUGHLIN
1937   The Flowering of New England. By VAN WYCK BROOKS
1938   The Road to Reunion, 1865-1900. By PAUL HERMAN BUCK
1939   A History of American Magazines. By FRANK LUTHER MOTT
1940   Abraham Lincoln: The War Years. By CARL SANDBURG
1941   The Atlantic Migration, 1607-1860. By MARCUS LEE HANSEN
1942   Reveille in Washington. By MARGARET LEECH
1943   Paul Revere and the World He Lived In. By ESTHER FORBES
1944   The Growth of American Thought. By MERLE CURTI
1945   Unfinished Business. By STEPHEN BONSAL
1946   The Age of Jackson. By ARTHUR MEIER SCHLESINGER JR.
1947   Scientists Against Time. By JAMES PHINNEY BAXTER 3D
1948   Across the Wide Missouri. By BERNARD DEVOTO
1949   The Disruption of American Democracy. By ROY FRANKLIN
        NICHOLS
1950   Art and Life in America. By OLIVER W. LARKIN
1951   The Old Northwest: Pioneer Period, 1815-1840. By R. CARLYLE
        BULEY
1952   The Uprooted. By OSCAR HANDLIN
1953   The Era of Good Feelings. By GEORGE DANGERFIELD
1954   A Stillness at Appomattox. By BRUCE CATTON
1955   Great River: The Rio Grande in North American History. By PAUL
        HORGAN
1956   Age of Reform. By RICHARD HOFSTADTER
1957   Russia Leaves the War: Soviet-American Relations, 1917-1920.
        By GEORGE F. KENNAN
1958   Banks and Politics in America: From the Revolution to the Civil
        War. By BRAY HAMMOND

BIOGRAPHY OR AUTOBIOGRAPHY

1917   Julia Ward Howe. By LAURA E. RICHARDS and MAUDE HOWE
        ELLIOTT assisted by FLORENCE HOWE HALL

1918   *Benjamin Franklin, Self-Revealed.* By WILLIAM CABELL BRUCE

1919   *The Education of Henry Adams.* By HENRY ADAMS

1920   *The Life of John Marshall,* 4 vols. By ALBERT J. BEVERIDGE

1921   *The Americanization of Edward Bok.* By EDWARD BOK

1922   *A Daughter of the Middle Border.* By HAMLIN GARLAND

1923   *The Life and Letters of Walter H. Page.* By BURTON J. HENDRICK

1924   *From Immigrant to Inventor.* By MICHAEL IDVORSKY PUPIN

1925   *Barrett Wendell and His Letters.* By M. A. DeWOLFE HOWE

1926   *The Life of Sir William Osler,* 2 vols. By HARVEY CUSHING

1927   *Whitman.* By EMORY HOLLOWAY

1928   *The American Orchestra and Theodore Thomas.* By CHARLES EDWARD RUSSELL

1929   *The Training of an American. The Earlier Life and Letters of Walter H. Page.* By BURTON J. HENDRICK

1930   *The Raven.* By MARQUIS JAMES

1931   *Charles W. Eliot.* By HENRY JAMES

1932   *Theodore Roosevelt.* By HENRY F. PRINGLE

1933   *Grover Cleveland.* By ALLAN NEVINS

1934   *John Hay.* By TYLER DENNETT

1935   *R. E. Lee.* By DOUGLAS S. FREEMAN

1936   *The Thought and Character of William James.* By RALPH BARTON PERRY

1937   *Hamilton Fish.* By ALLAN NEVINS

1938   *Pedlar's Progress.* By ODELL SHEPARD

           Andrew Jackson, 2 vols. By MARQUIS JAMES

1939   *Benjamin Franklin.* By CARL VAN DOREN

1940   *Woodrow Wilson, Life and Letters,* Vols. VII and VIII. By RAY STANNARD BAKER

1941   *Jonathan Edwards.* By OLA ELIZABETH WINSLOW

1942   *Crusader in Crinoline.* By FORREST WILSON

1943   *Admiral of the Ocean Sea.* By SAMUEL ELIOT MORISON

1944   *The American Leonardo: The Life of Samuel F. B. Morse.* By CARLETON MABEE

1945   *George Bancroft: Brahmin Rebel.* By RUSSEL BLAINE NYE

1946   *Son of the Wilderness.* By LINNIE MARSH WOLFE

1947   *The Autobiography of William Allen White.*

1948   *Forgotten First Citizen: John Bigelow.* By MARGARET CLAPP

1949   *Roosevelt and Hopkins.* By ROBERT E. SHERWOOD

1950   *John Quincy Adams and the Foundations of American Foreign Policy.* By SAMUEL FLAGG BEMIS

1951   *John C. Calhoun: American Portrait.* By MARGARET LOUISE COIT

1952 *Charles Evans Hughes.* By MERLO J. PUSEY
1953 *Edmund Pendleton 1721-1803.* By DAVID J. MAYS
1954 *The Spirit of St. Louis.* By CHARLES A. LINDBERGH
1955 *The Taft Story.* By WILLIAM S. WHITE
1956 *Benjamin Henry Latrobe.* By TALBOT FAULKNER HAMLIN
1957 *Profiles in Courage.* By JOHN F. KENNEDY
1958 *George Washington,* 7 vols. Vols. I-VI By DOUGLAS SOUTHALL FREEMAN; Vol. VII written by John Alexander Carroll and Mary Wells Ashworth after Dr. Freeman's death in 1953. The project was completed with the publication of Vol. VII in 1957. In recognition of Dr. Freeman's dominant part in the work, the $500 went to his estate.

POETRY

NOTE: *Previous to the establishment of this prize in 1922, the following awards had been made from gifts provided by the Poetry Society:*
1918 *Love Songs.* By SARA TEASDALE
1919 *Old Road to Paradise.* By MARGARET WIDDEMER
      Corn Huskers. By CARL SANDBURG

The Pulitzer poetry prizes follow:
1922 *Collected Poems.* By EDWIN ARLINGTON ROBINSON
1923 *The Ballad of the Harp-Weaver; A Few Figs from Thistles; Eight Sonnets in American Poetry, 1922, A Miscellany.* By EDNA ST. VINCENT MILLAY
1924 *New Hampshire: A Poem with Notes and Grace Notes.* By ROBERT FROST
1925 *The Man Who Died Twice.* By EDWIN ARLINGTON ROBINSON
1926 *What's O'Clock.* By AMY LOWELL
1927 *Fiddler's Farewell.* By LEONORA SPEYER
1928 *Tristram.* By EDWIN ARLINGTON ROBINSON
1929 *John Brown's Body.* By STEPHEN VINCENT BENET
1930 *Selected Poems.* By CONRAD AIKEN
1931 *Collected Poems.* By ROBERT FROST
1932 *The Flowering Stone.* By GEORGE DILLON
1933 *Conquistador.* By ARCHIBALD MACLEISH
1934 *Collected Verse.* By ROBERT HILLYER
1935 *Bright Ambush.* By AUDREY WURDEMANN
1936 *Strange Holiness.* By ROBERT P. TRISTRAM COFFIN
1937 *A Further Range.* By ROBERT FROST
1938 *Cold Morning Sky.* By MARYA ZATURENSKA

1939   *Selected Poems.* By JOHN GOULD FLETCHER
1940   *Collected Poems.* By MARK VAN DOREN
1941   *Sunderland Capture.* By LEONARD BACON
1942   *The Dust Which Is God.* By WILLIAM ROSE BENET
1943   *A Witness Tree.* By ROBERT FROST
1944   *Western Star.* By STEPHEN VINCENT BENET
1945   *V-Letter and Other Poems.* By KARL SHAPIRO
1946   No award.
1947   *Lord Weary's Castle.* By ROBERT LOWELL
1948   *The Age of Anxiety.* By W. H. AUDEN
1949   *Terror and Decorum.* By PETER VIERECK
1950   *Annie Allen.* By GWENDOLYN BROOKS
1951   *Complete Poems.* By CARL SANDBURG
1952   *Collected Poems.* By MARIANNE MOORE
1953   *Collected Poems 1917-1952.* By ARCHIBALD MacLEISH
1954   *The Waking.* By THEODORE ROETHKE
1955   *Collected Poems.* By WALLACE STEVENS
1956   *Poems—North & South.* By ELIZABETH BISHOP
1957   *Things of This World.* By RICHARD WILBUR
1958   *Promises: Poems 1954-1956.* By ROBERT PENN WARREN

SPECIAL CITATIONS

1944   *Oklahoma!* By RICHARD RODGERS and OSCAR HAMMERSTEIN, 2D
1957   A special citation is awarded to KENNETH ROBERTS for his historical novels which have long contributed to the creation of greater interest in our early American history.

MUSIC

1943   WILLIAM SCHUMAN for his *Secular Cantata No. 2, A Free Song,* performed by the Boston Symphony Orchestra and published by G. Schirmer, Inc., New York.

1944   HOWARD HANSON for his *Symphony No. 4, Opus 34,* performed by the Boston Symphony Orchestra on December 3, 1943.

1945   AARON COPLAND for his *Applachian Spring,* a ballet written for and presented by Martha Graham and group, commissioned by Mrs. E. S. Coolidge, first presented at the Library of Congress, Washington, D. C., October, 1944.

1946   LEO SOWERBY for *The Canticle of the Sun,* commissioned by the Alice M. Ditson Fund, first performed by the Schola Cantorum in New York, April, 1945.

1947 CHARLES IVES for his *Symphony No. 3*, first performed by Lou Harrison and Chamber Orchestra in New York, April, 1946.

1948 WALTER PISTON for his *Symphony No. 3*, first performed by the Boston Symphony Orchestra in Boston, January, 1948.

1949 VIRGIL THOMPSON for his music for the film *Louisiana Story*, released in 1948 by Robert Flaherty Productions.

1950 GIAN-CARLO MENOTTI for his music in *The Consul*, produced at the Barrymore Theatre, New York.

1951 DOUGLAS S. MOORE for his music in *Giants in the Earth*, produced by the Columbia Opera Workshop March 28, 1951.

1952 GAIL KUBIK for his *Symphony Concertante*, performed at Town Hall, January 7, 1952.

1953 No award.

1954 QUINCY PORTER for *Concerto for Two Pianos and Orchestra*, first performed by the Louisville Symphony Orchestra, March 17, 1954. This was one of the works commissioned under a grant of the Rockefeller Foundation for new American compositions for orchestra, or soloists and orchestra.

1955 GIAN-CARLO MENOTTI for *The Saint of Bleecker Street*, an opera first performed at the Broadway Theatre, New York, December 27, 1954.

1956 ERNST TOCH for his *Symphony No. 3*, first performed by the Pittsburgh Symphony Orchestra, December 2, 1955.

1957 NORMAN DELLO JOIO for his *Meditations on Ecclesiastes*, first performed at the Juilliard School of Music on April 20, 1956.

1958 SAMUEL BARBER for the score of *Vanessa*, an opera in four acts, first presented at the Metropolitan Opera House on January 15, 1958. (The libretto is by Gian-Carlo Menotti.)

IV. MEMBERS OF THE PULITZER PRIZE ADVISORY BOARD

1958

PRESIDENT GRAYSON KIRK	*Columbia University*
BARRY BINGHAM	*Louisville Courier-Journal*
ERWIN D. CANHAM	*Christian Science Monitor, Boston, Mass.*
HODDING CARTER	*The Delta Democrat-Times, Greenville, Miss.*
TURNER CATLEDGE	*The New York Times*

NORMAN CHANDLER	*The Los Angeles Times*
J. D. FERGUSON	*Milwaukee Journal*
KENNETH MACDONALD	*The Register & Tribune, Des Moines, Iowa*
BENJAMIN M. MCKELWAY	*The Evening Star, Washington, D. C.*
W. D. MAXWELL	*Chicago Tribune*
PAUL MILLER	*Gannett Newspapers, Inc., Rochester, N. Y.*
JOSEPH PULITZER JR.	*St. Louis Post-Dispatch*
LOUIS B. SELTZER	*Cleveland Press*
JOHN HOHENBERG, *Secretary*	*Graduate School of Journalism, Columbia University.*

FROM 1912

BARRY BINGHAM	*Louisville Courier-Journal*	1956-1960
SAMUEL BOWLES	*Springfield Republican*	1912-1915
SEVELLON BROWN	*The Providence Journal*	1938-1956
JOHN STEWART BRYAN	*Richmond News Leader*	1923-1924
NICHOLAS MURRAY BUTLER	*Columbia University*	1912-1945
ERWIN D. CANHAM	*Christian Science Monitor, Boston*	1958-1962
HODDING CARTER	*Delta Democrat-Times, Greenville, Miss.*	1949-1961
TURNER CATLEDGE	*The New York Times*	1955-1959
NORMAN CHANDLER	*Los Angeles Times*	1956-1961
ROBERT CHOATE	*The Boston Herald*	1943-1958
KENT COOPER	*The Associated Press*	1931-1956
GARDNER COWLES, JR.	*Des Moines Register-Tribune*	1947-1958
DWIGHT D. EISENHOWER	*Columbia University*	1948-1950
FRANK D. FACKENTHAL	*Columbia University*	1946-1948
J. D. FERGUSON	*Milwaukee Journal*	1952-1961
SOLOMON B. GRIFFIN	*Springfield Republican*	1916-1925
JULIAN HARRIS	*Enquirer Sun, Columbus, Ga.; Atlanta Constitution; Chattanooga Times*	1927-1942
WALTER M. HARRISON	*The Daily Oklahoman, Oklahoma City*	1938-1946
JOHN LANGDON HEATON	*The New York World*	1912-1934
ALFRED HOLMAN	*The Argonaut, San Francisco*	1924-1931

Arthur M. Howe	Brooklyn Daily Eagle	1912-1920
Palmer Hoyt	The Denver Post	1920-1946
George S. Johns	St. Louis Post-Dispatch	1947-1949
Frank R. Kent	The Baltimore Sun	1928-1953
Grayson Kirk	Columbia University	1950-
John S. Knight	Knight Newspapers, Inc., Detroit, Mich.	1944-1958
Arthur Krock	The New York Times	1940-1954
Robert Lathan	Ashville (N.C.) Citizen and Times	1932-1937
Victor Fremont Lawson	Chicago Daily News	1912-1925
Kenneth MacDonald	Des Moines Register & Tribune	1958-1962
Benjamin McKelway	The Washington (D.C.) Evening Star	1951-1959
St. Clair McKelway	Brooklyn Daily Eagle	1912-1922
William R. Mathews	The Arizona Daily Star, Tucson	1943-1956
W. D. Maxwell	Chicago Tribune	1958-1962
Charles Ransom Miller	The New York Times	1912-1922
Paul Miller	Gannett Newspapers, Inc., Rochester, New York	1956-1960
Edward Page Mitchell	The New York Sun	1912-1927
Robert Lincoln O'Brien	The Boston Herald	1920-1941
Rollo Ogden	The New York Times	1924-1936
Stuart H. Perry	The Adrian (Mich.) Telegram	1928-1956
Marlen E. Pew	Editor and Publisher, New York	1933-1936
Harold S. Pollard	New York World-Telegram	1937-1951
Joseph Pulitzer	St. Louis Post-Dispatch	1921-1955
Joseph Pulitzer Jr.	St. Louis Post-Dispatch	1955-1959
Ralph Pulitzer	The New York World	1912-1939
Whitelaw Reid	New York	1912
Roy A. Roberts	Kansas City Star	1943-1946
Louis B. Seltzer	Cleveland Press	1956-1960
Melville Elijah Stone	The Associated Press	1912-1930
Charles H. Taylor	Boston Globe	1912-1921
Samuel Calvin Wells	Philadelphia Press	1912-1922
William Allen White	Emporia (Kan.) Gazette	1937-1943

WALTER WILLIAMS	*University of Missouri*	1931-1932
CASPER S. YOST	*St. Louis Globe-Democrat*	1927-1930

EXECUTIVE SECRETARIES

JEROME LANDFIELD	1925-1929
R. A. PARKER	1930-1931
DEAN CARL W. ACKERMAN	1933-1954
JOHN HOHENBERG	1955-

PERMISSIONS

The author wishes to express his appreciation for the friendly cooperation of the following:

Milburn P. Akers of the Chicago *Sun-Times;* Eric Allen Jr. of the Medford *Mail Tribune;* Harry Ashmore of the *Arkansas Gazette;* Marvin Berger of the New York *Post;* Barry Bingham of the Louisville *Courier-Journal;* Buford Boone of the Tuscaloosa *News;* Hodding Carter of the *Delta Democrat-Times;* Horace Carter of the Tabor City *Tribune;* Lenoir Chambers of the *Virginian-Pilot;* Norman Chandler of the Los Angeles *Times;* Robert B. Choate of the Boston *Herald Traveler;* Richard W. Clarke of the New York *Daily News;* Tom Collins of the Chicago *Daily News;* J. W. Colt of the Kansas City *Star;* James M. Cox of the Canton *Daily News;* Ralph B. Curry of the Flint *Journal.*

Sam H. Day of the New York *Journal-American;* Arthur C. Deck of the Salt Lake *Tribune;* Thomas W. Dewart of Communications Advisors, Inc.; Coleman A. Harwell of the Nashville *Tennessean;* William Randolph Hearst Jr. of the Hearst Corporation; Jack R. Howard of the Scripps-Howard Newspaper Alliance; Earl J. Johnson of United Press International; Malcolm Johnson of Hill & Knowlton, Inc.; Alfred H. Kirchhofer of the Buffalo *Evening News;* L. S. Levy of the Oakland *Tribune;* Wallace Lomoe of the Milwaukee *Journal.*

Kenneth MacDonald of the Des Moines *Register and Tribune;* R. L. McGrath of the Seattle *Times;* Martha MacInnes of the Christian Science Publishing Co.; Reg Manning of the McNaught Syndicate; W. D. Maxwell of the Chicago *Tribune;* John A. Meising of the Press Publishing Co.; A. V. Miller of the New York *Herald Tribune;* Charles W. Mixer of the Columbia University Libraries; John Mosedale of the North American Newspaper Alliance; Scott Newhall of the San Francisco *Chronicle;* Newbold Noyes Jr. of the Washington *Star;* John T. O'Rourke of the Washington *Daily News;* Alicia Patterson of *Newsday;* Harvey Patton of the Detroit *News;* John D. Paulson of the Fargo *Forum;* Joseph Pulitzer Jr. of the St. Louis *Post-Dispatch.*

V. D. Ringwald of the Alice *Echo;* Carlos P. Romulo of the *Philippines Herald;* Thomas N. Schroth of the *Congressional Quarterly;* Frank J. Starzel of the Associated Press; Walker Stone of the Scripps-Howard Newspaper Alliance; Ivan Veit of the New York *Times;* Philip M. Wagner of the Baltimore *Sun;* Frederick Ware of the Omaha *World-Herald;* W. L. White of the Emporia *Gazette;* J. Russell Wiggins of the Washington *Post and Times-Herald;* Lee Wood of the New York *World-Telegram and Sun.*

Index

369